Palgrave Macmillan Studies in Banking and Financial Institutions

Series Editor
Philip Molyneux
University of Sharjah
Sharjah, United Arab Emirates

The Palgrave Macmillan Studies in Banking and Financial Institutions series is international in orientation and includes studies of banking systems in particular countries or regions as well as contemporary themes such as Islamic Banking, Financial Exclusion, Mergers and Acquisitions, Risk Management, and IT in Banking. The books focus on research and practice and include up to date and innovative studies that cover issues which impact banking systems globally.

More information about this series at
http://www.palgrave.com/series/14678

Sunduzwayo Madise

# The Regulation of Mobile Money

## Law and Practice in Sub-Saharan Africa

palgrave
macmillan

Sunduzwayo Madise
University of Malawi
Zomba, Malawi

ISSN 2523-336X ISSN 2523-3378 (electronic)
Palgrave Macmillan Studies in Banking and Financial Institutions
ISBN 978-3-030-13830-1 ISBN 978-3-030-13831-8 (eBook)
https://doi.org/10.1007/978-3-030-13831-8

Library of Congress Control Number: 2019932925



Cover illustration: Donald Iain Smith/Getty Images

This Palgrave Macmillan imprint is published by the registered company Springer Nature Switzerland AG
The registered company address is: Gewerbestrasse 11, 6330 Cham, Switzerland

*Dedicated to my wife, Rhosalyn*

# Foreword

Mobile payments seem to be the future of finance. Banks and other financial and quasi-financial service providers are partnering with technology companies to allow consumers to transact using electronic gadgets within the confines of their homes or in conditions of their choice. Among the many technological advancements that abound, mobile money is more likely to have a huge impact on the economies of sub-Saharan Africa.

This book looks at the legal aspects of regulating mobile money. A law-in-context approach is undertaken, with insights drawn both from practice and scholarly perspectives. Unlike most works that have written on the subject, the book takes a rather different approach, examining issues that are interdisciplinary and multidisciplinary on law, technology and finance. The book provides a critical analysis of novel challenges regarding the regulation of "new forms of money" such as mobile money.

A central thesis of the book is that the current financial service regulatory architecture in many sub-Saharan African countries is ill-equipped to regulate emerging financial services such as mobile money. Although the author, Dr. Madise, refers mainly to developments in his home country, Malaŵi, as a case study, the issues raised in the book are pertinent to many parts of sub-Saharan Africa and other emerging markets. A comparative analysis, for example, between Malawi and other jurisdictions within the region, including Kenya's standard setting *M-Pesa*, enriches the book.

The writing of this book has benefitted greatly from the author's unique background in matters of financial services regulation. I first met Dr. Madise when he was reading for his Master of Laws (LL.M.) degree programme at the University of Western Cape in South Africa, where I continue to serve periodically as Visiting Professor of Law. His chosen research area of specialisation was financial services regulation. I, together with Professor Rieke Wandrag, supervised Dr. Madise's LL.M. dissertation. And Dr. Madise's enthusiasm to explore linkages between his other area of expertise, namely engineering, and financial services regulation stems from his early years at the University of Western Cape.

Dr. Madise obtained his LL.M. (with distinction) at the University of Western Cape before pursuing his Ph.D. studies in the UK. I was privileged to act as Dr. Madise's referee when he applied for admission to carry out doctoral research studies in financial services regulation at the University of Warwick, where I taught in the 1990s.

And so, I am pleased and honoured to provide this Foreword. Dr. Madise has written an exceptional book, and I would recommend it, without hesitation, to all scholars, practitioners and researchers in law, technology and finance.

Kenneth Kaoma Mwenda Ph.D., LL.D., D.Sc. (Econ.)
Rhodes Scholar

South Africa — Extraordinary Professor of Law, University of Pretoria

USA — Adjunct Professor of Law, American University Washington College of Law

Washington, DC, USA — Program Manager, The World Bank

# Preface

This book is a result of research done from 2013 to 2017 for my doctoral studies. The book covers regulation of mobile money and uses case studies from Malaŵi. Although Malaŵi is used as a case study, the issues raised in this book would apply to most cases where disruptive and transformative technology like mobile money are being introduced. Before enrolling as a law student, I worked as an Electronics Engineer for almost a decade. My passion therefore lies in the intersection between law and technology. The book is therefore a convergence of law, technology and finance. The book is recommended for all scholars, researchers and practitioners in the fields of law, economics, finance, engineering and development.

I am immensely grateful to Professor Dalvinder Singh and Professor Abdul Paliwala under whose supervision and mentorship my doctoral thesis was prepared. I sincerely hope I have repaid, in some small way, the faith that they put in me by accepting to be my supervisors. This project would not have been possible without the financial assistance provided by the Commonwealth Scholarship Commission who funded my doctoral studies at the University of Warwick, in the UK. I should also acknowledge Dr. Chikosa Silungwe, a fellow Warwickan, who encouraged me in many ways and was always available to advise me on my journey. Finally, I must thank my sister Professor Nyovani Madise for her inspiration and support and my son Hlekwayo, who was my companion on my Ph.D. journey and bore most of the blunt of my bad days.

Zomba, Malawi — Sunduzwayo Madise

# Contents

# About the Author

**Sunduzwayo Madise** first read Mathematics and Physics at the University of Malaŵi graduating in 1991. For almost a decade, he worked as an engineer for Department of Posts and Telecommunications and the Electricity Supply Corporation of Malaŵi. In 2004, he enrolled for a Bachelor of Laws Honours programme, at the same University and graduated in 2009. After leaving law school, Sundu briefed worked as a State Defence Attorney in the Department of Legal Aid before joining the Faculty of Law of the University of Malaŵi. Sundu has been admitted to the Malaŵi Bar to practise law as an Advocate of the Malaŵi Supreme Court of Appeal and the High Court. In 2010, Sundu went to pursue a Master of Laws programme in International Trade and Business Law at the University of Western Cape, in South Africa, under an Australia Aid and Government of Malaŵi scholarship, graduating *cum laude* in 2011. In 2011, he interned for 3 months at SNR Denton LL.P. in London under the flagship International Lawyers for African (ILFA) Programme. In 2013, Sundu was accepted to pursue doctoral research studies at the University of Warwick, in the UK, and was awarded a full Commonwealth Scholarship. Sundu finished his doctoral studies in 2017. As Ph.D. candidate, Sundu also tutored at the University of Warwick and also served as a Resident Tutor, and Sundu also worked as a volunteer for the award-winning charity, Brilliant Club, teaching students in both primary and secondary schools in the Midlands. Sundu has held various academic and administrative positions in the University of Malaŵi including Head of Department, Coordinator of the LL.M. Commercial Law Programme and Dean of Students. From 1 January 2019, Sundu took up the position of Dean of the Faculty of Law, at the University of Malaŵi.

# Abbreviations and Glossary

| | |
|---|---|
| AML/CTF | Anti-money laundering/counterterrorism financing |
| Anon | Anonymous (used in footnotes and bibliography) |
| BAM | Bankers Association of Malaŵi |
| CAMA | Consumers Association of Malaŵi |
| CBK | Central Bank of Kenya |
| CDD | Customer due diligence |
| CEO | Chief Executive Officer |
| CFTC | Competition and Fair Trading Commission (Malaŵi) |
| E-commerce | Electronic commerce |
| E-money | Electronic money |
| E-value | Electronic value |
| FATF | Financial Action Task Force |
| FCA | Financial Conduct Authority (UK) |
| FDIC | Federal Deposit Insurance Corporation (US) |
| FDIS | Federal Deposit Insurance Scheme (US) |
| FIA | Financial Intelligence Agency (Malaŵi): from February 2017 |
| FIU | Financial Intelligence Unit (Malaŵi): to February 2017 |
| FPC | Financial Policy Committee (UK) |
| FSA | Financial Services Authority (UK) |
| FSCS | Financial Services Compensation Scheme Limited (UK) |
| GDP | Gross domestic product |
| GSM | *Groupe Speciale Mobile*/Global System for Mobile Communication |
| HDI | Human development index |
| ICT | Information communication technology |
| IFI | Index of financial inclusion |

| | |
|---|---|
| KYC | Know your customer |
| M2U/Me2U | Me to you |
| MACRA | Malaŵi Communications Regulator Authority |
| Malswitch | Malaŵi Switch Limited |
| MBC | Malaŵi Broadcasting Corporation |
| MITASS | Malaŵi's Interbank Funds Transfer and Settlement System |
| MLA | Money Laundering Act 2016 (Malaŵi)[1] |
| MNO | Mobile network operator |
| MOU | Memorandum of understanding |
| M-Pesa | Mobile Pesa |
| MPTC | Malaŵi Posts and Telecoms Corporations |
| NatSwitch | National Switch (Malaŵi) |
| NPC | National Payment Committee (Malaŵi) |
| NPS | National Payment System (Malaŵi) |
| P2P | Peer-to-peer/person-to-person |
| PBR | Principle-based regulation |
| PIN | Personal identification number |
| PMG | Postmaster General |
| PRA | Prudential Regulation Authority (UK) |
| RBA | Risk-based assessment |
| RBM | Reserve Bank of Malaŵi |
| RICA | Regulation of Interception of Communications and Provision of Communication-Related Information Act (South Africa) |
| SIM | Subscriber identification module |
| SMS | Small messaging service |
| SPV | Special purpose vehicle |
| Telco(s) | Telecommunication (s)/telecommunication operator |
| TNM | Telekom Networks Malaŵi Limited |
| UK | United Kingdom |
| USA/US | United States of America |

## Non-English Words

| | |
|---|---|
| *Khusa M'manja* | Cheŵa (Malaŵi) phrase for "money in the hands" Khusa is colloquial for money |
| *Mpamba* | Cheŵa (Malaŵi) word for money as in "start-up-capital" |
| *Pesa* | Swahili (Kenya and Tanzania) word for money |

[1]Money Laundering, Proceeds of Serious Crime, and Terrorist Financing Act 2016 (Malaŵi).

## Currencies

| | |
|---|---|
| $ | Dollar (USA) |
| £ | Pound Sterling (UK) |
| K | Kwacha (Malaŵi), t—Tambala (Malaŵi) \| K1 = 100t \| £1 = K947.09[2] |

[2]XE (2018) 'XE Currency Converter' (XE), https://www.xe.com/currencyconverter/convert/?Amount=1&From=GBP&To=MWK. 10 November 2018.

# List of Figures

# List of Tables

CHAPTER 1

# Introduction

Across sub-Saharan Africa, a region that has faced infrastructural challenges for fixed phone lines, the introduction of mobile technology has seen the region "leap-frog the land-line en route to the 21st century".[1] Mungai captured it very well when she said that in Africa, "the mobile phone comes first; before electricity, water, toilets or even food".[2] With the advent of mobile phones has come a horde of add-on services. One such service is mobile money. Most African countries have now some form of mobile money service based largely on the successful *M-Pesa*,[3] a mobile money service provided by Safaricom in Kenya.[4] Mobile money, despite its name, is not part of mobile banking. It is not an extension of one's bank account accessible by the mobile phone or other

[1] William Jack and Tavneet Suri (2011) *Mobile Money: The Economics of M-PESA* (National Bureau of Economic Research, Cambridge, MA), p. 3, http://www.nber.org/papers/w16721. 15 December 2018.

[2] Christine Mungai (2015) 'The Mobile Phone Comes First in Africa; Before Electricity, Water, Toilets or Even Food' *Mail & Guardian Africa* (Johannesburg, 3 March 2015), http://mgafrica.com/article/2015-03-03-mobile-come-first-in-africa-before-electricity-water-toilets-or-even-food. 9 March 2018.

[3] M for Mobile and *Pesa* is Swahili for Money. *M-PESA* therefore translates to "Mobile Money" see Peter Etelej (2011) 'About M-PESA', http://blog.theonlinekenyan.com/about-mpesa. 28 March 2018.

[4] Also, available under the same name Tanzania, but as will be seen later, with limited success.



S. Madise, *The Regulation of Mobile Money*, Palgrave Macmillan Studies in Banking and Financial Institutions,
https://doi.org/10.1007/978-3-030-13831-8_1

Internet-based gadget. It uses the mobile phone as a payment device. It is a revolutionary form of payment as it does not require the opening of a bank account.[5] It is part of the family of electronic money or electronic value. The mobile phone is used as the payment device and unlike the use of plastic money (debit or credit card), there is instantaneous transfer of value without the need of an intervening device such as a point of sale terminal.

Mobile network operators are uniquely placed to offer mobile money services. They already are in the mobile telephone business, they have experience with agent distribution who sell airtime (credit) and have a well-built brand and marketing structure in place.[6] In offering these add-on services, the mobile network operators have demonstrated a radical business gambit by adding a lucrative second stream of revenue in addition to the existing communications backbone. Developing countries have seen a boom in the growth of the mobile money service where it has acted as a tool for achieving financial inclusion and a key part of the development agenda.[7] As opposed to traditional banking, where efforts to increase the number of the banked are purely additive, mobile money is transformative.[8] It targets those who the banking sector would normally ignore.[9] Transformational banking also means that the banking facilities are not limited in space and time. Customers can be registered by agents outside the normal banking hours, and far from any banking premises.[10] Customers can also transact in the comfort of their

[5] Bill Maurer (2011) 'Mobile Money Regulation: A Story Arc of Best Practices and Emerging Realizations' *Notes from the Field* (December 2011), http://faculty.sites.uci.edu/wmmaurer/files/2011/12/Note_Dec2011_IMTFI.pdf. 15 December 2018.

[6] Simone Di Castri (2013) *Mobile Money: Enabling Regulatory Solutions* (GSMA, London), p. 12, http://www.gsma.com/publicpolicy/wp-content/uploads/2013/02/GSMA2013_Report_Mobilelectronicmoney-EnablingRegulatorySolutions.pdf. 20 February 2018.

[7] Malcom Webb and others (2014) *Mobile Money Regulation* (WebbHenderson, Sydney), p. 1, http://webbhenderson.com/wp-content/uploads/2015/06/Mobilelectronicmoney-Regulation-April-2014.pdf. 9 February 2018.

[8] David Porteous (2006) *The Enabling Environment for Mobile Banking in Africa* (Report Commissioned by Department for International Development [DFID], Boston), p. 17, http://bankablefrontier.com/wp-content/uploads/documents/ee.mobil_.banking.report.v3.1.pdf. 14 September 2018.

[9] Ibid.

[10] Ibid., p. 34.

homes and at any time of their choosing. As long as the mobile service is available, customers can potentially transact without limit. Apart from the easiness of transacting, it is also a much more safe way of dealing with payments. The statistics that support the case for mobile money are sobering. While the high-income countries had 91% household penetration of deposit accounts in 2010, sub-Saharan Africa only had 12%.[11] The average across other regions was 40%.[12] Sub-Saharan Africa also had a low automated teller machine density of 5 per 100,000 adults as opposed to 29 for all developing countries.[13] These statistics are evidence that the traditional model of financial inclusion has failed to work in sub-Saharan Africa.

Mobile money turns a phone into a mobile wallet.[14] It allows a user to send and receive money, make withdrawals and purchase goods and services.[15] Through agents employed by mobile network operators, customers exchange their cash for electronic value or electronic money.[16] The cash given to the agents is deposited into a trust or pool account in a bank.[17] The value of mobile money, a form of electronic money, should always match the deposits.[18] The mobile money service acts as a conduit to get money in and out of the financial system in a simple, efficient and user-friendly manner.[19] Although mobile money performs this

[11] CPSS (2012) *Innovations in Retail Payments* (Bank for International Settlements [Committee on Payment and Settlement Systems], Basel, Switzerland), p. 33, http://www.bis.org/cpmi/publ/d102.pdf. 20 February 2018.

[12] Ibid.

[13] Ibid.

[14] Airtel (2013) 'Airtel Money Launch in Malawi' (Airtel), http://africa.airtel.com/wps/wcm/connect/africarevamp/malawi/home/personal/airtel-money. 15 December 2018.

[15] Ibid.

[16] Bill Maurer (2012) 'Regulation as Retrospective Ethnography: Mobile Money and the Arts of Cash' 27 (2) *Banking and Finance Law Review* 299, p. 306, http://www.imtfi.uci.edu/files/docs/2012/bankingfinance_law_review_27.2_maurer.pdf. 15 December 2018.

[17] Ibid.

[18] Nick Hughes and Susie Lonie (2007) 'M-PESA: Mobile Money for the "Unbanked" Turning Cellphones into 24-Hour Tellers in Kenya' 2 (1–2) *Innovations* 63, p. 69, http://www.mitpressjournals.org/doi/pdf/10.1162/itgg.2007.2.1-2.63. 15 December 2018.

[19] Ernesto M Flores-Roux and Judith Mariscal (2010) 'The Enigma of Mobile Money Systems' (79) *Communications & Strategies*, p. 52, ftp://ftp.repec.org/opt/ReDIF/RePEc/idt/journl/CS7903/CS79_MARISCAM_FLORES-ROUX.pdf. 14 February 2018.

seemingly simple task, in reality the mobile money ecosystem is significantly complex.[20] It includes various actors, such as mobile network operators, customers, banks, retailers and merchants.[21] This diversity needs to be taken on board when designing a regulatory framework for mobile money.[22] Webb et al. argue that what mobile money needs is "a carefully considered regulatory framework that facilitates rapid deployment and easy access to mobile money, while also appropriately protecting the integrity and stability of the financial system".[23] Mobile money has a potential to positively impact on the financial inclusion agenda by providing financial services to the unbanked sections of the population but in doing so it raises regulatory and competition issues.[24] For example, deposit-taking has always been a mainstay of the banking business. By taking money directly from consumers, mobile money issuers are offering a direct challenge and wading into banking territory.

This book aims to analyse the regulatory framework of mobile money by looking at the regulatory approaches that have been used in the financial sector. Mobile money being a service that straddles the communication and financial sectors has its own regulatory challenges. Williams has argued that:

> Telecom regulators are passive to regulating mobile money, which is a positive. However, the financial regulators regulate mobile money based on how they perceive mobile money, either as a core or non-banking service.[25]

In most countries where mobile money has proven to be successful, such as Malaŵi and Kenya, the central bank, regulator of the financial sector considers mobile money as a non-banking service. This has huge

[20] Ibid.

[21] Ibid.

[22] Di Castri (2013), p. 34.

[23] Webb and others (2014), p. 1.

[24] Michael U Klein and Colin Mayer (2011) *Mobile Banking and Financial Inclusion: The Regulatory Lessons* (Policy Reserach Working Paper, The World Bank), p. 4, http://documents.worldbank.org/curated/en/docsearch/document-type/620265. 14 February 2018.

[25] Idongesit Williams (2013) 'Regulatory Frameworks and Implementation Patterns for Mobile Money in Africa: The Case of Kenya, Ghana and Nigeria' (*ICT Conference*, Accra, Ghana), p. 1, http://www.academia.edu/download/42068100/Regulatory_frameworks_and_Implementation20160204-17000-9tcws1.pdf. 17 February 2018.

ramifications for the regulatory approach taken to supervise mobile money. Since the target for the mobile money service is the poor unbanked and under banked in rural areas,[26] mobile money is a key developmental tool towards achieving financial inclusion. The question that arises is whether the traditional financial regulatory architecture is best suited to regulating a new form of money such as mobile money. Klein and Mayer argue that this may be the most important regulatory struggle facing an emerging service such as mobile money.[27] They argue that ideally, the best way is to desegregate the service into its constituent components and then structure the regulation to mirror this.[28] This leads to the question: What type of regulation would best suit each component? In the case of mobile money, although it is an emerging service, lessons from other financial services are crucial in formulating a regulatory framework for the service.

For mobile money services, there is a distinction between the telco-led[29] and bank-led[30] models. Telco-led (from telecommunication led) are associated with light touch while the bank-led are associated with prudential regulation. Light touch is a reference to a regulatory environment which is not strictly controlled or supervised. Chapter 4 discusses different types of regulation. Both the central banks of Kenya and Malaŵi allowed mobile money services to operate through a "Letter of No Objection".[31] This instrument was

[26] Rajanish Dass and Sujoy Pal (2011) 'Exploring the Factors Affecting the Adoption of Mobile Financial Services Among the Rural Under-Banked' (*European Conference on Information Systems*, Helsinki), http://aisel.aisnet.org/ecis2011/246. 26 April 2018.

[27] Klein and Mayer (2011), p. 5.

[28] Ibid.

[29] Such as *M-Pesa*, Airtel Money and *Mpamba*.

[30] Such as WIZZIT and MTN Money in South Africa.

[31] Kenya has since enacted the National Payment System Act 39 of 2011 of the Laws of Kenya 2011, http://kenyalaw.org/kl/fileadmin/pdfdownloads/Acts/NationalPaymentSystemsAct__No39of2011.pdf. 19 February 2018. Section 12 expressly for authorisation of payment service providers.

Rasheda Sultana (2009) 'Mobile Banking: Overview of Regulatory Framework in Emerging Markets' (*4th Communication Policy Research, South Conference*) Negombo, Sri Lanka, pp. 9–10, http://papers.ssrn.com/sol3/papers.cfm?abstract_id=1554160. 14 February 2018.

Gerald Nyaoma (2009) 'Regulating Mobile Money: The Case of M-Pesa in Kenya' (Global Policy Forum, Nairobi, 16 September 2009), http://www.afi-global.org/sites/default/files/GPF_Gerald_Nyaoma.pdf. 20 May 2018.

issued in the absence of a statutory framework for regulation and licensing "as an interim means of permitting mobile money services to operate".[32] The Kenyan and Malaŵian models of mobile money are telco-led. They are called telco-led because they are set up by telecommunications operators and run as an add-on service.[33] Bank-led models involve non-banks and banks working in partnership.[34] Will the creation of mobile money services potentially expose the financial system to risk, from both prudential and conduct of business fronts, and result in having companies that are too big to fail?[35] As noted, the regulation of mobile money potentially includes more than one regulator. The question that naturally arises is whether plurality of regulators is helpful or hinders that growth of such an emerging service.

As a new service, mobile money presents regulators with a challenge. Most are slow to appreciate that they are dealing with a fundamentally new species of electronic payment instruments.[36] Unlike other payments methods, the means of effecting the mobile money payment system are through the mobile phone device.[37] Regulating the service as if it were just a financial service overlooks the technical aspects of the service. The danger with this approach is an improperly regulated service. Unless properly regulated, the attainment of critical mass and interconnectivity of the mobile money ecosystem could pose problems for the national payment system. There is also the potential risk posed by an increase of

Guidelines for Mobile Payment Systems (2011) (Reserve Bank of Malaŵi), http://www.rbm.mw/documents/payment_systems/Mobile%20Payments%20Systems%20Guidelines.pdf. 13 March 2018.

[32] Webb and others (2014), p. 2.

[33] Maurer (2011).

[34] Sultana (2009), p. 12.

[35] For the concept of too big to fail, see generally James R. Barth and Class Wihlborg (2016) 'Too Big to Fail and Too Big to Save: Dilemmas for Banking Reform' (235) *National Institute Economic Review*, http://journals.sagepub.com/doi/pdf/10.1177/002795011623500113. 9 February 2018.

[36] Simon L Lelieveldt (1996) 'How to Regulate Electronic Cash: An Overview of Regulatory Issues and Strategies' 46 *American University Law Review* 1163, p. 1166, http://heinonline.org/hol-cgi-bin/get_pdf.cgi?handle=hein.journals/aulr46&section=39. 17 March 2018.

[37] Ibid., p. 1168.

mobile money on money supply, which may be inflationary.[38] However, a balance needs to be found that allows the service to roll out without being unduly suffocated by a stringent regulatory framework.

Malaŵi has witnessed an exponential surge in mobile phone users with two dominant mobile network operators, Telekom Networks Malawi (TNM) and Airtel. TNM was the first player in the mobile phone business and largely benefitted from the unbundling of the communications sector.[39] Airtel, owned by the Bharti Group of India,[40] was previously known as Zain and Celtel before.[41] With the advent of mobile phones has come a horde of add-on services. One such service is mobile money. The two mobile network operators have launched Airtel Money[42] also called *Khusa M'manja*[43] and TNM *Mpamba*.[44] Both have strong parallels with the Kenyan *M-Pesa*.[45]

This book argues that the current regulatory framework for mobile money, based on the traditional architecture of financial service regulation, does not address the specific issues and challenges posed by mobile

[38]William Jack and Tavneet Suri (2011) 'Mobile Money: The Economics of M-PESA', p. 11 (National Bureau of Economic Research), http://www.nber.org/papers/w16721. 15 December 2018.

George Ngigi (2012) 'M-Pesa Linked to Rise in Inflation' *Business Daily* (14 February 2012), http://www.businessdailyafrica.com/M-Pesa-linked-to-rise-in-inflation/-/539552/1327538/-/13rogmr/-/index.html. 23 February 2018.

See also Will Mutua (3 June 2012) 'How M-Pesa Disrupts Entire Economies', http://memeburn.com/2012/03/how-m-pesa-disrupts-entire-economies/. 28 March 2018.

[39]Author's personal knowledge having worked for the Department of Posts and Telecommunications.

[40]'Bharti Airtel' (Bharti Airtel, 2017), http://www.airtel.in/about-bharti/about-bharti-airtel. 30 May 2018.

[41]Anon (2008) 'Celtel Morphs into Zain' (TeleGeography, 2008), https://www.telegeography.com/products/commsupdate/articles/2008/08/04/celtel-morphs-into-zain/. 30 May 2018. Anon (2010) 'Airtel Swallows Zain' (Vanguard Media Limited, 2010), http://www.vanguardngr.com/2010/11/airtel-swallows-zain/. 30 May 2018.

[42]Launched on 29 February, 2012—'Airtel Money Launch in Malawi' (Airtel, 2013), http://africa.airtel.com/wps/wcm/connect/africarevamp/malawi/home/personal/airtel-money. 15 December 2018.

[43]Literally meaning 'money in the hands.' *Khusa* is colloquial for money and *m'manja* means "in the hands".

[44]*Mpamba* correctly means "start-up-capital" but is also used to refer to money.

[45]Tanzania also has *M-Pesa* but the service in Tanzania is nowhere as successful as its Kenyan counterpart.

money as an emerging service. As a solution, it proposes principles of an appropriate regulatory framework for mobile money, using Malaŵi as a case study, by analysing the local context and taking cognisance of the need not to over regulate nor to create regulatory risks for an emerging industry. The importance of mobile money is not only in its role as a development tool for achieving financial inclusion, but also the reality that it is a service that in most developing countries has come to stay.[46] The underlying assumption is that the current regulatory architecture of the financial service is incoherent and not ideally suitable for an emerging and hybrid service such as mobile money. Therefore the service requires a different regulatory approach.

At the root of the problem is that the introduction of mobile money did not witness an accompanying regulatory shift to embrace it. The same old rules were essentially realigned to accommodate the new service. Therefore, there is a need for an effective and efficient mobile money regulatory framework, which would protect consumers, allow innovative growth and ensure financial soundness. Consumer protection is crucial in a country like Malaŵi with low literacy (66%),[47] and financial literacy levels (57%).[48] The fear is that those who are not financially literate are vulnerable and much more open to market abuse.[49] This book argues for a regulatory framework that takes cognisance of the fact that the mobile money service is not only a communications service but a financial service as well. Its uniqueness requires a unique regulatory approach.

In effect then, the book sets out to answer the question: *How can mobile money be effectively regulated to achieve financial inclusion, financial stability and financial integrity?* To answer this question, the book will analyse the development aspects of mobile money and how this can lead to financial inclusion without posing a financial risk. In terms of

[46] Kevin P Donovan (2012) 'Mobile Money, More Freedom? The Impact of M-PESA's Network Power on Development as Freedom' 6 *International Journal of Communication* 2647, p. 2647, http://ijoc.org/index.php/ijoc/article/view/1575. 20 May 2018.

[47] 73.02% male and 59.03 female—UNESCO (2016) 'Malawi' (UNESCO Institute for Statistics), http://uis.unesco.org/en/country/mw. 17 February 2018.

[48] Phillip Dzikanyanga (2016) 'Reserve Bank of Malawi to Launch Financial Literacy Strategy' *Nyasa Times* (20 May 2016), http://www.nyasatimes.com/reserve-bank-of-malawi-to-launch-financial-literacy-strategy/#sthash.vWN1Njlb.dpuf. 17 February 2018.

[49] Porteous (2006), p. 31.

methodology, the approach taken in this book is to break down the central question into the following sub-questions:

- How does mobile money fit into the financial system?
- What risk does an unregulated mobile money service pose, to consumers and the financial system?
- How can the law achieve financial stability and integrity as well as financial inclusion?
- How can the regulator discharge its duty so that the interests of consumers are balanced with those of mobile money issuers?
- To what extent is the focus on development and provision of financial services for the poor? Is there a contradiction between efficient regulation of mobile money and services for the poor?
- How does the global anti-money laundering regime affect the operation of mobile money?

The study of mobile money and its effect on financial inclusion is important for countries in sub-Saharan Africa. For example, in Malaŵi, in 2008, 19% of the adult population was banked and 55% was categorised as financially excluded.[50] By 2014, there was a slight increase in the percentage of the banked increasing to 27 while 51% were still financially excluded.[51] The number of financially included includes those with bank accounts plus those with access to formal financial services even though they may have no accounts. Access to financial services seems to be the preserve of the rich.[52] High levels of inflation have also prevented poor people from accessing finance.[53] In the midst of all this, however, mobile money is seen as a possible solution. The success in Kenya of *M-Pesa*, which managed to recruit 50% of the adult population in under 4 years, has given hope of replication

[50] Finscope (2014) *FinScope Consumer Survey Malawi 2014* (Finmark Trust, Midrand, Johannesburg), p. 19, http://www.finmark.org.za/wp-content/uploads/2016/08/FS-Malawi-2014-Launch-presentation.pdf. 5 May 2017.

[51] Ibid.

[52] Peter Dittus and Michael Klein (2011) *On Harnessing the Potential of Financial Inclusion* (BIS Working Papers No. 347, Bank of International Settlements, Basel), p. 1, http://www.bis.org/publ/work347.pdf. 20 February 2018.

[53] Alka Bhatia and Peter Mwanakatwe (2016) 'Malawi 2016' (Africa Economic Outlook, OECD Development Centre), p. 2, http://www.africaneconomicoutlook.org/sites/default/files/2016-05/Malawi_GB_2016%20WEB.pdf. 9 March 2018.

in other countries.[54] If *M-Pesa*'s success can be replicated in Malaŵi, even if not to the same extent, the mobile phone can become a prime driver to lift people out of poverty.[55]

On a rather sad note, although mobile money initially targeted the unbanked, this is no longer the case. A variety of "niche-market" services such as electricity and water, car fuel and pay television subscription have been added to the service.[56] The advantage of the mobile money service is that more people, banked and unbanked, are likely to resort to using the mobile money service to transact.

## 1.1 Chapter Outline

Chapter 2 is an introduction to money. In a way, this provides a framework of analysis as the chapter starts to answer the question; what is being regulated? To place the study into context, it analyses the evolution of money, central banks, the regulation of money and the financial services. Apart from providing an overview of the historical development of money, it looks at emerging forms of money and the challenges these new forms of money present. For example, most forms of digital forms of money such as Bitcoin are private money and not state-regulated. What does this mean for the future of money? The chapter also analyses the nature of payment system.

Chapter 3 analyses the development of the mobile phone and how this has uniquely led to the success of the mobile money service, especially in sub-Saharan Africa. It looks at how mobile network operators have used mobile money as a solution to the remittance dilemma. It examines how the mobile money payment system interacts with the national payment system.

Chapter 4 looks at the different types of regulation. It analyses the various approaches to regulation and theories of regulation and their application to the financial services. The chapter employs the notion of

[54] Dittus and Klein (2011), p. 1.

[55] Ibid., p. 2.

[56] TNM (2017) 'Mpamba, TNM Mobile Money' (Telekom Networks Malawi), https://www.tnmmpamba.co.mw/. 12 March 2017. Airtel (2013).

Selipha Kihagi (2013) 'Malawians to Pay for Fuel Services Using Airtel Money' (HumanIPO), http://www.humanipo.com/news/36717/malawians-to-pay-for-fuel-services-using-airtel-money/. 12 March 2018.

regulatory space as the lens through which to analyse regulatory issues. The chapter argues that regulation must be responsive to the regulated environment to be effective.

Chapter 5 analyses the regulation of money and the many issues that such a regulatory framework presents. It also narrows down to approaches that may be useful in regulating mobile money. The chapter notes that in most jurisdiction, light-touch regulation has been used as the preferred model for mobile money. The chapter analyses the various issues that may arise in regulating a new service such as mobile money based on the existing regulatory architecture of the financial system.

Chapter 6 discusses the concept of financial inclusion. The chapter argues that financial inclusion as a concept suffers from being associated with only the formal financial system. It attempts to locally contextualise the concept and draw interlinks between mobile money and the financial inclusion. Using the study of a local village bank, as a case in point, it argues for a redefinition of the concept of financial inclusion to reflect local contexts.

Chapter 7 undertakes a comparative study of mobile money in Kenya and Malaŵi. It also examines the factors that have led *M-Pesa* to be very successful in Kenya but not in other jurisdictions like Tanzania. It suggests that mobile money developments are more likely to follow the Tanzania growth model as opposed to the Kenyan one. It also examines the differences in operation between telco-led and bank-led models and concludes that the regulatory choices are the reason for the success of the former.

Chapter 8 analyses the existing regulatory framework around mobile money in Malaŵi. In analysing the plurality of regulators involved with mobile money, it concludes that the traditional banking architecture is ill-suited for mobile money and that the plurality of regulators may lead to a lack of regulatory focus and regulatory arbitrage. The hybrid nature of mobile money is at the centre of the regulatory incoherence. Mobile money while being a financial service also is a service that rides on the rail of the telecommunication service. Since in most countries, mobile money is offered by mobile network operators, regulating it offers a challenge to the financial regulator and the communications regulator.

Chapter 9 proposes an alternative regulatory framework for mobile money. It conducts an analysis of the regulatory arena and the key participants and lays out two possible routes: an independent agency or streamlining existing regulators. The chapter proposes setting up an autonomous agency within the central bank to regulator not only mobile money but all forms of electronic money which are outside banking supervision.

Chapter 10 provides the conclusion for the book and analyses the challenges that setting up an autonomous agency may present and how these can be overcome. The chapter also highlights some issues which are likely to arise once mobile money in the post-financial inclusion phase.

## References


Airtel (2013) 'Airtel Money Launch in Malawi', http://africa.airtel.com/wps/wcm/connect/africarevamp/malawi/home/personal/airtel-money. 15 December 2018.

Airtel swallows Zain (Vanguard Media Limited, 2010), http://www.vanguardngr.com/2010/11/airtel-swallows-zain/. 30 May 2018.

Alka Bhatia and Peter Mwanakatwe (2016) 'Malawi 2016' (Africa Economic Outlook, OECD Development Centre), http://www.africaneconomicoutlook.org/sites/default/files/2016.

Anon (2008) 'Celtel Morphs into Zain' (TeleGeography, 2008), https://www.telegeography.com/products/commsupdate/articles/2008/08/04/celtel-morphs-into-zain/. 30 May 2018. Anon (2010).

Bharti Airtel (Bharti Airtel, 2017), http://www.airtel.in/about-bharti/about-bharti-airtel. 30 May 2018.

Bill Maurer (2011) 'Mobile Money Regulation: A Story Arc of Best Practices and Emerging Realizations' *Notes from the Field* (December 2011), http://faculty.sites.uci.edu/wmmaurer/files/2011/12/Note_Dec2011_IMTFI.pdf. 15 December 2018.

Bill Maurer (2012) 'Regulation as Retrospective Ethnography: Mobile Money and the Arts of Cash' 27 (2) *Banking and Finance Law Review* 299, http://www.imtfi.uci.edu/files/docs/2012/bankingfinance_law_review_27.2_maurer.pdf. 15 December 2018.

Christine Mungai (2015) 'The Mobile Phone Comes First in Africa; Before Electricity, Water, Toilets or Even Food' *Mail & Guardian Africa* (Johannesburg, 3 March 2015), http://mgafrica.com/article/2015-03-03-mobile-come-first-in-africa-before-electricity-water-toilets-or-even-food. 9 March 2018.

CPSS (2012) *Innovations in Retail Payments* (Bank for International Settlements [Committee on Payment and Settlement Systems], Basel, Switzerland), http://www.bis.org/cpmi/publ/d102.pdf. 20 February 2018.

Ernesto M Flores-Roux and Judith Mariscal (2010) 'The Enigma of Mobile Money Systems' (79) *Communications & Strategies*, ftp://ftp.repec.org/

opt/ReDIF/RePEc/idt/journl/CS7903/CS79_MARISCAM_FLORES-ROUX.pdf. 14 February 2018.

Finscope (2014) *FinScope Consumer Survey Malawi 2014* (Finmark Trust, Midrand, Johannesburg), http://www.finmark.org.za/wp-content/uploads/2016/08/FS-Malawi-2014-Launch-presentation.pdf. 5 May 2017.

George Ngigi (2012) 'M-Pesa Linked to Rise in Inflation' *Business Daily* (14 February 2012), http://www.businessdailyafrica.com/M-Pesa-linked-to-rise-in-inflation/-/539552/1327538/-/13rogmr/-/index.html. 23 February 2018.

Gerald Nyaoma (2009) 'Regulating Mobile Money: The Case of M-Pesa in Kenya' (Global Policy Forum, Nairobi, 16 September 2009), http://www.afi-global.org/sites/default/files/GPF_Gerald_Nyaoma.pdf. 20 May 2018.

Guidelines for Mobile Payment Systems (2011) (Reserve Bank of Malaŵi), http://www.rbm.mw/documents/payment_systems/Mobile%20Payments%20Systems%20Guidelines.pdf. 13 March 2018.

Idongesit Williams (2013) 'Regulatory Frameworks and Implementation Patterns for Mobile Money in Africa: The Case of Kenya, Ghana and Nigeria' (*ICT Conference*, Accra, Ghana), http://www.academia.edu/download/42068100/Regulatory_frameworks_and_Implementation20160204-17000-9tcws1.pdf. 17 February 2018.

James R Barth and Class Wihlborg (2016) 'Too Big to Fail and Too Big to Save: Dilemmas for Banking Reform' (235) *National Institute Economic Review*, http://journals.sagepub.com/doi/pdf/10.1177/002795011623500113. 9 February 2018.

Kevin P Donovan (2012) 'Mobile Money, More Freedom? The Impact of M-PESA's Network Power on Development as Freedom' 6 *International Journal of Communication* 2647, http://ijoc.org/index.php/ijoc/article/view/1575. 20 May 2018.

Malcom Webb and others (2014) *Mobile Money Regulation* (WebbHenderson, Sydney), http://webbhenderson.com/wp-content/uploads/2015/06/Mobilelectronicmoney-Regulation-April-2014.pdf. 9 February 2018.

Michael U Klein and Colin Mayer (2011) *Mobile Banking and Financial Inclusion: The Regulatory Lessons* (Policy Research Working Paper, The World Bank), http://documents.worldbank.org/curated/en/docsearch/document-type/620265. 14 February 2018.

National Payment System Act 39 of 2011 of the Laws of Kenya 2011, http://kenyalaw.org/kl/fileadmin/pdfdownloads/Acts/NationalPaymentSystemsAct__No39of2011.pdf. 19 February 2018.

Nick Hughes and Susie Lonie (2007) 'M-PESA: Mobile Money for the "Unbanked" Turning Cellphones into 24-Hour Tellers in Kenya' 2 (1–2) *Innovations* 63, http://www.mitpressjournals.org/doi/pdf/10.1162/itgg.2007.2.1-2.63. 15 December 2018.

Peter Dittus and Michael Klein (2011) *On Harnessing the Potential of Financial Inclusion* (BIS Working Papers No. 347, Bank of International Settlements, Basel), http://www.bis.org/publ/work347.pdf. 20 February 2018.

Peter Etelej (2011) 'About M-PESA', http://blog.theonlinekenyan.com/about-mpesa. 28 March 2018.

Phillip Dzikanyanga (2016) 'Reserve Bank of Malawi to Launch Financial Literacy Strategy' *Nyasa Times* (20 May 2016), http://www.nyasatimes.com/reserve-bank-of-malawi-to-launch-financial-literacy-strategy/#sthash.vWN1Njlb.dpuf. 17 February 2018.

Rajanish Dass and Sujoy Pal (2011) 'Exploring the Factors Affecting the Adoption of Mobile Financial Services Among the Rural Under-Banked' (*European Conference on Information Systems*, Helsinki), http://aisel.aisnet.org/ecis2011/246. 26 April 2018.

Rasheda Sultana (2009) 'Mobile Banking: Overview of Regulatory Framework in Emerging Markets' (*4th Communication Policy Research, South Conference*) Negombo, Sri Lanka, http://papers.ssrn.com/sol3/papers.cfm?abstract_id=1554160. 14 February 2018.

Selipha Kihagi (2013) 'Malawians to Pay for Fuel Services Using Airtel Money' (HumanIPO), http://www.humanipo.com/news/36717/malawians-to-pay-for-fuel-services-using-airtel-money/. 12 March 2018.

Simon L Lelieveldt (1996) 'How to Regulate Electronic Cash: An Overview of Regulatory Issues and Strategies' 46 *American University Law Review* 1163, http://heinonline.org/hol-cgi-bin/get_pdf.cgi?handle=hein.journals/aulr46&section=39. 17 March 2018.

Simone Di Castri (2013) *Mobile Money: Enabling Regulatory Solutions* (GSMA, London), http://www.gsma.com/publicpolicy/wp-content/uploads/2013/02/GSMA2013_Report_Mobilelectronicmoney-EnablingRegulatorySolutions.pdf. 20 February 2018.

TNM (2017) 'Mpamba, TNM Mobile Money' (Telekom Networks Malawi), https://www.tnmmpamba.co.mw/. 12 March 2017.

UNESCO (2016) 'Malawi' (UNESCO Institute for Statistics), http://uis.unesco.org/en/country/mw. 17 February 2018.

Will Mutua (3 June 2012) 'How M-Pesa Disrupts Entire Economies', http://memeburn.com/2012/03/how-m-pesa-disrupts-entire-economies/. 28 March 2018.

William Jack and Tavneet Suri (2011) *Mobile Money: The Economics of M-PESA* (National Bureau of Economic Research, Cambridge, MA), http://www.nber.org/papers/w16721. 15 December 2018.

CHAPTER 2

# Introduction to Money

## 2.1 Introduction

As a form of value, mobile money raises the immediate question of whether anything other than fiat money could be money. Fiat money refers to the money that circulates in countries under the legal decree of the issuing country.[1] The biggest problem of regulation of money arises because of the way in which money or credit supply in various forms has expanded in ways which national and global regulators find difficult to control. Braithwaite and Drahos have referred to money as "the root of all financial regulation".[2] An analysis of money and mobile money is therefore a fitting place to start unpacking the regulatory issues of mobile money. The underlying question for the regulation of emerging forms of money, such as mobile money, is the extent to which they create new or different risks, and whether forms of control would endanger the very prospect of financial inclusion they seem to promote.

The historical development of money illustrates that there were other forms of money issued by non-state authorities in the past before the

[1] Abba P Lerner (1947) 'Money as a Creature of the State' 37 (2) *The American Economic Review* 312, p. 314, http://www.jstor.org/stable/pdf/1821139.pdf. 29 April 2018.

[2] John Braithwaite and Peter Drahos (2000) 'Finacial Regulation' in *Global Business Regulation* (Cambridge University Press, Cambridge), p. 88.



S. Madise, *The Regulation of Mobile Money*, Palgrave Macmillan Studies in Banking and Financial Institutions,
https://doi.org/10.1007/978-3-030-13831-8_2

advent of fiat money. One example is the use of the *denarius*, or silver penny by the Hanseatic League (1400–1800), a commercial non-state confederation of cities in Germany.[3] Another example is the Maria Theresa Thaler (dollar), used in world trade from the fifteenth century issued by the Empress of the Astro-Hungarian Empire.[4] It was used in trade across parts of the Mediterranean and Arabia, and Thaler coins were, as late as 1974, found on the East African Coast.[5] The German Mark only replaced the Thaler in 1873.[6] It would seem the emergence of the Mark, the Spanish Peso and Pound Sterling heralded the emergence of the era of world currencies. Although the US Dollar is arguably the dominant currency, it was only introduced in 1875, and as a way of delinking the new country from the British dominion.[7] Recently, there has been the emergence of new forms of money such as Bitcoin and mobile money. The emergence of new forms of money which are not state-issued has raised questions as to whether anything that does not have state guarantee can effectively serve as money, and if so how can they maintain their value?

This chapter looks at the origins of money and the evolution of the central bank, as an issuer of money and regulator of financial services. The chapter is divided into four main sections. The first looks at the origins of money and the emergence of central banks, the second section discusses the emergence of regulation of money and the regulatory issues around money. The third section analyses various emerging forms of money, and the fourth section looks at the nature of the payment system.

[3] Stephen Halliday (2009) 'The First Common Market? The Hanseatic League' 59 (7) *History Today*, http://www.historytoday.com/stephen-halliday/first-common-market-hanseatic-league. 13 September 2018.

[4] Peter Harrigan (2003) 'Tales of a Thaler' 54 (1) *ARAMCO World* 14, http://archive.aramcoworld.com/issue/200301/tales.of.a.thaler.htm. 13 September 2018.

[5] Ibid.

[6] Robert A Leonard (1994) 'Money and Language' (55) *Money: Lure, Lore, and Literature* 1, p. 4, https://www.unc.edu/~salemi/Econ006/Leonard.pdf. 13 September 2018.

[7] Ibid., p. 5.

## 2.2 Origins and Nature of Money

Money has been around for millennia although its origin has been the subject of academic debate for centuries.[8] There are two main theories of how money emerged. The dominant theory states that money is a creation of the market, emerging out of barter and serving fundamentally to facilitate commodity exchange.[9] States only embraced money because of the power it gave them, such as the monopoly to issue legal tender.[10] The alternative theory argues that money actually is the deliberate and positive creation of the state and that barter succeeded money and was not the precursor.[11] Proponents of this theory, such as Graeber, assert that the essential nature of money is credit or debt.[12] There are two common strands of thought within this theory: the idea that money originated as a unit of account for debt and the proposition that money creation involves the simultaneous creation of money and debt. A detailed discussion of these theories is outside the scope of this book, but a reading of Graeber's work[13] would be recommended to anyone interested in theories of money. Suffice to say, this theory posits that debt is the real money. Under this theory therefore, the regulation of debt becomes crucial since an unregulated debt market can lead to inflation. This book adopts the dominant theory of the evolution of money.

Money has changed form, and although it may have been a different commodity in different societies, it has always maintained the same

[8] Carl Menger (1892) *On the Origins of Money (2009 repr)* (Ludwig von Mises Institute, Auburn, Alabama), p. 45.

Glyn Davies (2002) 'From Primitive and Ancient Money to the Invention of Coinage, 3000–600 BC' in *A History of Money: From Ancient Times to the Present Day* (University of Wales Press, Cardiff), Chapter 2.

Nigel Dodd (2014) *The Social Life of Money* (Princeton University Press, Princeton, NJ), p. 15.

Braithwaite and Drahos (2000), p. 88.

[9] Michael Hudson (2004) 'The Archaeology of Money: Debt Versus Barter Theories of Money's Origins' in Randal L. Wray (ed) *Credit and State Theories of Money* (Edward Elgar, Cheltenham), p. 99.

[10] David Graeber (2011) *Debt: The First 5,000 Years* (Melville House, Brooklyn, New York), p. 49.

[11] Hudson (2004), p. 107.

[12] Graeber (2011), p. 22.

[13] Ibid.

basic function, that of serving to facilitate exchange and trade. As societies developed and civilisations flourished, money also evolved with time. Montesquieu, in his seminal work, wrote in 1748 that money is a "sign which represents the value of all merchandise".[14] As an example, take the local farmer in the old days. Suppose he harvested corn and put it into bags, ordinarily, he would go to the marketplace to exchange his produce with goods, which he needed. However, suppose he wanted a rabbit to cook, he would then have to take a portion of the corn in exchange for the rabbit. However, what if the hunter wanted eggs instead? An exchange was not possible unless the farmer first exchanged with another person who had something that the hunter desired. Even if the hunter wanted the corn, how much corn would be exchangeable for the rabbit? What is clear is that in the marketplace, everyone is looking for something and they are prepared to exchange their produce or wares. However, supply and demand do not always "quantitatively coincide".[15] In the marketplace, "there may be many people wanting, and many possessed those things wanted" so barter will only occur where there is a "double coincidence".[16] The coincidence of wants is crucial in a barter economy.[17] As this is not always possible, then a third, somewhat, neutral commodity may just be the answer.

If "$X$" refers to this neutral commodity, then the farmer may demand a certain multiple of $X$ to trade with his bag of corn. On the other hand, the hunter may demand a fraction of $X$ to exchange with his rabbit. The farmer can then exchange his bag of corn for a certain multiple of $X$, and since the hunter is also looking for a fraction of $X$, it allows the farmer and hunter to trade directly. Assuming the corn exchanges at $5X$ and the rabbit at $X$, the farmer can trade with the hunter and still have $4X$ left for use to exchange for other commodities he needs or keep the change. It is this commodity, $X$, that became *money*. Money took up the function as a medium of exchange.[18] It also offered a means of setting up

[14] Charles de Secondat Baron de Montesquieu (1748) 'Of Laws in Relation to the Use of Money' in *The Spirit of Laws (2001 repr)* (Batoche Books, Ontario), p. 407.

[15] Menger (1892), p. 20.

[16] William Stanley Jevons (1875) 'Barter' in *Money and the Mechanism of Exchange* (D. Appleton and Company, New York), p. 3.

[17] Braithwaite and Drahos (2000), p. 88.

[18] RTS (1854) *Money; Its Nature, History, Uses, and Responsibilities* (The Religious Tract Society, London), p. 75.

the standard of value.[19] Using the above example, therefore, it can be said that the value of a rabbit would be a fifth of that of a bag of corn; or a bag of corn would procure 5 rabbits. This allowed each commodity brought to the marketplace to be converted to its money equivalent and thereby to set up its price. Money became a "common denominator or common measure of value in terms of which [to] estimate the value of all other goods so that their value becomes capable of the [easiest] comparison".[20] Money also allowed goods and services which could not be subdivided to be monetised, such as the product of a tailor.[21]

For a commodity to perform the function of money, it had to be readily saleable or liquid.[22] Liquidity is a measure of how quickly and easily something can be traded and is "determined by the demand and supply of immediacy".[23] When compared, other commodities brought to the marketplace are all less liquid than the commodity that functions as a money, making it an attractive commodity to all.[24] Menger used the Latin expression *percuniam habens, habet omnem rem quem vult habere* translated as when you've got money you have got everything you want.[25] The corollary is therefore that if one comes to the marketplace with anything other than money, then one places themselves at a disadvantage, compared to the one who comes to the marketplace with a stock of money.[26] Whatever it is, money is that commodity that is accepted by all as a medium of exchange. It serves as a facilitator of exchange. As a unit of exchange, it also provides a solution to the question: *at what rate will an exchange be made?*[27] Money becomes the unit of exchange. Money also performs another key function, that of storing

[19] Ibid.

[20] Jevons (1875), p. 5.

[21] Ibid., p. 6.

[22] Menger (1892), p. 39.

[23] Sanford J Grossman and Merton H Miller (1988) 'Liquidity and Market Structure' 43 (3) *The Journal of Finance*, p. 617, http://onlinelibrary.wiley.com/doi/10.1111/j.1540-6261.1988.tb04594.x/pdf. 6 October 2018.

[24] Menger (1892), p. 39.

[25] Ibid., 40; Translation from 'Can Anyone Translate This Latin for Me?' (Yahoo! 2011), https://answers.yahoo.com/question/index?qid=20110704153951AAed8Dn. 7 November 2018.

[26] Ibid., pp. 39, 40.

[27] Jevons (1875), p. 5.

value. A trader can sell his goods at the marketplace but need not be under pressure to buy anything. He may keep his money until the day he wants to buy something he desires. This allows one to temporarily convey and transform value from one form to another, using money as a common denominator.[28]

Money in the classical sense must perform three core functions. As a medium of exchange, it must facilitate the payments.[29] It must also be able to facilitate the transfer of property by having a purchasing power, and it does this through storing value.[30] Money must also serve as a unit of account and the standard measure of value.[31] The ability to maintain its purchasing power over time is an attribute of good money.[32] The first items of the commodity to serve as money were precious metals and rare articles or stones.[33] Although the Egyptians, Chaldeans and Assyrians had used metals for thousands of years, King Alyattes of Lydia (Turkey) created the earliest known minted coin in 600 BC.[34] However, there is evidence of the Zhou Dynasty in China perfecting bronze casting and making replicas as a form of money in 1100 BC.[35] China is also accredited with the invention of paper money.[36]

[28] Ibid., p. 6.

[29] Thomas H Greco Jr (1997) 'New Money: A Creative Opportunity for Busines' 11 (3) *Global Development Research Centre [First Published in Perspectives on Business and Global Change* (World Business Academy), http://www.gdrc.org/icm/new-money.html. 14 November 2018.

Robleh Ali and others (2014b) 'The Economics of Digital Currencies' 54 *Quarterly Bulletin* (Bank of England), p. 278, http://www.bankofengland.co.uk/publications/Documents/quarterlybulletin/2014/qb14q3digitalcurrenciesbitcoin2.pdf. 14 September 2018.

[30] Ibid.

[31] Ibid.

[32] Alaxander P Reed Jr (1998) *Money and the Global Economy* (Woodhead Publishing, Cambridge), p. 17.

[33] RTS (1854), p. 77.

[34] Rebecca Burn-Callander (2014) 'The History of Money: From Barter to Bitcoin' *The Telegraph* (20 October 2014), http://www.telegraph.co.uk/finance/businessclub/money/11174013/The-history-of-money-from-barter-to-bitcoin.html. 13 September 2018.

[35] Ibid.

[36] Braithwaite and Drahos (2000), p. 88.

Money has always been controlled by those in authority, either as kings, queens or as state authorities. The natural hierarchical position of the early rulers made it possible to have decrees whereby any issued coins would circulate within each dominion as money. This control was vital in establishing coins as a form of organised money.[37] The natural scarcity of precious minerals plus the cost of their extraction and processing ensured the stability of value.[38] They benefited from the fact that precious metals were both homogeneous and fungible.[39] There was a one-to-one match in value between the commodity and the value of money it represented. The money could never be more than it was *worth*.[40] In a way, selling and buying are bartering. However, unlike other commodities of barter, money offers convenience in trading.[41] It gives the holder a bargaining advantage and control as he has what everyone in the marketplace covets, resulting in the superiority of the buyer (who has the money) over the seller (who covets the money).[42] It is also a store of surplus value.

With the passage of time, money soon became recognised in the form of minted coins, made by turning smelted precious metal into discs usually emblazoned with the sovereign's crest or features. Coinage served two important purposes, an assurance that the coins were genuine and that through general circulation they served as a recognisable demonstration of the authority of the state.[43] It soon became clear that the coins were susceptible to wear and tear.[44] They were also costly to produce since the value in the metal usually represented the value of the coin.[45] The valuable coin was also susceptible to being lost or destroyed.[46] Although the coin was valuable, in trade it served no valuable utility except as a medium of exchange, such that if a cheaper payment system

[37] John F Chown (1994) 'Some Concepts of Money' in *A History of Money from AD 800* (Routledge, London), p. 8.

[38] RTS (1854), p. 78.

[39] Menger (1892), p. 49.

[40] RTS (1854), p. 77.

[41] Ibid., p. 80.

[42] Menger (1892), pp. 42, 43.
Dodd (2014), p. 18.

[43] Menger (1892), p. 51.

[44] RTS (1854), p. 111.

[45] Ibid.

[46] Ibid.

was devised, and accepted, it could serve the same function.[47] This eventually led to the introduction of paper money, mostly riding on the industrial revolution that led to the development of the printing press as well as coins made of cheaper metal.[48]

### 2.2.1 Evolution of Central Banks

Normal et al. say early forms of banking can be traced to "the mid-seventeenth century [when] a network of … goldsmith 'bankers' was issuing notes and lending funds".[49] These notes were also called gold certificates.[50] The issuance of these certificates was in exchange for gold deposits.[51] Cooper says the gold was in the form of coins, "checked as it was deposited, and the depositor issued with a paper certificate of deposit".[52] The certificate was evidence that the holder had a certain amount of gold deposits with the issuing bank and could "present the certificate back to the bank, who would, on demand, exchange it for the same amount of gold coins originally deposited".[53] The shrewd gold bankers soon realised that the traffic of gold deposits and gold withdrawals either cancelled each other or favoured deposits.[54] They started issuing paper to merchants who needed finance for their businesses.[55] Therefore, very early on, the gold bankers harnessed the power of creating money by the process of issuing paper against gold deposits based on the belief that its depositors would not turn up and withdraw the gold.

[47] Ibid.

[48] Edward W Kelley Jr (1999) 'The Future of Electronic Money: A Regulator's Perspective' 34 *Spectrum* (IEEE), http://spectrum.ieee.org/telecom/standards/the-future-of-electronic-money-a-regulators-perspective. 14 September 2018.

[49] Ben Norman, Rachel Shaw and George Speight (2011) *The History of Interbank Settlement Arrangements: Exploring Central Banks' Role in the Payment System* (Bank of England Working Paper, London), p. 8, http://ssrn.com/abstract=1863929. 30 May 2018.

[50] George Cooper (2010) 'Money, Banks and Central Banks' in *The Origin of Financial Crises: Central Banks, Credit Bubbles and the Efficient Market Fallacy* (Harriman House Limited, Petersfield, Hampshire), p. 47.

[51] Norman et al. (2011), p. 8.

[52] Cooper (2010), p. 48.

[53] Ibid.

[54] Norman et al. (2011), p. 8; Cooper (2010), p. 48.

[55] Norman et al. (2011), p. 8.

As such, banks embarked on intermediation of funds. From the deposit business, banks developed the lending business.[56]

According to Norman, initially, these banks could "not redeem on each other, offering to transfer funds only across their own accounts and/or refusing to accept notes issued by other banks".[57] Arrangements by banks to start accepting each other's notes are the basis of the modern-day inter-bank settlement or payment system. The process was gradual though, with acceptance of notes issued by "banks within their local area".[58] However, not all banks allowed claims on other banks, and these "pressures on banks to accept claims on each other" soon led to a need for a better system of inter-bank settlement and the establishment of central banks.[59]

The earliest recorded bank to emerge as a central bank is the Swedish Riksbank.[60] "It was established in 1668 to lend the government funds and act as a clearing house for commerce".[61] The Bank of England was founded as a private company in 1694 to buy government debt.[62] Braithwaite and Drahos say that the bank was established essentially to finance a war against the French.[63] Bordo says other banks followed later in Europe based on the same principle: chartered to raise funds for the government "though some were established to deal with monetary disarray".[64] The establishment of the Banque de France, for example, in 1800 was primary for currency stabilisation resulting from the financial turmoil of the French Revolution.[65] Therefore, from inception, the governments

[56] Ibid.

[57] Ibid., p. 9.

[58] Ibid., p. 11.

[59] Ibid., p. 27.

[60] Michael D Bordo (2007) 'A Brief History of Central Banks' *Economic Commentary* (Federal Reserve Bank of Cleveland), p. 1, https://www.clevelandfed.org/en/newsroom-and-events/publications/economic-commentary/economic-commentary-archives/2007-economic-commentaries/ec-20071201-a-brief-history-of-central-banks.aspx. 24 May 2018.

[61] Ibid.

[62] Ibid.

[63] Braithwaite and Drahos (2000), p. 89.

[64] Bordo (2007), p. 1.

[65] Ibid.

naturally favoured these central banks.[66] The banks soon developed a higher "financial standing relative to other banks".[67] As central banks started issuing their own money, this was considered "a superior form of money to the notes of any other bank".[68]

Commercial banks also soon realised that they need someone or something to help them during times of financial distress. According to Cooper, the central bank, as a bank of banks, became the solution to "support troubled institutions, and [create a] system of firewalls to prevent trouble at one bank from spreading into a general panic throughout the entire system".[69] They became the lender of last resort.[70] The idea of a lender of last resort had existed in relation to sovereigns, but with regard to central banks, it was the formulation of two Englishmen, Henry Thornton[71] and Walter Bagehot[72] who established it as a cornerstone in central bank business in the nineteenth century. In return for this fiscal support, Cooper says the banks "gave up the right to issue their own gold depository certificates [in favour of] only one permitted type of depository certificate … printed by the government" with all banks depositing their gold with the central bank.[73] On the other hand, since the central bank came to "represent the ultimate source of liquidity", commercial banks found in this some form of insurance.[74] To avoid moral hazard (risky behaviours by bank managers, assured of this insurance), central banks began to exercise some control over these banks or, as is called today, regulate and supervise the banking system.[75]

[66] Charles Goodhart (1988) *The Evolution of Central Banks* (MIT Press Books, Cambridge), p. 4.

[67] Norman et al. (2011), p. 15.

[68] Ibid., p. 13.

[69] Cooper (2010), p. 56.

[70] Henry Thornton (1939) *An Enquiry into the Nature and Effects of the Paper Credit of Great Britain (1802)* (Frank Cass & Co Ltd, London), Chapter IV.

[71] Charles Goodhart and Gerhard Illing (2002) *Financial Crises, Contagion, and the Lender of Last Resort, a Reader* (Oxford University Press, Oxford), p. 1.

[72] Walter Bagehot (1873) *Lombard Street: A Description of the Money Market* (Henry S King & Co., London), Chapter II.

[73] Cooper (2010), p. 61.

[74] Goodhart (1988), p. 7.

[75] Ibid.

The relationship between central banks and the government meant the government, through them, had a monopoly on printing money.[76] This also provided the government with another tool of monetary control. While before, the government had to recall all coinage to issue new coins, with the new system all it needed to do was a simple adjustment to the amount of gold that was now exchangeable with the circulating certificates.[77] In doing so, governments avoided the unpopular decision of debasing the currencies by reducing the metal content on reissue.[78] Through fiat, the state could create or destroy money.[79] All that was required was "a short parliamentary decree announcing a new rate of conversion to gold".[80]

Such money is not backed up by any valuable deposits but by the power of the issuing state.[81] Since the government now had a monopoly over money printing, it also meant it could "print itself some more money to pay off its debts", but because this was not backed by any gold deposits, the eventual result was inflation and devaluation.[82] Politically, this proved to be less messy. In the old days, kings would engage in currency debasing for profiteering. They would withdraw money and issue new money with a reduced content of the metal in the money, but present it as containing the same value, with the sovereign keeping the rest and making a profit and plundering their subjects.[83] Debasement, therefore, is not a new phenomenon at all. It is as old as the history of coined money.[84] Monopoly in power to issue coinage by the sovereign meant that there was no opportunity for an honest competitor to check the sovereign's profiteering.[85] Although central banks became to be controlled

[76] Cooper (2010), p. 62.

[77] Ibid.

[78] Ibid., p. 63.

[79] Lerner (1947), p. 314.

[80] Cooper (2010), p. 62.

[81] Charles Goodhart (1998) 'The Two Concepts of Money: Implications for the Analysis of Optimal Currency Areas' 14 *European Journal of Political Economy* 407, p. 417, http://www.sciencedirect.com/science/article/pii/S0176268098000159. 29 April 2018.

[82] Cooper (2010), p. 63 but cf with Goodhart (1998), p. 424.

[83] Greco Jr (1997), p. 2; Chown (1994), p. 10.

[84] Chown (1994), p. 10.

[85] Greco Jr (1997), p. 2.

by the government, this was a gradual process of assuming control.[86] Norman et al. have reduced the core functions of the central bank to bank of bankers, monitoring or regulating commercial banks, monopoly of currency issue, conducting monetary policy and lender of last resort.[87]

However, these functions did not just accrue to the central banks; they evolved over time. For example, central banks were not initially tasked with supervisory and regulatory functions. According to Grossman, very few central banks were "given a monopoly of domestic note-issue at the time of their founding" and the Bank of England, for example, only got this 150 years later.[88] Grossman also argues that even the role of bankers' bank and lender of last resort came in later.[89] However, making the central bank a lender of last resort was fundamental as it discouraged it from competing with commercial banks.[90] By being a bankers' bank, the central bank is the anchor of the payment system by having mutual obligations of banks settled in central bank money.[91] Since banks hold accounts with the central bank, they use these to settle payment obligations, just as customers do with their banks.[92] A more detailed discussion of the payment system and the role of the central bank is provided towards the end of this chapter.

Being a bank of bankers meant that the central bank was a repository for banks, thereby acquiring large reserves and effectively serving the functionality of lender of last resort during financial distress.[93] The lender of last resort function has been criticised by Norman et al. for "encouraging more risky lending inadvertently" destabilising the very

[86] Bordo (2007), p. 3.

[87] Norman et al. (2011), p. 20. See also Goodhart (1988), Chapter 7 'Why Banks Need a Central Bank.'

[88] Richard Grossman (2006) *The Emergence of Central Banks and Banking Regulation in Comparative Perspective* (Wesleyan Economics Working Papers, Wesleyan University), p. 11, http://repec.wesleyan.edu/pdf/rgrossman/2006021_grossman.pdf. 1 June 2018.

[89] Ibid.

[90] Ibid., p. 13.

[91] Norman et al. (2011), pp. 6, 19.

[92] Ibid., p. 21.

[93] Bordo (2007), p. 1; Heidi Mandanis Schooner and Mark W Taylor (2010) *Global Bank Regulation: Principles and Policies* (Academic Press, Burlington, Massachusetts), pp. 53–5; Goodhart (1988), p. 7.

credit system which the central bank was created to stabilise.[94] To ensure that this tendency by bankers to engage in moral hazard is monitored, regulation of the banks becomes paramount, especially in relation to the creation of credit within the banking system.[95] For example, in the years 1825–1857, there were major panics in England, which were caused by the central bank's refusal to aid commercial banks in financial distress.[96] The central bank responded to criticism but to discourage risky lending by banks, adopted the responsibility doctrine.[97] Bordo says:

> [This] required the bank to subsume its private interest to the public interest of the banking system as a whole. The bank began to … lend freely on the basis of any sound collateral offered – but at a penalty rate to prevent moral hazard. The bank learned its lesson well. No financial crisis occurred in England for nearly 150 years after 1866. It wasn't until August 2007 that the country experienced its next crisis.[98]

The reference by Bordo to 2007 is to the bank run that plagued Northern Rock at the peak of the 2007–2008 financial crisis. However, Campbell and Lastra have insisted that what central banks do is "provide liquidity but not provide capital".[99] This distinction is crucial. Injection of central bank liquidity is meant to be for the short and immediate term, and any long-term assistance must be left to the relevant treasury organs.[100] The two authors have therefore aptly termed it emergency liquidity assistance.[101] Timely injection of emergency and adequate liquidity will ordinarily arrest impending financial crises.[102] From the theory espoused by Thornton and Bagehot, they isolate 4 pillars of lender of last resort or as they would call it, emergency liquidity assistance:

[94] Norman et al. (2011), p. 59.

[95] Ibid., p. 88.

[96] Bordo (2007), p. 2.

[97] Ibid.

[98] Ibid.

[99] Andrew Campbell and Rosa Lastra (2009) 'Revisiting the Lender of Last Resort' 24 (3) *Banking and Finance Law Review* 453, p. 457, http://0-search.proquest.com.pugwash.lib.warwick.ac.uk/docview/218867839?accountid=14888. 10 December 2018.

[100] Ibid., p. 470.

[101] Ibid., p. 454.

[102] Ibid., p. 464.

i. Emergency liquidity assistance must be given to banks which although illiquid are, however, solvent;
ii. Liquidity must be freely provided, but at a penalty rate;
iii. Any institution with "good collateral" must be accommodated;
iv. The central bank must make it known that all emergency liquidity assistance is discretionary and not obligatory.[103]

### 2.2.2 *From the Gold Standard to Fiat Money*

The gold standard arose out of a need for an international monetary system up to the outbreak of the First World War.[104] According to Bordo, the classical gold standard was a way in which "each country defined its currency in terms of a fixed weight of gold".[105] This price was supposed to be fixed,[106] or rather "pegged within narrow bands" called "gold points" within which it was allowed to fluctuate.[107] Earlier standards had used a bimetallic system of gold and silver.[108] Bordo and Kydland say gold was eventually chosen "because of its intrinsic value and desirable properties".[109] By the end of the nineteenth century, most major currencies were based on the gold standard.[110] After the end of the Second World War, at the Bretton Woods Conference, in the USA, an agreement

[103] Ibid., pp. 465–6.

[104] Jeffry A Frieden (1993) 'Dynamics of International Monetary Systems: International and Donmestic Factors in the Rise, Reign, and Demise of the Classical Gold Standard' in Jack Snyder and Robert Jervis (eds) *Coping with Complexity in the International System* (Westview Press, Boulder), p. 137.

[105] Bordo (2007), p. 1.

[106] Michael D Bordo and Finn E Kydland (1997) 'The Gold Standard as a Rule' in Barry Eichengreen and Marc Flandreau (eds) *The Gold Standard in Theory and History* (Routledge, London), p. 71.

[107] Tamim Bayoumi and Barry Eichengreen (1995) *The Stability of the Gold Standard and the Evolution of the International Monetary System* (IMF Working Paper, Washington, DC), p. 1, https://papers.ssrn.com/sol3/papers.cfm?abstract_id=883236. 1 May 2018.

See also John Maynard Keynes (1997) 'The Significance of the Gold Points' in Barry Eichengreen and Marc Flandreau (eds) *The Gold Standard in Theory and History* (Routledge, London), p. 95.

[108] Bordo and Kydland (1997), p. 71.

[109] Ibid., p. 73.

[110] Frieden (1993), p. 142.

was reached to peg all major world currencies to the US Dollar ($).[111] This followed a failure to reconstitute the gold standard after the outbreak of war and following the depression of the 1930s.[112] The Dollar itself was then set at a fixed price of $35 per ounce of gold thereby creating, what Cooper describes as a unitary global "gold standard monetary system".[113] By 1971, most Dollars in global circulation were not backed by any actual gold reserves.[114] Fearing that the holders would demand conversion into gold, the USA stopped using the Dollar as a gold certificate, thereby sounding a death-knell to the gold standard.[115]

The demise of the gold standard heralded the birth of fiat money.[116] Fiat money is the name given to "the new currency regime, without a gold exchange rate".[117] While with the gold standard, devaluations were in relation to gold reserves, fiat money can be created "from thin air" and the government is under no liability to pay out anything as an equivalent sum of money.[118] It is the money created by fiat. Of course, in most countries, there may be regulations and restrictions on how the state can issue fiats to create money, reduced in statute or some other decree. Fiat money is usually distinguishable from other forms of money on the basis that it is legal tender.[119] It means one can use such money to settle pecuniary debts and obligations within a particular jurisdiction in which the said money is issued and that it would be deemed unlawful for anyone to reject it.[120] Normally when used, the term *money* refers to fiat money. Sometimes, the words cash or paper money and coins are used to distinguish it with other forms of money. The principle that a state has monetary sovereign was made sacrosanct in international law by the Permanent Court of International Justice in 1929 in the *Serbian Loans*

[111] Cooper (2010), p. 65.

[112] Frieden (1993), p. 155.

[113] Cooper (2010), p. 65.

[114] Ibid., p. 68.

[115] Ibid.

[116] Lerner (1947), p. 314.

[117] Cooper (2010), p. 69.

[118] Ibid.

[119] Goodhart (1998), p. 417.

[120] Jevons (1875), p. 75.

*Case* where the Court said "it is indeed a generally accepted principle that a state is entitled to regulate its own currency".[121]

Modern paper money is in a form of a promissory note or an IOU (I owe you). As Maurer says, it is not money until someone accepts it.[122] In this case, it is money because society within a jurisdiction is obligated to accept it by legal decree. An example of the paper money of England, Malaŵi and USA brings the point home. The notes issued by the Bank of England have the words: "I promise to pay the bearer on demand the sum of [X] Pounds". The note issued by the Reserve Bank of Malaŵi says: "Promise to pay the bearer the sum of [Y] Kwacha". The question that arises therefore is if these are promises to pay (promissory notes), then where is the *real money*? On the other hand, the note issued by the Federal Reserve in the USA is worded somewhat differently manifesting the legal character of the note: "This note is legal tender for all debts, public and private". So what then is money? Maybe Graeber provides the most plausible way out that money can be reduced to "the promise to pay *something* of the same value as an ounce of gold".[123] Of course, with the abandonment of the gold standard, the *something* has value based on the trust that the public has in the state issuing it.[124] It is submitted that apart from economic factors of production, it is the value attached to the issuing state that distinguishes values of various currencies. This may explain why the pronouncements of key world leaders may affect certain global currencies.

With fiat money, it is no longer essential that money exists as a chattel or a physical concept.[125] Graeber argues that money now is an abstract concept although it may still be issued in physical form by the state.[126]

[121] *Case Concerning the Payment of Various Serbian Loans Issued in France (France v. Serbia) and Payment in Gold of the Brazilian Federal Loans Contracted in France (France v. Brazil)* PCIJ Rep Series A Nos 20–21 (Judgment of 12 July 1929), 'Summaries of Judgments, Advisory Opinions and Orders of the Permanent Court of International Justice' (United Nations, 2012), http://legal.un.org/PCIJsummaries/documents/english/PCIJ_FinalText.pdf. 7 November 2018.

[122] Bill Maurer (2012) 'Payment: Forms and Functions of Value Transfer in Contemporary Society' 30 *Cambridge Anthropology* 15, p. 17.

[123] Graeber (2011), p. 46.

[124] Ibid.

[125] Charles Proctor (2012) *Mann on the Legal Aspect of Money* (7th edn, Oxford University Press, Oxford), pp. 40–41.

[126] Ibid.

State authority now defines, through legislation, what is to serve as money within the jurisdiction of the state. In *Mann on the Legal Aspect of Money*, Proctor describes 3 elements comprising the legal definition of money:

a. It must be expressed by reference to a name and denominated by reference to a unit of account prescribed by the law.
b. The currency and unit must be intended to serve as the generally accepted measure of value and medium of exchange within the state.
c. The legal framework for the currency must include a central bank or monetary authority responsible for the issue of the currency, appropriate institutional provisions for its management through the conduct of monetary policy and the oversight of payment systems.[127]

### 2.2.3 *Money as a Creation of the Marketplace?*

Traditionally money has always been viewed as a creation of the sovereign or national governments. It has, however, been argued that the sovereign merely adopted money "on account of its intrinsic utility".[128] This school of thought argues that money is in fact a creation of the marketplace and not a construct of the state. Menger has argued that actually government edicts do not create money; it is rather the market marketplace that creates money.[129]

> No accident, nor the consequence of state compulsion, nor voluntary convention of traders effected this. It was just apprehending of their individual self-interest which brought it to pass, that all the more economically advanced nations accepted the precious metals as money as soon as a sufficient supply of them had been collected and introduced into commerce.[130]

Money is not a creature of the law and "sanction by the authority of the state is a notion alien to it", but through state sanction and recognition (and regulation), "money has been perfected and adjusted to

[127] Ibid., p. 41.
[128] RTS (1854), p. 77.
[129] Menger (1892), p. 8.
[130] Ibid., p. 49.

the manifold and varying needs of an evolving commerce, just as customary rights have been perfected and adjusted by statute law".[131] It is, however, the power to regulate the supply of money that creates value. Money, like any commodity, will only be valuable and useful "when supplied in moderate quantities, and at the right time".[132]

### 2.2.4 *Standards and Qualities of Money*

As has been noted above, the standard test of classical money is threefold: a medium of exchange, store of value and unit of account. It is, however, argued that these three attributes satisfy the requirement for what can be termed *economic money*. However, to satisfy the requirements of *legal money*, state sanction and a legal framework enabling the issuing of currency needs to be in place. This section looks at the framework comprising the standards and qualities of money and then develops a framework for assessing whether any commodity can function as money based on this framework.

#### *2.2.4.1 Utility and Value*

As noted, with time, money was no longer valuable by itself. However, because it was a coveted commodity, it became valuable because of its utility. The piece of paper or coin that represents a Pound Sterling or One Kwacha may itself not be worth much, especially in the case of paper money. It is therefore not the worthiness of the money itself that prompts people to take it but the fact that people accept that it has utility to stand as a standard payment system and facilitate by its passing the transfer of property.[133]

#### *2.2.4.2 Portability*

Money must not only be valuable but must also be easy to carry and store. In this regard, paper money is much easier to carry than heavier coin money. Portability therefore allows large amounts to be transferred across space with ease and at minimal cost (relative to the value of the money).[134]

[131] Ibid., p. 51.

[132] Jevons (1875), p. 9.

[133] Menger (1892), p. 31.

[134] Ibid., p. 34.

### 2.2.4.3 *Indestructibility*

Money must not be easily destroyed or lost to the elements. Extremely put, it "must no evaporate like alcohol, nor putrefy like animal substances, nor decay like wood, nor rust like iron".[135] The substance used as money must therefore be able to withstand the elements.

### 2.2.4.4 *Homogeneity*

The commodity that is used as money must be uniform in all aspects. This ensures that it maintains the same value across time and space. So although originally this was easy with precious metals (their weight gave the value), with token money, the key thing is for the money to maintain the same value by its representation.

### 2.2.4.5 *Divisibility*

Money must be able to be divided into smaller denominations. But what is more fundamental is that the reverse must also equally hold true. The "aggregate value ... after division should be ... exactly the same as before division".[136]

### 2.2.4.6 *Stability of Value*

The value of money must be stable over space and time. But this does not mean that money cannot lose value. It is an intrinsic nature of money to lose value over time. The concept referred to as time value of money essentially means money will gradually lose value (depreciate) over time. In order to compensate for the loss of money of time, something must be done to the present value (PV) to make it equal to the future value (FV). This *something* is the rate of interest r at which PV must grow over a time t so that the value of FV has the same purchasing power. Therefore, the formula for calculating the value of money at a future time would be $FV_t = PV + (1 + r)^t$. In *Bryant v Foot*, it was said the court must take judicial notice that the value of money has fallen since 1189; it being the year set to represent time immemorial.[137] This characteristic of money is important as it is the one that makes banking a profitable business for all. The figure below shows that the value of money is not static over time and that in order to maintain real stability in value, one has to factor in the rate of interest over time (Fig. 2.1).

[135] Ibid., p. 35.

[136] Ibid., p. 37.

[137] *Bryant v Foot* [1868] LR 3 497 QB.

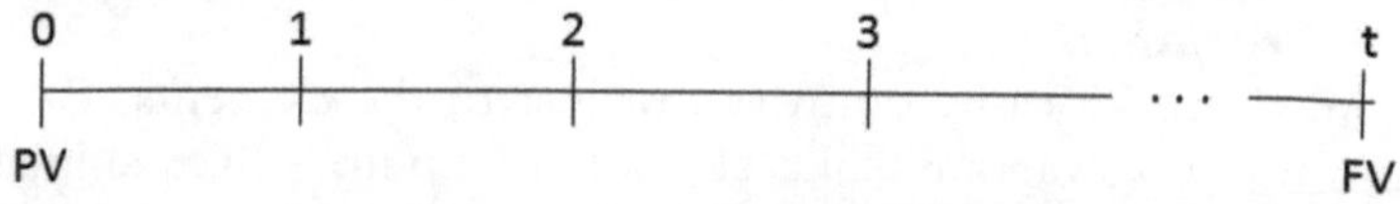


**Fig. 2.1** Scale representing value of money over a time *t* (*Source* Author)

So although it is an intrinsic characteristic of money to lose value over time, fiat money will face exchange rate fluctuations when traded with other currencies. An example would be the sudden plunge of the British Pound on the announcement of the referendum result that Britain would leave the European Union.[138] Another example is the downward spiral of the Iranian *Rial* upon the re-imposition of economic sanction by the USA.[139] Therefore, while it may maintain its face value, its real value (purchasing power) may be affected by a whole array of factors.[140]

#### *2.2.4.7 Tangibility*

Tangibility is a key feature of money. Everyone wants to satisfy themselves that what they have, what they have been given, or what they have given out is money. Money is something everyone can see, feel and for newly printed paper money even smell! Invariably, it must also be deemed to be genuine and not a counterfeit.

#### *2.2.4.8 Cognizability*

The commodity that is used as money must be easily recognisable by all. Usually, this will be manifested by an impression representing the issuing authority as well as a mark setting its value. Now whether form money is, a key point is that it must be coinable. Strictly speaking, this

[138] Angela Monaghan (2016a) 'Sterling Hits New 31-Year Low Against the Dollar' *The Guardian* (6 July 2016), https://www.theguardian.com/business/2016/jul/06/brexit-pound-plunges-to-30-year-lows-as-eu-fears-bite-into-global-markets-again. 13 September 2018.

[139] Reuters (2018) 'Iran Currency Extends Record Fall as U.S. Sanctions Loom' (29 July 2018), https://www.reuters.com/article/us-iran-nuclear-currency/iran-currency-extends-record-fall-as-us-sanctions-loom-idUSKBN1KJ0DY. 4 November 2018.

[140] Angela Monaghan (2016b) 'First Post-Brexit Vote Data Shows UK Inflation Rose to 0.6% in July' *The Guardian* (16 August 2016), https://www.theguardian.com/business/2016/aug/16/first-post-brexit-data-shows-uk-inflation-rose-to-06-in-july. 13 September 2018.

**Table 2.1** Qualities of money[a]

| *Quality* | *Elements* |
|---|---|
| Utility and value | • Money is no longer valuable by itself, but as it is coveted, its utility gives it value<br>• People accept money because it has utility to stand as a standard payment system and facilitate by its passing, the transfer or rights in the property |
| Portability | • Money must be easy to carry and store<br>• It must allow transfer of large amounts with ease and minimal costs |
| Homogeneity | • Money must be uniform in all aspects to ensure the stability of value across time and space |
| Divisibility | • Money must be divisible into smaller denominations and vice versa without loss of value |
| Stability of value | • The value of money must be stable over space and time |
| Cognoscibility | • Money must be easily recognisable, usually through impressions representing the issuing authority as well as a mark setting its value<br>• Good money must be difficult to counterfeit |

[a]*Source* Jevons (1875), pp. 31, 34, 37, 39, 58 and Kelley Jr (1999), p. 21

term was used to refer to coins. However, it is submitted that the concept can be used for all types of money. In other words, once issued, "according to proper regulations with the impress of the state" it must "be known to all as good and legal currency". A key factor in coinage is that good money should not only be difficult to counterfeit but must also reflect the "artistic and historical monument" of the issuer as well as its users.

In coming up with a framework that embraces the evolution of money over time and embracing advances in technology, several of the characteristics or attributes may safely be left out of such a framework. For example, the requirement of indestructibility may be dispensed with when dealing with money in other forms as opposed to an actual chattel. The same also applies to the requirement that money must be tangible. Table 2.1 summarises the key qualities and elements of money that can be used taking into account the evolution of money over time.

From the above table, a framework may be drawn (table below) on identifying money and this framework will be used later in assessing whether

**Table 2.2** Framework for identifying money

| *Type of money* | *Medium of exchange* | *Store of value* | *Unit of account* | *Utility and value* | *Portable* | *Homogeneity* | *Divisible* | *Cognizable* | *Legal tender* |
|---|---|---|---|---|---|---|---|---|---|
| Fiat | x | x | x | x | x | x | x | x | x |

anything that is used as money, such as mobile money, fits the billing. The basis of compassion for the framework is fiat money or cash (Table 2.2).

## 2.3 Money the Oil That Drives the Financial System

A discussion of money inevitably must be done in conjunction with a discussion of the banking and financial system. As Padoa-Schioppa says:

> Why do we dub banking as a "system", while we do not use this notion for the steel or chemical industries, or even for the insurance and securities industries? Firstly, banks are interconnected through the payment system, whose essential feature is currency-specificity. It refers to the circulation of one and the same money, which is completely fungible throughout the economy.[141]

In relation to the financial system and the central role played by the central bank, he adds:

> A financial system may, and usually does, remain segmented to some extent. However, if a liquidity need emerges in a specific segment of it, it is always the central bank that bears ultimate responsibility. Hence, all the answers to why banking is a "system" have to do with the singleness of the currency and the central bank. This also shows that – with or without formal supervisory functions – the central bank is a key part of the financial system and responsible for its smooth functioning.[142]

It may be argued that regulation of money, the banking and financial system is a three-pronged exercise because of the centrality of banking within the financial system and the role of money within both the banking and financial system. The fact that central banks are issuers of money makes them the premier institution in ensuring financial stability, and in monitoring "the quality of their counterparts".[143]

[141] Tommaso Padoa-Schioppa (2003) 'Central Banks and Financial Stability: Exploring the Land in Between' in Vitor Gaspar, Philipp Hartmann and Olaf Sleijpen (eds) *Second ECB Central Banking Conference: The Transformation of the European Financial System* (European Central Bank), p. 274.

[142] Ibid.

[143] Ibid., pp. 278–9.

### 2.3.1 A Brief Overview of Malaŵi's Financial Sector

Malaŵi's financial sector remains small and dominated by banking. Her capital markets are not well developed, and the only stock exchange is highly illiquid.[144] These banks offer a variety of services but are mostly located in urban areas. Although the country has high lending costs,[145] this does not translate to high yields for savers. For example, in the first quarter of 2015, the central bank (policy) rate was at 25%, the (commercial lending) base rate at 33% while the savings rate was at a meagre 7%.[146] Such low savings returns are not conducive to cultivating a saving culture. It may be argued that this leads to a vicious cycle. Low returns mean savers would rather hold on to their money or invest in other higher yielding investments. This results in a limited pool, which banks can utilise for intermediation. In the absence of an injection of cheap liquidity by the state, there is a rise in the cost of borrowing with an increased demand for finance. The other intervening factor that leads to high costs of finance is borrowing by the government. The World Bank estimates the fiscal deficit in 2014/2015 of 5.9% to continue in 2015/2016.[147] The government is forced to borrow domestically to finance this deficit thereby pushing rates up.

Other players in the financial sector include insurance firms and pension funds. Recently, there has been an emergence of discount and clearing houses, although most of them have since registered as banks.[148] Hitherto, the country's payment system has been comprised mainly of the banking service. Because of the dominance of the banking sector, it is no surprise that the central bank plays a dominant role. Its governor is the registrar of financial institutions, and the central bank is the single regulator of the financial services.[149] It also regulates and operates as the

[144] It is not unheard of for the MSE to register no trading at all in a whole week. Generally trading is low—see MSE (2014) 'Daily Stock News' (Malawi Stock Exchange), http://www.mse.co.mw/current/daily.pdf. 17 June 2014.

[145] RBM (2015) *Financial and Economic Review* (Reserve Bank of Malawi), p. 10, https://www.rbm.mw/Home/GetContentFile?ContentID=7492. 14 December 2018.

[146] Ibid.

[147] World_Bank (2015) 'Malawi—Overview' (World Bank), http://www.worldbank.org/en/country/malawi/overview. 21 December 2018.

[148] First Discount House (FDH) is now FDH Bank and Commercial Discount House (CDH) is CDH Bank.

[149] Section 8 Financial Services Act (Malaŵi, 2010).

gatekeeper of the payment system.[150] In the section that follows, a brief overview of the institutional framework of Malaŵi's central bank is provided. While it is appreciated that this does not present the traditional central bank model, such as the Bank of England model, for example, its discussion is to highlight the central role that the central bank plays in the financial system and in the control of money and money supply.

### 2.3.2 *Structure of Malaŵi's Central Bank*

In Malaŵi, the country's president exclusively appoints the central bank's governor, deputy governors and the board of the central bank.[151] In a rather strange arrangement, the governor of the central bank chairs the board of the central bank.[152] This is an arrangement which raises serious accountability and corporate governance issues. What this illustrates is that the central bank is de facto and de jure under the executive. It brings to question the independence of the central bank. Since independence in 1964, Malaŵi has had 5 presidents.[153] The central bank has had 12 governors since its inception in 1965.[154] The longest-serving governor was John Tembo,[155] who served during the one-party rule.[156] The shortest was the first governor, A. G. Perrin, who only served a year.[157] In 2008, the average term of a governor was approximately

[150] Section 4 Payment Systems Act (Malaŵi, 2016).

[151] Section 12 Reserve Bank of Malaŵi Act (1989).

[152] Section 11 Reserve Bank of Malaŵi Act (1989).

[153] Kamuzu Banda, Bakili Muluzi, Bingu wa Mutharika, Joyce Banda (who completed the term of Bingu wa Mutharika after his death) and Peter Mutharika (younger brother to Bingu).

[154] See Lukes Kalilombe (2008) 'Central Bank Governance, Accountability and Independence: The Case of Reserve Bank of Malawi' (MA, University of Kwazulu-Natal), p. 40, http://researchspace.ukzn.ac.za/handle/10413/575. 5 May 2018. But add Perks Ligoya (2009–2012), Charles Chuka (2012–2017 [April]) and Dalitso Kabambe (April 2017–Present).

[155] (1971–1984) Tembo was until last year President of the Malaŵi Congress Party, a party led by Kamuzu Banda. It is submitted this may have been the case in the John Tembo governorship, who was Dr Banda's 'right-hand' man.

[156] Kalilombe (2008), p. 40.

[157] He was seconded from the Bank of England—Ibid., p. 40. See RBM (2017) 'Reserve Bank of Malawi', https://www.rbm.mw/. 24 April 2018.

4.7 years, almost equal to the 5-year post-one-party political cycle.[158] An examination of the rate of turnover of governors after the advent of multiparty democracy[159] to 2008 indicates a drop to 4.5 years.[160] In 2014, it has further dropped to 3.8 years.[161] Notably, a governor is replaced within a year after an election[162] or change in the presidency.[163] For example, Mathews Chikaonda replaced Francis Pelekamoyo as governor in 1995 soon after the 1994 elections.[164] Elias Ngalande replaced Chikaonda in 2000 after the 1999 elections while Victor Mbewe replaced Ngalande in 2005 after the 2004 elections.[165] Perks Ligoya replaced Mbewe, months after the 2009 general elections.[166] After President Bingu wa Mutharika's sudden death in April 2012, Charles Chuka replaced Ligoya within days of Mutharika's death.[167] Chuka would seem to be the only one to have run out a full term. Dalitso Kalilombe has since replaced him and was appointed by Peter Mutharika, young brother to Bingu.[168]

On average, each post-one-party era presidential term ushers in a new governor. It can be inferred that currently, the job of the governor does not provide much security of tenure. The governor of the Bank

[158] Kalilombe (2008), p. 40.

[159] Referendum was in 1993 and first post one-party era General Elections were held in 1994.

[160] Kalilombe (2008), p. 40.

[161] 12 governors over a 46-year period (1968–2014).

[162] Kalilombe (2008), p. 41.

[163] Except for Chuka who has been retained by the current President after the 2014 elections.

[164] Kalilombe (2008), p. 41.

[165] Ibid.

[166] In September 2009 Gregory Gondwe (2011) 'Reserve Bank of Malawi Appoints New Governor' (Biz Community), http://www.bizcommunity.com/Article/415/87/40038.html. 3 March 2018.

[167] Catherine Snowdon (2012) 'Malawi President Axes Central Bank Governor' (Central Banking), http://www.centralbanking.com/central-banking/news/2170162/malawi-president-axes-central-bank-governor. 3 March 2018.

[168] 'Public Appointment: Reserve Bank Governor' (2017) *Government of Malaŵi*, https://www.facebook.com/malawigovernment/?hc_ref=PAGES_TIMELINE&fref=nf. 21 April 2018.

of Zambia has proposed that ensuring that the central bank governor does not drink from the same poisonous presidential term chalice would enhance professionalism, remove patronage and ensure the security of tenure.[169] A solution may lie in having asymmetrical or non-coincidental terms between those of the governor and the president. It would also be helpful if it were enshrined in legislation that an independent body, such as a non-partisan professional committee, can only remove the governor. However, Lukes Kalilombe has cautioned at making linear conclusions from these figures:

> Care should be taken in interpreting these values because low turnover sometimes may mean lower independence of the central bank. A subservient governor may stay in the seat for a longer time if he does what the politicians want him to do.[170]

In fact, it must be put on record that in most jurisdictions, the governor of the central bank, or as in the USA, the Chairman of the Federal Reserve, is appointed by the head of state. In the UK, the governor of the Bank of England is appointed by the sovereign, currently Queen Elizabeth II, although in actual fact the appointment (or nomination) is made by the prime minister but approved by the sovereign. In presidential systems, this is usually the prerogative of the president. However, what may contrast different governance structures of central banks is how the central government, treasury and the central bank operate, and how they relate to each other. It is therefore submitted that where there are robust checks and balances, a governor of a central bank is more likely to be appointed on merit than on cronyism.

## 2.4 The Nature of Payment Systems

There is an intrinsic link between money and payment systems.[171] For anything that performs the function of money to perform as a medium of exchange, it requires a secure means of being transferred or conveyed

[169] Kenneth Kaoma Mwenda (2010) *Legal Aspects of Banking Regulation: Common Law Perspectives from Zambia* (PULP, Pretoria), p. 82.

[170] Kalilombe (2008), p. 20.

[171] Ali and others (2014a), p. 263.

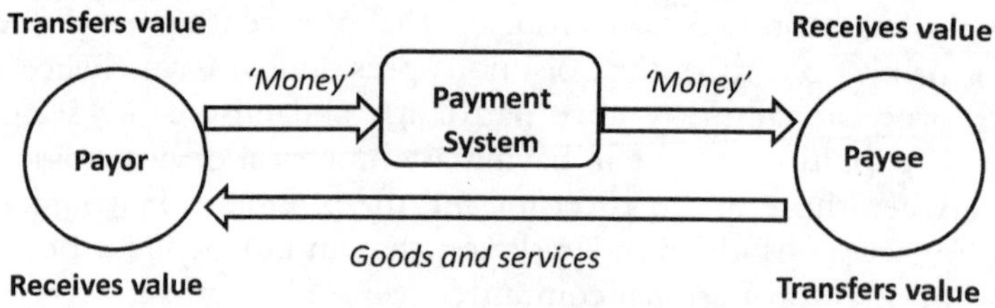


**Fig. 2.2** Showing the mutual transfer of value (*Source* Author)

across time and space.[172] The payment system is the one that ensures such transfer. The Bank for International Settlements has defined it as "a set of instruments, procedures and rules for the transfer of funds among system participants".[173] Payment systems ensure that the payment cycle functions to the satisfaction of all parties in a payment chain. The parties are typically the payor (payer) and a payee using an intermediary, usually a bank. A payment system can be defined as a way in which a buyer (payor) and a seller (payee) agree to transfer value in a transaction.[174] The *thing* that is used as *money* is what distinguishes payment systems. Money can include commodities, cash, cheques or electronic value.[175] Regardless of the type of *money* employed, the payment system operates as a means of clearing and settlement (Fig. 2.2).[176]

The figure above illustrates a simple payment cycle. The payor pays money to the payee which is processed via the payment system in exchange for goods and services. Often, the payor and payee pay little attention to processes that occur to ensure that the payment cycle has been completed. As long as the payor has received his goods or services and the payee his money, whatever happens in between (payment system) is not of prime concern to either. However, should the cycle be

[172] Ibid., p. 264.

[173] CPSS (2001) *Core Principles for Systemically Important Payment Systems* (BIS, Committee on Payment and Settlement Systems), p. 14, http://www.bis.org/cpmi/publ/d43.pdf. 17 February 2018.

[174] David B Humphrey (1995) *Payment Systems: Principles, Practice, and Improvements* vol 23 (World Bank Publications, Washington, DC), p. 3.

[175] Ibid., p. 4.

[176] Ibid.

broken because of some failure in the payment system processes, then issues begin to arise. Clearing and settlement will depend on the instrument that has been used to transfer value and may not be instant, as in the case of a cheque. As the figure above shows, as between the person paying and the person receiving the payment, money moves in the opposite direction to the goods or services. There are three main elements in a payment system:

i. Payment initiation by payor (debtor) to payee (creditor);
ii. Transfer of payment information among banks enabling the payor's bank to debit the payor's account and the payee's bank to credit the payee's account; and
iii. Settlement of the transfer of funds between banks, usually through accounts held by the banks at the central bank.[177]

If payment is by cheque, the payee deposits it with his bank which then presents the cheque to the payor's bank for settlement.[178] This is usually done via the central bank, by debiting and crediting their clearing or reserve requirement balances through accounts, which the local banks have with the central bank.[179] At the close of business, each local bank's credits and debits are grossed or netted.[180] To ensure that the system is reliable, the payor is not allowed to reverse a transaction.[181] If there has been an error, this is rectified by initiating a new transaction.[182] Ordinarily, the payor's bank would want to ensure that the payor has enough credit funds to satisfy the cheque.[183] If satisfied, the payee's bank will credit the payee's account by transferring "good and final funds" to

[177] Setsuya Satåo and David B Humphrey (1995) *Transforming Payment Systems: Meeting the Needs of Emerging Market Economies* (World Bank Discussion Papers, World Bank), p. 1.

[178] The process of inter-bank clearance and settlement may involve actual delivery of the cheque and an inter-bank transfer or indeed transmission of an electronic image.

[179] Satåo and Humphrey (1995), p. 24.

[180] Grossing is bilateral (real time) and usually while netting is multilateral (end-of period).

[181] Satåo and Humphrey (1995), p. 26.

[182] Ibid.

[183] Or has at least made prior arrangements as in the case for over-draft or other loan.

complete the transaction.[184] In the event of non-availability of funds, the cheque will be returned to the payee's bank and on to the payee (and back to the payor).[185] Humphrey defines settlement is the act of transferring "good and final funds".[186]

Clearing refers to the depositing, presentation, checking, sorting and the ancillary processes.[187] It is done between banks while settlements typically through the central bank.[188] Payment systems are important because the instrument transferring value is not typically the value itself. The corollary is that where the instrument transferring value represents the value itself, there is no need for a settlement or clearing. Payment involving barter trade, commodity money[189] or cash represents a transfer of "good and final funds", thereby removing the need for settlement or clearing.[190]

The figure below illustrates the payment cycle of a typical transaction involving at least two separate banks and using an instrument of value transfer such as a cheque (Fig. 2.3).

Looking at the above, the central role that the central bank plays in the payment system becomes evident. It houses the clearing house or process centres and ensures grossing or netting of transactions between various players. Every country has a payment system reflecting its level of "development of money and capital markets and implementation of monetary policy".[191] Its main purpose "is to provide low cost, timely, and secure payments for both enterprises and households".[192] Increasingly now, with technological advancements, there is a global acceleration in non-cash transactions, with Asia registering the highest growth, and Africa coming second.[193] A growth in non-cash transactions

[184] Humphrey (1995), p. 4.

[185] Satåo and Humphrey (1995), p. 8.

[186] Humphrey (1995).

[187] Ibid., p. 4.

[188] Ibid., p. 7.

[189] Commodity money is money whose value comes from the constitutive commodity of which it is made. Unlike fiat money, it consists of objects that have value in themselves as well as value in their use as money.

[190] Humphrey (1995).

[191] Ibid., pp. 1, 11.

[192] Ibid.

[193] Ganesh Samvaran Vudayagiri and others (2016) *World Payments Report* (Capgemini and BNP Paribas), p. 6, http://www.astrid-online.it/static/upload/worl/world_payments_report_wpr_2016.pdf. 10 March 2018.

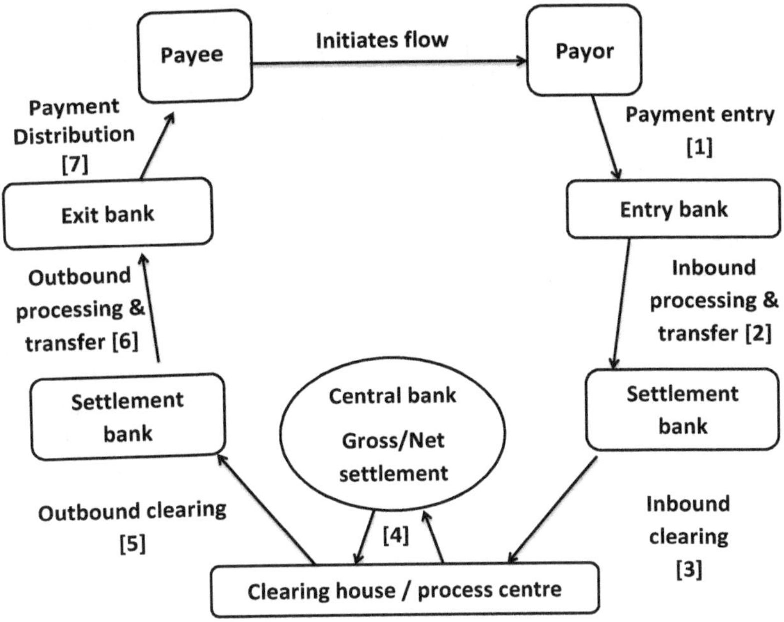


**Fig. 2.3** Showing the complete payment cycle (*Source* Adapted from Satåo and Humphrey [1995], p. 22, Figure 2: Payment cycle for non-cash payment)

depicts that settlement of obligations is increasingly being done by payments other than cash.

Although commercial firms have tried to gain access to the payment system, this has always been resisted. The grounds are that banking and other forms of commerce must remain apart to ensure the integrity of the banking system, to limit possible disruption of the money supply or the payment system itself and to provide a means of protecting deposits.[194] This implies that commercial firms such as mobile network operators have to approach banks to access the payment system platform since banks have a monopoly on the provision of payment services.[195] However, with mobile money, mobile network operators may just have devised a way, piggybacking on banks, to get on the national payment system platform or at least to develop an alternative payment system.

[194] Ibid., p. 33.

[195] Ibid.

The central bank as regulator must ensure the soundness of the counterparties to ensure integrity in the payment system.[196] The central bank also needs to have a mechanism of firewalling against shocks which may be caused by an unreliable counterparty. Ensuring that counterparty hold adequate reserves with the central bank is one way of ensuring that mutual obligations are settled at the end of the business day.[197] Since most transactions are now electronic, having a robust and redundant backbone to ensure reliability and reduced downtime is vital for the efficient operation of the payment system. Apart from the central bank investing in the appropriate technology and expertise, it may require a similar investment by the counterparts. While every country will have in place institutions to regulate the financial sector, Satåo and Humphrey say it is important that any such framework "permit new and cost-effective payment instruments to develop and evolve if they meet better the payment needs of households and enterprises in a market economy".[198]

## 2.5 The Malaŵi Payment System

In its Financial Sector Development Strategy for 2010–2015, the Malaŵi Government prioritised the promotion of savings mobilisation and building an inclusive payment system as tenets to achieve financial inclusion.[199] The Reserve Bank of Malaŵi, the National Payments Council[200] and Bankers Association of Malaŵi are the organisations behind the operation of the National Payment System. In 2008, the Reserve Bank of Malaŵi and National Payments Council issued a vision and strategy framework with a broad objective "to attain a safe, efficient, and harmonised national payment system that effectively contributes to

[196] Padoa-Schioppa (2003), p. 305.

[197] Goodhart (1988), p. 85.

[198] Satåo and Humphrey (1995), p. 17.

[199] *Financial Sector Development Strategy: 2010–2015* (2015) (Government of Malaŵi), pp. 33–4, http://www.finance.gov.mw/fspu/index.php/financial-sector-laws/strategy-documents/55-malawi-financial-sector-development-strategy-2010-2015/file. 21 December 2018.

[200] Established in 1993 under the IMF assisted modernisation programme of the financial sector—BIS (1997) *The Payment System in Malawi* (Bank of International Settlements), p. 67, https://www.bis.org/cpss/paysys/Malawi.pdf. 20 February 2018.

the country's financial stability".[201] Under the law, the Reserve Bank of Malaŵi has a statutory duty to promote a sound financial infrastructure in Malawi, including payment and clearing systems.[202]

### 2.5.1 Development of the National Payment System

In 1999, the Reserve Bank of Malaŵi embarked on the Malaŵi Switch Centre (Malswitch) project.[203] The project was later incorporated into a company.[204] Malswitch linked all major banks in Malaŵi and acted as a switch as well as a central point for electronic cheque clearing services.[205] Malswitch had the goal of linking inter-bank and retail electronic fund transfers but the latter never took off nationwide.[206] The payment infrastructure comprises the Malaŵi Inter-Bank Transfer and Settlement System, the Electronic Cheque Clearing House and the National Switch (NatSwitch) which has taken the role of Malswitch.[207] NatSwitch was set up, as a partnership with the Bankers Association of Malaŵi, with funding from the World Bank.[208] Its aim was to establish an automated

[201] RBM (2008) *Malawi National Payment System Vision Strategy Framework for the Period 2009–2013* (Reserve Bank of Malawi), p. 4, http://www.rbm.mw/documents/payment_systems/NPS%20Vision%20%20Strategy%20Framework%20December%202008%20Final.pdf. 10 February 2018.

The first one only came out as recent as 2001—Ibid., p. 5.

[202] Section 4(*e*) Financial Crimes Act (Malaŵi, 2017).

[203] Edwin Saidi (2009) 'Mobile Opportunities, Mobile Problems: Assessing Mobile Commerce Implementation Issues in Malawi' 14 (1) *Journal of Internet Banking and Commerce* 1, p. 1.

[204] Malswitch Malswitch (Malawi Switch Centre Limited), http://www.malswitch.mw/malswitch/. 10 February 2018.

[205] Saidi (2009).

[206] Ahmed Dermish, Joel Phiri and Caitlin Sanford (2012) *Mapping the Retail Payment Services Landscape Malawi* (FinMark Trust), p. 13, http://www.finmark.org.za/wp-content/uploads/pubs/Rep_RPS_landscape_Malawi_2012.pdf. 10 February 2018.

[207] Ibid., p. 10. NatSwitch has replaced Malswitch.

[208] SADC (2013) 'Payment Systems Progress Report to Committee of Central Bank Governors (CCBG) for the period April 2011 to March 2012 (Malawi)' (Southern Africa Development Community [SADC] Bankers Association), http://www.sadcbankers.org/subcommittees/PaySystem/media/Documents/Newsletters/Vulindlela_Nov2012/Malawi.pdf. 10 February 2018.

transfer system to process real-time transactions settlement on a gross basis.[209] Its target is to achieve interoperability of automated teller machines (ATMs) and point of sale devices, owned or operated by different banks or financial institutions.[210] The bankers association, through its membership, owns the NatSwitch.[211]

At its launch, NatSwitch promises reduced transaction fees and overall benefits to customers as the interoperability platform will allow sharing of point of sale devices and ATMs, among others.[212] All the commercial banks in Malaŵi are now connected to the NatSwitch, and most have Visa Card and MasterCard interconnectivity. One can access money at any ATM irrespective of the owner of the ATM.[213] However, there is still a transactional fee that is charged across banks. However, compared to the position before NatSwitch started operating, there has been a sharp decrease in transactions fees across ATMs of rivals' banks of almost a tenth.[214] There is still debate on whether investing in a completely new switch was wise, with a consumer rights body lamenting that the interconnectivity benefits are not being passed on to consumers of the service.[215]

Efforts by Malswitch to operate the national switch were rebuffed by the central bank. Lack of interoperability has been arguably one of the reasons why Malswitch never achieved all its intended goals. The central bank attributes this to failure to connect enough banks to the switch. Although Malswitch had built up capacity and expertise, it had a narrow platform in that only a handful of bankers signed up to the switch. With

[209] Ibid.

[210] Ibid.

[211] Taonga Sabola (2015) 'Banks Switch on Payment System' *Daily Times* (17 February 2015), http://timesmediamw.com/banks-switch-payment-system/. 7 October 2018.

[212] Chikondi Chiyembekeza (2013) 'National Switch: A Long Overdue Project or a Waste?' *The Nation* (5 September 2013), http://mwnation.com/national-switch-long-overdue-project-waste/. 10 February 2018.

[213] Grace Khombe (2015) 'National Switch Connects ATMs to All' *Zodiak Online* (16 February 2015), http://www.zodiakmalawi.com/top-stories/national-switch-connects-atms-to-all. 15 December 2018.

[214] Before NatSwitch, only ATMs of banks on the Visa platform were interoperable. The transaction fee was K700. With NatSwitch it is now K200.

[215] Grace Thipa (2016) 'Banks Faulted on Natswicth' *Daily Times* (4 May 2016), http://www.times.mw/banks-faulted-on-natswitch/. 7 October 2018.

the coming in of Nat-switch, Malswitch has left the switching business and is now "an integrated technologies business with core activities in the areas of electronic payment, information technology infrastructure, and data communication services". [216]

Though a private company, Malswitch is still owned by state organs. The change of business focus means its switching equipment is now inoperative and of little utility. Nat-switch invited Malswitch to bid for the operation of the new national switch but opted to operate it on its own. Malswitch is of the view that it was never in the running. Commenting on whether it had the capacity to manage the Nat-switch, Malswitch's Head of Business and Sales, Goodwin Chinseu said this was evidenced by the fact that Nat-switch employed the bulk of their engineers to operate their switch. Interesting, however, among the older ATM, when one draws cash across banks, the information displayed indicates that it is going through Malswitch. Whether this is a sign of obsolete equipment still in use or failure to reprogramme the system is unknown.

## 2.6 Emerging Forms of Money

New forms of money seem to emerge from a reversal of the concept of monetary sovereignty. Traditionally, states and central banks have issued and controlled money. In doing so, money has been used in the power relations between those with power and those without it. Emerging forms of money seem to challenge the monopoly of central banks, the decentralised issuing of money and leading to what can be described as *liberation of money*.[217] It is imperative to point out at the outset that although electronic banking is a rapid developing means of processing payments, this is not a new form of money but rather, as Kelley puts it, "a new way to access a number of traditional bank services with traditional money" using new technologies.[218] Electronic banking is therefore not part of emerging forms of money, and for this reason, the discussion that follows excludes it.

[216] Goodwin Chimseu (Head of Business Development and Sales, Malswitch), 20 August 2015 (Interview).

[217] Greco Jr (1997).

[218] Kelley Jr (1999), p. 21.

### 2.6.1 *Electronic Money and Virtual Currencies*

While the terms electronic money and virtual currency may sometimes be used interchangeably, the two are technically different. Electronic money "is a digital representation of fiat currency used to electronically transfer value denominated in fiat currency".[219] It always maintains a one-to-one ratio with fiat money.[220] Electronic money is an electronic representation of a currency, which itself serves as legal tender.[221] The most known examples of electronic money are debit and credit cards. Another example of electronic money is mobile money, discussed in detail in the next chapter. There is also another form of value, airtime, which may be said to be a derivative of electronic money. Although it has many attributes of electronic money and has been used as value in countries such as Tanzania (see Chapter 3), it is not issued as electronic money and is not generally regarded as such.

The European Banking Authority (EBA) defines a virtual currency a "digital representation of value that is neither issued by a central bank or public authority but is used as a means of exchange and can be transferred, stored or traded electronically".[222] It can be digitally traded as, and functions as money, but is not legal tender.[223] Since any state authority does not issue it, it has no state guarantee and operates as money on the basis that the community, which uses it, accepts it.[224] The European Central Bank has provided this definition for a virtual currency:

> A type of unregulated, digital money issued and usually controlled by its developers, and used and accepted among members of a specific virtual community.[225]

[219]FATF (2014) *Virtual Currencies Key Definitions and Potential AML/CFT Risks* (Financial Action Task Force), p. 4, http://www.fatf-gafi.org/media/fatf/documents/reports/Virtual-currency-key-definitions-and-potential-aml-cft-risks.pdf. 14 September 2018.

[220]Ibid.

[221]Ibid.

[222]EBA (2014) *Opinion on 'Virtual Currencies'* (European Banking Authority), p. 10, http://www.eba.europa.eu/documents/10180/657547/EBA-Op-2014-08+Opinion+on+Virtual+Currencies.pdf. 15 April 2018.

[223]Ibid., p. 4.

[224]Ibid.

[225]ECB (2012) *Virtual Currency Schemes* (European Central Bank), p. 5, https://www.ecb.europa.eu/pub/pdf/other/virtualcurrencyschemes201210en.pdf. 15 April 2018.

The famous Internet-based payment system, PayPal is not a virtual currency. While a virtual account is created of users, PayPal does not issue any currency within the PayPal community and funding is via "credit transfer from a bank account or by a credit card payment".[226] PayPal operates within the banking system and its regulations.[227] Apple Pay is also like PayPal and is thus not a virtual currency. It works by cloning credit or debit cards and facilitating payment by bringing the Apple mobile device near the point of sale terminal.[228] It employs a new technology called near-field communication, which just requires a tap for information transmission.[229] A more famous example of virtual currency is Bitcoin. Bitcoin is also a type of what are called cryptocurrencies and is discussed below.

#### *2.6.1.1* Cryptocurrency

This is a decentralised virtual currency, based on a mathematical formula that is protected by cryptography.[230] Cryptography ensures that the digital currency is secure and protected from being interfered with by third parties. It also prevents the duplicate or multiple uses of the same currency so that once it is used in a transaction it cannot be used again.[231] There are already estimated to be over a hundred cryptocurrencies in operation.[232]

The most famous cryptocurrency is Bitcoin. Despite its name, there are no coins in Bitcoin. It comprises "unique strings of numbers and

[226] Ibid., p. 17.

[227] Ibid.

[228] Apple (2016) 'Apple Pay' (Apple Inc), http://www.apple.com/uk/apple-pay/. 9 March 2018.

[229] Cameron Faulkner (2015) 'What Is NFC? Everything You Need to Know', http://www.techradar.com/news/phone-and-communications/what-is-nfc-and-why-is-it-in-your-phone-948410. 9 March 2018.

[230] EBA (2014), p. 5.

[231] Félix Brezo and Pablo G Bringas (2012) 'Issues and Risks Associated with Cryptocurrencies Such as Bitcoin' (*SOTICS 2012: The Second International Conference on Social Eco-informatics*), p. 21, https://www.thinkmind.org/download.php?articleid=sotics_2012_1_40_30101. 14 September 2018.

[232] Mitsuru Iwamura, Yukinobu Kitamura and Tsutomu Matsumoto (2014) 'Is Bitcoin the Only Cryptocurrency in the Town? Economics of Cryptocurrency and Friedrich A. Hayek' *SSRN*, p. 7, http://papers.ssrn.com/sol3/papers.cfm?abstract_id=2405790. 14 September 2018.

letters that constitute units of the currency".[233] Bitcoins have no value in themselves and are not issued and backed by any central bank. While central banks use monetary policy to regulate the currency they issue, Bitcoin achieves this by a clever complex mathematical algorithm.[234] This is done through what is called block-chain technology.[235] The block-chain or Nakamoto *consensus protocol* (named after its inventor) regulates transactions in Bitcoins among users.[236] The production of new Bitcoins is through a block-chain-led process called *mining*.[237] This process allows Bitcoins to be introduced into the system depending on demand. The demand is measured by the energy expended in digitally mining the Bitcoins using computing power.[238] The protocol reacts to changes in mining power and will discourage further mining by increasing the level of difficulty in mining new Bitcoins.[239]

In this way, the algorithm supervises the value of Bitcoin as a currency.[240] Bitcoin is Internet based, requiring no intermediation by banks.[241] It is privately owned, but not by one individual, but all the anonymous participants of this distributed payment system.[242] The

[233] EBA (2014), pp. 5–6.

[234] The algorithm is said to have been written by Satoshi Nakamoto, Bitcoin's inventor in 2009. It is not known whether this is a real person. Recently a person came out in Australia to claim to be the elusive Satoshi Nakamoto: Michael Safi (2016) 'Australian Craig Wright Claims He Is Bitcoin Founder Satoshi Nakamoto' *The Guardian* (2 May 2016), https://www.theguardian.com/technology/2016/may/02/craig-wright-bitcoin-founder-satoshi-nakamoto-claim. 14 September 2018.

[235] Ittay Eyal and others (2016) 'Bitcoin-NG: A Scalable Blockchain Protocol' (*13th USENIX Symposium on Networked Systems Design and Implementation [NSDI'16] March 16–18, 2016* Santa Clara, California), p. 45, https://www.usenix.org/system/files/conference/nsdi16/nsdi16-paper-eyal.pdf. 3 April 2018.

[236] Ibid., p. 47.

[237] Ibid.

[238] Ibid., p. 50.

[239] Ibid.

[240] Ibid.

[241] Robleh Ali and others (2014a) 'Innovations in Payment Technologies and the Emergence of Digital Currencies' 54 *Quarterly Bulletin* (Bank of England), p. 265, http://www.bankofengland.co.uk/publications/Documents/quarterlybulletin/2014/qb14q3digitalcurrenciesbitcoin1.pdf. 21 July 2018.

[242] Ibid.

distributed ledger concept is what makes Bitcoin unique.[243] Its value lies in the fact that people will accept it as payment. Social acceptance is, therefore, crucial for its existence. Since it can be accepted, it can be bought and paid for using cash.[244]

Normally, operations in the digital domain always leave a trace or a footprint. However, thanks to cryptography, Bitcoin allows users to trade with a high degree of anonymity.[245] In this respect, Bitcoin mimics cash. When one gets a banknote, for example, the note does not contain an information trail of who else has handled it or where it has gone through. The closest one can get is to identify, if possible, the last holder of the note, such one if one receives the note from another person. But even that does not reveal much about the note or its passage over time. Bitcoin goes a step further and shields all its users. Because of this, Bitcoins have become attractive to criminals including those dealing in illicit financing.[246] The recent *Ransomware* attack that occurred in 2017, where hackers got into the systems of several global institutions, including the UK's National Health Service and threatened to permanently lock data unless a ransom was paid in Bitcoins is a further testimony of this.[247]

Bitcoins can be subdivided and split into smaller denominations, and each split denomination carries with it a unique digital signature as part of its encryption that makes it impossible to forge.[248] To avoid double spending, Bitcoin uses a time-stamp as part of its encryption.[249] Double

243 Eyal and others (2016), p. 45.

244 EBA (2014), p. 6.

245 Ibid.

246 The *Silk Road* is a hidden website (part of the so-called 'dark web)' designed to enable users to buy and sell illegal drugs, weapons, etc. anonymously and beyond the reach of the law; romanticised as the *Amazon of illegal drugs*—Brezo and Bringas (2012), p. 23.

247 Rowland Manthorpe (2017) 'Live Tracker Reveals How Much NHS Hackers Are Making from Their Ransomware Demands' *Wired* (15 May 2017), http://www.wired.co.uk/article/nhs-hackers-bitcoin-value. 29 May 2018.

248 Anon (2013) 'Digital Currencies: A New Specie' *The Economist* (13 April 2013), http://www.economist.com/news/leaders/21576104-regulators-should-keep-their-hands-new-forms-digital-money-such-bitcoin-new-specie. 9 March 2018.

249 Iwamura et al. (2014), p. 2.

spending is possible in digital currencies because digital information can be easily copied and edited.[250] Once processed, Bitcoins transactions are irreversible.[251] Vendors adore this because it ensures that they are paid and are not exposed to the risk of fraud.[252] On the other hand, if a Bitcoins owner were to be defrauded, the irreversibility of the transaction would mean this would be irrecoverable. In a way, this is no different from losing cash to an unknown fraudster or thief.

Unlike electronic money, which is cash-tied, a virtual currency like Bitcoin may suffer from the instability of value.[253] In terms of its algorithm, Bitcoin is a finite currency with a concrete ceiling of 21 million Bitcoins.[254] It may be argued that as the concrete ceiling is approached, the value of Bitcoins is likely to rise. However, should a competing and more successful cryptocurrency emerge, the opposite may well be the result. Using an analysis based on the three attributes of money, Yermack exposes Bitcoin's weaknesses as a currency by arguing that fails to satisfy the classical attributes of a currency.[255]

### *2.6.2 Cash and Digital Currencies Contrasted*

As noted earlier, the main difference between cash and the digital currencies is that the former is legal tender and the only obligatory method of payment within a jurisdiction. Apart from fulfilling any legal requirements, cash is subject to prudential regulation. A country's central bank will usually be charged with monetary policy including setting up its value and fixing its supply. Table 2.3 summarises the differences between cash and digital currencies.

[250] Ali and others (2014a), p. 267.

[251] Anon (2013).

[252] Ibid.

[253] Iwamura et al. (2014), p. 4.
Maurer (2011).

[254] Anon (2013).

[255] David Yermack (2015) 'Is Bitcoin a Real Currency? An Economic Appraisal' in David KC Lee (ed) *Handbook of Digital Currency* (Elsevier), pp. 31–44.

**Table 2.3** Differences between virtual currency and electronic money[a]

| | *Cash* | *Digital currencies* | |
|---|---|---|---|
| | | *Electronic money* | *Virtual currency* |
| Unit of account | Traditional currency with legal issue | Traditional currency with legal issue | Invented currency |
| Acceptance | Mandatory acceptance within a jurisdiction | By undertakings other than the issuer | Usually within a specific virtual community |
| Nature and legal status | Public—issued by fiat | Private but tied to a particular currency | Private and no direct links to a particular currency |
| Regulation and supervision | Yes | Yes | No |
| Supply of money | Fixed | Fixed | Not fixed (depends on issuer's decisions) |
| Possibility of redeeming funds | Self-guarantee | Guaranteed (at par value to cash) | Not guaranteed |

[a]ECB (2012), p. 16

## 2.7 Conclusion

This chapter has provided an overview of the development of money and what qualities need to be satisfied for a commodity to function as money. The journey back to the origins of money was necessary to appreciate the evolution of money and the emergence of new forms of money, such as mobile money. This chapter also discussed the evolution of the central bank and its central role within the financial system and its interlinks with the payment system. However, the development of other virtual currencies like Bitcoin evidences a shift in the sovereign foundations of money. These new currencies also question the importance of state guarantee in the issuance of money. Fundamentally, this also raises the question of how these emerging forms of money can maintain value independent of state guarantee. Furthermore, due to their extra-territorial nature, questions now arise as to how these emerging forms of money may be regulated. Will they require cross-border licences and corroboration by regulators of different countries? Where does the fiscal buck-stop lie?

## References

Abba P Lerner (1947) 'Money as a Creature of the State' 37 (2) *The American Economic Review* 312, http://www.jstor.org/stable/pdf/1821139.pdf. 29 April 2018.

Ahmed Dermish, Joel Phiri and Caitlin Sanford (2012) *Mapping the Retail Payment Services Landscape Malawi* (FinMark Trust), http://www.finmark.org.za/wp-content/uploads/pubs/Rep_RPS_landscape_Malawi_2012.pdf. 10 February 2018.

Alexander P Reed Jr (1998) *Money and the Global Economy* (Woodhead Publishing, Cambridge).

Andrew Campbell and Rosa Lastra (2009) 'Revisiting the Lender of Last Resort' 24 (3) *Banking and Finance Law Review* 453, http://0-search.proquest.com.pugwash.lib.warwick.ac.uk/docview/218867839?accountid=14888. 10 December 2018.

Angela Monaghan (2016a) 'Sterling Hits New 31-Year Low Against the Dollar' *The Guardian* (6 July 2016), https://www.theguardian.com/business/2016/jul/06/brexit-pound-plunges-to-30-year-lows-as-eu-fears-bite-into-global-markets-again. 13 September 2018.

Angela Monaghan (2016b) 'First Post-Brexit Vote Data Shows UK Inflation Rose to 0.6% in July' *The Guardian* (16 August 2016), https://www.theguardian.com/business/2016/aug/16/first-post-brexit-data-shows-uk-inflation-rose-to-06-in-july. 13 September 2018.

Anon (2013) 'Digital Currencies: A New Specie' *The Economist* (13 April 2013), http://www.economist.com/news/leaders/21576104-regulators-should-keep-their-hands-new-forms-digital-money-such-bitcoin-new-specie. 9 March 2018.

Apple (2016) 'Apple Pay' (Apple Inc), http://www.apple.com/uk/apple-pay/. 9 March 2018.

Ben Norman, Rachel Shaw and George Speight (2011) *The History of Interbank Settlement Arrangements: Exploring Central Banks' Role in the Payment System* (Bank of England Working Paper, London), http://ssrn.com/abstract=1863929. 30 May 2018.

Bill Maurer (2011) 'Mobile Money Regulation: A Story Arc of Best Practices and Emerging Realizations' *Notes from the Field* (December 2011), http://faculty.sites.uci.edu/wmmaurer/files/2011/12/Note_Dec2011_IMTFI.pdf. 15 December 2018.

Bill Maurer (2012) 'Payment: Forms and Functions of Value Transfer in Contemporary Society' 30 *Cambridge Anthropology* 15.

BIS (1997) *The Payment System in Malawi* (Bank of International Settlements), https://www.bis.org/cpss/paysys/Malawi.pdf. 20 February 2018.

*Bryant v Foot* [1868] LR 3 497 QB.

Cameron Faulkner (2015) 'What Is NFC? Everything You Need to Know', http://www.techradar.com/news/phone-and-communications/what-is-nfc-and-why-is-it-in-your-phone-948410. 9 March 2018.

Carl Menger (1892) *On the Origins of Money (2009 repr)* (Ludwig von Mises Institute, Auburn, Alabama).

*Case Concerning the Payment of Various Serbian Loans Issued in France (France v. Serbia) and Payment in Gold of the Brazilian Federal Loans Contracted in France (France v. Brazil)* PCIJ Rep Series A Nos 20–21 (Judgment of 12 July 1929), 'Summaries of Judgments, Advisory Opinions and Orders of the Permanent Court of International Justice' (United Nations, 2012), http://legal.un.org/PCIJsummaries/documents/english/PCIJ_FinalText.pdf. 7 November 2018

Catherine Snowdon (2012) 'Malawi President Axes Central Bank Governor' (Central Banking), http://www.centralbanking.com/central-banking/news/2170162/malawi-president-axes-central-bank-governor. 3 March 2018.

Charles de Secondat Baron de Montesquieu (1748) 'Of Laws in Relation to the Use of Money' in *The Spirit of Laws (2001 repr)* (Batoche Books, Ontario).

Charles Goodhart (1988) *The Evolution of Central Banks* (MIT Press Books, Cambridge).

Charles Goodhart (1998) 'The Two Concepts of Money: Implications for the Analysis of Optimal Currency Areas' 14 *European Journal of Political Economy* 407, http://www.sciencedirect.com/science/article/pii/S0176268098000159. 29 April 2018.

Charles Goodhart and Gerhard Illing (2002) *Financial Crises, Contagion, and the Lender of Last Resort, a Reader* (Oxford University Press, Oxford).

Charles Proctor (2012) *Mann on the Legal Aspect of Money* (7th edn, Oxford University Press, Oxford).

Chikondi Chiyembekeza (2013) 'National Switch: A Long Overdue Project or a Waste?' *The Nation* (5 September 2013), http://mwnation.com/national-switch-long-overdue-project-waste/. 10 February 2018.

CPSS (2001) *Core Principles for Systemically Important Payment Systems* (BIS, Committee on Payment and Settlement Systems), http://www.bis.org/cpmi/publ/d43.pdf. 17 February 2018.

David B Humphrey (1995) *Payment Systems: Principles, Practice, and Improvements* vol 23 (World Bank Publications, Washington, DC).

David Graeber (2011) *Debt: The First 5,000 Years* (Melville House, Brooklyn, New York).

David Yermack (2015) 'Is Bitcoin a Real Currency? An Economic Appraisal' in David K. C. Lee (ed) *Handbook of Digital Currency* (Elsevier, Amsterdam).

EBA (2014) *Opinion on 'Virtual Currencies'* (European Banking Authority), http://www.eba.europa.eu/documents/10180/657547/EBA-Op-2014-08+Opinion+on+Virtual+Currencies.pdf. 15 April 2018.

ECB (2012) *Virtual Currency Schemes* (European Central Bank), https://www.ecb.europa.eu/pub/pdf/other/virtualcurrencyschemes201210en.pdf. 15 April 2018.

Edward W Kelley Jr (1999) 'The Future of Electronic Money: A Regulator's Perspective' 34 *Spectrum* (IEEE), http://spectrum.ieee.org/telecom/standards/the-future-of-electronic-money-a-regulators-perspective. 14 September 2018.

Edwin Saidi (2009) 'Mobile Opportunities, Mobile Problems: Assessing Mobile Commerce Implementation Issues in Malawi' 14 (1) *Journal of Internet Banking and Commerce* 1.

FATF (2014) *Virtual Currencies Key Definitions and Potential AML/CFT Risks* (Financial Action Task Force), http://www.fatf-gafi.org/media/fatf/documents/reports/Virtual-currency-key-definitions-and-potential-aml-cft-risks.pdf. 14 September 2018.

Félix Brezo and Pablo G Bringas (2012) 'Issues and Risks Associated with Cryptocurrencies such as Bitcoin' (*SOTICS 2012: The Second International Conference on Social Eco-informatics*), https://www.thinkmind.org/download.php?articleid=sotics_2012_1_40_3010. 14 September 2018.

Financial Crimes Act (Malaŵi, 2017).

Financial Sector Development Strategy: 2010–2015 (2015) (Government of Malaŵi), http://www.finance.gov.mw/fspu/index.php/financial-sector-laws/strategy-documents/55-malawi-financial-sector-development-strategy-2010-2015/file. 21 December 2018.

Financial Services Act (Malaŵi, 2010).

Ganesh Samvaran Vudayagiri and others (2016) *World Payments Report* (Capgemini and BNP Paribas), http://www.astrid-online.it/static/upload/worl/world_payments_report_wpr_2016.pdf. 10 March 2018.

George Cooper (2010) 'Money, Banks and Central Banks' in *The Origin of Financial Crises: Central Banks, Credit Bubbles and the Efficient Market Fallacy* (Harriman House Limited, Petersfield, Hampshire).

Grace Khombe (2015) 'National Switch Connects ATMs to All' *Zodiak Online* (16 February 2015), http://www.zodiakmalawi.com/top-stories/national-switch-connects-atms-to-all. 15 December 2018.

Grace Thipa (2016) 'Banks Faulted on Natswicth' *Daily Times* (4 May 2016), http://www.times.mw/banks-faulted-on-natswitch/. 7 October 2018.

Gregory Gondwe (2011) 'Reserve Bank of Malawi Appoints New Governor' (*Biz Community*), http://www.bizcommunity.com/Article/415/87/40038.html. 3 March 2018.

Glyn Davies (2002) 'From Primitive and Ancient Money to the Invention of Coinage, 3000–600 BC' in *A History of Money: From Ancient Times to the Present Day* (University of Wales Press, Cardiff), Chapter 2.

Henry Thornton (1939) *An Enquiry into the Nature and Effects of the Paper Credit of Great Britain (1802)* (Frank Cass & Co Ltd, London), Chapter IV.

Ittay Eyal and others (2016) 'Bitcoin-NG: A Scalable Blockchain Protocol' (*13th USENIX Symposium on Networked Systems Design and Implementation (NSDI '16) March 16–18, 2016* Santa Clara, California), https://www.usenix.org/system/files/conference/nsdi16/nsdi16-paper-eyal.pdf. 3 April 2018.

Jeffry A Frieden (1993) 'Dynamics of International Monetary Systems: International and Domestic Factors in the Rise, Reign, and Demise of the Classical Gold Standard' in Jack Snyder and Robert Jervis (eds) *Coping with Complexity in the International System* (Westview Press, Boulder).

John Braithwaite and Peter Drahos (2000) 'Financial Regulation' in *Global Business Regulation* (Cambridge University Press, Cambridge).

John F Chown (1994) 'Some Concepts of Money' in *A History of Money from AD 800* (Routledge, London).

John Maynard Keynes (1997) 'The Significance of the Gold Points' in Barry Eichengreen and Marc Flandreau (eds) *The Gold Standard in Theory and History* (Routledge, London).

Kenneth Kaoma Mwenda (2010) *Legal Aspects of Banking Regulation: Common Law Perspectives from Zambia* (PULP, Pretoria).

Lukes Kalilombe (2008) 'Central Bank Governance, Accountability and Independence: The Case of Reserve Bank of Malawi' (MA, University of Kwazulu-Natal), http://researchspace.ukzn.ac.za/handle/10413/575. 5 May 2018.

Malswitch (Malawi Switch Centre Limited), http://www.malswitch.mw/malswitch/. 10 February 2018.

Michael D Bordo (2007) 'A Brief History of Central Banks' *Economic Commentary* (Federal Reserve Bank of Cleveland), https://www.clevelandfed.org/en/newsroom-and-events/publications/economic-commentary/economic-commentary-archives/2007-economic-commentaries/ec-20071201-a-brief-history-of-central-banks.aspx. 24 May 2018.

Michael D Bordo and Finn E Kydland (1997) 'The Gold Standard as a Rule' in Barry Eichengreen and Marc Flandreau (eds) *The Gold Standard in Theory and History* (Routledge, London).

Michael Hudson (2004) 'The Archaeology of Money: Debt Versus Barter Theories of Money's Origins' in Randal L Wray (ed) *Credit and State Theories of Money* (Edward Elgar, Cheltenham).

Michael Safi (2016) 'Australian Craig Wright Claims He Is Bitcoin Founder Satoshi Nakamoto' *The Guardian* (2 May 2016), https://www.theguardian.com/technology/2016/may/02/craig-wright-bitcoin-founder-satoshi-nakamoto-claim. 14 September 2018.

Mitsuru Iwamura, Yukinobu Kitamura and Tsutomu Matsumoto (2014) 'Is Bitcoin the Only Cryptocurrency in the Town? Economics of Cryptocurrency and Friedrich A. Hayek' *SSRN*, http://papers.ssrn.com/sol3/papers.cfm?abstract_id=2405790. 14 September 2018.

MSE (2014) 'Daily Stock News' (Malawi Stock Exchange), http://www.mse.co.mw/current/daily.pdf. 17 June 2014.

Nigel Dodd (2014) *The Social Life of Money* (Princeton University Press, Princeton, NJ).

Payment Systems Act (Malaŵi, 2016).

Peter Harrigan (2003) 'Tales of a Thaler' 54 (1) *ARAMCO World* 14, http://archive.aramcoworld.com/issue/200301/tales.of.a.thaler.htm. 13 September 2018.

Public Appointment: Reserve Bank Governor (2017) *Government of Malaŵi*, https://www.facebook.com/malawigovernment/?hc_ref=PAGES_TIMELINE&fref=nf. 21 April 2018.

RBM (2008) *Malawi National Payment System Vision Strategy Framework for the Period 2009–2013* (Reserve Bank of Malawi), http://www.rbm.mw/documents/payment_systems/NPS%20Vision%20%20Strategy%20Framework%20December%202008%20Final.pdf. 10 February 2018.

RBM (2017) 'Reserve Bank of Malawi', https://www.rbm.mw/. 24 April 2018.

RBM (2015) *Financial and Economic Review* (Reserve Bank of Malawi), https://www.rbm.mw/Home/GetContentFile?ContentID=7492. 14 December 2018.

Rebecca Burn-Callander (2014) 'The History of Money: From Barter to Bitcoin' *The Telegraph* (20 October 2014), http://www.telegraph.co.uk/finance/businessclub/money/11174013/The-history-of-money-from-barter-to-bitcoin.html. 13 September 2018.

Reserve Bank of Malaŵi Act (1989).

Reuters (2018) 'Iran Currency Extends Record Fall as U.S. Sanctions Loom' (29 July 2018), https://www.reuters.com/article/us-iran-nuclear-currency/iran-currency-extends-record-fall-as-us-sanctions-loom-idUSKBN1KJ0DY. 4 November 2018.

Richard Grossman (2006) *The Emergence of Central Banks and Banking Regulation in Comparative Perspective* (Wesleyan Economics Working Papers, Wesleyan University), http://repec.wesleyan.edu/pdf/rgrossman/2006021_grossman.pdf. 1 June 2018.

Robert A Leonard (1994) 'Money and Language' (55) *Money: Lure, Lore, and Literature* 1, https://www.unc.edu/~salemi/Econ006/Leonard.pdf. 13 September 2018.

Robleh Ali and others (2014a) 'Innovations in Payment Technologies and the Emergence of Digital Currencies' 54 *Quarterly Bulletin* (Bank of England), http://www.bankofengland.co.uk/publications/Documents/quarterlybulletin/2014/qb14q3digitalcurrenciesbitcoin1.pdf. 21 July 2018.

Robleh Ali and others (2014b) 'The Economics of Digital Currencies' 54 *Quarterly Bulletin* (Bank of England), http://www.bankofengland.co.uk/publications/Documents/quarterlybulletin/2014/qb14q3digitalcurrenciesbitcoin2.pdf. 14 September 2018.

Rowland Manthorpe (2017) 'Live Tracker Reveals How Much NHS Hackers Are Making from Their Ransomware Demands' *Wired* (15 May 2017), http://www.wired.co.uk/article/nhs-hackers-bitcoin-value. 29 May 2018.

RTS (1854) *Money; Its Nature, History, Uses, and Responsibilities* (The Religious Tract Society, London).

SADC (2013) 'Payment Systems Progress Report to Committee of Central Bank Governors (CCBG) for the Period April 2011 to March 2012 (Malawi)' (Southern Africa Development Community [SADC] Bankers Association), http://www.sadcbankers.org/subcommittees/PaySystem/media/Documents/Newsletters/Vulindlela_Nov2012/Malawi.pdf. 10 February 2018.

Sanford J Grossman and Merton H Miller (1988) 'Liquidity and Market Structure' 43 (3) *The Journal of Finance* 617, http://onlinelibrary.wiley.com/doi/10.1111/j.1540-6261.1988.tb04594.x/pdf. 6 October 2018.

Setsuya Satåo and David B Humphrey (1995) *Transforming Payment Systems: Meeting the Needs of Emerging Market Economies* (World Bank Discussion Papers, World Bank).

Stephen Halliday (2009) 'The First Common Market? The Hanseatic League' 59 (7) *History Today*, http://www.historytoday.com/stephen-halliday/first-common-market-hanseatic-league. 13 September 2018.

Tamim Bayoumi and Barry Eichengreen (1995) *The Stability of the Gold Standard and the Evolution of the International Monetary System* (IMF Working Paper, Washington, DC), https://papers.ssrn.com/sol3/papers.cfm?abstract_id=883236. 1 May 2018.

Taonga Sabola (2015) 'Banks Switch on Payment System' *Daily Times* (17 February 2015), http://timesmediamw.com/banks-switch-payment-system/. 7 October 2018.

Thomas H Greco Jr (1997) 'New Money: A Creative Opportunity for Business' 11 (3) *Global Development Research Centre [First Published in Perspectives on Business and Global Change]* (World Business Academy), http://www.gdrc.org/icm/new-money.html. 14 November 2018.

Tommaso Padoa-Schioppa (2003) 'Central Banks and Financial Stability: Exploring the Land in Between' in Vitor Gaspar, Philipp Hartmann and Olaf Sleijpen (eds) *Second ECB Central Banking Conference: The Transformation of the European Financial System* (European Central Bank).

Walter Bagehot (1873) *Lombard Street: A Description of the Money Market* (Henry S King & Co., London), Chapter II.

William Stanley Jevons (1875) 'Barter' in *Money and the Mechanism of Exchange* (D. Appleton and Company, New York).

World Bank (2015) 'Malawi—Overview' (World Bank), http://www.worldbank.org/en/country/malawi/overview. 21 December 2018.

CHAPTER 3

# Developments in Mobile Technology and the Emergence of Mobile Money

## 3.1 Introduction

To fully appreciate the ingenuity of the development of mobile money (mobile money) as a service, there is a need to start by analysing how the mobile phone developed. If the home is an Englishman's castle, then the mobile phone may be said to be a modern person's sanctuary. In the mobile phone, the subscriber identification module (SIM)[1] may well be said to be its heart, memory bank and nerve centre combined. The subscriber identity module is used by phones using the Groupe Speciale Mobile (GSM) family of protocols.[2] It "contains encryption keys, secures the user's personal identification number (PIN) on entry, and drives the phone's menu".[3] Developed in the early 1980s as a European standard, the GSM has quickly become a global standard.[4]

While the developed world has been laying expensive cables for landlines, in Africa, the mobile phone has been the solution of connectivity bottlenecks. With an exponential increase in usage, the mobile phone

[1] Also called sim card.

[2] GSMA (2017) 'Brief History of GSM & the GSMA' (GSM Association), http://www.gsma.com/aboutus/history. 10 March 2017.

[3] Ignacio Mas and Daniel Radcliffe (2011) 'Mobile Payments Go Viral: M-PESA in Kenya' 32 *The Capco Institute Journal of Financial Transformation* 169, p. 170.

[4] GSMA (2017).



S. Madise, *The Regulation of Mobile Money*, Palgrave Macmillan Studies in Banking and Financial Institutions,
https://doi.org/10.1007/978-3-030-13831-8_3

has by far superseded the landline in Africa.[5] Africa's mobile penetration stood at 67% in 2015[6] and is expected to grow to 79% by 2020.[7] Aker and Mbiti say, "as telecommunications markets mature, mobile phones in Africa are evolving from simple communication tools to service delivery platforms".[8] Porteous in 2006 postulated that the number of mobile phone users may have exceeded that of the banked.[9] It is submitted, the correct current position is that it has now exceeded that of the banked.

The proliferation of the mobile phone has led to the introduction of several add-on services. While the first mobile phones were used only for voice telephony, it soon became apparent that the service could be used for much more. The introduction of the interactive short messaging service (SMS), a data channel available on phones using the GSM platform proved to be a game-changer.[10] Using the mobile phone to access financial services and transact was therefore only an event waiting to happen. The mobile phone essentially mimics key ingredients that are essential for the offer of banking services.[11] The SIM can authenticate users and the phone can also be employed as a point of sale terminal.[12]

The emergence of the mobile phone also revolutionised the telephone transmission theory, which in effect says any transmission system should have an energy source, a medium of transmission and a receiving device.[13] The medium of transmission was for a long-time a conductor-wire. This ensured direct connectivity between any two

[5]Jenny Aker and Isaac Mbiti (2010) 'Mobile Phones and Economic Development in Africa' 24 (3) *Journal of Economic Perspectives* 207, p. 4, https://www.aeaweb.org/atypon.php?doi=10.1257/jep.24.3.207. 13 December 2018.

[6]Adeyemi Adepetun (2015) 'Africa's Mobile Phone Penetration Now 67%' *The Guardian*, http://www.ngrguardiannews.com/2015/06/africas-mobile-phone-penetration-now-67/. 12 December 2018.

[7]Anon (2015) 'Why Africa Mobile Phone Penetration Rising to 79% by 2020 Is Good News' (Amgoo Telecom Co., Ltd.), http://www.amgoo.com/blog/why-africa-mobile-phone-penetration-rising-to-79-by-2020-is-good-news. 12 December 2018.

[8]Aker and Mbiti (2010), p. 3.

[9]Porteous (2006), p. 3.

[10]Jack and Suri (2011), p. 7.

Mas and Radcliffe (2011), p. 170.

[11]Mas and Radcliffe (2011), p. 170.

[12]Ibid., p. 172.

[13]CF Myers and LS Crosby (1953) *Principles of Electricity Applied to Telephone and Telegraph Work* (American Telephone and Telegraph Company, New York), p. 154.

communication points. In energy studies, it is trite that energy cannot be created from nothing, it just changes form. So ideally transmission over a telephone line requires an energy source at the origin (usually a voltaic cell) which converts speech into an electric current (microphone). The electric current has to be transmitted through a wire (requiring more energy) and at the other end will be needed a device to convert the electric current back into sound, usually via a speaker or earpiece.

The introduction of the mobile phone introduced a new transmission medium; air.

One important element of air is that it allows for waves to flow more freely. What is required is energy to broadcast the signal. For the receiving device, what is required is the energy to receive the signal and decode it, if it has been coded. Apart from getting rid of wires, the mobile phone is also more energy efficient. When energy is being transmitted through a conductor, there is always some energy lost in overcoming the resistance within the conductor.[14] This loss of energy arises because most wires, and all metals in general, are not perfect conductors. On the other hand, since air is virtually free,[15] and offers less resistance, this also contributed to lowering of costs.[16]

This chapter opens with a discussion of the development of telephones and how this technology gave birth to mobile phones. The chapter then analyses the birth of the mobile money service, as an added on service to the repertoire of mobile phone services. Using the Kenyan *M-Pesa* as the standard, it analyses how mobile money works.

## 3.2 Development of the Telephone

For most developed countries, mobile phones may have developed as a means of technological advancement. However, for most countries in sub-Saharan Africa, mobile phones developed out of sheer necessity. In order to appreciate this, it is imperative to provide a brief historical overview of the development of the telephone.

Traditionally communication was over telephone lines. These lines principally were composed of copper wire. Copper is preferred because it is a very good conductor, durable, resistant to corrosion, ductile and

[14] Ibid., p. 165.

[15] Of course, licences must be procured to be allowed to transmit radio signals.

[16] Myers and Crosby (1953), p. 165.

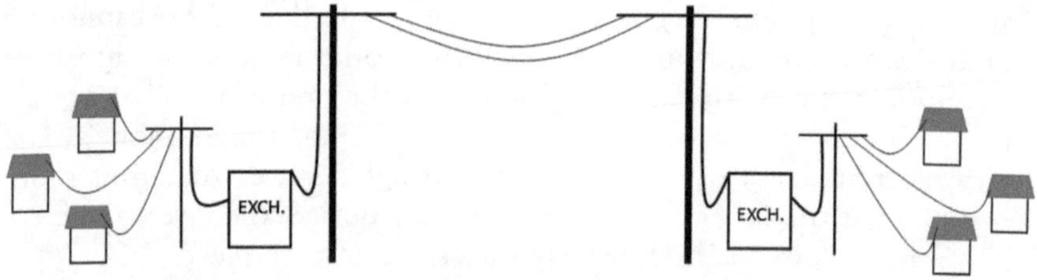


**Fig. 3.1** Telephone lines using wires (*Source* Author)

infinitely recyclables. This also makes copper ideal for residential purposes. Houses were connected by a pair of copper wires to a line (usually on a pole). In the early times, the line ran from the house to the local exchange. There was therefore a stream of wires connecting poles up to the exchange. At the exchange, the signals from the wires would be added together (multiplexed) using a switch and the output would be a pair or more (depending on the capacity) which would be used to connect exchanges. At the other end, the process would be reversed; the exchange would de-multiplex the signals and distribute them to the houses under its catchment area. In time, some low-level form of multiplexing started being done at the pole so that from the pole to the exchange, there were fewer lines. While technological advances ensured that more signals could be sent over fewer lines, the need to actually have a physical connection from point A to point B meant that telephone communication was expensive. The figure below shows a typical telephone connection system using copper wires (Fig. 3.1).

It soon emerged that running copper cables across the country was not only expensive, it was also unsustainable. The initial step was the replacement of long-distance copper wires between exchanges with microwave radio links. The figure below shows this development (Fig. 3.2).

Although they travel through the air, radio waves are not sound waves; they are electromagnetic waves and can travel at the speed of light.[17] The antenna acts as a transceiver, performing dual functions of a transmitter and a receiver.[18] Since radio signals travel unidirectional,

[17]Christopher Haslett (2008) *Essentials of Radio Wave Propagation* (Cambridge University Press, Cambridge), p. 1.

[18]Ibid., p. 3.

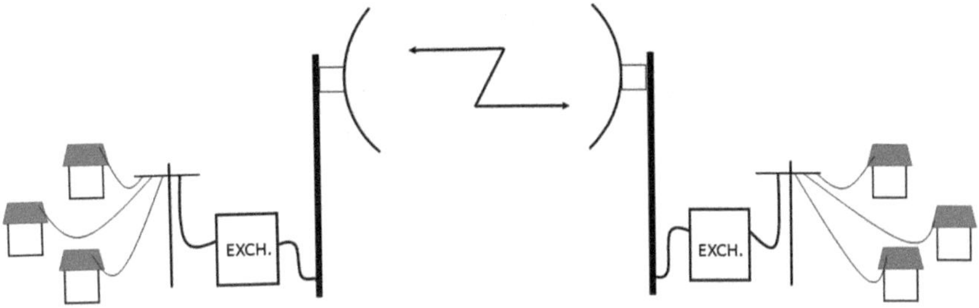


**Fig. 3.2** Telephone lines utilising radio (parabolic dishes) (*Source* Author)

there must be a line of sight between the transmitting and receiving antenna to ensure no loss of signal.[19] Therefore, any obstacle including bad weather affects this form of communication. The same also applies where there are long distances separating a transmitter and a receiver which cannot be overcome by using repeater transceivers. In this case, satellite communication is employed. A hyperbolic, dish not so much unlike the microwave antenna, acts as a transceiver but this time connect with a satellite orbiting in space.

So as an example, suppose one wished to communicate from Zomba in Malaŵi to Coventry in the UK using this system, this is how the communication would be routed.

i. When the caller in Zomba picks up his phone, the local exchange will detect this, and when he dials the UK, the local exchange will realise that this is an international call.
ii. It will then direct the call to the international gateway. The route to the gateway maybe via copper wire to the local exchange and then microwave radio to the international gateway.
iii. At the international gateway, this call will be routed with other calls going to the UK via a communications satellite hovering above the orbit in Malaŵi.
iv. The satellite will simply relay the signal (which is also in the form of a microwave radio wave) to the international gateway (acting as a recipient) in the UK.

[19]Joel Young (2009) 'Weird & Wireless: RF "Line of Sight"' *Electronics Weekly* (21 October 2009), http://www.electronicsweekly.com/blogs/electro-ramblings/weird-wireless/weird-wireless-rf-line-of-sight-2009-10/. 10 March 2018.

v. Here, the process is then reversed. The international gateway will route the call to Coventry and may use microwave radio links until the call terminates in the local exchange in Coventry.
vi. From here, it will be transferred to the specific telephone number that has been called.

Although the process looks complicated, it is actually done in microseconds. A typical telltale sign of this method of communication is that there is usually a moment of delay and one also hears an echo over the line.

Bad weather naturally also affects this type of satellite communication. This has now been solved by the introduction of a fibre optic network that is now almost global. An optical fibre system is similar to other transmission systems and the same transmission theory applies. The difference is that the instead of an energy source, there is an optical or light source.[20] The device at the source will encode (modulate) a signal to produce light pulses. This light travels through an optical fibre cable and is then received at the other end by an optical detector, a device which can decode (demodulate) the information in the light.[21] There is therefore electrical-light conversion at the modulation stage and light-electric conversion at the demodulation stage.[22] Transmission is achieved by varying the light pulses, and usually, in the now more established digital modulation format, this is a series of on and off pulses.[23]

As the optical fibre is basically made up of smaller glass strands (typically the diameter of a human hair), this medium offers a more secure medium than would free air but at the same time does not have some of the bottlenecks that affect metal wires.[24] They are much lighter than wires, there is low transmission loss and they are more rugged and flexible, offering a higher reliability with a low cost of maintenance.[25] Unlike

[20] John M Senior (1951) *Optical Fiber Communications* (Prentice-Hall International, Inc.), p. 6.

[21] Ibid., p. 6.

[22] Ibid.

[23] Ibid.

[24] Ibid., p. 7.

[25] For a comparison between optical fibre and copper see: 'Submarine Cable Map' (PriMetrica, Inc., 2015), http://www.submarinecablemap.com/#/. 5 May 2018.

precious copper wires which are usually the target of vandals and those interesting in smelting the copper, optical fibre presents no such value and can therefore be buried in the ground and left untouched. Since there is no electricity conduction occurring, optical fibre is also safe to be laid under the sea bed or laid over areas which would otherwise be hazardous to electric transmission.[26]

Despite its competitive advantage, others feel that the future of communications in Africa lies with wireless technologies because of the continent's geographical spread.[27] Therefore, while the fibre optic network may be the backbone for continental and regional connections, wireless may be the technology that ensures last-mile connectivity.

## 3.3 Development of the Mobile Phone

The basic mobile phone principle is based on the concept of wireless communication. Mobile phones actually use radio waves.[28] The development of the mobile or cell phone seems to have taken place simultaneously in the USA and in the Nordic countries. In the USA, the technology evolved from military technology of the Handie-Talkie and Walkie-Talkie two-way radios.[29] In Europe, the Nordic countries teamed up to develop the GSM protocol in Stockholm in 1992.[30] As a mobile telephone standard, the GSM completely revolutionalised mobile telephony technology. Starting as a European protocol for the digital cellular phone system, it has is now become the standard setter across the globe.[31] The key to mobile phone telephony is the cell. A cell comprises a base station and mobile phones within its geographical

[26] See ibid.

[27] Gabriella Mulligan (2015) 'Is Fibre Optic Cable Key to Africa's Economic Growth?' BBC Business News (London, 31 March 2015), http://www.bbc.co.uk/news/business-32079649. 9 May 2018.

[28] 'Mobile Phone Base Stations—How Mobile Phone Networks Work' (Ofcom 2001), http://www.ofcom.org.uk/static/archive/ra/topics/mpsafety/school-audit/mobilework.htm. 27 March 2018.

[29] Jon Agar (2003) *Constant Touch: A Global History of the Mobile Phone* (Icon Books, Cambridge) Chapter 4.

[30] Ibid., Chapter 7.

[31] Ibid.

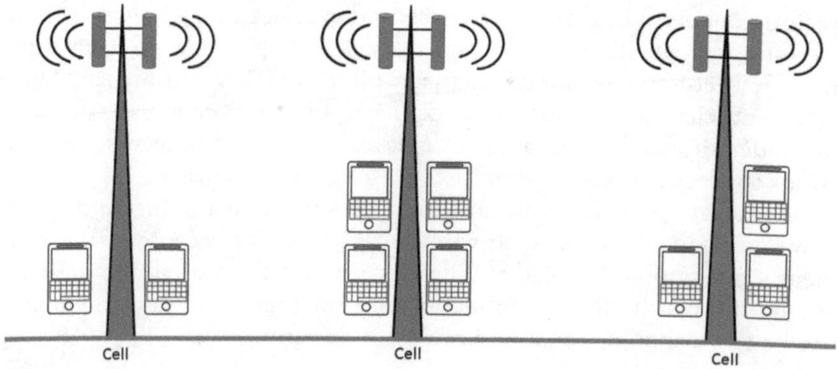


**Fig. 3.3** Cells comprising base stations and mobile phones (*Source* Author)

coverage.[32] Both the base station and the mobile phones communicate via radio waves, with the base communicating with other bases or the main station thereby linking the mobile phone users to other users within the network.[33] Interconnectivity between the main stations with other telephony providers, including those for fixed line, ensures that mobile phone users can communicate across networks. When they first came out, mobile phones were aptly called cellular phones (cell phones). The figure below shows a simplified representation of the multiplying factor of the cell technology. While base stations can communicate with each other within a reasonable distance, another means of connectivity, usually optical fibre, is used to connect them over long distances or with main stations. This is where mobile telephony benefits from the superior connectivity of fibre optic cables which can transmit signals to far away base stations efficiently and cheaply. Comparing the 3 towers in the figure below, it becomes clear that cell technology offers the best means of communication. It uses less hardware and allows for mobility of the user (Fig. 3.3).

For Sub-Saharan Africa, the cell phone was, therefore, a godsend. It meant that telecommunications companies could forgo the expensive

[32] Ofcom (2001) 'Mobile Phone Base Stations—How Mobile Phone Networks Work' (Office of the Communications Regulator, UK), http://www.ofcom.org.uk/static/archive/ra/topics/mpsafety/school-audit/mobilework.htm. 12 December 2018.

[33] Ibid.

investment of laying down copper cables and having exchanges all over the country. By installing base stations in or near communities, people who would have otherwise been cut from the telephone network are now able to communicate. The mobile phone has become ubiquitous, thanks to an influx of cheap phones.[34] The mobile phone has been warmly embraced in sub-Saharan Africa. From 11 million subscribers in 2000 across the whole of Africa,[35] it was at a staggering 680 million by mid-2015[36] and projected to reach just under a billion by 2019 in sub-Saharan Africa alone.[37] The mobile phone revolution has been said to be "an engine for development, inclusive growth, and reform".[38]

## 3.4 A New Service Is Born: Mobile Money

The use of the mobile phone to access financial services and transactions was an event waiting to happen. The mobile phone achieves this using the interactive SMS, a data-messaging channel available on phones using the GSM platform.[39] The mobile phone essentially mimics key ingredients that are essential for the offer of banking services. The SIM can authenticate users.[40] Mobile money services are set up by telecommunication companies and operate as add-on services to the normal telecommunication services. There is a direct correlation between mobile money

[34]David Smith (2014) 'Internet Use on Mobile Phones in Africa Predicted to Increase 20-fold' *The Guardian* (5 June 2014), http://www.theguardian.com/world/2014/jun/05/internet-use-mobile-phones-africa-predicted-increase-20-fold. 10 March 2018.

[35]ITU (2009) *Information Society Statistical Profiles 2009—Africa* (International Telecommunications Union), p. 1, http://www.itu.int/dms_pub/itu-d/opb/ind/D-IND-RPM.AF-2009-PDF-E.pdf. 12 December 2018.

[36]GSMA (2015) *The Mobile Economy Sub-Saharan Africa 2015*, https://www.gsmaintelligence.com/research/?file=721eb3d4b80a36451202d0473b3c4a63&download. 12 December 2018.

[37]Smith (2014).

[38]Giridaran Saubramaniam (2013) 'Mobile Money: A Theoretical Study of Alternative Media of Exchange, and an Empirical Study with Respect to M-Pesa in Kenya' (Toulouse School of Economics), p. 6, http://papers.ssrn.com/sol3/papers.cfm?abstract_id=2278679. 15 December 2018.

[39]Mas and Radcliffe (2011), p. 170.

[40]Ibid., p. 172.

and access to a mobile phone.[41] It follows, that mobile money is likely to be more widespread where there is a good mobile network.[42]

The mobile or cell phone was first introduced in Malaŵi in 1995.[43] At that time, the main means of remitting money was through the postal services network (formal), friends and relatives (informal). There have been infrastructural and development changes since 1995, but it is argued that so far, at least, until what the author terms the "revolutionary solution", there was no answer to the remittance dilemma.

### 3.4.1 The Remittance Dilemma

Transferring money across geographically spread locations is a problem in most developing countries. Ironically as a service, remittances benefit when families are split. Ideally, they target the "urban migrant population who seek better employment options and send money regularly to relatives in rural kins".[44] Heyer and Mas found a direct correlation between remittances and rate of urbanisation.[45] The problems faced by migrant workers in sending money home are not unique to Africa. In the Middle East and Asia, the *Hawala* has been used for a long time as an informal way of sending not only domestic but also international remittances.[46] *Hawala*, developed in India, works as an alternative remittance system that transfers money without moving the money.[47] In fact, *Hawala* is an ancient remittance system which predates the introduction of Western banking.[48] Its strength lies in its network of members:

[41] Porteous (2006), p. 44.

[42] Ibid.

[43] Author's personal knowledge.

[44] Amrik Heyer and Ignacio Mas (2009) *Seeking Fertile Grounds for Mobile Money* (Mobile Money for the Unbanked, GSMA, London), p. 5, http://www.gsma.com/mobilefordevelopment/wp-content/uploads/2012/03/fertile_grounds_mobile_money55.pdf. 14 February.

[45] Ibid., p. 5.

[46] Ibid., p. 10.

[47] Patrick M Jost and Harjit Singh Sandhu (2003) *The Hawala Alternative Remittance System and Its Role in Money Laundering* (Interpol), p. 2, https://www.peacepalacelibrary.nl/ebooks/files/hawala.pdf. 14 February 2018.

[48] Ibid.

using family or regional affiliations.[49] On its part, Malaŵi has had money remittance problems, especially in the rural areas. These problems are mainly rooted in the country's infrastructural and institutional bottlenecks.

#### *3.4.1.1 Road Network*

A World Bank survey done on Malaŵi in 2009 established the following:

> Quality of the trunk road network is not a major constraint but differences in the quality of feeder roads connecting villages to the main road network have a bearing on transport costs. And costs due to poor feeder roads are exacerbated by low volumes of trade between rural locations and market centers. With empty backhauls and journeys covering small distances, only a few transport service providers enter the market, charging disproportionately high prices to cover fixed costs and maximize mark-ups.[50]

All forms of remittances relying on the road network are not only expensive but also unreliable. Due to bad or non-existent feeder roads, access to rural areas may just be impossible. It is not easy to remit money to remote areas because of inaccessibility. Even formal means of remittance are expensive because of high accessibility costs.

#### *3.4.1.2 Inaccessibility of Banking Services*

Bank charges in Malaŵi are generally high across all platforms.[51] Apart from bank charges, it is expensive to operate a bank account in Malaŵi because of several factors. Most banks are concentrated in the main cities and towns and usually have agencies in the smaller towns. People in the rural areas must travel long distances to access banking services. Only one bank, OIBM operated a physically mobile banking service.[52]

[49] Ibid.

[50] Somik V Lall, Hyoung Wang and Thomas Munthali (2009) *Explaining High Transport Costs Within Malawi—Bad Roads or Lack of Trucking Competition?* (Policy Research Working Paper 5133, World Bank Publications), http://elibrary.worldbank.org/doi/pdf/10.1596/1813-9450-5133. 11 March 2018.

[51] Chris Chibwana (2010) 'The High and the Hidden Costs of Banking in Malawi', http://chibwana.com/2010/04/05/costs-of-banking-in-malawi/. 11 March 2018.

[52] Geetha Nagarajan (July 2010) 'Money in a Pot: Has OIBM Altered Savings in Rural Malawi?' (Financial Service Assessment), http://www.fsassessment.umd.edu/notes/savings-rural.html. 11 March 2018.

Unfortunately, this bank was facing financial problems and has since been taken over by another bank, First Merchant Bank (FMB).[53] It is unclear whether FMB[54] will continue operating the mobile banking service. Most banks also require a minimum credit balance to open and operate a savings account. Some also charge a ledger fee for current accounts. Some banks also impose limits per day and per month, not only for amounts of money withdrawn but also for the number of transactions. All banks have onerous know your customer requirements. Malaŵi has just embarked on a national identity system and it is difficult for people in rural arrears or those in the informal sector to obtain identification papers acceptable by the banks.[55]

Although transferring money may be free when using the same bank, lack of holding an account may be a barrier. The banking sector is effectively one serving the middle and upper classes. Statistics in 2014 show only 33% (up from 19% in 2008) of the population was banked.[56] The rural population was at 86% in 2014,[57] up from 80% in 2010,[58] a trend that may point to either reverse-urbanisation or an increased rate of reproduction among the rural population. Figures for 2016 put the rural population at 84%.[59] This means those who are banked in rural areas, in the absence of local banking services, must trek to urban centres to access banking services. On the other hand, it may well be that the percentage of those banked does not represent the actual number of people but rather of bank accounts. If this is so, then the actual population

[53] Kelvin Chaguza (2017) 'Opportunity International Bank of Malawi (OIBM) to Trim Its Staff This Year' *Face of Malawi* (26 January 2017), http://www.faceofmalawi.com/2017/01/opportunity-bank-of-malawi-oibm-to-trim-its-staffs-this-year/. 10 March 2018.

FMB 'First Merchant Bank to Acquire Opportunity International Bank of Malawi' (27 June 2017), http://www.fmbmalawi.com/first-merchant-bank-to-acquire-opportunity-international-bank-of-malawi/. 18 July 2018.

[54] Which has now rebranded to First Capital Bank.

[55] Legislation to enable national identification system was passed: National Registration Act (Malaŵi 2010), but efforts to operationalise it only started in 2015—Malaŵi Government (2015).

[56] Finscope (2014), p. 5.

[57] Ibid., p. 2.

[58] Anon (2014) 'Rural Population in Malawi' *Trading Economics*, http://www.tradingeconomics.com/malawi/rural-population-wb-data.html. 19 May 2018.

[59] UNESCO (2016).

banked may be even less as it is common for most people to hold multiple accounts. The current banking services, illustrate the class division in society. The last state-owned bank, which had targeted rural communities, was sold in 2015 thereby reinforcing the private banking system.[60]

#### *3.4.1.3 Expensive Remittance Services*

There are several remittance services operating in Malaŵi, apart from those exclusively offered by the postal services. These include MoneyGram and Western Union. MoneyGram charges a fee of K4,200.00 for any amount up to K35,000.00, K5,250.00 from then on to K70,000.00 and K7,000.00 from K70,001.00 to K140,000.00 and so on.[61] These charges are not only high but deter remittance of small amounts. [£1 = K943.71].[62] It may be argued, however, that the higher the amount to be transferred, the lower the transaction costs becomes. The economies of scale balance out when higher amounts are transferred. This, however, disadvantages those who transfer small amounts. These money remittance services are useful for international and regional remittances but not for small amounts. For domestic remittances, they are the least ideal because of high transaction costs.

#### *3.4.1.4 Unreliable but Relatively Expensive Postal Services*

One could in the old days, put money in an envelope and post it. Posting money, this way was prohibited but this did not stop the risk-takers. Now, the risk of an envelope containing money going missing is so great it would be foolhardy to even dare. The postal service has always operated remittance services. The postal service has a service called Fast Cash, and still, operate money or postal order services.[63] However, there are post offices that do not have a sufficiently large enough cash float to enable them to pay out.[64] Therefore, if one sent money to via a rural

[60] Chipiliro Kansilanga (2015) 'Malawi Savings Bank Finally Sold' *Daily Times* (2 July 2015), http://www.times.mw/malawi-savings-bank-finally-sold-2/. 20 July 2018.

[61] 'MoneyGram' (MoneyGram International Limited), https://m.moneygram.com/mgomobile/site/costEstimator.html#CostEstimatorResults. 11 March 2018.

[62] XE (2018).

[63] MPC (2017) 'Financial, Retail & Agency Services' (Malawi Posts Corporation), http://malawiposts.com/finance.html. 10 March 2018.

[64] Vince Kumwenda (2012) 'Malawi Posts Corporation's Fast Cash Money Transfer', http://vincekumwenda.blogspot.co.uk/2012/05/malawi-posts-corporations-fast-cash.html. 23 February 2018.

post office, chances are that the post office in question may not have the money to pay out the full amount.

#### *3.4.1.5 Unreliable Friends and Relatives*

It is common for people to send money to relatives living in another village using friends or other family members going there. The risk here is that the friend or relative may not deliver the money, possibly claiming that they had lost the money or that it was stolen. They might also claim that the money was lost through magic. The local word used to describe this phenomenon is *chitaka*.[65] Cases of *chitaka* seem to be on the decline, and this has been attributed to improved financial literacy.[66]

### *3.4.2 The "Revolutionary Solution": Mobile Money Remittance*

Following on from the groundbreaking innovation of *M-Pesa* by Safaricom in Kenya, mobile network operators have introduced what the author terms the *revolutionary solution*: the mobile money service. Mobile money is not just a money service, it also offers other financial products and takes deposits, which has become a game-changer since deposit-taking is the mainstay of banks. Mobile money is therefore a complete payment system. There is still debate whether deposit, as understood by mobile network operators in their marketing messages, carries the same meaning as in the banking sense. It is submitted that at present it does not. By addressing the remittance challenges, mobile network operators have devised a unique network of solutions to the remittance dilemma using the mobile money payment system:

*Localise everything*—mobile network operators already have agents with an established presence in most parts of the country who sell airtime or credit.[67] By using the same agents as mobile money agents, the service will be easily accepted by the community.

[65] *Chitaka* is a collective word (Chewa) all forms of magic tricks usually associated with stealing of money.

[66] (2012) *Study on Informal and Non-formal Rural Financial Services 2012* (Concern Universal Malawi), p. 13, http://concern-universal.org/wp-content/uploads/2014/07/CUMO-Study-of-Rural-Finance-Summary.pdf. 7 October 2018.

[67] Although the agent low agent penetration is still perceived as a barrier that needs to be overcome.

*Reduce transactions costs*—the charges for sending and receiving money are low and affordable. In fact, the charges are so minimal that the other money remittance services are now in danger to adapt or die.[68]

*Load a new money service on an existing and familiar telecommunication services*—Mobile money services use the same telecommunication platform already built by the mobile network operators and the same interface that mobile phone users are already accustomed to. It is based on the SMS, which is a well-known feature and has been around since the advent of the mobile phone.

*Take advantage of the ubiquitous nature of the mobile phone*—the mobile phone is now found almost anywhere and everywhere. It is trusted too. If one can trust it to send a message across hundreds and thousands of kilometres, one may be easily convinced to use the same device for other services such as sending and receiving money or buying goods and services. It is also a convenient tool.

*Develop a vibrant ecosystem*—mobile money issuers have collaborated with the major utility service providers so that customers are encouraged to procure or pay their bills via mobile money. The electricity and water utilities are some of the utility companies that are part of the mobile money ecosystem. The inclusion of retail fuel providers and pay television services indicates that the target is beyond merely the unbanked.[69]

One can use the mobile money service, just like one uses one's phone, for regular every day (text-based) communication, not only to send and receive money but also to procure goods and services. It invariably also means that one can use the service to receive payments for goods and services sold. The service makes it much easier, safer, faster and cheaper to send money. The user of the service need not have a bank account or pass the other stringent know your customer checks that one may be subjected to before being able to open a bank account. There are some rudimentary checks that are done when a person is registering for mobile money and the checks escalate with increased amounts of transactions, but these checks are nothing compared to what banks require. Mobile money then presents the very first, but crucial step towards getting those who were financially excluded into the formal financial sector. Mas and Radcliffe argue that this has opened a completely new way of transacting

[68] For example, the remittance fee is K50 regardless of the amount for *Mpamba*.

[69] Kihagi (2013). See also TNM (2017).

effectively, replacing methods such as personal trips, and using friends as couriers, public courier, postal systems, and public transport networks.[70] Camner et al. found that after *M-Pesa* was launched in Kenya, there was a "massive reduction in using hand-delivery, bus travel, or courier companies for remittances".[71]

Malaŵi has experienced a sharp rise in Internet and mobile banking. In 2015, mobile banking led by mobile network operators registered an annual 141% increase with a corresponding 180% growth in value (48 billion Kwacha, from just under 17 billion Kwacha).[72] The popularity of utility bill payments plus aggressive marketing by the two mobile money issuers was attributed to this increase.[73] The total number of registered subscribers for mobile payment services grew by 156% (12.5 million from 4.9 million).[74] It is important, however, to caution that this figure most likely is the aggregate of all mobile payments and includes both mobile banking and mobile money payments. As is seen later, the total figure of mobile phones subscribers is way below this figure. The central bank puts the total number of subscribers of non-bank mobile payments at 3.6 million as at December 2016.[75] In 2014, just a year or two after mobile network operators had started offering mobile payment services, the central bank noted that:

> Mobile network operator [MNO] led mobile payments services have grown at a very significant rate, in fact at a much faster rate than the mobile banking services offered by the commercial banks, in terms of both transactions (volumes and value) and a number of subscribers. This development confirms the potential for MNO-led microfinance service as a significant tool in the financial inclusion agenda, as they cater for a wider section of the population including the unbanked.[76]

Maurer has described the mobile money system in this manner:

[70] Mas and Radcliffe (2011). See also Aker and Mbiti (2010), p. 20.

[71] Donovan (2012), p. 2653.

[72] RBM (2015), p. 14.

[73] Ibid.

[74] Ibid.

[75] RBM (2017), p. 1.

[76] RBM (2015), p. 14.

> [An agent] starts by depositing cash via [an] MNO into a pooled account at a bank that is partnered with the MNO. The MNO next creates for the [agent] an electronic money account equivalent to his share of the pooled account on deposit with the bank, which he can access via his mobile phone. He now has a share of electronic credits with the MNO. When a customer wants to send money to another person, the customer can come to the [agent] and provide cash in the amount to be transferred to another person, plus a commission. The [agent] receives the cash and transfers to the customer's mobile phone some of his own electronic money on account with the MNO. The MNO records the transfer of electronic money to the [agent's] customer. The [agent] can then deposit the cash in his bank account, which will top up his supply of MNO-issued electronic money. This maintains a one-to-one correspondence between the money on deposit in the bank and the electronic money in the system.[77]

Put simply, customers give fiat money to an agent who issues them with mobile money in the form of "a code. The code can then be given to [an agent] anywhere else in the country, and redeemed for cash".[78] To emphasise the need to match mobile money and the physical money, Hughes and Lonie say, it "must exactly match the real money or we could find ourselves in the unfortunate situation of creating currency".[79] In fact were it not to match, it would also create runaway inflation, as there would be mobile money, which cannot be backed by deposits. The pooled funds are held in a bank in the name of the mobile money issuer and not individual customers.[80] This means the accounts that the individual mobile money customers have are with the mobile network operators. These accounts are tied to the subscriber telephone numbers allocated by the parent mobile phone operator. The system works under the peer-to-peer platform.[81] Subject to any interoperability constraints, this allows anyone with a mobile phone to send money to another

[77] Maurer (2012), p. 306.

[78] Brendan Greeley (2013) 'One Good Paper: Monopoly Power in Mobile Money' *Bloomberg Businessweek*, http://www.businessweek.com/articles/2013-03-13/one-good-paper-monopoly-power-in-mobilelectronicmoney. 28 March 2018.

[79] Hughes and Lonie (2007), p. 69.

[80] Di Castri (2013), p. 15.

[81] Ibid.

person with a mobile phone.[82] The mobile money application resides on the phone's SIM for authentication.[83]

The ingenuity of mobile money as a service lies in the fact that its interface is the same as that of regular every day text-based communication. If one can procure goods and services, it invariably means one can also receive payments for goods and services sold. Since there is no requirement to possess a bank account,[84] this is what makes mobile money a game changer in the financial inclusion agenda. Although mobile money has been touted as a positive development in most African countries, there are fears that it may have an impact on inflation. For example, in Kenya, the African Development Bank has raised concerns that mobile money may possibly be the cause of rising inflation.[85] The argument is that mobile money impacts on the velocity of money. There is an "increased pace of monetary transactions while increasing cash in circulation, looping more people into the financial sector and leading to demand for goods and services outstripping supply".[86]

Jenkins says despite its manifestation, mobile money is real and not "pseudo money".[87] Hughes and Lonie have called the mobile money service "turning cell phones into 24-hour tellers".[88] Jenkins says mobile money has the benefit of reducing "the cost and risk inherent in dealing with cash".[89] The ranges of transactions and services, which can be accessed by the mobile phone, are limitless thereby resulting in significant implications for economic activity across the world.[90] Maurer says mobile money "represents a collision of two ubiquitous technologies,

[82] Mas and Radcliffe (2011), p. 171.

[83] Donovan (2012), p. 2648.

[84] A customer due diligence is however done.

[85] George Ngigi, 'M-Pesa Linked to Rise in Inflation' *Business Daily* (14 February 2012), http://www.businessdailyafrica.com/M-Pesa-linked-to-rise-in-inflation/-/539552/1327538/-/13rogmr/-/index.html. 28 March 2018.

[86] Ibid.

[87] Beth Jenkins (2008) 'Developing Mobile Money Ecosystems' (Washington, DC: International Finance Corporation and Harvard Kennedy School), p. 21, http://ww.gsma.com/mobilefordevelopment/wp-content/uploads/2012/06/report_30_mobilemoney.pdf. 13 December 2018.

[88] Hughes and Lonie (2007), p. 63.

[89] Jenkins (2008), p. 5.

[90] Ibid.

each with similar but internally contradictory set of symbolic associations and social practices".[91] He argues both represents modernity: mobile money an "index of technological savvy" and the flashing of money a symbol of importance.[92] Using mobile money, therefore, helps bring into the formal system money that is kept in the informal system. Imagine the impact of raking into the formal economy all those millions of Kwachas that Malaŵians have kept in their safe deposit boxes buried deep into the ground.[93]

Malaŵi has two dominant mobile network operators, Airtel and TNM. Airtel is a regional mobile player and has presence in Africa and India.[94] TNM is a Malaŵian company which emerged from the deregulation that unbundled the telecommunications sector. Each of the mobile network operators has its own mobile money service. Airtel has Airtel Money or *Khusa M'manja* (colloquial for *money in the hands* in the widespread local language, Chicheŵa). TNM has *Mpamba* (colloquial for money). Their set-up shows that they are largely modelled on the Kenyan *M-Pesa*. The reference to mobile money in this book may therefore be general, but unless specifically distinguished, must be understood in the context of these 3 mobile money services. This is important because as Chapter 7 will show, the mobile money services have different models and there is anecdotal evidence that the models have an impact on how successful they become.

#### 3.4.2.1 *Analysis of Mobile Money Using the Framework for Identifying Money*

In Chapter 2, a framework was developed of analysing money, based on the concept of economic money as well as legal money. Using this framework, this section analyses the attributes of mobile money and how they fit into the framework of money.

Utility and Value

The greater the number of those accepting payments via mobile money, the more mobile money mimics the qualities of cash. Within its

[91] Maurer (2012), p. 308.

[92] Ibid.

[93] Reference to a common manner of keeping money safe in rural areas of Malaŵi.

[94] 'Bharti Airtel' (Bharti Airtel 2017), http://www.airtel.in/about-bharti/about-bharti-airtel. 30 May 2018.

ecosystem, mobile money is accepted as a medium of exchange. It is not accepted because it represents a valued commodity, but it begets its value from its utility. Although it is a digital representation, that representation manifests itself as a store of value. One can transfer the value to another person, peer to peer, and the person who receives such transferred value are at liberty to deal with it in any manner. The storage of value is also closely tied to the fact that it is a representation of cash.

Unit of Account
Mobile money has a one-to-one ratio with cash deposited in an account domiciled at a commercial bank. This ensures that it serves as a unit of account. The expression of the value of mobile money is the same as that of cash. As noted above, the mobile money issuer opens a pool account with a bank where cash from customers is deposited.[95] The issuer then issues out mobile money backed by these deposits and the mobile money circulates within its ecosystem. Customers exchange cash for mobile money and vice versa. Mobile money therefore retains the same properties of a unit of account as cash does.

Portability
The ubiquitous nature of the mobile phone has meant that mobile money can also be carried virtually anywhere, and in a cost-effective manner too. As a service, it is inseparable from the mobile phone containing the SIM to which it is tied. The user information embedded in the SIM is also replicated in computer servers of the mobile money issuer as well as the mobile phone operator. Compared to cash, mobile money is safer to carry around. When one produces a wallet full of notes, one attracts attention. When one produces a mobile phone and transacts on it, no one pays attention. Although mobile phones are increasingly valuable and can be stolen, the basic yet effective security features for the mobile money service will protect the mobile money in such instances. In this case, mobile money is not only portable but also a convenient way of carrying money around.

Homogeneity
As it has a one-to-one ratio with fiat money, mobile money is homogeneous. It maintains the same value by representation, ensuring uniformity

[95] Di Castri (2013), p. 15.

across time and space. It is easily divisible into smaller units. In Malaŵi, the currency is divided into Kwacha and Tambala. It is possible to divide mobile money into Kwacha and Tambala, as well as to aggregate it. 1 Kwacha equals 100 Tambala. When used within its ecosystem, mobile money does not lose its value when it moves around. Any loss of value occurs mostly at the point of transition between cash and mobile money, usually at the point of cashing out. A transaction fee is levied on the service.

Cognoscibility
Within its ecosystem, mobile money is easily recognised and accepted. The recognition manifests itself after a transaction has been completed and someone has been paid. In this way, it may be said the recognition is ex-post facto. It is credited after the transaction. On the other hand, with cash, once it is presented, it is cognizable at that level, even before the vendor puts it into the cash box. This in a way is like payment via electronic money generally, such as in the case of debit cards.

Legal Tender
Although easily accepted within its ecosystem, there is nothing to obligate anyone to accept payment via mobile money. Outside the mobile money ecosystem, it is not acceptable at all. It thus lacks a key feature of fiat money—no state authority to make it legal tender. It can be said that while it may be regarded as *social tender* it is definitely not legal tender. With growth in the ecosystem, mobile money is more likely to gain traction and become the norm. In Kenya, this is already the case. However, even when it becomes customary to make payments via mobile money, this will still not make it legal tender. In a way, this mirrors plastic money as evidenced in debit and credit cards. A vendor would be within his rights to refuse payment via debit or credit card and insist on cash.

### *3.4.3 Airtime*

The technical definition of airtime is "the amount of broadcasting time that someone has on television or radio".[96] For mobile phones, which are radio devices, this is equivalent to the amount of *talk time* that one has. With technological advances, airtime or airtime credit is now not

[96] 'Airtime' (2016) Cambridge University Press, http://dictionary.cambridge.org/dictionary/english/airtime. 27 June 2018.

restricted to talk time only, but may also be used for text messaging and data transmission. With time, airtime has emerged not only as a means of communication but also as a form of value which can be transferable. So although airtime was never conceived as a money service, in the same way that mobile money was, it has through local adaptation and innovation gained an ancillary role of a form of money. Popular among mobile phone users in sub-Saharan Africa is a peer-to-peer facility called *me to you* (Me2U or M2U) which allows transfer of airtime credit between users.[97] This can be for gratis but may also be in exchange for cash or another form of payment.[98] It is this that has led others to suggest that airtime is a form of money or at least an alternative currency.[99] Airtime also has another unique monetary attribute; it can be transferred without loss of value through the peer-to-peer scheme. So similarly to mobile money, as long as the airtime credit is within the ecosystem of a particular mobile network operator, it retains its value. This is how Sambaza, the M2U service operated by Kenya's Safaricom,[100] was described by Peter Day of the BBC when it was launched:

> What [Safaricom] has actually done is to create a new currency - a cyber-currency that can be sent anywhere in the country at the press of a button, without needing a bank account or incurring high bank charges.[101]

It is submitted that Peter Day may have exaggerated somewhat what airtime is or does. However, what he says underscores the fact that airtime has value, which can be transferred efficiently and in a cost-effectively.

[97] Airtel (2016) 'Me2U' (Airtel, Malawi), http://africa.airtel.com/wps/wcm/connect/africarevamp/malawi/home/personal/voice-and-text/phone-services/me2u. 21 May 2018.

TNM (2013) 'Me2u Service' (Telekom Networks Malawi), http://www.tnm.co.mw/index.php/me2u.html. 21 May 2018.

Safaricom Call Theirs 'Sambaza': Safaricom (2017) 'Sambaza' (Safaricom, Kenya), https://www.safaricom.co.ke/personal/calls-sms/prepay/sambaza. 17 February 2018.

[98] As where two persons are in a remote area far from any airtime vendor and one of them needs to top up his or her airtime.

[99] Porteous (2006), p. 23.

[100] Safaricom (2017).

[101] Peter Day (2005) 'Mutual Benefits of Profits from Poverty' BBC News (4 July 2005), http://news.bbc.co.uk/1/hi/business/4648049.stm. 17 February 2018.

#### *3.4.3.1 Analysis of Airtime Using the Framework for Identifying Money*

Across Africa, Airtel has a regional mobile telephony product called *One Network*.[102] This allows seamless use of Airtel services within its footprint. One can purchase airtime in country X, travel to country Y and use it. Better still, one can be in country D and purchase airtime in country E if one has the means. This aspect makes airtime unique and easily transferable across borders. Initially, Airtel, like TNM used to denominate airtime units in Dollars. Procurement was in local currency but the value was fixed at a set rate of the Kwacha to the Dollar. Following complaints by consumer groups as well as the local communications regulator, this has stopped and the airtime units are now in Kwacha.

An example of my own experience will demonstrate the across border remittance capacity of airtime. In 2008, I went to Uganda to participate in a University Challenge completion sponsored by Zain, the predecessor company to Airtel. I took both my Airtel and TNM phones. In Uganda, the TNM phone was able to recognise the local network, Uganda Telecom but I could not do much with it. When I tried to send a text message it could not go through. It required a reconfiguration of settings. I gave up. The Airtel phone, however, immediately provided a message, "Welcome to Airtel Uganda" and informed me of the keys I had to use to access certain information. I noted that except for a few differences, this was very similar to what I was used. I was able to send messages back home at the same rate as though I was home and even receive calls from home. For the people calling me from Malaŵi, they were being charged the local call rate. That is when I realised the uniqueness and enormity of the one network service by Airtel. But I soon run out of airtime and was unable to go outside to buy more airtime credit. So I thought of using my mobile banking application, called MO626, running on the mobile phone platform, to procure more airtime credit using funds in my bank account in Malaŵi.[103] I was not sure if this would work though and proceeded with utmost caution by buying a small value of airtime. When I received the code, I used the

[102] Airtel (2017) 'One Network Countries' (Airtel Ghana), http://africa.airtel.com/wps/wcm/connect/africarevamp/Ghana/Home/personal/premier/one-network/PG_One-Network-Countries/. 29 May 2018.

[103] The MO6262 is a mobile platform service operated by the National bank of Malaŵi. Almost all banks now have a similar service that extends the bank account to the mobile phone platform.

same value entering system as I would in Malaŵi and *voila* credit topped up! I then realised that several people had also run-out of airtime and were either sending people to procure airtime using Uganda Shillings or they were just out of communication. I offered to exchange airtime with them for whatever of value they had which I could use. So I procured airtime from Malaŵi using my local account and gave the codes or used the M2U service to transfer the airtime credit to others. In return I received money, in various currencies or goods and services that I coveted. Since at the time the Dollar rate was fixed in Malaŵi by the central bank, if I received US Dollars, these Dollars would be worth more than the Kwacha equivalent upon my return to Malaŵi.

The above example illustrates that airtime can be transmitted across borders. This means that if the airtime has value, this value can also be transmitted. This transmission of value does not go through any foreign exchange regulatory agency or intermediary. It is all via the telecommunication network of the mobile phone provider. So airtime is a commodity capable of serving as a medium of exchange. It could be used to exchange with other commodities such as currencies of other countries, goods or services. However, it still needs to be emphasised that although it serves this purposes, its main use is not as a medium of exchange. Its use as a medium of exchange is ancillary.

The *dollarization* of airtime had its benefit as it allowed it to maintain a unit of value across borders. One Dollar of airtime had the same value in country X as it had in country Y although the local monetary equivalent varied. In 2008, airtime was still *dollarized*. It therefore not only stored but maintained its value. However, even now, although the airtime is no longer denominated in dollars, it still serves as a unit of account and a store of value. This is because the value in the airtime represents the value in fiat money. Instead of sending fiat or mobile money, one may therefore send airtime to a relative in the village. The relative may decide to redeem the airtime from whosoever needs it (commodity of want) or even exchange it for other goods and services. This value is one-to-one although not always. An example may help to illustrate this feature.

Suppose one has an abundance of airtime in a village where there are no agents or vendors selling airtime. In this case, one can be able to exchange the commodity of airtime with other commodities that maybe exchangeable, including fiat money. It also means that potentially One Hundred Kwacha value of airtime may in an area where there is no airtime credit available, or where there is scarcity of airtime credit, be able to be exchanged for a value greater than K100. If we apply the flip-side economic argument of supply and demand, it follows, that where there is plenty of supply for airtime credit, and one wants to exchange his credit, he may have to do so at a loss of value. This deviation in value that demonstrates that airtime is a form of money and that it mimics the trading that takes place between two forms of money such as in the case of a foreign exchange transaction.

Utility and Value

The value of airtime is in its usage as a communications enabler. It is primarily coveted because, without it, one's mobile phone is just another useless device.[104] It is only the mobile phone that is connected to the right network that will recognise the value of airtime credit in it. Its value, therefore, comes from its usage and its utility. However, airtime can store value and this storage is almost perpetual.[105] As noted above, the value can also be transferred without loss through the peer-to-peer facility.

Medium of Exchange

The value in the airtime has an equivalent value in cash. Instead of sending cash, one may send airtime to a relative in the village. Therefore, in places where cash may not be easily remitted, it can operate as an effective medium of exchange.[106] The recipient may redeem the airtime from whosoever needs it, as a commodity of want, or exchange it for goods and services. However, the value is not always one to one with cash. The use of airtime as a currency has been found to be common in Tanzania. Camner and Sjöblom have described the process as follows:

> The sender buys an airtime voucher, scratches it in order to see the code then texts the code in a text message to the person supposed to receive the money. It is then up to the recipient to go out and sell the code to people who wants [sic] to buy airtime, or resellers and shops that in turn will sell it to people wanting airtime. The value of the voucher is reduced when

[104] This may not be necessary true, however, in the age of Wi-fi technology and for the so-called smart phones which are able to connect to this technology and still operate, on a reduced level though.

[105] Porteous (2006), p. 23.

[106] Ibid.

selling it the second time, most often by 10% but in some cases even up to 40%.[107]

The airtime code seems to mimic tradable and negotiable financial instruments used in the discounting or factoring business. This is interesting because Tanzania has the mobile money service, *M-Pesa*, a counterpart of the Kenyan model.[108] Despite *M-Pesa* being cheaper in transactional fees, Camner and Sjöblom say "this informal way of sending money through airtime vouchers has been generally accepted as a value transfer service in Tanzania".[109] There has not been documented evidence of a similar widespread occurrence in Kenya, where *M-Pesa* originated or in Malaŵi.

Unity of Value and Homogeneity

Airtime also maintains uniformity of value. It is homogeneous over space and time, mainly because it is expressed in terms of the unit used for cash and not in terms of time units.[110] Airtime can also be unbundled into smaller parts. It is possible for one who has 100 Kwacha worth of airtime to equally divide and transmit this to ten people, airtime worth Ten Kwacha each. There is no service charge for this service making it perfectly divisible. Although the mobile network operators provide coupons with specific values, airtime agents have devised means of breaking the values in the coupons further. For example, suppose the minimum value of a coupon is Fifty Kwacha, agents can load this into their phone and then sell a fraction to a customer who may not have the Fifty Kwacha. The balance can then be sold to other customers or combined with other vouchers to create a higher value. This is possible because the mobile network operators sell the vouchers to the agents at a discount.[111]

[107] Gunnar Camner and Emil Sjöblom (2009) *Can the Success of M-PESA Be Repeated?—A Review of the Implementations in Kenya and Tanzania*, pp. 7–8, http://emil.sjoblom.com/pdf/M-Pesa_implementations_Ke_Tz.pdf. 15 December 2018.

[108] M-Pesa is short for Mobile Pesa. Pesa is a Swahili (spoken in both Kenya and Tanzania) word for money. M-Pesa then directly translates to Mobile Money.

[109] Camner and Sjöblom (2009).

[110] Porteous (2006), p. 23.

[111] Personal experience having been an agent before, at Chancellor College in Zomba (2006–2008).

Portability and Cognoscibility
Airtime is tied to a particular mobile phone with its information embedded in the SIM and servers of the mobile network operator. Presented as a coupon, the airtime is easily recognisable in Malaŵi. However, the coupons merely contain the airtime code. Commonly, however, the coupon has grown to represent airtime. The production of coupons mirrors what the mint does when producing money and the unique number of the coupon is akin to unique banknote serial numbers. Furthermore, the coupon producer needs a database, which links with the mobile network operator servers so they can recognise and accept as value any airtime validly issued. Conversely, the system must be able to reject unofficially issued coupons. On its own, airtime is cognizable when shown as a balance on one's phone or when transferred peer to peer.

Legal Tender
Airtime is not traditionally used to pay for goods and services even within a mobile phone ecosystem. It cannot be redeemed for cash at par value.[112] In fact, its face value masks the fact that airtime is usually sold via agents at a discount. But this is not different from other money instruments which are sold at a discount such as treasury bills. The only difference is that with treasury bills, they have a maturity when the face value is redeemable while the face value of airtime is redeemable at purchase. Importantly though, it means no one can be obligated to accept it in settlement of any debt. It is not legal tender. Unlike mobile money, it is not even considered as social tender. In most countries, airtime also attracts a tax,[113] something that is not normally associated with money.

### 3.4.4 *Analysing Mobile Money and Airtime Using the Money Framework*

The Table 3.1 summarises the analysis of mobile money and airtime and compares these forms of value with fiat money.

[112] Porteous (2006), p. 23.

[113] James M Kenani, Stan G Kaunda and Chiyembekezo Chafuwa (2014) 'Taxation Policy and Performance in Malawi Since Independence' (*Inaugural ECAMA Research Symposium,* Lilongwe), http://www.slideshare.net/IFPRIMaSSP/taxation-policy-and-performance-in-malawi-since-independence-by-sg-kaunda-j-kenani. 17 February 2018.

Porteous (2006), p. 24.

**Table 3.1** Analysis of mobile money and airtime

| *Type of money* | *Medium of exchange* | *Store of value* | *Unit of account* | *Utility and value* | *Portable* | *Homogeneity* | *Divisible* | *Cognizable* | *Legal tender* |
|---|---|---|---|---|---|---|---|---|---|
| Fiat | X | X | X | X | X | X | X | X | X |
| Mobile money | X | X | X | X | X | X | X | X | |
| Airtime | | X | X | X | X | X | X | X | |

Mobile money fails to satisfy the requirements of fiat money, as it is not legal tender. Airtime fails because it is not primarily a medium of exchange and is not legal tender. However, if one removes the legal tender column, mobile money would be included in the category of money. Airtime, however, would not fully qualify, because as it has been noted, its use as a medium of exchange is accidental or ancillary. From the discussion of money, it can be said that mobile money and airtime are forms of value. Mobile money is electronic money as it is backed on a one-to-one ratio with fiat money. Airtime is not electronic money as it lacks this characteristic. In answering the question whether mobile money and airtime are money, it may be said that in the classical sense they are not. However, as Bitcoin has proved, the future may lie in the decentralisation of sovereign monetary power. Being legal tender may no longer be the yardstick for money. It can be said that mobile money and airtime are emerging forms of money. How successfully they will fulfil the function of money will depend on how they develop. As has been shown earlier, the evolution of money has been a constant attribute of money from its origins. With advances in technology, demands of society and changes in procurement habits, money will continue to evolve.[114] So far, however, it would seem that it is only mobile money that has demonstrated the capacity and capability of functioning as money.

## 3.5 Mobile Money in Operation

The mobile money service is essentially modelled on the cell infrastructure. If we look at Fig. 3.3, anyone with a mobile phone not only has access to other users but can also potentially financially interact with them. One can order products within and outside one's geographical area. When a mobile phone user is within a particular base station, the base station detects the user's presence in real time including all communications done and this information is relayed to the main station.[115] This digital footprint can prevent people from denying, for example, liability for debts arising from mobile money transactions based on a false alibi.

[114] Kelley Jr (1999), p. 22.

[115] In the recent criminal case of *R v Kumwembe* et al. Criminal Case No. 65 of 2013 (Lilongwe Registry), the High Court convicted the accused persons based on evidenced that was mainly provided by a mobile network provider.

Mobile money services allow the smooth conversion from cash to electronic value and back to cash.[116] It also allows transfer of e-value between users.[117] It, therefore, works as a 3 steps remittance system:

- Convert cash to electronic value;
- Transfer electronic value between accounts;
- Convert electronic value to cash.

Each customer, apart from registering with the mobile network operator for the mobile service, also registers with the mobile money service and by so doing holds an account. The transfers are therefore conducted between these accounts. Camner and Sjöblom say mobile network operators are uniquely placed to run mobile money services "because they have a great number of both banked and unbanked customers and an established network of airtime resellers which can be turned into agents".[118]

So far, the growth phase of mobile money is still what Jenkins calls an "emerging or chaos phase".[119] He adds, for mobile money to emerge as a universal and omnipresent service there is a need to develop solid ecosystems since "for something to be ubiquitous, the foundations need to be very strong".[120] He argues that if mobile money is to become the service which every consumer wants, there is need first to develop a "critical mass of mobile money" and some degree of interoperability is crucial for this.[121] Mas and Radcliff call this the chicken-and-egg trap.[122] For it to sell as a viable service to customers, there is need to bring on board merchants and utility providers to serve them.[123] However, for these to get on board, they need assurance of a critical mass of customers.[124] For an effective mobile money ecosystem, there is need to rope in a

[116] Heeks (2012).

[117] Ibid.

[118] Camner and Sjöblom (2009), p. 3.

[119] Jenkins (2008), p. 11 quoting Fundamo CEO Hannes van Rensburg.

[120] Ibid., p. 12 quoting Hans Wijiyasuriya, CEO of Sri Lanka's Dialog Telekom.

[121] Ibid., pp. 13, 15.

[122] Mas and Radcliffe (2011), p. 177.

[123] Ibid.

[124] Ibid.

cross-section and a wide range of players. These include the mobile network operators, banks, agents, shops, service providers and utilities.[125]

Since mobile payments are made remotely, they require a verification process beyond the physical signature. The electronic signature includes the PIN and sometimes, biometric data.[126] This is important as where an e-signature is invalid; it may be rejected or if not, challenged, thereby exposing agents and payees to the risk of fraud or repudiation.[127] The role of agents and their ability to act as the front end of the business is crucial for the ecosystem. Heyer and Mas argue that a relaxed regulatory regime on who can be an agent is key for mobile money.[128] Unless the business has attained profitability, imposing licensing fees and other requirements on agents may be a hindrance.[129] In most countries, these agents are also airtime sellers for the mobile network operators. The advantage is that the agents already have the experience in dealing with mobile technology, although Heyer and Mas argue that mobile money does appreciably require "higher capital movements and ... treasury management expertise".[130]

The success of the mobile money service lies in its simplicity: as an add-on service based on the SMS platform. Having the SMS as a forerunner has its advantages. On its own, Heyer and Mas caution that the mobile money service is a service that could potentially "intimidate and confuse people who have only used their phones to talk".[131] However, the SMS has already overcome this, thereby laying a foundation on which mobile money can ride on. The beauty of the SMS lies in the fact that it can be used on the most basic mobile phone. Even among those already banked the mobile money service "overcomes the tyranny of distance to banking infrastructure – captured by both distance and time to a bank branch".[132]

[125] Jenkins (2008), p. 7.

[126] Porteous (2006), p. 31.

[127] Ibid.

[128] Heyer and Mas (2009), p. 13.

[129] Ibid.

[130] Ibid., p. 15.

[131] Ibid., p. 13.

[132] Subramaniam (2013), p. 7.

Although mobile money has been touted as a positive development in most African countries, others have expressed fear that it may have an impact on inflation.[133] The inflation risk has, however, been downplayed by the Governor of the Bank of Tanzania who argued that instead the mobile money service had eased tracking transactions as well as money in circulation.[134] Indeed unless, the mobile money is not fully backed up by deposits, it is difficult to imagine how inflation can be triggered since the mobile network operators are not creating money in the traditional banking sense.[135] In any event, in the greater scheme of things, m-mobile is still insignificant to affect monetary supply or policy.[136] The Bank of International Settlements says:

> Although electronic money has become more important in some countries, the impact of these developments on the composition of the monetary base is considered negligible thus far… Most central banks therefore judge that the influence of innovations in retail payments on monetary policy is neutral or of low importance.[137]

To recap, mobile money needs an ecosystem of agents, registered customers, mobile network operators, and a bank. The mobile money is usually issued in bulk through a cascading system of agents and the agents must deposit cash with the mobile network operator.[138] The mobile network operator records all transfers to ensure that there is always a one-to-one correspondence between the money in the pool or trust account and electronic money in the system.[139] Mobile money can be used to pay for a wide range of things such as school fees or wages

[133] Ngigi (2012).

[134] Gantala Hawaiju (2013) *The Impact of Mobile Money Transfer Technology* (Clknet Policy Brief No. 12), http://docplayer.net/14873424-Curriculum-vitae-giuseppe-travaglini.html. 11 November 2018.

[135] Di Castri (2013), p. 10.

[136] Ibid.

[137] CPSS (2012), p. 58.

[138] Maurer (2012), p. 306.

[139] Ibid.

of low-income workers.[140] The service therefore helps in the following ways:

a. Ease of convenience as users can access the service from the comfort of their homes or in the case of a farmer, in the field.
b. Since the transactions are digital, there is a sense of safety and dependability.
c. Users have greater control of the services and are not limited by the normal limitations of the formal banking service such as time of the transaction.[141]

An ethnographic study of the mobile money service in Kenya by Mas and Ng'weno showed that "customers in town understood that [it] was for sending money whereas those in the rural areas understood it was for receiving".[142] The typical remitter is the urban businessman or worker living in the city, most likely a migrant.[143] The typical recipient is a rural-based woman.[144]

## 3.6 Mobile Money and the National Payment System

The linkage between mobile money and payment systems can be summarised using a Venn diagram and set theory analogy.[145] The payment systems may be deemed as the unit set—the sum of all the different systems within it.[146] Inside it would be other subsystems such as paper or

[140] William Jack, Tavneet Suri and Robert M Townsend (2010) 'Monetary Theory and Electronic Money: Reflections on the Kenyan Experience' 96 (1) *Federal Reserve Bank of Richmond Economic Quarterly* 83, p. 89, https://www.richmondfed.org/publications/research/economic_quarterly/2010/q1/townsend. 15 December 2018.

[141] Heyer and Mas (2009), p. 9.

[142] Ignacio Mas and Amolo Ng'weno (2010) Three Keys to M-PESAss Success: Branding, Channel Management and Pricing (GSMA), p. 6, http://www.www.oneapigw.gsma.com/mobilefordevelopment/wp-content/uploads/2012/06/keystompesassuccess-4jan69.pdf. 15 December 2018.

[143] Camner and Sjöblom (2009), p. 4.

[144] Ibid.

[145] Robert R Stoll (1961) *Set Theory and Logic* (Dover Publications, New York) Chapter 1.

[146] Ibid., pp. 4–5.

Fig. 3.4 Venn diagram of the payment system (*Source* Author)

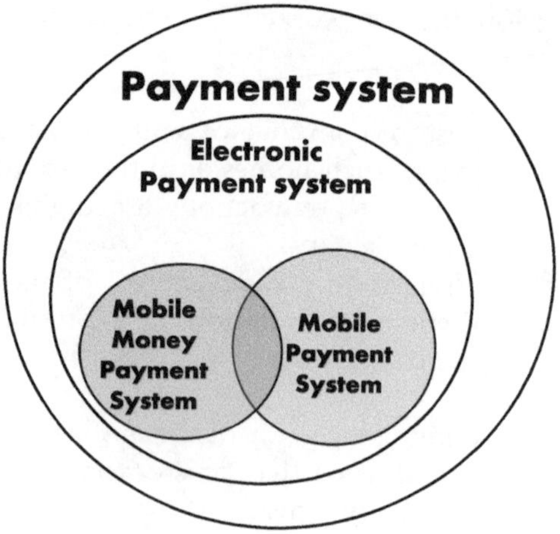


electronic payment systems. Inside the electronic payment systems would be several payment systems such as electronic transfer of funds and mobile payment systems. While there may be an intersection between mobile payment systems and mobile money payment systems, as in the case of a bank-led mobile money model, there are also differences as in the case of the telco-led model. One cannot separate the mobile money payment system from the national payment system because the former is an integral part of the latter. The Venn diagram figure below illustrates the relationship between the mobile money payment system and the national payment system but omits other subsystems not directly related to mobile money (Fig. 3.4).

Operationally, the mobile money platform rides on the telecommunications platform of the mobile network operators. As discussed earlier, once money has been deposited into the pool account, mobile money can be issued on a one-to-one ratio. In this sense, mobile money is private money issued by a mobile money service provider but backed up fully by fiat money in an account (the pool or trust account) domiciled with a commercial bank. Settlement of obligations and clearances are done using the pool account within the banking system. However, mobile money issuers have now adopted an integrated approach where transactions are in real time and clients do not have to go to an agent to obtain electronic value. Clients can transact between their bank accounts and mobile money accounts and settle their obligations or remit money without physically moving.[147]

This has huge ramifications for the agency distribution network. Agents may be cut off from the transactions chain and lose out on the commission that they receive. For some agents, who perceived the commissions as their main source of income, this loss of revenue may prove catastrophic. Although such agents also usually sell airtime, increasingly, the mobile network operators are linking with banks to allow bank customers to buy airtime using the banking applications that are available on mobile phones or through the automated teller machines. The jury is still out whether, in relation to mobile money, this will result in reduced transaction fees for customers. However, it would be too early to prophesy the death of the agency relationship, as agents are still needed to register customers as well as help customers without a bank account, who incidentally were the prime targets of mobile money. Therefore, while clearance and settlement are still within the banking system, the integration allows the mobile money issuers to offer new innovative products and to circulate value within their ecosystem. This then raises the issue whether this telco-led model is now mimicking the bank-led model since a direct linkage to the bank account is the hallmark of the latter. A discussion of these two models is done in Chapter 7.

Airtel Money says integration helps to create a seamless web of transactions between depositing money into the pool account and creation of electronic value to match the deposits.[148] However, it would seem that first tier banks were initially reluctant to have a fully integrated system with mobile network operators.[149] Using its first mover advantage, Airtel Money decided to approach the second tier of banks who were more receptive.[150] It was only when the first tier banks realised they were losing out on the intermediation benefits of trust accounts that they came knocking on the door, "wanting a share of the pie".[151] On its part, Airtel Money used this as an opportunity to negotiate full integration with the

[147] Mkoloma (2015), Mbekeani (2015).

[148] Mkoloma (2015).

[149] Ibid.

[150] Ibid.

[151] Ibid.

bank; as well as negotiate higher returns thereby ensuring a win-win situation.[152]

The ideal situation for mobile money issuers would be that once electronic value has been created, it stays within the ecosystem. This would also mean that the mobile money issuers would have reduced transactions fees paid to national switches such as NatSwitch. Appreciably, there is a cost to integration. Banks and mobile network operators use different technologies for their operations. Integrating can be challenging and costly. It involves procuring equipment and software that can act as a switch between the two systems. Where the mobile network operators wish to integrate with various banks, this compounds the issues and increases the costs. It is submitted that some banks may also feel uncomfortable to have a fully integrated system with a third party, which they cannot control, and which is not prudentially regulated.

It must be pointed out, however, that although the mobile money payment system can be linked to the national payment system, the two can exist outside each other. In fact, the mobile money payment system can operate entirely outside the banking system.[153] Once electronic value is created, the mobile money payment system has a life of its own. Users can remit funds directly to each other, procure goods and services and settle in real time independently of the banking system.[154] The fact that the system is instantaneous and can bypass the clearing bottlenecks of the banking system gives it an advantage.[155] It raises the possibility of whether it may start posing a direct challenge to the payment system operated by banks. In fact, were the two mobile money issuers to set up a joint system with full interoperability, it may well start encroaching into the territory of the banking payment system.

### *3.6.1 Role of the Regulator: Authorising Mobile Money Operations*

Since the central bank is tasked with ensuring that there is financial stability, it is always on the lookout for any potential risk posed to the

[152] Ibid.

[153] Klein and Mayer (2011), p. 14.

[154] Ibid.

[155] Ibid.

national payment system. Central banks are keen to regulate mobile money because it:

- promotes financial inclusion;
- Expands the range of payment choices;
- Helps in anti-money laundering and counter-terrorism financing by channelling cash into the formal system;
- Aids national socio-economic development.[156]

Central banks may also be keen to regulate mobile money to avoid any danger that it may pose to financial stability. Any mobile money service must be authorised before it can roll out. This is the legal and operating framework obtaining in Kenya and Malaŵi. To allow for the framework of authorisation and regulation, the Reserve Bank of Malaŵi issued Mobile Payment Systems Guidelines in 2011.[157] Chapter 8 discusses these guidelines. What can be said now is that Malaŵi's central bank seems to have adopted a light-touch regulatory model on mobile money. This may very well be a deliberate undertaking to allow the service to grow and gain traction. It may also be a learning curve for the regulator considering that the mobile money service is unique in that it combines elements of a financial service and a communication service. It must also be appreciated that the mobile money ecosystem is a complex payment system because it can connect with other payment systems. However, even where a regulator starts with a laissez-faire attitude, eventually the regulator will have to start considering certain pertinent questions.[158] For example, who is dispensing cash, what type of transactions should be permitted and how can liability be limited or capped.[159] Much more important, however, will the vulnerable consumer be protected?[160] A more detailed discussion of regulation and regulatory approaches follows in the next chapter.

[156] Jenkins (2008), p. 8.

[157] Guidelines for Mobile Payment Systems (Malaŵi, 2011).

[158] Tonny K Omwansa (2009) 'M-PESA: Progress and Prospects' *Innovations* 107, p. 121, https://profiles.uonbi.ac.ke/tomwansa/files/innov-gsma-omwansa.pdf. 1 December 2018.

[159] Ibid.

[160] Ibid.

What can be said at this point, however, is the 2011 Guidelines, while providing the building blocks may soon be deemed insufficient as the service grows in quantum leaps. This is hardly surprising. The technology driving mobile telephony is changing rapidly that the regulator is likely to play catch-up for some time. The guidelines also illustrate a common feature among regulators of mobile money; a certain degree of non-appreciation of what the system is all about and how to regulate it.[161] This again is not surprising as mobile money is not the usual customer that the financial service regulator must deal with. Malaŵi recently enacted the Payment Systems Act 2016, a law which provides the framework for the national and other payment systems within the country as well as how the mobile money is to be regulated. While previously the Reserve Bank of Malaŵi allowed operations based on a "Letter of No Objection" which had no express statutory backing, the law now requires a prior application for a licence or authorisation before rolling out.[162]

### *3.6.2 The Mobile Money Ecosystem*

Kennedy defines the mobile money ecosystem as (Fig. 3.5):

> The networks of organizations that must be in place for mobile money services to take root, proliferate, and go to scale. Nazerono explains, "The objective is ubiquity. The 3 rules of retail are location, location, location. In mobile money, they're partnering, partnering, partnering. We need to create a mesh of partnerships covering various networks of relationships".[163]

The figure above illustrates a simple mobile money ecosystem looking at a closely knit and localised network. The figure underscores 3 key points:

1. The customer does not need to open and operate a bank account to become a part of the ecosystem;
2. Customers can remit money to other customers, peer to peer without having to cash out and

[161] For a similar scenario in Kenya, see ibid.

[162] Section 12(1) Payment Systems Act (Malaŵi, 2016).

[163] Jenkins (2008), p. 8.

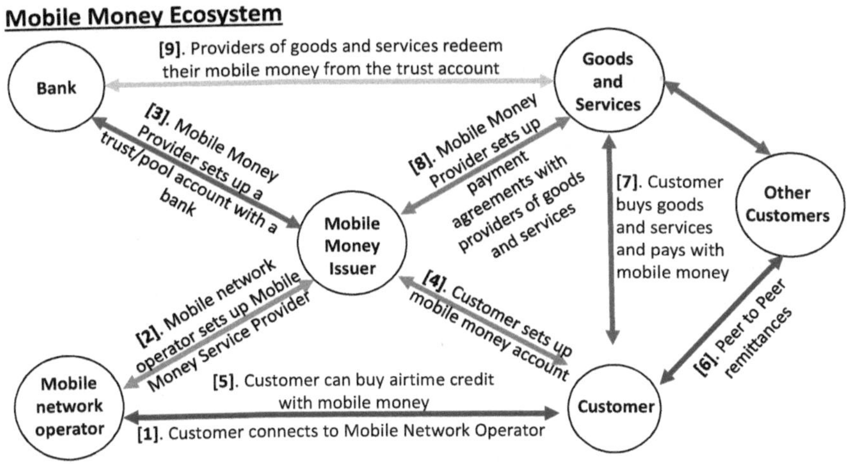


**Fig. 3.5** Showing a simple mobile money ecosystem (*Source* Author)

3. Mobile money is a payment system. Therefore, the mobile money ecosystem does provide a means of attaining some level of financial inclusion.

The simplified figure omits the fact that providers of goods and services do not have to cash out their mobile money. They can use it to procure goods and services. Therefore, the mobile money issuer is not only a subsidiary of the mobile network operator, but also acts as an agent and outlet of the mobile network operator. Customers can procure goods and services such as airtime and handsets, which can be paid for by mobile money. The figure also excludes injection of cash via third parties as well as the role of the various regulators.

Both mobile money issuers in Malaŵi are now members of NatSwitch, the national switch which is owned by the association of bankers.[164] Airtel Money and *Mpamba* have indicated they are considering creating their own mobile money payment system, linked to NatSwitch.[165] Were this to happen, it has the potential to minimise transaction costs paid to

164 Mbekeani (2015).
165 Mkoloma (2015), Mbekeani (2015).

NatSwitch and allow only clearing and settlement to be done using the trust account. Hopefully, any financial benefits received from this will be passed on to consumers and result in reduced transactional fees. It would mean once created, the electronic value would circulate within the ecosystem and only the aggregate surplus or deficit would be settled with fiat money. An efficient and encompassing ecosystem would be a critical element of such a dedicated payment system.

For a couple of years now, Airtel Money and *Mpamba* have been discussing interoperability so that customers across the two platforms can transact as if they were on one platform.[166] The biggest hurdle was that the initial route required interoperability of the telecommunications platform between the two mobile network operators first. Interoperability is, however, not a simple issue. It is subject to competition and corporate political interests. For example, the fact that the two mobile network operators do not have an equal market share may affect any agreement and it may require the regulator's intervention to implement such an arrangement.[167] However, the two mobile money operators have now announced that customers can send and receive mobile money across the two services. This has been possible by using the NatSwitch platform. This means *Mpamba* customers can send money to Airtel Money customers and vice versa, subject to transactional fees. In a way, this is a game-changer and a momentous step in the mobile money evolution. For the customer, it is a much more convenient way of transacting using the mobile money platform. For the aggregate mobile money ecosystem, this means almost a doubling of liquidity within the ecosystem.

### *3.6.3 Mobile Money Not Yet Systemically Important*

When dealing with payment systems, there is a distinction between services that are systemically important and those that are not. According to the Committee on Payment and Settlement Systems of the Bank of International Settlements, the test whether a payment system is systemically important is:

[166] Ibid.

[167] Airtel claims to have ¾ share of the mobile market—Mkoloma (2015).

> If the system were insufficiently protected against risk, disruption within it could trigger or transmit further disruptions among participants or systemic disruptions in the financial area more widely.[168]

For a payment system to be systemically important, its failure must trigger disruptions or transmit shocks within the financial system.[169] To be systemically important, a payment system must satisfy one of the following criteria:

a. Be the sole or principal payment system;
b. Handle mainly payments of high value;
c. Be used for the settlement of financial market transactions or for the settlement of other payment systems.[170]

Analysing the Malaŵi payment system using this standard, the national payment system operated through the NatSwitch qualifies as systemically important on all 3 levels. The Reserve Bank of Malaŵi in fact has stated that the Malaŵi's Interbank Funds Transfer and Settlement System (MITASS) is "the sole systemically important payment system".[171] The mobile money payment system does not meet any of the criteria. In fact, the mobile money payment system uses the national payment system for settlement. Mobile money values are also limited and low in value. For example, the December 2016 report by the central bank shows that mobile money only formed 2% of the daily value settled by MITASS.[172] In 2014, Ali et al., of the Bank of England, concluded that digital currencies do not yet pose a systemic risk as "the total value of all digital currencies is too small to pose a threat ... at present".[173] In his study of mobile money in Kenya, Muthiora found that although it forms "a very important part of the financial system ... mobile money does not

[168] CPSS (2001), p. 5.

[169] Ibid.

[170] Ibid.

[171] RBM (2015), p. 10.

[172] RBM (2016) *Monthly National Payments System Report: December 2016* (Reserve Bank of Malaŵi), p. 1, https://www.rbm.mw/PaymentSystems/GetContentFile/?ContentID=12148pdf. 17 February 2018.

[173] Ali and others (2014), p. 8.

introduce systemic risk to the financial system".[174] Di Castri agrees that in comparison to banking, mobile money does not pose a systemic risk.[175] Evaluation of data available in Kenya showed that mobile money only had a 6.5% stake in the national payment system in 2015. If at a 6.5%, mobile money is not considered a systemic risk, a fortiori 2% for Malaŵi? These low figures may largely be attributed to the fact that electronic money is used mostly in the retail payment system as opposed to the wholesale payment system.[176] Another reason may be that the banking system becomes more attractive in terms of transaction costs the higher the amount of transfer. When mobile money starts attracting wholesale payments, the risk assessment is likely to change. The interoperability that has been set up between *Mpamba* and Airtel Money, for example, also means that the aggregate value of the mobile money ecosystem which is connected to the national payment system is likely to grow. Such widespread usage and growth could make the mobile money payment system systemically important.[177]

## 3.7 Conclusion

This chapter has discussed the development of the mobile phone and how innovations in the small messaging service have given birth to the mobile money service. The mobile phone, it would seem was made to address some of sub-Saharan unique communications challenges which the landline had failed to address for decades. The chapter analysed how mobile network operators came up with a radical and revolutionary business solution to the remittance dilemma. The chapter also analyses mobile money as an emerging form of money and how it, and airtime credit, compare to the standard set by fiat money. The chapter also looked at the mobile money ecosystem and the linkage between the

[174]Brian Muthiora (2015) *Enabling Mobile Money Policies in Kenya: Fostering a Digital Financial Revolution* (GSMA), pp. 8, 12, https://www.itu.int/en/ITU-T/focusgroups/dfs/Documents/2015_MMU_Enabling-Mobilelectronicmoney-Policies-in-Kenya.pdf. 17 February 2018.

[175]Di Castri (2013), p. 8.

[176]Boon-Chye Lee and Olujoke Longe-Akindemowo (1999) 'Regulatory Issues in Electronic Money: A Legal-Economics Analysis' 1 (1) *Netnomics* 53, p. 63.

[177]Ibid.

mobile payment system and the national payment system. Looking at the mobile money ecosystem, it becomes clear that mobile money is not just a money service but a complete payment system. Although mobile money is connected to the national payment system, it has the capacity to exist outside the system. Compared to the national payment system, it has the advantage of offering an instantaneous settlement of obligations. However, although mobile money has grown in its usage, it is not yet systemically important. This is largely because the volume of transactions and value compared to bank deposits is still very small. This may change with time, especially as more people resort to mobile money as the premier means of settling their obligations or making payments.

## References

Adeyemi Adepetun (2015) 'Africa's Mobile Phone Penetration now 67%' *The Guardian*, http://www.ngrguardiannews.com/2015/06/africas-mobile-phone-penetration-now-67/. 12 December 2018.

Airtel (2016) 'Me2U' (Airtel, Malawi), http://africa.airtel.com/wps/wcm/connect/africarevamp/malawi/home/personal/voice-and-text/phone-services/me2u. 21 May 2018.

Airtel (2017) 'One Network Countries' (Airtel Ghana), http://africa.airtel.com/wps/wcm/connect/africarevamp/Ghana/Home/personal/premier/one-network/PG_One-Network-Countries/. 29 May 2018.

Airtime (2016) Cambridge University Press, http://dictionary.cambridge.org/dictionary/english/airtime. 27 June 2018.

Amrik Heyer and Ignacio Mas (2009) *Seeking Fertile Grounds for Mobile Money* (Mobile Money for the Unbanked, GSMA, London), http://www.gsma.com/mobilefordevelopment/wp-content/uploads/2012/03/fertile_grounds_mobile_money55.pdf. 14 February 2018.

Anon (2014) 'Rural Population in Malawi' *Trading Economics*, http://www.tradingeconomics.com/malawi/rural-population-wb-data.html. 19 May 2018.

Anon (2015) 'Why Africa Mobile Phone Penetration Rising to 79% by 2020 Is Good News' (Amgoo Telecom Co., Ltd.), http://www.amgoo.com/blog/why-africa-mobile-phone-penetration-rising-to-79-by-2020-is-good-news. 12 December 2018.

Beth Jenkins (2008) 'Developing Mobile Money Ecosystems' (Washington, DC: International Finance Corporation and Harvard Kennedy School), http://ww.gsma.com/mobilefordevelopment/wp-content/uploads/2012/06/report_30_mobilemoney.pdf. 13 December 2018.

Bill Maurer (2012) 'Payment: Forms and Functions of Value Transfer in Contemporary Society' 30 *Cambridge Anthropology* 15.

Boon-Chye Lee and Olujoke Longe-Akindemowo (1999) 'Regulatory Issues in Electronic Money: A Legal-Economics Analysis' 1 (1) *Netnomics* 53.

Brendan Greeley (2013) 'One Good Paper: Monopoly Power in Mobile Money' *Bloomberg Businessweek*, http://www.businessweek.com/articles/2013-03-13/one-good-paper-monopoly-power-in-mobilelectronicmoney. 28 March 2018.

Brian Muthiora (2015) *Enabling Mobile Money Policies in Kenya: Fostering a Digital Financial Revolution* (GSMA), https://www.itu.int/en/ITU-T/focusgroups/dfs/Documents/2015_MMU_Enabling-Mobilelectronicmoney-Policies-in-Kenya.pdf. 17 February 2018.

'Brief History of GSM & the GSMA' (GSM Association), http://www.gsma.com/aboutus/history. 10 March 2018.

CF Myers and LS Crosby (1953) *Principles of Electricity Applied to Telephone and Telegraph Work* (American Telephone and Telegraph Company, New York).

Chipiliro Kansilanga (2015) 'Malawi Savings Bank Finally Sold' *Daily Times* (2 July 2015), http://www.times.mw/malawi-savings-bank-finally-sold-2/. 20 July 2018.

Christopher Haslett (2008) *Essentials of Radio Wave Propagation* (Cambridge University Press, Cambridge).

Chris Chibwana (2010) 'The High and the Hidden Costs of Banking in Malawi', http://chibwana.com/2010/04/05/costs-of-banking-in-malawi/. 11 March 2018.

CPSS (2001) *Core Principles for Systemically Important Payment Systems* (BIS, Committee on Payment and Settlement Systems), http://www.bis.org/cpmi/publ/d43.pdf. 17 February 2018.

CPSS (2012) *Innovations in Retail Payments* (Bank for International Settlements [Committee on Payment and Settlement Systems], Basel, Switzerland), http://www.bis.org/cpmi/publ/d102.pdf. 20 February 2018.

CU (2012) *Study on Informal and Non-formal Rural Financial Services 2012* (Concern Universal Malawi), http://concern-universal.org/wp-content/uploads/2014/07/CUMO-Study-of-Rural-Finance-Summary.pdf. 7 October 2018.

David Porteous (2006) *The Enabling Environment for Mobile Banking in AFRICA* (Report Commissioned by Department for International Development [DFID], Boston), http://bankablefrontier.com/wp-ontent/uploads/documents/ee.mobil_banking.report.v3.1.pdf. 14 September 2018.

David Smith (2014) 'Internet Use on Mobile Phones in Africa Predicted to Increase 20-fold' *The Guardian*, (5 June 2014) http://www.theguardian.com/world/2014/jun/05/internet-use-mobile-phones-africa-predicted-increase-20-fold. 10 March 2018.

Edward W Kelley Jr (1999) 'The Future of Electronic Money: A Regulator's Perspective' 34 *Spectrum* (IEEE), http://spectrum.ieee.org/telecom/standards/the-future-of-electronic-money-a-regulators-perspective. 14 September 2018.

Finscope (2014) *FinScope Consumer Survey Malawi 2014* (Finmark Trust, Midrand, Johannesburg), http://www.finmark.org.za/wp-content/uploads/2016/08/FS-Malawi-2014-Launch-presentation.pdf. 5 May 2017.

FMB 'First Merchant Bank to Acquire Opportunity International Bank of Malawi' (27 June 2017), http://www.fmbmalawi.com/first-merchant-bank-to-acquire-opportunity-international-bank-of-malawi/. 18 July 2018.

Gabriella Mulligan (2015) 'Is Fibre Optic Cable Key to Africa's Economic Growth?' BBC Business News (London, 31 March 2015), http://www.bbc.co.uk/news/business-32079649. 9 May 2018.

Gantala Hawaiju (2013) *The Impact of Mobile Money Transfer Technology* (Clknet Policy Brief No. 12), http://docplayer.net/14873424-Curriculum-vitae-giuseppe-travaglini.html. 11 November 2018.

Geetha Nagarajan (July 2010) 'Money in a Pot: Has OIBM Altered Savings in Rural Malawi?' (Financial Service Assessment), http://www.fsassessment.umd.edu/notes/savings-rural.html. 11 March 2018.

George Ngigi, 'M-Pesa Linked to Rise in Inflation' *Business Daily* (14 February 2012), http://www.businessdailyafrica.com/M-Pesa-linked-to-rise-in-inflation/-/539552/1327538/-/13rogmr/-/index.html. 28 March 2018.

Giridaran Subramaniam (2013) 'Mobile Money: A Theoretical Study of Alternative Media of Exchange, and an Empirical Study with Respect to M-Pesa in Kenya' (Toulouse School of Economics), http://papers.ssrn.com/sol3/papers.cfm?abstract_id=2278679. 15 December 2018.

GSMA (2015) *The Mobile Economy Sub-Saharan Africa 2015*, https://www.gsmaintelligence.com/research/?file=721eb3d4b80a36451202d0473b-3c4a63&download. 12 December 2018.

GSMA (2017) 'Brief History of GSM & the GSMA' (GSM Association), http://www.gsma.com/aboutus/history. 10 March 2017.

Guidelines for Mobile Payment Systems (Malaŵi, 2011).

Gunnar Camner and Emil Sjöblom (2009) *Can the Success of M-PESA Be Repeated?—A Review of the Implementations in Kenya and Tanzania*, http://emil.sjoblom.com/pdf/M-Pesa_implementations_Ke_Tz.pdf. 15 December 2018.

Ignacio Mas and Amolo Ng'weno (2010) 'Three Keys to M-PESA's Success: Branding, Channel Management and Pricing' (GSMA), http://www.www.oneapigw.gsma.com/mobilefordevelopment/wp-content/uploads/2012/06/keystompesassuccess4jan69.pdf. 15 December 2018.

Ignacio Mas and Daniel Radcliffe (2011) 'Mobile Payments Go Viral: M-PESA in Kenya' 32 *The Capco Institute Journal of Financial Transformation* 169.

Interview with Bigboy Mkoloma Product and Development Manager, Airtel Money (7 August 2015).

Interview with Webster Mbekeani Head, Mobile Money Division, TNM (20 August 2015).

ITU (2009) *Information Society Statistical Profiles 2009—Africa* (International Telecommunications Union), http://www.itu.int/dms_pub/itu-d/opb/ind/D-IND-RPM.AF-2009-PDF-E.pdf. 12 December 2018.

James M Kenani, Stan G Kaunda and Chiyembekezo Chafuwa (2014) 'Taxation Policy and Performance in Malawi Since Independence' (*Inaugural ECAMA Research Symposium*, Lilongwe), http://www.slideshare.net/IFPRIMaSSP/taxation-policy-and-performance-in-malawi-since-independence-by-sg-kaunda-j-kenani. 17 February 2018.

Jenny Aker and Isaac Mbiti (2010) 'Mobile Phones and Economic Development in Africa' 24 (3) *Journal of Economic Perspectives* 207, https://www.aeaweb.org/atypon.php?doi=10.1257/jep.24.3.207. 13 December 2018.

Joel Young (2009) 'Weird & Wireless: RF "Line of Sight"' *ElectronicsWeekly* (21 October 2009), http://www.electronicsweekly.com/blogs/electro-ramblings/weird-wireless/weird-wireless-rf-line-of-sight-2009-10/. 10 March 2018.

John M Senior (1951) *Optical Fiber Communications* (Prentice-Hall International, Inc., Upper Saddle River).

Jon Agar (2003) *Constant Touch: A Global History of the Mobile Phone* (Icon Books, Cambridge).

Kelvin Chaguza (2017) 'Opportunity International Bank of Malawi (OIBM) to Trim Its Staff This Year' *Face of Malawi* (26 January 2017), http://www.faceofmalawi.com/2017/01/opportunity-bank-of-malawi-oibm-to-trim-its-staffs-this-year/. 10 March 2018.

Kevin P Donovan (2012) 'Mobile Money, More Freedom? The Impact of M-PESA's Network Power on Development as Freedom' 6 *International Journal of Communication* 2647, http://ijoc.org/index.php/ijoc/article/view/1575. 20 May 2018.

Michael U Klein and Colin Mayer (2011) *Mobile Banking and Financial Inclusion: The Regulatory Lessons* (Policy Research Working Paper, The World Bank), http://documents.worldbank.org/curated/en/docsearch/document-type/620265. 14 February 2018.

Mobile Phone Base Stations—How Mobile Phone Networks Work (*Ofcom*, 2001), http://www.ofcom.org.uk/static/archive/ra/topics/mpsafety/school-audit/mobilework.htm. 27 March 2018.

'MoneyGram' (MoneyGram International Limited), https://m.moneygram.com/mgomobile/site/costEstimator.html#CostEstimatorResults. 11 March 2018.

MPC (2017) 'Financial, Retail & Agency Services' (Malawi Posts Corporation), http://malawiposts.com/finance.html. 10 March 2018.

Nick Hughes and Susie Lonie (2007) 'M-PESA: Mobile Money for the "Unbanked" Turning Cellphones into 24-hour Tellers in Kenya' 2 (1–2) *Innovations* 63, http://www.mitpressjournals.org/doi/pdf/10.1162/itgg.2007.2.1-2.63. 15 December 2018.

Ofcom (2001) 'Mobile Phone Base Stations—How Mobile Phone Networks Work' (Office of the Communications Regulator, UK), http://www.ofcom.

org.uk/static/archive/ra/topics/mpsafety/school-audit/mobilework.htm. 12 December 2018.

Patrick M Jost and Harjit Singh Sandhu (2003) *The Hawala Alternative Remittance System and Its Role in Money Laundering* (Interpol), https://www.peacepalacelibrary.nl/ebooks/files/hawala.pdf. 14 February 2018.

Payment Systems Act (Malaŵi, 2016).

Peter Day (2005) 'Mutual Benefits of Profits from Poverty' BBC News (4 July 2005), http://news.bbc.co.uk/1/hi/business/4648049.stm. 17 February 2018.

RBM (2015) *Financial and Economic Review* (Reserve Bank of Malawi), https://www.rbm.mw/Home/GetContentFile?ContentID=7492. 14 December 2018.

RBM (2016) *Monthly National Payments System Report: December 2016* (Reserve Bank of Malaŵi), https://www.rbm.mw/PaymentSystems/GetContentFile/?ContentID=12148pdf. 17 February 2018.

RBM (2017) 'Reserve Bank of Malawi', https://www.rbm.mw/. 24 April 2018.

Richard Heeks (2012) 'Why M-Pesa Outperforms Other Developing Country Mobile Money Schemes' *ICTs for Development*, http://ict4dblog.wordpress.com/2012/11/24/why-mpesa-outperforms-other-developing-country-mobilelectronicmoney-schemes/. 8 May 2018.

Robert R Stoll (1961) *Set Theory and Logic* (Dover Publications, New York) Chapter 1.

Robleh Ali and others (2014) 'The Economics of Digital Currencies' 54 *Quarterly Bulletin* (Bank of England), http://www.bankofengland.co.uk/publications/Documents/quarterlybulletin/2014/qb14q3digitalcurrenciesbitcoin2.pdf. 14 September 2018.

Safaricom (2017) 'Sambaza' (Safaricom, Kenya), https://www.safaricom.co.ke/personal/calls-sms/prepay/sambaza. 17 February 2018.

Selipha Kihagi (2013) 'Malawians to Pay for Fuel Services Using Airtel Money' (HumanIPO), http://www.humanipo.com/news/36717/malawians-to-pay-for-fuel-services-using-airtel-money/. 12 March 2018.

Simone Di Castri (2013) *Mobile Money: Enabling Regulatory Solutions* (GSMA, London), http://www.gsma.com/publicpolicy/wp-content/uploads/2013/02/GSMA2013_Report_Mobilelectronicmoney-EnablingRegulatorySolutions.pdf. 20 February 2018.

Somik V Lall, Hyoung Wang and Thomas Munthali (2009) *Explaining High Transport Costs Within Malawi—Bad Roads or Lack of Trucking Competition?* (Policy Research Working Paper 5133, World Bank Publications), http://elibrary.worldbank.org/doi/pdf/10.1596/1813-9450-5133. 11 March 2018.

'Submarine Cable Map' (PriMetrica, Inc, 2015), http://www.submarinecablemap.com/#/. 5 May 2018.

TNM (2013) 'Me2u Service' (Telekom Networks Malawi), http://www.tnm.co.mw/index.php/me2u.html. 21 May 2018.

TNM (2017) 'Mpamba, TNM Mobile Money' (Telekom Networks Malawi), https://www.tnmmpamba.co.mw/. 12 March 2017.

Tonny K Omwansa (2009) 'M-PESA: Progress and Prospects' *Innovations* 107, https://profiles.uonbi.ac.ke/tomwansa/files/innov-gsma-omwansa.pdf. 1 December 2018.

UNESCO (2016) 'Malawi' (UNESCO Institute for Statistics), http://uis.unesco.org/en/country/mw. 17 February 2018.

Vince Kumwenda (2012) 'Malawi Posts Corporation's Fast Cash Money Transfer', http://vincekumwenda.blogspot.co.uk/2012/05/malawi-posts-corporations-fast-cash.html. 23 February 2018.

William Jack and Tavneet Suri (2011) *Mobile Money: The Economics of M-PESA* (National Bureau of Economic Research, Cambridge, MA), http://www.nber.org/papers/w16721. 15 December 2018.

William Jack, Tavneet Suri and Robert M Townsend (2010) 'Monetary Theory and Electronic Money: Reflections on the Kenyan Experience' 96 (1) *Federal Reserve Bank of Richmond Economic Quarterly* 83, https://www.richmondfed.org/publications/research/economic_quarterly/2010/q1/townsend. 15 December 2018.

XE (2018) 'XE Currency Converter' (XE), https://www.xe.com/currencyconverter/convert/?Amount=1&From=GBP&To=KES. 28 December 2018.

CHAPTER 4

# Different Types of Regulation

## 4.1 Introduction

The term regulation refers to a set of binding rules issued by a private or public body.[1] In its most generic form, it represents an "intervention between the parties to a transaction".[2] Fleuriot says that regulation aims at the maintenance of a balance or equilibrium and the task of the regulator is to maintain the various balances among the different actors.[3] Ogus refers to regulation as the "sustained and focused control exercised by a public agency over activities that are valued by a community".[4] These are "obligations imposed by public law designed to

[1] Kenneth Kaoma Mwenda (2006) *Legal Aspects of Financial Services Regulation and the Concept of a Unified Regulator* (World Bank, Washington, DC), p. 5.

[2] César Córdova-Novion and Deirdre Hanlon (2002) 'Regulatory Governance: Improving the Institutional Basis for Sectoral Regulators' 2 (3) *OECD Journal on Budgeting*, p. 60, https://www.oecd.org/gov/budgeting/43505850.pdf. 15 February 2018.

[3] Pierre Fleuriof (1997) 'Financial Regulation as the Safeguard of Balances in a Global Context' in Alain Jeunemaitre (ed) *Financial Markets Regulation* (Macmillan, Basingstoke), p. 34.

[4] Anthony I Ogus (1994) *Regulation: Legal Form and Economic Theory* vol 152 (Clarendon Press Oxford, Oxford), p. 1 citing Philip Selznick and Philippe Nonet (1978) *Law and Society in Transition: Toward Responsive Law* (Harper and Row, New York), p. 363.



S. Madise, *The Regulation of Mobile Money*, Palgrave Macmillan Studies in Banking and Financial Institutions,
https://doi.org/10.1007/978-3-030-13831-8_4

induce individuals and firms to outcomes which they would not voluntarily reach".[5] It is the threat of some form of punishment or sanction that underpins regulatory enforcement.[6] In relation to economic activities, one of the motivations for putting in place regulations is market failure.[7] It is trite that a pinnacle tenet of a free market is to leave it to regulate itself and find its own equilibrium. Yet, there will be times when the market may fail to do this, either due to exogenous or endogenous shocks or factors. The reason why the market usually will want less regulation is that it is perceived as an economic cost. According to Dumez and Jeunemaitre, "regulation will be preferred to *laissez faire* whenever the cost of regulation is less than the transaction costs due to regulation plus the market failure costs".[8]

Different societal systems will have different regulatory standards and objectives. For the financial sector, three things are associated with the need for regulation: correcting information asymmetry, maintaining trust in the financial system and avoiding systemic risk or contagion.[9] All these are considered public goods.[10] In most economic enterprises, there is information asymmetry between the consumers and the suppliers in favour of the latter.[11] This is more so where consumers are dealing with institutions that have a network or web of interconnected ties, which the average consumer cannot fathom.[12] Statutory requirements obliging suppliers to disclose information related to their service or product are part of this correction.[13] Apart from consumer interests, there are also

[5] Anthony Ogus (2009) 'Regulation Revisited' (2) *Public Law*, p. 333, http://repub.eur.nl/pub/16031/A.%20Ogus,%20Regulation%20Revisited.pdf. 19 May 2018.

[6] Ibid.

[7] Herve Dumez and Alain Jeunemaitre (1997) 'Financial Regulation: From Economic Analysis to Practical Experience' in Alain Jeunemaitre (ed) *Financial Markets Regulation* (Macmillan, Basingstoke), p. 4.

[8] Ibid., p. 5.

[9] Ibid., p. 4.

[10] Marc Quintyn and Michael W Taylor (2002) *Regulatory and Supervisory Independence and Financial Stability* (International Monetary Fund, Washington, DC), p. 8, https://www.imf.org/external/pubs/ft/wp/2002/wp0246.pdf. 1 February 2018.

[11] Dumez and Jeunemaitre (1997), p. 4.

[12] Boon-Chye Lee and Olujoke Longe-Akindemowo (1999) 'Regulatory Issues in Electronic Money: A Legal-Economics Analysis' 1 (1) *Netnomics* 53, p. 60, http://link.springer.com/article/10.1023/A:1011445620486. 12 March 2018.

[13] Dumez and Jeunemaitre (1997), p. 4.

state interests at play such as ensuring system security and good financial management. Trust is a prerequisite for consumers to procure the service.[14] To gain trust, a system must be seen to be working in a fair and an orderly way.[15] On the other hand, trust can only be built if the consumers have confidence in the system. Therefore, the two operate as one continuous cycle, a break in one causing the whole cycle to crumble.

Systemic risk is crucially important in financial services because risk has a tendency to adopt a domino effect, or lead to a phenomena called contagion, whereby a problem in one financial institution may become infectious and quickly spread and cause panic within the whole financial system. For example, the collapse of one firm may instil fear within the financial system leading to a collapse of other related firms.[16] Firms engaged in banking and quasi-banking services are at greater risk of systemic risk than others.[17] Because of the domino effect of extending loans to consumers from deposits, banking is considered in some cases too important to fail.[18] A good example of when the domino effect may kick in is when there is default in loan repayment affecting one bank. The affected bank will then not have enough money to pay all its depositors on demand. After all, as was noted in Chapter 2, the traditional banking business is that of an intermediary of funds. It collects deposits, usually demand deposits, from depositors and then lends it to borrowers, at a premium. Ordinarily of course, depositors will not descend on a bank and ask for their deposits unless they have cause for concern or expect it to fail.[19] Knowledge of adverse news about the bank may trigger this.[20] Sometime a malicious or ill-timed rumour can also have the same effect. The phenomena are called psychological contagion.[21] Since the financial

[14] Ibid., pp. 4–5.

[15] Ibid., p. 4.

[16] Ibid., p. 5.

[17] Avinash Persaud (2015) 'Why Do We Regulate Finance?' in *Reinventing Financial Regulation* (Apress, New York), p. 13.

[18] Ibid.

[19] Douglas W Diamond and Philip H Dybvig (1983) 'Bank Runs, Deposit Insurance, and Liquidity' 91 (3) *Journal of Political Economy* 401, p. 401, http://www.journals.uchicago.edu/doi/pdfplus/10.1086/261155. 27 April 2018.

[20] Persaud (2015), p. 14.

[21] Tom de Swaan and Others (1995) *The Supervision of Financial Conglomerates* (Tripartite Group of Bank, Securities and Insurance Regulators, Mardrid), p. 18, https://www.iosco.org/library/pubdocs/pdf/IOSCOPD47.pdf. 3 October 2018.

system in most countries is highly integrated and interlinked, cause for concern in one bank can quickly spread to other banks. The inter-bank market also means problems in one bank can easily spread to other connected banks.[22] Prudential rules are usually set up to ensure the stability and integrity of the financial system and in doing so minimising systemic risk and protect depositors.[23]

### *4.1.1 Public Interest Theory*

Shleifer says that the regulatory theory of public interest or helping hand is premised on the fact that markets fail when they are left to their own devices.[24] Posner adds that the theory evolved on the assumption that markets are extremely fragile and are likely to operate inefficiently if not regulated.[25] He says regulation is a manifestation of existing imperfections in the market.[26] Shleifer says regulation can be used to discourage anti-competitive behaviour.[27] The theory, which Morgan and Yeung refer to as the *welfare economic approach* aims at "promoting the general welfare of the community".[28] Posner however argues that this theory is flawed. He argues that:

> Were this theory of regulation correct, we would find regulation imposed mainly in highly concentrated industries (where the danger of monopoly is greatest) and in industries that generate substantial external costs or benefits. We do not.[29]

[22] Ibid.

[23] Dumez and Jeunemaitre (1997), p. 5.

[24] Andrei Shleifer (2005) 'Understanding Regulation' 11 (4) *European Financial Management* 439, p. 440, http://scholar.harvard.edu/files/shleifer/files/02_eufm00121.pdf?m=1360042225. 19 May 2018.

[25] Richard A Posner (1974) 'Theories of Economic Regulation' 5 (2) *Bell Journal of Economics and Management Science* 335, p. 336, http://www.thecre.com/oira/wp-content/uploads/2016/03/Posner.pdf. 1 February 2018.

[26] Posner (1974), p. 336.

[27] Shleifer (2005), p. 444.

[28] Bronwen Morgan and Karen Yeung (2007) *An Introduction to Law and Regulation* (Cambridge University Press, Cambridge), p. 18.

[29] Posner (1974), p. 336.

He argues that the theory ignores the "linkage or mechanism by which a perception of the public interest is translated into legislative action".[30] What is perceived to be in the public interest may not be what is on the mind of politicians and the legislature. In fact, it begs the question, how is the public interest measured? Who decides that a particular legislation is in the public interest? It is this vagueness of the theory that may have led to Posner's critique. Posner's evaluation is that there is no positive correlation between monopolistic market structure and regulation.[31] It is submitted that, however measured, financial stability is in the public interest. In this regard, regulating a service such as mobile money is likely to be in the public interest.

Persaud has also cautioned that to equate the emergence of regulation with market failures is to oversimplify the matter.[32] He argues that if that were true, the corollary would be that where there is no market failure, there would be no need for regulation.[33] Yet, Persaud argues, the practice reveals that in almost all jurisdictions, regulation occurs with or without market failures.[34]

### *4.1.2 Capture Theory*

The regulatory capture theory was first posited as an economic theory in the seminal work by Stigler.[35] It is premised on the concept that regulation is a cost, which must be managed.[36] According to Posner, the capture theory is the antithesis of the public interest theory.[37] This theory essentially argues that in any regulatory environment, the rules that regulate the state of play eventually end up favouring the industry, or at least the strong players in the industry. According to Posner, "regulation is supplied in response to the demands of interest groups struggling

[30] Ibid., p. 340.

[31] Ibid., p. 336.

[32] Persaud (2015).

[33] Ibid., p. 8.

[34] Ibid.

[35] George J Stigler (1971) 'The Theory of Economic Regulation' *The Bell Journal of Economics and Management Science* 3, http://hsecon.tripod.com/stigler-regulation.pdf. 1 February 2018.

[36] Ibid.

[37] Posner (1974), p. 341.

among themselves to maximise the incomes of their members".[38] The arena within which these interest groups contest is referred to as regulatory space and is discussed below.

Capture is achieved by the subtle power that the industry exerts on the regulator, which in time results in the regulator regulating the industry by the dictates of the industry.[39] However, the regulator is unconscious of this fact, believing instead that the regulation is good for the public.[40] The result is that the regulator and the regulation have in effect been captured by the industry. Quintyn and Taylor summarised it in this manner:

> Agencies that suffer from capture come to identify industry interests with the public interest. Just like political pressure, industry capture can undermine the effectiveness of regulation. Rules may be formulated with a view to minimize industry costs, rather than strike an appropriate balance between those costs and public benefits. Rules may also be applied inconsistently, with individual firms winning case-by-case exemptions from regulatory requirements.[41]

Capture is possible because regulation is, like any other commodity, affected by the economic factors of supply and demand.[42] Seen as an economic cost, it is to the advantage of the interest groups who wish to minimise costs to have a regulatory regime that is least costly. Using Stigler's work as a basis, Peltzman argued that "what is at stake in regulatory processes is a transfer of wealth, [This is] rarely in cash, but rather in the form of a regulated price".[43] Shleifer says the result is that there is capture not only of the regulator, but also of the "political process of regulation".[44] The end result is that instead of breaking

[38] Ibid., pp. 335–6.

[39] Stigler (1971), p. 3.

[40] Ibid.

[41] Quintyn and Taylor (2002), p. 9.

[42] Posner (1974), p. 344.

[43] Sam Peltzman (1976) 'Toward a More General Theory of Regulation' 19 (2) *The Journal of Law and Economics* 211, pp. 213–4, http://www.journals.uchicago.edu/doi/pdfplus/10.1086/466865. 1 February 2018.

[44] Shleifer (2005), p. 441.

down monopolies, regulation sustains them.[45] The capture theory has been criticised on the basis that it wrongly assumes that the regulator and the regulated (regulatee) are supposed to be at polar ends of the regulatory matrix, with power concentrated in the regulator. Scott, Hancher and Moran argue that where this power is decentralised and dispersed, the notion of capture does not even arise.[46] It is however submitted that while decentralisation and dispersion of regulatory power reduced chances of capture, to argue that capture does not occur, would be to ignore the reality of the dynamism and highly contested nature of the regulatory space environment.

## 4.2 The Regulatory Spectrum

Regulation as a topic usually attracts a bipolar reaction depending on where one standing with regard to the market. Either there is no regulation at all or there is a degree of regulation. However, no regulation is in itself a form of regulation. It arises out of a deliberate construction of a market in which other interests such as state or consumer cannot intervene, with power left to those involved in the market. The choice not to regulate is therefore, a regulatory choice. Where regulation is done positively, it is perceived differently by different sections of society. For the industry, especially in market economies, there is usually a perception or view that there is over-regulation and too much red tape or bureaucracy.[47] On the other hand, according to Ogus, the public seems to have "a perception of regulatory failure in relation to entrepreneurial excesses and financial distress and a call for more rigorous controls".[48] Balancing these two competing views lies at the centre of the continuous reforming of regulation. Different approaches to regulation can be analysed to identify the stages of development on the regulatory journey,

[45] Ibid.

[46] Colin Scott (2001) 'Analysing Regulatory Space: Fragmented Resources and Institutional Design' *Public Law* 329, http://researchrepository.ucd.ie/bitstream/handle/10197/6785/AnalysingRegSpace.pdf?sequence=2. 1 December 2018.

Leigh Hancher and Michael Moran (1998) 'Organizing Regulatory Space' in Robert Baldwin, Colin Scott and Christopher Hood (eds) *A Reader in Regulation* (Oxford University Press, Oxford).

[47] Ogus (2009), p. 341.

[48] Ibid.

and sometimes these approaches overlap, creating a regulatory spectrum.[49] The starting point is the realisation that in certain industries, the command and control theory (discussed below) of regulation may not be ideal and that law can only regulate through some other form of regulation, which involves an element of self-regulation. How this self-regulation is achieved is where theories differ.

The main theories that this books look at are responsive regulation and reflexive regulation. The thesis of responsive regulation is based on changes that occur within the law due to internal dynamics within the legal system while reflexive regulation considers changes both from internal and external social forces or variables.[50] Reflexive regulation is most associated with the theory of autopoiesis, as espoused by Gunther Teubner. However, it is argued that autopoiesis is also the basis for the emergence of responsive regulation theory. The problem may arise from the fact that they both arise from the need to move away from command and control towards some form of self-regulation, mainly because of regulatory failure. Teubner says this failure arises due to what he called a regulatory ***trilemma***; a three-way dilemma; incongruence between the regulator and the regulated system, over-regulation and over-socialisation by the regulator, which leads to capture.[51]

In looking at regulation, there is also need to look at the behaviour of the various market actors. Julia Black argues that the neoclassical economic theory that man is always a utility maximiser no longer always holds true and that there are other social factors that can make a regulatee abide and play by the rules other than pure economic gain.[52]

[49] Anthony Ogus (1995) 'Rethinking Self-Regulation' 15 (1) *Oxford Journal of Legal Studies* 97, p. 100, http://ojls.oxfordjournals.org/content/15/1/97.full.pdf. 19 May 2018.

[50] Selznick and Nonet (1978), p. 20.

Gunther Teubner (1983) 'Substantive and Reflexive Elements in Modern Law' *Law and Society Review* 239, pp. 245, 258 and 259, http://www.jstor.org/stable/3053348. 18 November 2018.

[51] Gunther Teubner (1986) 'After Legal Instrumentalism? Strategic Models of Post-regulatory Law' in Gunther Teubner (ed) *Dilemmas of Law in the Welfare State* (Walter de Gruyter, New York), p. 311.

[52] Julia Black (2013) *Seeing, Knowing, and Regulating Financial Markets: Moving the Cognitive Framework from the Economic to the Social* (LSE Law, Society and Economy Working Papers 24/2013), pp. 6, 9, www.lse.ac.uk/collections/law/wps/WPS2013-24_Black.pdf. 19 May 2018.

Regulators need to build new frameworks which are different to the way economists perceive financial markets otherwise there is a risk of regulatory mirage, a false image of the financial market and its constitute elements.[53] According to Black, there must be a "social conception of financial markets so that regulators regulate markets responsively".[54] However, as a caveat, profit-motive or the survival instinct must never be underestimated. Maytz argues that regulation "in principle motivates behaviour which is dependent upon personal initiative, innovation and positive commitment".[55] However, where the law comes into direct conflict with the profit motive or in questions of business survival in the face of bankruptcy, there is little chance of the law being obeyed.[56] How a regulatee will respond to regulation is more complex than simply the profit motive and includes normative values,[57] social licence,[58] the nature of their interactions with the regulator and their ability and capacity to comply.[59] Furthermore, the effect of power relations needs to be factored in, as "enforcement of regulatory rules is as much about power as it is about interpretation".[60]

### *4.2.1 Command and Control*

The command and control concept has its origins in the military.[61] In law, it is largely associated with the Austinian theory prevalent in criminal law where law is seen as an instrument of control, by a higher body (the sovereign or the state) of a lower body (the citizens) at the pain of sanctions.[62] Ogus says, where a regulated party fails to comply with

[53] Ibid., p. 2.

[54] Ibid.

[55] Quoted by Gunther Teubner (1993) *Law as an Autopoietic System* (Blackwell, Oxford/Cambridge), p. 91.

[56] Ibid.

[57] Whether they agree with the regulatory requirements or not.

[58] Their interpretive framework and 'peer pressure.'

[59] Black (2013), p. 19.

[60] Ibid., p. 45.

[61] David S Alberts and Richard E Hayes (2006) 'Reader Orientation' in *Understanding Command and Control* (CCRP Publishing, Washington, DC), Chapter 2.

[62] See generally John Austin (1832) *The Province of Jurisprudence Determined* (John Murray, London).

laid down rules, this may lead to sanctions, but usually as a last resort.[63] However, this presents a problem because in truth regulatory breaches do not result in penal sanctions but attract some form of sanction, which is civil in nature.[64] Ogus argues that the use of criminal law terminology did not happen by chance, at least in England. It followed a period where enforcement of regulation was via criminal or quasi-criminal legislation and agencies.[65] The Crown created inspectorates to supervise various economic activities, but denied these agencies prosecutorial powers.[66] Ogus says, the agencies therefore "developed an enforcement strategy in which ultimate resort to the courts played only a small role".[67] The result is a model in which legislation is enacted under which those to be regulated must obey the dictates as prescribed under pain of sanction. This sanction is usually a fine, but it may sometimes be of a criminal nature. For example, in Malaŵi, the Financial Services Act (2010) has provisions for administrative penalties.[68] However, despite these being administrative penalties, failure to pay or comply with them may lead to criminal conviction.[69] The United Kingdom's (UK) Financial Services Act (2012) also has provisions where a person may be found guilty of an offence in circumstances which would otherwise attract a civil censure.[70]

Command and control theory is associated with rigidity, heavy handedness or rules-based regulation and statutory law backed enforcement. It manifests itself in most prescriptive legislation. Black laments that unfortunately this has been equated "with nit-picking bureaucracy in which compliance with detailed provisions is more important than the attainment of an overall outcome".[71] Command and control, which

[63] Ogus (1994), p. 79.

[64] Ibid., p. 80.

[65] Ibid., pp. 80–1.

[66] Ibid., p. 81.

[67] Ibid.

[68] Section 75 Financial Services Act (Malaŵi, 2010).

[69] Section 75(3), ibid.

[70] Section 92 Financial Services Act (United Kingdom: Chapter 21, 2012), http://www.legislation.gov.uk/ukpga/2012/21/pdfs/ukpga_20120021_en.pdf. 2 June 2018.

[71] Julia Black (2010) *The Rise, Fall and Fate of Principles Based Regulation* (LSE Law, Society and Economy Working Papers, London School of Economics and Political Science), p. 3, http://eprints.lse.ac.uk/32892/1/WPS2010-17_Black.pdf. 27 April 2018.

Baldwin et al. refer to as deterrence and compliance[72] is usually contrasted with principles-based regulation also known as light-touch regulation and self-regulation.

### *4.2.2 Principles-Based Regulation*

Black, a leading proponent of principles-based regulation defines it as approach that is:

> Moving away from reliance on detailed prescriptive rules and relying more on high level, broadly stated rules or principles to set the standards by which regulated firms must conduct business.[73]

Apart from moving away from detailed rules, the approach focuses on outcomes and increases responsibility on senior management.[74] The underlying argument is that it is management, not regulators, who are best placed to determine what needs to be done to achieve set outcomes.[75] The duty of the regulator is therefore to define these outcomes and vet the people who take up senior management positions.[76] As an approach, principles-based regulation attained recognition when the Financial Services Authority (FSA), the then sole unified regulator in the UK, embraced it as its preferred regulatory approach.[77] It origins, however, can be traced to the times when Alan Greenspan was Chairman of the Federal Reserve (USA) and Gordon Brown was Chancellor of the Exchequer (UK).[78] Principles-based regulation allows flexibility and

[72] Robert Baldwin, Martin Cave and Martin Lodge (2011) *Understanding Regulation: Theory, Strategy, and Practice* (2nd edn, Oxford University Press, Oxford), p. 259.

[73] Julia Black (2007) 'Principles Based Regulation: Risks, Challenges and Opportunities' (Principles Based Regulation, University of Sydney, Sydney), p. 3, http://eprints.lse.ac.uk/62814/. 28 April 2018.

[74] Ibid.

[75] Ibid., p. 5.

[76] Ibid., pp. 5, 6.

[77] Ibid., pp. 2, 5.

Black (2010), p. 3.

[78] Roger Alford (2010) *Some Help in Understanding Britain's Banking Crisis, 2007–09* (LSE Financial Markets Group Paper Series, London School of Economics, London), p. 28, http://www.lse.ac.uk/fmg/workingPapers/specialPapers/PDF/SP193.pdf. 9 February 2018.

encourages innovation by firms thereby enhancing completion.[79] Instead of ticking boxes, or engaging in creative compliance,[80] firms focus more on substantive compliance by emphasising on and improving their own conduct.[81] Regulators are also able to innovate and rapidly respond to the regulated environment.[82]

Black says since principles-based regulation is "based on responsibility, mutuality, and trust", any breakdown on the underlying assumptions lead to paradoxes.[83] Therefore, despite being a higher form of regulation, these paradoxes make principles-based regulation vulnerable.[84] Black has identified 7 paradoxes:

i. *Interpretive* caused by impreciseness of principles.[85]
ii. *Communicative* caused by the regulator not being clear on its guidance.[86]
iii. *Compliance* caused by conservativeness by firms.[87]
iv. *Supervisory and enforcement* caused by over-enforcement.[88]
v. *Internal management* caused by overloading of senior management.[89]
vi. *Ethical* caused by an erosion of ethics.[90]
vii. *Trust* caused by its breakdown.[91]

[79] Black (2007), p. 2.

[80] Compliance with the letter but not the spirit of the lure—ibid., p. 4.
Julia Black (2008) *Forms and Paradoxes of Principles Based Regulation* (LSE Law, Society and Economy Working papers, London School of Economics and Political Science, London), p. 3, http://eprints.lse.ac.uk/23103/1/WPS2008-13.pdf. 28 April 2018.

[81] Black (2007), p. 2.

[82] Black (2008), p. 3.

[83] Ibid., pp. 8, 4–5.

[84] Ibid., p. 36.

[85] Ibid., p. 25.

[86] Ibid.

[87] Ibid., p. 28.

[88] Ibid., p. 29.

[89] Ibid., p. 32.

[90] Ibid., p. 33.

[91] Ibid., p. 35.

Black says the trust paradox is probably the ultimate one in that "principles based regulation can help create trust, but it itself has to be founded on trust if it is ever to operate effectively".[92] As the then FSA's Hector Sants stated, principles-based regulation "does not work with individuals who have no principles".[93] The principles-based regulation approach by the FSA was based on a broader risk-based regulation approach under the Advanced Risk Responsive Operating Framework (ARROW).[94] Black has, however, argued that there is a dissonance between risk-based regulation and principles-based regulation and it is unclear how the two approaches interact.[95] She argues that for risk-based regulation, risk, not rules, is the starting point while for principles-based regulation, it is principles.[96] In risk-based regulation, rules only come during enforcement to mitigate risk.[97] The lack of complementarity and mismatch highlights a critical regulatory lacuna.[98] As Joanna Gray rightly observes, the problem with risk is to distinguish between "knowable and *ex ante* ascertainable risk and genuine unknowns and uncertainty".[99]

The main criticism of principles-based regulation is that it encourages firms to backslide leading to erosion of adequate consumers and stakeholders' protection.[100] The other criticism is that principles by nature lack certainty and predictability.[101] The balance therefore seems to be

[92] Ibid., p. 36.

[93] Hector Sants (2009) 'Delivering Intensive Supervision and Credible Deterrence' (Finacial Services Authority), http://www.fsa.gov.uk/pages/Library/Communication/Speeches/2009/0312_hs.shtml. 28 April 2018.

[94] Joanna Gray (2009) 'Is It Time to Highlight the Limits of Risk-Based Financial Regulation?' 4 (1) *Capital Markets Law Journal* 50, p. 52, https://doi.org/10.1093/cmlj/kmn035. 28 April 2018.

Julia Black (2005) 'The Emergence of Risk-Based Regulation and the New Public Risk Management in the United Kingdom' *Public Law* 510, pp. 526–34, https://www.academia.edu/1295947/The_emergence_of_risk-based_regulation_and_the_new_public_risk_management_in_the_United_Kingdom?auto=download. 28 April 2018.

[95] Black (2010), p. 23.

[96] Ibid.

[97] Gray (2009), p. 53.
Black (2010), p. 24.

[98] Black (2010), pp. 23, 24.

[99] Gray (2009), p. 59.

[100] Black (2007), p. 2.

[101] Black (2008), p. 3.

between the latitude that the regulators can provide for firms to innovate and the engagement of the regulatees, especially at senior level with regulatory issues.[102] According to Black, it is the "presence of the shotgun behind the door" that ensures compliance in principles based regulation,[103] and which may counter the view of it as "lax regulation".[104] Or as Ayres and Braithwaite refer to it, the benign gun, is the one that compels compliance.[105]

While principles-based regulation was seen as the solution pre-2007/2008 financial crisis, it was later isolated as the source of the problem, after the crisis.[106] Lord Turner of the FSA testified before the House of Commons Treasury Committee, in its enquiry after the 2008 financial crisis, that the FSA had been criticised before the crisis for adopting a regulation strategy that was deemed heavy handed instead of being more light touch.[107] There was, therefore, pressure on the

[102] Black (2007), pp. 19, 20.

[103] Ibid., p. 22.

[104] Black (2008), p. 1.

[105] Ian Ayres I and John Braithwaite (1992) Responsive Regulation: Transcending the Deregulation Debate (Oxford University Press, Oxford).

[106] Black (2010), p. 3.

Roman Tomasic (2010) 'Beyond "Light Touch" Regulation of British Banks After the Financial Crisis' in MacNeil IG and O'Brien J (eds), The Future of Financial Regulation (Hart Publishing, Portland), p. 104.

Anon (2012) 'Light Touch No More' *The Economist* (1 December 2012), http://www.economist.com/news/21567399-britains-financial-regulators-are-getting-much-tougher-light-touch-no-more. 9 February 2018.

Brooke Masters (2011) 'Regulator's "Light Touch" Led to Failure' *Financial Times* (12 December 2011), https://www.ft.com/content/2bf14c52-24ce-11e1-bfb3-00144feabdc0. 9 February 2018.

Andrew Hill and Joe Leahy (2009) 'FSA Bids Farewell to Light-Touch Financial Regulation' *Financial Times* (19 March 2009), http://www.ft.com/cms/s/0/da208b14-1426-11de-9e32-0000779fd2ac.html?ft_site=falcon&desktop=true#axzz4YBrB0BUq. 9 February 2018.

Light Touch regulation see Lucia Quaglia (2010) 'Completing the Single Market in Financial Services: The Politics of Competing Advocacy Coalitions' 17 (7) *Journal of European Public Policy* 1007, pp. 15, 25, http://aei.pitt.edu/33124/1/quaglia._lucia_(2).pdf. 17 October 2018.

[107] House of Commons Treasury Committee (2009) *Banking Crisis: Regulation and Supervision* (Parliament, London), p. 11, https://www.publications.parliament.uk/pa/cm200809/cmselect/cmtreasy/767/767.pdf. 3 February 2018.

regulatory, by the industry for less regulation based on the notion that the market knew best. However, although light touch is deemed attractive to investors, Tomasic argues that it leads to regulatory arbitrage which may lead to a race to the bottom with regulators competing to offer the bare minimum supervision.[108]

So, although the post-financial crisis regulatory financial framework has moved from principles-based regulation, it would seem that the approach is still favoured in the regulation of mobile money, but the name commonly used is light touch.[109] In principles-based regulation or light-touch regulation, outcomes define principles and senior management is given some latitude. According to Black, lessons learnt from the last financial crisis are that there is a need for a more "intensive and sceptical supervisory process that looks at how systems operate in practice".[110]

### *4.2.3 Self-Regulation*

Black says self-regulation essentially combines a definition of two concepts, "disciplining of one's own conduct by oneself and regulation by a collective group of the conduct of its members".[111] It therefore stands in sharp contrast to command and control.[112] At the centre of self-regulation is the concept that the best way of regulating any industry is to have the industry participants themselves come up with their own rules to regulate their conduct.[113] As Black puts it, self-regulation disciplines

[108]Tomasic (2010), p. 112.

[109]Richard Heeks (2012) 'Why M-Pesa Outperforms Other Developing Country Mobile Money Schemes' (ICTs for Development, 24 November 2012), http://ict4dblog.wordpress.com/2012/11/24/why-m-pesa-outperforms-other-developing-country-mobilelectronicmoney-schemes/. 8 May 2018.

For a discussion of Light Touch regulation see Quaglia (2010), pp. 15, 25.

[110]Black (2010), p. 15.

[111]Julia Black (1996) 'Constitutionalising Self-Regulation' 59 (1) *The Modern Law Review* 24, p. 27, http://onlinelibrary.wiley.com/doi/10.1111/j.1468-2230.1996.tb02064.x/full. 19 May 2018.

[112]Ibid.

[113]Willem J. Witteveen (2005) 'A Self-Regulation Paradox: Notes Towards the Social Logic of Regulation' 9 (1) *Electronic Journal of Comparative Law*, p. 2, http://www.ejcl.org/91/art91-2.PDF. 19 May 2018.

own conduct through tailor-made regulation.[114] Teubner has argued, "the only way of regulating complex organizations from the outside is to grant them a high degree of autonomy and to lay down only general structural guidelines to regulate the context of action".[115] Autonomy is, therefore, key to self-regulation. Witteveen adds that, "rather than centralized regulation by distant bureaucracies, self regulation promise[s] dialogically formulated and locally effective regulation by actors with a stake in the work processes and their outcomes".[116] Since the various actors within the regulatory arena have differences in the resources and power that they possess, and sometimes these actors compete to gain an advantage and self-regulation usually reflects this contestation.[117]

There are three main forms of self-regulation; enforced, consensual and co-regulation.[118] Ayres and Braithwaite, have argued that enforced self-regulation is an element of responsive regulation.[119] Ogus posits that consensual regulation requires bargaining within the various actors before the regulation can be rolled out.[120] Black says co-regulation requires "industry-association self regulation with some oversight or ratification by government".[121]

Since self-regulation is premised on the regulated industry making the rules, Witteveen argues that self-regulation as a concept leads to a paradox.[122] He asks the question; "how can one obey the rule and at the same time be a law unto oneself?"[123] Ogus also warns that some actors may use self-regulation if they feel threatened by regulation and feel there are considerable benefits to be gained "if they are allowed themselves to formulate and enforce the relevant controls".[124] Ogus further criticises self-regulation on the basis that self-regulatory organisations

[114] Black (1996), p. 26.

[115] Teubner (1993), p. 142.

[116] Witteveen (2005), p. 3.

[117] Ibid., p. 2.

[118] Ayres and Braithwaite (1992), p. 101; Ogus (1995), p. 101; Black (1996), p. 26.

[119] Ayres and Braithwaite (1992), p. 101.

[120] Ogus (1995), p. 101.

[121] Black (1996), p. 26.

[122] Witteveen (2005).

[123] Ibid., p. 6.

[124] Ogus (1995), p. 98.

may not consistently enforce rules against recalcitrant members.[125] Furthermore, powerful actors within the industry may influence the self-regulatory organisations to restrict entry of new members and "enable incumbent practitioners to earn supra-competitive profits".[126] However, this is based on the assumption that self-regulation and public regulation are discrete concepts. Ogus argues that actually they are not and are part of "a spectrum containing different degrees of legislative constraints".[127] Therefore, while there may be a fear that self-regulation may lead to reduced oversight, Baldwin et al. argue that in fact it benefits from the expertise and efficiency within the industry.[128]

### 4.2.4 *Responsive Regulation*

Responsive regulation is based on the concept that the regulator is more likely to get compliance from the regulatees if the regulator has the means to enforce compliance.[129] Ayres and Braithwaite are the main proponents of the theory of responsive regulation, and the escalation pyramid aptly summarises the theory.[130] Understandably, Braithwaite calls the pyramid "the most distinctive part of responsive regulation".[131] The pyramid has several layers of enforcing and ensuring compliance. The broad base is made up of persuasion while the apex is the ultimate punishment, resulting in licence revocation which ultimately would lead to cessation of business.[132] According to this theory, much of the regulatory effort should focus on persuasion but there must be no fear to escalate the punishment although the incidences of such must reduce as one moves up to the apex.[133] However, the base should never be mistaken

[125] Ibid., p. 99.

[126] Ibid.

[127] Ibid., p. 100.

[128] Baldwin et al. (2011), p. 139.

[129] Ayres and Braithwaite (1992), p. 35.

[130] Ibid.

[131] John Braithwaite (2002) 'Responsive Regulation' in *Restoraive Justice and Responsive Regulation* (Oxford University Press, Oxford), p. 30.

[132] Ayres and Braithwaite using an 'escalation' pyramid to illustrate this with the apex being the most punitive and the base comprising persuasion—See Ayres and Braithwaite (1992), Fig. 2.1, p. 35.

[133] Baldwin et al. (2011), p. 259.

as representing a state of deregulation. Ogus calls it "a base of benign advice", implying that any advice given has to be seriously considered by the regulated.[134] The regulator therefore has some latitude between the base and the apex to secure compliance.[135] The presence of the "benign big gun" aids this compliance.[136] Quintyn and Taylor argue that the regulator's power "is much more persuasive if they can threaten to remove the licence".[137] One would add that threats on their own may not amount to much unless they are backed by potential enforcement by the regulator.

Mascini and Van Wijk summarise responsive regulation as "the assumption that enforcers should not shift to coercing before it has become clear that persuading does not work".[138] Responsive regulation requires "broad political participation and institutional redesigns that ensure adequate representation of various interests in the core organisations of society".[139] Witteveen says "responsiveness is an institutional virtue: it requires an adequate and purposive institutional reaction to the problems and challenges it is facing".[140] He adds that, "responsive regulation is more problem centred than rule centred, more persuasive than coercive".[141] Cooperation is therefore the essence of a responsive legal order.[142] So in essence, the regulatory framework is one that is based on cooperation by all actors. Any rules that are made reflect the needs of the industry and the society. However, should any of the actors fail to play by the rules; the regulator retains the power to enforce those rules.[143] Witteveen argues that the "willingness to consider new solutions to recurring problems" is a key distinguishing feature of responsive regulation.[144]

[134] Ogus (2009), p. 339.

[135] Ibid.

[136] Ayres and Braithwaite (1992), p. 19.

[137] Quintyn and Taylor (2002), p. 19.

[138] Mascini and Wijk (2009), p. 27.

[139] Teubner (1983), p. 269 referring to Selznick and Nonet (1978), p. 95.

[140] Witteveen (2005), p. 8.

[141] Ibid.

[142] Ibid.

[143] Ibid.

[144] Ibid., p. 9.

Braithwaite insists that ideally all negotiations ought to start at the base of the pyramid but has acknowledged that there may be situations where there may be a need to start at another level.[145] He says the pyramid is a dynamic model made up of presumptions.[146] Therefore, this presumption can be overridden depending on the severity of the breach.[147] Black has criticised the general theory of responsive regulation as formulated by Ayres and Braithwaite and argues that it does not go far enough. Regulation must be responsive "in the sense of understanding how markets and market actors are operating, how regulators should respond to (or even anticipate) those operations, and recognising the effects that the regulators' own edicts and activities are having on their operation".[148] She calls for "developing a socially enriched way of seeing and knowing markets [as] central to the ability of market regulators, including financial regulators, to be able to regulate in a 'really responsive way'."[149] Black and Baldwin have called regulation that responds in this way, "really responsive regulation".[150] However, one may argue that Black and Baldwin are not really proposing a new theory or indeed disagreeing with Ayres and Braithwaite at all. In fact, what they refer to really responsive regulation may just be an extension of responsive regulation.

### 4.2.5 *Reflexive Regulation*

Reflexive regulation is a theory proposed by the German legal philosopher Gunther Teubner based on the legal theory of autopoiesis.[151] Maturana and Varela first developed autopoiesis as a biological

[145] Braithwaite (2002), p. 30.

[146] Ibid.

[147] Ibid.

[148] Black (2013), p. 2.

[149] Ibid.

Robert Baldwin and Julia Black (2008) 'Really Responsive Regulation' 71 (1) *The Modern Law Review* 59, p. 69, http://onlinelibrary.wiley.com/doi/10.1111/j.1468-2230.2008.00681.x/full. 18 November 2018.

[150] Baldwin and Black (2008).

[151] Teubner (1993).

theory.[152] Niklas Luhmann, another German philosopher, applied the theory to the law in his proposition of systems theory.[153] It needs to be stated however, that both systems theory and autopoiesis are complex theories and it is not the intention of this book to provide a comprehensive expose of these theories. It would seem that maybe to understand both Teubner and Luhmann, one needs to read Ralf Rogowski's book, *Reflexive Labour Law in the World Society*[154] and an article by Ana Lourenço 'Autopoietic Social Systems Theory: The Co-Evolution of Law and the Economy'.[155] Rogowski argues that at the centre of systems theory is the realisation that "society is a system of communication" which has undergone functional differentiation and is no longer segmented and stratified.[156]

It may be argued that even the systems or subsystems within society have undergone second order functional differentiation. For example, in law one can find functional subsystems such as contract law, administrative law, commercial law and other branches. There may be cases of further differentiation where the law intersects and interacts with other branches of knowledge to create subsystems like economic law, financial law, environmental law and others similar. Lourenço says Luhmann provides a paradigm shift in the way the legal system relates to other

[152] Francisco G Varela, Humberto R Maturana and Ricardo Uribe (1974) 'Autopoiesis: The Organization of Living Systems, Its Characterization and a Model' 5 (4) *Biosystems* 187, http://homepages.math.uic.edu/~kauffman/MUV.pdf. 19 May 2018.

Humberto R Maturana and Francisco J Varela (1980) *Autopoiesis and Cognition: The Realization of the Living* (Springer Netherlands, Dordrecht).

[153] Niklas Luhmann (1991) 'Operational Closure and Structural Coupling: The Differentiation of the Legal System' 13 *Cardozo Law Review* 1419, http://heinonline.org/hol-cgi-bin/get_pdf.cgi?handle=hein.journals/cdozo13&section=94. 19 May 2018.

Niklas Luhmann (1990) 'The Autopoiesis of Social Systems' in *Essays on Self-Reference* (Columbia University Press, New York).

Niklas Luhmann (2004) 'The Location of Legal Theory' in *Law as a Social System* (Oxford University Press, Oxford).

[154] Ralf Rogowski (2013) *Reflexive Labour Law in the World Society* (Edward Elgar Publishing, Cheltenham).

[155] Ana Lourenço (2010) 'Autopoietic Social Systems Theory: The Co-evolution of Law and the Economy' 35 *Australian Journal of Legal Philosophy* 35, http://heinonline.org/hol-cgi-bin/get_pdf.cgi?handle=hein.journals/ajlph35&section=6, p. 35. 19 May 2018.

[156] Rogowski (2013), p. 3.

societal systems.[157] In systems theory, law, economic, politics are all social systems and while relating to each other, they are in effect closed systems.[158] They are normatively closed but cognitively open to each other.[159] It means while each system may be influenced by its environment (cognitively open) only the system itself can trigger and institute any changes to the system (normatively closed).[160]

Baxter says a system is cognitively open if it has the possibility of observing its environment or the world beyond its boundaries, but this observation is conditioned by its own code or programming.[161] The effect of the environment on cognitively open systems is therefore indirect.[162] Black argues that a system is normatively closed when the only norms it recognises and understands to be valid are those norms which it itself has produced.[163] Simply put, the legal system, as a closed system, can only internally communicate in a language, which only it understands, and similarly the economic system can only communicate internally in a language that only the economic system understands. The law communicates in terms of the language of the law while economics engages in the language of prices.[164] Any form of intersystem communication is therefore noise and can only be received if it is coded, decoded, and recoded by the system using its own communication code.[165]

For a system to evolve, it needs to be cognitively open, otherwise it would forever be inward looking, using its own code as a point of reference. However, each system depends on its own self-referentiality, self-reproduction and recursivity to maintain its autopoietic nature.[166] This means the system looks upon itself (inward looking) as a point of

157 Lourenço (2010).

158 See generally Luhmann (1991).

159 Ibid.

160 Rogowski (2013), pp. 33–4.

161 Hugh Baxter (1998) 'Autopoiesis and the "Relative Autonomy" of Law' 19 *Cardozo Law Review* 1987, pp. 2009–10, http://heinonline.org/hol-cgi-bin/get_pdf.cgi?handle=hein.journals/cdozo19&section=76. 2 February 2018.

162 Black (1996), p. 44.

163 Ibid.

164 Teubner (1993), p. 102.
Luhmann (1991), p. 1435.

165 Lourenço (2010), p. 39.

166 Teubner (1993), p. 15.

reference (self-referential), and only reproduces based on itself (self-reproduction) and depends on indefinite reproduction (recursivity). This does not mean that systems do not influence or affect each other, as according to Teubner, changes in the system reflect "an internal dynamic, which, is affected by external stimuli and, in turn, influences the external environment".[167] Therefore, although an autopoietic system is a complete stand-alone system, this does not mean that it is immune from development. Interactions with other systems lead to its evolution or mutation, but any such changes are internally orchestrated, notwithstanding that they may be the result of external stimuli or intersystem friction (what Teubner refers to as perturbations). Lourenço argues that because of this, autopoietic theory is therefore also a theory of cognition.[168]

As already noted, and as others such as Black have rightly observed, the theory of autopoiesis is a complex one,[169] and therefore, this book does not intend to delve into it much further. The overview is however crucial in understanding reflexive regulation which is premised on this theory. Teubner posits that responsive law cannot achieve its aim unless it is reflexive.[170] Lourenço argues that "cognitive openness is a condition for the responsiveness of regulation" since the perturbations between systems allow systems to respond to these perturbations, but any such response is self-driven by the system.[171] According to Selznick and Nonet, the broad view of responsive law is that it is a "purposive, oriented undertaking" of the law to become part of society.[172] The closed nature and autonomy of systems mean that since their points of self-reference are internal, intervention by direct legislation is unlikely to succeed.[173] Black states that:

> [L]aw cannot simply require the economic system to act in the way the law demands. It has to regulate by observing and recognising the autopoiesis

[167] Teubner (1983), p. 249.

[168] Lourenço (2010), p. 37.

[169] Black (1996), p. 44.

[170] Teubner (1983).

[171] Lourenço (2010), p. 44.

[172] Selznick and Nonet (1978), pp. 78, 95.

[173] Teubner (1993), p. 77.

> of other systems; by assessing their process of self-production and self-reference and adapting its intervention accordingly.[174]

Reflexive regulation may be said to be Teubner's response to responsive regulation. It calls for inducing action not through commands but through decentralised mechanisms of self-regulation by the system that the law intends to regulate.[175] Teubner argues that although responsive law combines two elements, substantive and reflexive, only the latter can truly develop into a neo-evolutionary theory of law.[176] Rogowski says:

> [T]he legal system becomes consciously reflexive when it recognises that the societal domains which it purports to regulate, and to which it seeks to respond, are themselves independent autopoietic systems.[177]

Reflexive regulation calls for a change of regulatory focus; from supervising the outcome of regulatory processes to concentrating on putting place proper self-regulatory mechanisms.[178] It means the instruments and means used to regulate must be different. According to Teubner, the law must view "itself as a system-in-an-environment" and must "take account of the limits of its own capacity as it attempts to regulate the functions and performances of other social subsystems".[179] Teubner argues that:

> [L]aw must improve its knowledge of the processes, function, and structures within the field of regulation. It must develop scientifically grounded models of the surrounding systems, and tailor its norms accordingly.[180]

Recursivity is central to any self-referential system.[181] So for example, only economics can truly regulate economics since economics can only use economics as a point of reference. The problem arises from the fact

[174] Black (1996), p. 45.

[175] Lourenço (2010), p. 51.

[176] Teubner (1983), pp. 250–7

[177] Rogowski (2013), p. 33.

[178] Teubner (1983), p. 239

[179] Ibid., p. 280.

[180] Teubner (1993), p. 81.

[181] See Luhmann (2004), p. 78.

that the domain being regulated is not just an economic domain but also a social, political, cultural and legal one. According to Teubner, any control by the law of a social action must be "indirect and abstract" determining only the "organizational and procedural premises of future action".[182] Put another way, the law can influence change, but the influence must trigger an inward reflexive action in the other system that the law wishes to affect.[183] To facilitate internal change within any system, what is required are not authoritative prescriptions by the law but structural premises that can facilitate the internal restructuring of and within the system itself.[184] So in order have a "conceptual readiness" that takes advantage of societal emerging "opportunity structures",[185] Teubner's thesis is that responsive law needs to be reflexive.[186] In a way, reflexive law is not only Teubner's response to responsive law but is a deconstruction and reconstruction of a new theory from it, effectively his interpretation and development of responsive law.

## 4.3 Analysis of the Regulatory Approaches

If command and control and self-regulation are seen as extreme ends, then a regulatory continuum can be constructed to illustrate how the various theories discussed above fit. In command and control, the state retains all the regulatory power. It is actively engaged, through state agencies in supervising the regulated market. Historically, the problem with this approach seems to be an attempt to regulate through changing the norms without addressing contextual dynamics of the environment. Because of its form, this has traditionally been through legislation, without reaching into the contextual dynamic of the system being regulated. On the other hand, self-regulation seems to suffer from some level of ambiguity. As an ideology, self-regulation seems to have two meanings, depending on which side of the Atlantic one is standing on. In America,

[182] Teubner (1983), p. 255.

[183] To appreciate the complexity of regulation of systems see John Paterson and Gunther Teubner (1998) 'Changing Maps: Empirical Legal Autopoiesis' 7 (4) *Social & Legal Studies* 451, http://sls.sagepub.com/content/7/4/451.short. 2 February 2018.

[184] Teubner (1983), p. 255.

[185] It is structural coupling that leads law, politics, and the economy to co-evolve—Rogowski (2013), p. 34.

[186] Teubner (1983).

self-regulation is understood in the neoliberal context to imply that the state has no control.[187] It stands on the extreme opposite end of command and control. Once the necessary requirements for entry have been satisfied and the relevant body issues a licence, then regulatees are pretty much left to manage their own affairs. In most ways, it came to imply deregulation.[188] Full autonomy is therefore the hallmark of this ideology.

On the other hand, this seems not to be the understanding of self-regulation in Europe. The approach is much subtler. The objective of regulation seems to be the centrepiece in formulating theory based on self-regulation. What needs to be regulated and in whose interest become key regulatory issues. Teubner, Black, Braithwaite and others look at self-regulation as one giving the regulatees some level of autonomy but with the regulator retaining power to supervise. Self-regulation is therefore a way of allowing the industry to innovate without leaving it to its own devices. The theories of responsive and reflexive regulation neatly fall into this ideology.

On the regulatory continuum, reflexive regulation and responsive regulation would therefore, be elements of self-regulation. In reflexive regulation, there is constant engagement between the regulator and the regulatee that dispenses with the need to conceive the pyramid enforcement structure of responsive regulation.[189] The constant communication between the regulator and regulatee allows the setting up of the regulatory boundaries within which the regulatee can self-regulate. However, this does not imply that there is no engagement in responsive regulation. Indeed, as demonstrated by the pyramid enforcement structure proposed by Ayres and Braithwaite, most of the time is spent on persuasion.[190]

[187] George Monbiot (2016) 'Neoliberalism—The Ideology at the Root of All Our Problems' *The Guardian* (15 April 2016), https://www.theguardian.com/books/2016/apr/15/neoliberalism-ideology-problem-george-monbiot. 25 April 2018.

Alvaro J de Regil (2001) *Neoliberalism and Its Dogma: The Implications of Its Philosophical Postulates* (TLWNSI Issue Essay Series, Jus Semper Global Alliance), http://www.jussemper.org/Resources/Economic%20Data/The%20Neo-Capitalist%20Assault/Resources/NeoliberalismPostulates.pdf. 25 April 2018.

[188] John Braithwaite (2005) *Neoliberalism or Regulatory Capitalism* (Occasional Paper 5 Regulatory Institutions Network, Australian National University, Canberra), p. 3, https://www.anu.edu.au/fellows/jbraithwaite/_documents/Articles/Neoliberalism_Regulatory_2005.pdf. 25 April 2018.

[189] Ayres and Braithwaite (1992), p. 35.

[190] Ibid.

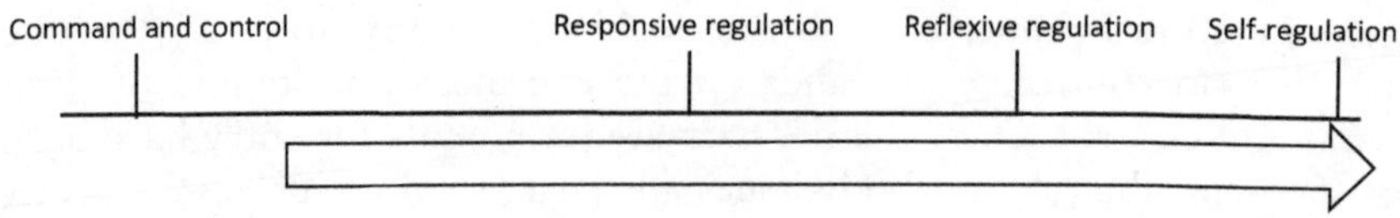


**Fig. 4.1** Regulatory continuum (*Source* Author)

If this fails, then there is escalation up the pyramid. This escalation is in itself a form of communication and sends a message not only to the organisation or firm targeted but also to the entire industry or sector. On the other hand, in reflexive regulation, there does not need to be escalation because the regulator is constantly engaged in self-regulation of its own rules while the regulatee is also engaged in self-regulation according to the regulatory boundaries set by the regulator. Both the regulator and the regulatee are therefore each engaged in self-regulation and each influences the other thereby diminishing the need for punitive intervention. Reflexive regulation therefore seems to be the higher level of responsive regulation.[191] The figure below illustrates the regulatory continuum. Throughout the continuum, the regulator may adopt the hard or light-touch approach or a variety of both. The regulatory framework is therefore always in a dynamic state (Fig. 4.1).

However, is the regulatory continuum the wrong way of analysing the regulatory framework? For a start, is there a real difference between responsive and reflexive regulation? Teubner himself acknowledges that reflexive regulation a form of responsive regulation, although typically as its champion, he refers to it as the superior form.[192] In responsive regulation, the pyramid structure is the central point.[193] This illustrates that while the regulatees are allowed room, the regulator retains the benign gun of enforcement.[194] At the centre of responsive regulation is the regulator's readiness to embrace change.[195] On the other hand, Teubner

[191] Teubner (1983), pp. 256–7.

[192] Ibid.

[193] Braithwaite (2002), p. 30.

[194] Ogus (2009), p. 339.

[195] Witteveen (2005), p. 9.

argues that once both the regulator and the regulatee are fully engaged in self-regulation, there is no need for the regulator to enforce regulation, as the regulatee is always aware of what has to be done. Ayres and Braithwaite require regulation to respond to the needs of the industry it is regulating to be effective. Although reflexive regulation draws its origins from systems theory and autopoietic theory of law, it is argued, that in effect, it has much more in common with responsive regulation. In fact, responsive regulation may be the dominant theory with reflexive regulation the theory that has evolved from it. However, both theories seem to concentrate on the regulator and the regulatee. Unfortunately, these are not the only stakeholders populating the regulatory arena. So, is there another theory that tries to address this shortfall?

Black and Baldwin seem to have further evolved the theory of responsive regulation to address these concerns. Black argues that regulation must not only respond to the dynamics of the regulator and regulatee but the entire market as a whole.[196] Anticipating how stakeholders will respond is key to this.[197] Black argues that for regulators to really respond there is need to develop mechanisms of analysing the market from all angles, including their social context.[198] If markets do this, this leads to really responsive regulation.[199] So really responsive regulation calls for a paradigm shift in the way the regulation framework is designed and formulated.

In the end it is submitted, there is not much difference between "responsiveness" and "reflexivity". What is important is who holds the balance of power in a regulatory balance, and this will ultimately decide which theory is dominant. If the regulator is too submissive to the regulatee, this shifts the balance towards the extreme end of self-regulation. If the centre of power resides in the regulator alone, then it shifts towards command and control. When the regulator starts to cede authority in response to market needs, then the shift is towards responsive and reflexive regulation. However, the level of involvement of the market players will determine whether the regulation is responsive or really responsive.

[196] Black (2013), p. 2.

[197] Ibid.

[198] Ibid.
Baldwin and Black (2008), p. 59.

[199] Ibid. Baldwin et al. (2011), p. 262.

The regulator must understand the day-to-day operations of the regulated environment otherwise; the power will shift to the regulatee. Regulation is not a two-way engagement between the regulator and regulatee, but must involve all market players and stakeholders. Therefore, regulation must respond to the needs of the market. It must understand the market and anticipate issues that may arise due to the regulatory framework being employed.[200] A regulatory that is anticipatory is much better placed to respond to issues that one that is reactionary. The regulatory task is to reach a higher level of responsiveness but that task will inherently be problematised by the fact that the regulators often fail to obtain a real understanding of the culture of the regulated.[201] This is partly an institutional problem because most regulators are state organs and act in the civil servant mode, which is at variance with the business approach of the regulatee. Apart from the service or goods providers, there is usually no involvement of other stakeholders and market players. One of the challenges therefore is the need of change to understand the culture of the regulated market. Real responsiveness requires a much finer and thorough understanding of the regulated environment.

It is submitted that really responsive regulation is the one that stands out for its ability not only to evolve and respond to the environment, but also to include in the regulatory process all stakeholders and market players. It is submitted that in really responsive regulation, the appropriate regulatory fit in the contemporary culture of the regulated environment is the main issue. The system is not static but is engaged in a process of continuous learning. The process means that new responses help to calibrate the system bit by bit. To achieve this, a crucial aspect is a reliable and robust information gathering, processing, disseminating and storage system. The regulator needs regular meetings with all the market players and stakeholders, which can act as reservoirs of information. The regulator can also broaden the information base, which the regulatees are required to provide. Where the system only provides for market players participation, the regulator needs to deliberately include all other stakeholders such as consumers and counterparties. The difference therefore is that with really responsive regulation, there is a shift in approach from macro norms to information norms. Santos may have captured the regulatory dilemma well when he said, "the solution lies neither in the

[200] Black (2013), p. 2.

[201] See Baldwin et al. (2011), p. 261.

**Fig. 4.2** Really responsive regulation approach (*Source* Author)

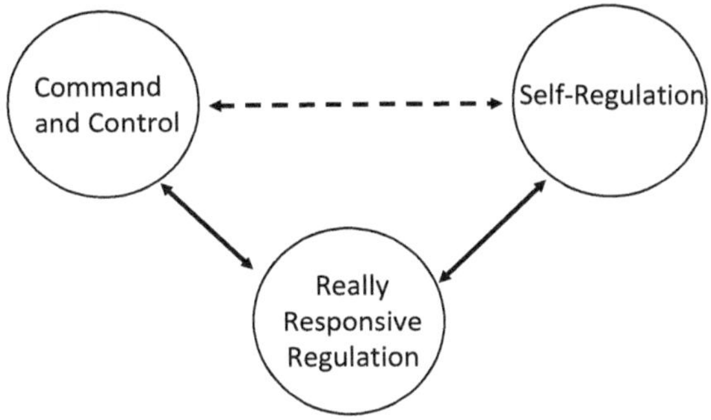


state nor in the market, but rather in a third type of organization form – collaborative networks involving firms and secondary associations".[202] Stakeholder collaboration is therefore, crucial (Fig. 4.2).

The figure above illustrates that really responsive regulation is the approach that best describes the proper balance that the regulation must aim to attain. As the figure shows, there are forces that will attempt to pull the framework towards the command and control or self-regulation. However, where the regulator adopts collaboration of all stakeholders within the framework, it is submitted that it will have a greater chance of withstanding these forces. In doing so, the regulator will also avoid dangers posed by industry capture. Collaboration is therefore one efficient way of minimising capture and decentralising regulatory power. Cunningham and Sinclair have referred to regulation that "embraces flexible, imaginative and innovative forms of control" as *smart* regulation.[203] Their conception is based on a revaluation of Braithwaite's pyramid enforcement mechanism. In effect therefore, smart regulation is what Black would term really responsive regulation.[204] It based on the notion of regulatory pluralism,[205] using a combination of various policy

[202] Boaventura De Sousa Santos (2005) 'Law, Politics, and the Subaltern in Counter-Hegemonic Globalization' in Boaventura De Sousa Santos and A. Rodriguez-Geravito César (eds) *Law and Globalization from Below* (Cambridge University Press, Cambridge), p. 7.

[203] Neil Gunningham and Darren Sinclair (2017) 'Smart Regulation' in Peter Drahos (ed) *Regulatory Theory: Foundations and Applications* (Australian National University Press, Canberra), p. 133.

[204] See Baldwin et al. (2011), p. 269.

[205] Gunningham and Sinclair (2017), p. 133.

instruments including command and control, self-regulation and voluntarism.[206] The smartness or really responsiveness lies in the fact that the regulation can combine several complimentary instruments to achieve the desired outcome. Baldwin et al. have observed that really responsive regulation is not without its problems as it makes "severe informational, analytical and resource demands" on the regulator.[207] However, this can be overcome if the regulator adopts a different mindset and adapts the approach to suit the economic and cultural environment in which they operate. It is therefore an approach, which is continuously learning.

## 4.4 Regulatory Space

Hancher and Moran coined the term *regulatory space* to describe the regulatory arena, which is populated by different players, including the regulator, regulatee, courts as well as consumer groups.[208] To Hancher and Moran, space matters because "regulation occurs … in particular places".[209] However, they argue that regulatory space is not a physical phenomenon but an analytical construct used to analyse a range of regulatory issues.[210] The issues that any particular regulatory space present will therefore define the type of regulatory framework that is developed. However, the issues that preoccupy the occupants of any regulatory space are not static and their dynamism leads to a continuous evolution of regulatory issues.[211] This also leads to a subsequent dilemma, what "is to be regulated, and by whom?"[212] This may require a regulator to evolve or the coming in of a new regulator. It may also require a reorganisation of the regulatory framework. Ogus says regulation is a process that involves a continuous "interaction, even a game, between the various actors, decisions being made by reference to the perceived costs

[206] Ibid., p. 140.

[207] Baldwin et al. (2011), p. 280.

[208] Generally, Hancher and Moran (1998).
Scott (2001), p. 330.
Morgan and Yeung (2007), pp. 59–60.

[209] Hancher and Moran (1998), p. 159.

[210] Ibid., p. 153.

[211] Ibid., p. 169.

[212] Ibid., p. 170.

and benefits of alternative strategies".[213] The concept of space inevitably lends itself to "occupation" and unequal power relations between participants.[214] Resultantly, there is a furious contest for advantage by the occupants.[215] According to Hancher and Moran, those organisations which have access to resources:

> [W]ill dominate regulatory space and the organisation that command the necessary resources at the historical moment when regulation is initiated has a good chance of exercising a continuing dominant influence.[216]

The regulator no longer monopolises regulatory authority in a regulatory space.[217] Understanding the dispersion or fragmentation of resources and the different power dynamics is key to understanding the concept of regulatory space.[218] Understanding the organisational dynamics and the relationships between organisations are central to understanding regulation.[219] In its simplest form, "regulation is by and through organisations".[220] How the regulator manages these relationships defines the regulatory framework. Because of the division of resources and power among participants, the relationship is largely horizontal as opposed to vertical.[221] The regulator that adopts a cooperative model is likely to succeed in overseeing a functioning framework.[222] It is submitted such collaborative model fits into the theory of really responsive regulation discussed above.

Viewed this way, Hancher and Moran argue that the idea of regulatory capture is synonymous with a view of a regulatory arena in which there is a dichotomy between the public regulatory authority and the regulated and that the two sides must remain apart.[223] Where you have

[213] Ogus (2009), p. 338.

[214] Hancher and Moran (1998), p. 153.

[215] Ibid.

[216] Ibid., pp. 159–60

[217] Scott (2001), p. 330.

[218] Ibid.

[219] Hancher and Moran (1998), p. 155.

[220] Ibid., p. 161.

[221] Ibid., p. 162.

[222] Ibid.

[223] Ibid., p. 150.

cooperation, the notion of capture does not arise. In fact, Scott argues that the fact that regulatory authority is dispersed makes capture of multiple institutions difficult.[224] Furthermore, Scott argues that once the concept of dispersed authority is accepted, then strict enforcement could never have been the intended method of regulating.[225]

## 4.5 Conclusion

This chapter has provided an overview of the different regulatory approaches being employed with a focus on the financial sector. Among the various theories and approaches, the chapter argues that the broad theory of responsive regulation is the one that envelopes most of them, but within this, the extension made by Julia Black and Robert Baldwin (really responsive regulation) makes the theory more flexible to the needs of the financial sector. Colin Scott calls the approach smart regulation. In a way, really responsive or smart regulation describes a framework that responds and regulates according to the needs of the market as a whole.

The chapter also looked at the concept of the regulatory space and argued that within this space, timing is very important. Those organisations and institutions that can seize the moment or already have influence within a would-be regulatory space will always be at an advantage. The concept of regulatory space therefore helps to identify the regulatory issues of concern. The main issue that arises from this chapter seems to be how law and regulation are defined. For example, law is increasingly seen as a mix of hard and soft law such that law as applied to regulation is not always command and control, but rather of autopoietic legal forms. Similarly, to suggest that the issue is purely between law and economics is succumbing to the law and economics ideology. Regulatory space is a complex space, which includes various types of institutions, including political, legal, social, cultural and economical, with different forms of power. Forms of regulation must be both responsive and reflexive considering these complexities in space, time and power. In the end, the question may therefore not being whether the regulator is susceptible to capture or not, but whether the regulatory framework is responsive enough.

[224] Scott (2001), p. 338.

[225] Ibid., p. 343.

## References


Alvaro J de Regil (2001) *Neoliberalism and Its Dogma: The Implications of Its Philosophical Postulates* (TLWNSI Issue Essay Series, Jus Semper Global Alliance), http://www.jussemper.org/Resources/Economic%20Data/The%20Neo-Capitalist%20Assault/Resources/NeoliberalismPostulates.pdf. 25 April 2018.

Ana Lourenço (2010) 'Autopoietic Social Systems Theory: The Co-evolution of Law and the Economy' 35 *Australian Journal of Legal Philosophy* 35, http://heinonline.org/hol-cgi-bin/get_pdf.cgi?handle=hein.journals/ajlph35&section=6. 19 May 2018.

Andrei Shleifer (2005) 'Understanding Regulation' 11 (4) *European Financial Management* 439, http://scholar.harvard.edu/files/shleifer/files/02_eufm00121.pdf?m=1360042225. 19 May 2018.

Andrew Hill and Joe Leahy (2009) 'FSA Bids Farewell to Light-Touch Financial Regulation' *Financial Times* (19 March 2009), http://www.ft.com/cms/s/0/da208b14-1426-11de-9e32-0000779fd2ac.html?ft_site=falcon&desktop=true#axzz4YBrB0BUq. 9 February 2018.

Anon (2012) 'Light Touch No More' *The Economist* (1 December 2012), http://www.economist.com/news/21567399-britains-financial-regulators-are-getting-much-tougher-light-touch-no-more. 9 February 2018.

Anthony I Ogus (1994) *Regulation: Legal Form and Economic Theory* vol 152 (Clarendon Press Oxford, Oxford).

Anthony I Ogus (1995) 'Rethinking Self-Regulation' 15 (1) *Oxford Journal of Legal Studies* 97, http://ojls.oxfordjournals.org/content/15/1/97.full.pdf. 19 May 2018.

Anthony I Ogus (2009) 'Regulation Revisited' (2) *Public Law*, http://repub.eur.nl/pub/16031/A.%20Ogus,%20Regulation%20Revisited.pdf. 19 May 2018.

Avinash Persaud (2015) 'Why Do We Regulate Finance?' in *Reinventing Financial Regulation* (Apress, New York).

Boaventura De Sousa Santos (2005) 'Law, Politics, and the Subaltern in Counter-Hegemonic Globalization' in Boaventura De Sousa Santos and A. Rodriguez-Geravito César (eds) *Law and Globalization from Below* (Cambridge University Press, Cambridge).

Boon-Chye Lee and Olujoke Longe-Akindemowo (1999) 'Regulatory Issues in Electronic Money: A Legal-Economics Analysis' 1 (1) *Netnomics* 53, http://link.springer.com/article/10.1023/A:1011445620486. 12 March 2018.

Bronwen Morgan and Karen Yeung (2007) *An Introduction to Law and Regulation* (Cambridge University Press, Cambridge).

Brooke Masters (2011) 'Regulator's "Light Touch" Led to Failure' *Financial Times* (12 December 2011), https://www.ft.com/content/2bf14c52-24ce-11e1-bfb3-00144feabdc0. 9 February 2018.

César Córdova-Novion and Deirdre Hanlon (2002) 'Regulatory Governance: Improving the Institutional Basis for Sectoral Regulators' 2 (3) *OECD Journal on Budgeting*, https://www.oecd.org/gov/budgeting/43505850.pdf. 15 February 2018.

Colin Scott (2001) 'Analysing Regulatory Space: Fragmented Resources and Institutional Design' *Public Law* 329, http://researchrepository.ucd.ie/bitstream/handle/10197/6785/AnalysingRegSpace.pdf?sequence=2. 1 December 2018.

David S Alberts and Richard E Hayes (2006) 'Reader Orientation' in *Understanding Command and Control* (CCRP Publishing, Washington, DC), Chapter 2.

Douglas W Diamond and Philip H Dybvig (1983) 'Bank Runs, Deposit Insurance, and Liquidity' 91 (3) *Journal of Political Economy* 401, http://www.journals.uchicago.edu/doi/pdfplus/10.1086/261155. 27 April 2018.

Financial Services Act (Malaŵi, 2010).

Financial Services Act (United Kingdom, 2012), http://www.legislation.gov.uk/ukpga/2012/21/pdfs/ukpga_20120021_en.pdf. 2 June 2018.

Francisco G Varela, Humberto R Maturana and Ricardo Uribe (1974) 'Autopoiesis: The Organization of Living Systems, Its Characterization and a Model' 5 (4) *Biosystems* 187, http://homepages.math.uic.edu/~kauffman/MUV.pdf. 19 May 2018.

George Monbiot (2016) 'Neoliberalism—The Ideology at the Root of All Our Problems' *The Guardian* (15 April 2016), https://www.theguardian.com/books/2016/apr/15/neoliberalism-ideology-problem-george-monbiot. 25 April 2018.

George J Stigler (1971) 'The Theory of Economic Regulation' *The Bell Journal of Economics and Management Science* 3, http://hsecon.tripod.com/stigler-regulation.pdf. 1 February 2018.

Gunther Teubner (1983) 'Substantive and Reflexive Elements in Modern Law' *Law and Society Review* 239, http://www.jstor.org/stable/3053348. 18 November 2018.

Gunther Teubner (1986) 'After Legal Instrumentalism? Strategic Models of Post-regulatory Law' in Gunther Teubner (ed) *Dilemmas of Law in the Welfare State* (Walter de Gruyter, New York).

Gunther Teubner (1993) *Law as an Autopoietic System* (Blackwell, Oxford/Cambridge).

Hector Sants (2009) 'Delivering Intensive Supervision and Credible Deterrence' (Financial Services Authority), http://www.fsa.gov.uk/pages/Library/Communication/Speeches/2009/0312_hs.shtml. 28 April 2018.

Herve Dumez and Alain Jeunemaitre (1997) 'Financial Regulation: From Economic Analysis to Practical Experience' in Alain Jeunemaitre (ed) *Financial Markets Regulation* (Macmillan, Basingstoke).

House of Commons Treasury Committee (2009) *Banking Crisis: Regulation and Supervision* (Parliament, London), https://www.publications.parliament.uk/pa/cm200809/cmselect/cmtreasy/767/767.pdf. 3 February 2018.

Hugh Baxter (1998) 'Autopoiesis and the "Relative Autonomy" of Law' 19 *Cardozo Law Review* 1987, http://heinonline.org/hol-cgi-bin/get_pdf.cgi?handle=hein.journals/cdozo19&section=76. 2 February 2018.

Humberto R Maturana and Francisco J Varela (1980) *Autopoiesis and Cognition: The Realization of the Living* (Springer Netherlands, Dordrecht).

Ian Ayres I and John Braithwaite (1992) Responsive Regulation: Transcending the Deregulation Debate (Oxford University Press, Oxford).

John Austin (1832) *The Province of Jurisprudence Determined* (John Murray, London).

John Braithwaite (2002) 'Responsive Regulation' in *Restorative Justice and Responsive Regulation* (Oxford University Press, Oxford).

John Braithwaite (2005) *Neoliberalism or Regulatory Capitalism* (Occasional Paper 5 Regulatory Institutions Network, Australian National University, Canberra), https://www.anu.edu.au/fellows/jbraithwaite/_documents/Articles/Neoliberalism_Regulatory_2005.pdf. 25 April 2018.

John Paterson and Gunther Teubner (1998) 'Changing Maps: Empirical Legal Autopoiesis' 7 (4) *Social & Legal Studies* 451, http://sls.sagepub.com/content/7/4/451.short. 2 February 2018.

Joanna Gray (2009) 'Is It Time to Highlight the Limits of Risk-Based Financial Regulation?' 4 (1) *Capital Markets Law Journal* 50, https://doi.org/10.1093/cmlj/kmn035. 28 April 2018.

Julia Black (1996) 'Constitutionalising Self-Regulation' 59 (1) *The Modern Law Review* 24, http://onlinelibrary.wiley.com/doi/10.1111/j.1468-2230.1996.tb02064.x/full. 19 May 2018.

Julia Black (2005) 'The Emergence of Risk-Based Regulation and the New Public Risk Management in the United Kingdom' *Public Law* 510, https://www.academia.edu/1295947/The_emergence_of_risk-based_regulation_and_the_new_public_risk_management_in_the_United_Kingdom?auto=download. 28 April 2018.

Julia Black (2007) 'Principles Based Regulation: Risks, Challenges and Opportunities' (Principles Based Regulation, University of Sydney, Sydney), http://eprints.lse.ac.uk/62814/. 28 April 2018.

Julia Black (2008) *Forms and Paradoxes of Principles Based Regulation* (LSE Law, Society and Economy Working Papers, London School of Economics and Political Science, London), http://eprints.lse.ac.uk/23103/1/WPS2008-13.pdf. 28 April 2018.

Julia Black (2010) *The Rise, Fall and Fate of Principles Based Regulation* (LSE Law, Society and Economy Working Papers, London School of Economics and Political Science), http://eprints.lse.ac.uk/32892/1/WPS2010-17_Black.pdf. 27 April 2018.

Julia Black (2013) *Seeing, Knowing, and Regulating Financial Markets: Moving the Cognitive Framework from the Economic to the Social* (LSE Law, Society and Economy Working Papers 24/2013), www.lse.ac.uk/collections/law/wps/WPS2013-24_Black.pdf. 19 May 2018.

Kenneth Kaoma Mwenda (2006) *Legal Aspects of financial Services Regulation and the Concept of a Unified Regulator* (World Bank, Washington, DC).

Leigh Hancher and Michael Moran (1998) 'Organizing Regulatory Space' in Robert Baldwin, Colin Scott and Christopher Hood (eds) *A Reader in Regulation* (Oxford University Press, Oxford).

Lucia Quaglia (2010) 'Completing the Single Market in Financial Services: The Politics of Competing Advocacy Coalitions' 17 (7) *Journal of European Public Policy* 1007, http://aei.pitt.edu/33124/1/quaglia._lucia_(2).pdf. 17 October 2018.

Marc Quintyn and Michael W Taylor (2002) *Regulatory and Supervisory Independence and Financial Stability* (International Monetary Fund, Washington, DC), https://www.imf.org/external/pubs/ft/wp/2002/wp0246.pdf. 1 February 2018.

Neil Gunningham and Darren Sinclair (2017) 'Smart Regulation' in Peter Drahos (ed) *Regulatory Theory: Foundations and Applications* (Australian National University Press, Canberra).

Niklas Luhmann (1990) 'The Autopoiesis of Social Systems' in *Essays on Self-Reference* (Columbia University Press, New York).

Niklas Luhmann (1991) 'Operational Closure and Structural Coupling: The Differentiation of the Legal System' 13 *Cardozo Law Review* 1419, http://heinonline.org/hol-cgi-bin/get_pdf.cgi?handle=hein.journals/cdozo13&section=94. 19 May 2018.

Niklas Luhmann (2004) 'The Location of Legal Theory' in *Law as a Social System* (Oxford University Press, Oxford).

Peter Mascini and Eelco Van Wijk (2009) 'Responsive Regulation at the Dutch Food and Consumer Product Safety Authority: An Empirical Assessment of Assumptions Underlying the Theory' 3 (1) *Regulation & Governance* 27, http://citeseerx.ist.psu.edu/viewdoc/download?doi=10.1.1.1001.348&rep=rep1&type=pdf. 19 May 2018.

Philip Selznick and Philippe Nonet (1978) *Law and Society in Transition: Toward Responsive Law* (Harper and Row, New York).

Pierre Fleuriof (1997) 'Financial Regulation as the Safeguard of Balances in a Global Context' in Alain Jeunemaitre (ed) *Financial Markets Regulation* (Macmillan, Basingstoke).

Ralf Rogowski (2013) *Reflexive Labour Law in the World Society* (Edward Elgar Publishing, Cheltenham).

Richard Heeks (2012) 'Why M-Pesa Outperforms Other Developing Country Mobile Money Schemes' *ICTs for Development*, http://ict4dblog.wordpress.com/2012/11/24/why-m-pesa-outperforms-other-developing-country-mobilelectronicmoney-schemes/. 8 May 2018.

Richard A Posner (1974) 'Theories of Economic Regulation' 5 (2) *Bell Journal of Economics and Management Science* 335, http://www.thecre.com/oira/wp-content/uploads/2016/03/Posner.pdf. 1 February 2018.

Robert Baldwin and Julia Black (2008) 'Really Responsive Regulation' 71 (1) *The Modern Law Review* 59, http://onlinelibrary.wiley.com/doi/10.1111/j.1468-2230.2008.00681.x/full. 18 November 2018.

Robert Baldwin, Martin Cave and Martin Lodge (2011) *Understanding Regulation: Theory, Strategy, and Practice* (2nd edn, Oxford University Press, Oxford).

Roger Alford (2010) *Some Help in Understanding Britain's Banking Crisis, 2007–09* (LSE Financial Markets Group Paper Series, London School of Economics, London), http://www.lse.ac.uk/fmg/workingPapers/specialPapers/PDF/SP193.pdf. 9 February 2018.

Roman Tomasic (2010) 'Beyond "Light Touch" Regulation of British Banks After the Financial Crisis' in MacNeil IG and O'Brien J (eds), The Future of Financial Regulation (Hart Publishing, Portland).

Sam Peltzman (1976) 'Toward a More General Theory of Regulation' 19 (2) *The Journal of Law and Economics* 211, http://www.journals.uchicago.edu/doi/pdfplus/10.1086/466865. 1 February 2018.

Tom de Swaan and Others (1995) *The Supervision of Financial Conglomerates* (Tripartite Group of Bank, Securities and Insurance Regulators, Madrid), https://www.iosco.org/library/pubdocs/pdf/IOSCOPD47.pdf. 3 October 2018.

Willem J Witteveen (2005) 'A Self-Regulation Paradox: Notes Towards the Social Logic of Regulation' 9 (1) *Electronic Journal of Comparative Law*, http://www.ejcl.org/91/art91-2.PDF. 19 May 2018.

CHAPTER 5

# Regulating Money

## 5.1 Introduction

Although historically, there have been non-sovereign forms of money, sovereigns and countries now monopolise the power to issue money and control its circulation.[1] The more important factor has always been the authority behind the issue, manifesting itself in proof of value. As discussed in Chapter 1, after the demise of the gold standard, the public has trust in the value of the currency because it has trust in the sovereign issuing it. Currency issuance has now been delegated to central banks as state agents. This sovereign power is however limited to the jurisdiction in which the sovereign exercises legal and political control. This allows state regulation of money issued within each jurisdiction. The Permanent Court of International Justice made the principle that a state has monetary sovereignty sacrosanct in international law in 1929 in the *Serbian Loans Case* when it said: "it is indeed a generally accepted principle that a state is entitled to regulate its own currency".[2]

[1] Friedrich August v Hayek (1990) *Denationalisation of Money—The Argument Refined: An Analysis of the Theory and Practice of Concurrent Currencies (3rd Ed)* (Institute of Economic Affairs, London) Chapter III.

[2] *Case Concerning the Payment of Various Serbian Loans Issued in France (France v. Serbia) and Payment in Gold of the Brazilian Federal Loans Contracted in France (France v. Brazil)* PCIJ Rep Series A Nos 20–21 Permanent Court of international Justice, http://legal.un.org/PCIJsummaries/documents/english/PCIJ_FinalText.pdf. 7 November 2018.



S. Madise, *The Regulation of Mobile Money*, Palgrave Macmillan Studies in Banking and Financial Institutions,
https://doi.org/10.1007/978-3-030-13831-8_5

Part of this sovereign power includes the power to withdraw money from circulation and issue new money. In modern times, the monetary policy of most central banks includes mopping up excess liquidity to control money circulation and to check inflation. It is the power to regulate the supply of money that creates value. Value therefore is directly related to quantity and timing of supply of money.[3] The sovereign power, however, works on the presumption of pre-existing trust. The subjects or citizens have to trust that the sovereign will guarantee the value and stability of the money. Trust and confidence are intrinsically linked to the stability of value.

The case of Zimbabwe demonstrates a scenario where loss of trust can be costly. First, the national currency, the Zimbabwe Dollar was debased and eventually abandoned and replaced by the US Dollar.[4] Due to a shortage of US Dollars, Zimbabwe has started printing bond notes, effectively introducing a new currency despite the central bank's insistence that this did not mean a return to the Zimbabwean Dollar.[5] Since the bond notes are issued at par value to the US Dollar, the challenge faced by the business community is one of trust.[6] Why would anyone want to exchange their US Dollar with a bond at par value when it is clear that the US Dollar as a global currency is easily negotiable in most countries. The fear was that "if they are difficult to get rid of and you can't spend them in shops", people may then not accept them.[7] On a brief visit to Zimbabwe in September 2018, I had the pleasure of meeting the full blunt of this quagmire. When I took my Visa Card shopping, the overpriced goods were charged at US Dollar value. However, when I had become wiser and obtained some bond notes, at a premium (typically 1 US Dollar = 1.4 bond note), I was able to use the bond notes to procure goods and services at the very same price marked as US Dollars but which is pegged at the US Dollar equivalent. What this evidences is

[3] Jevons (1875), p. 9.

[4] Joseph Noko (2011) 'Dollarization: The Case of Zimbabwe' 31 (2) *Cato Journal* 339, https://www.ciaonet.org/attachments/18686/uploads. 14 September 2018.

[5] Andrew England (2016) 'Zimbabwe to Print "Bond Notes" to Tackle Cash Shortage' *Financial Times* (5 May 2016), http://www.ft.com/cms/s/0/90a66462-12da-11e6-91da-096d89bd2173.html#axzz4AKE4BM9k. 1 June 2018.

[6] Ibid.

[7] Ibid.

that despite any assurance by the state that the bond note is at par with the US Dollar, the citizens of Zimbabwe know better.

Therefore, the imprimatur of the state underlines the issue of authentication and social acceptance. It is submitted both are important, but fundamentally, it is social acceptance, which may allow the operation of non-state money. An example of a currency based on social acceptance and trust is the Bristol Pound.[8] The Bristol Pound is not issued by the Bank of England (or Bank of Bristol) but still operates within the city of Bristol. It has attained social acceptance. The Bristol Pound can be traded electronically within Bristol as a private currency.[9]

### 5.1.1 *Regulating the Financial Sector*

Governments regulate the financial sector for two main reasons: consumer protection and to maintain financial integrity and stability, clear public goods that justify a more elaborate framework of regulation and supervision.[10] Singh describes financial stability as "a catch-all phrase referring to a whole host of factors, both positive and negative, that have an impact on the efficiency with which an economy or financial system performs".[11] This is achieved "through cooperation between the central bank, other safety-net players and financial regulators".[12] The ability to accurately assess financial risk by the central bank is a precondition for financial stability as well as integrity.[13] Prevention of fraud and ensuring that the markets are not tainted or associated with proceeds of crime is crucial in maintaining financial integrity.[14] Quintyn and Taylor have

[8] Mona Naqvi and James Southgate (2013) 'Banknotes, Local Currencies and Central Bank Objectives' *Bank of England Quarterly Bulletin* Q4 322, http://www.bankofengland.co.uk/publications/Documents/quarterlybulletin/2013/qb130403.pdf. 4 October 2018.

Ruby Szarowicz (2016) 'Bringing Bristol Pound to Massive Attack at the Downs' *Bristol Pond Our City Our Money* (Bristol, 6 September 2016), http://bristolpound.org/blog/. 13 September 2016.

[9] Anon (2016) 'What Is the Bristol Pound?' (*Bristol City*), http://bristolpound.org/what. 13 September 2018.

[10] Quintyn and Taylor (2002), p. 8.

[11] Dalvinder Singh (2007) *Banking Regulation of UK and US Financial Markets* (Ashgate Publishing, Aldershot, Hampshire), p. 2.

[12] Ibid., p. 3.

[13] Ibid.

[14] Ibid., p. 22.

summarised the objectives of regulation as, avoiding monopolies, promoting financial stability and consumer protection.[15] They argue that unlike other sectors, financial regulation requires a more elaborate framework because of the central role that the sector plays in the economy.[16]

Although at times used interchangeably, the terms regulation and supervision mean different things despite the fact that for most countries, their functions are subsumed into one agency.[17] Supervision has to do with promoting and ensuring safety and soundness of institutions.[18] According to Burton and Brown, the supervisor's role is a "continuous oversight to ensure that [financial institutions] are operated prudently and in accordance with statutes and regulations".[19] This supervision may be in situ or ex situ.[20] In situ entails sending supervisors to examine and assess the condition of institutions and ascertain if they comply with laid down regulations.[21] On the other hand, regulators are tasked with preparing and issuing regulations and promoting a culture of compliance.[22] Burton and Brown say regulation aims at establishing "a framework for … behaviour that fosters the maintenance of a safe and sound [financial] system and the fair and efficient delivery of services to … customers".[23] One may look at regulation as an effort to restrict some activity which would occur but for the regulation.[24] In summary, regulation: defines permissible activities; determines reserves that financial institutions must hold in relation to any deposits and ensures fair treatment of consumers of financial products and services.[25]

[15] Quintyn and Taylor (2002), p. 8.

[16] Ibid., p. 8.

[17] As in the UK, or Malaŵi (Part II of the Financial Services Act, Malaŵi says the Registrar is to Regulate and Supervise Financial Institutions)—see also Mwenda (2006), p. 5.

[18] Maureen Burton and Bruce Brown (2014) *The Financial System and the Economy: Principles of Money and Banking* (Routledge, Abingdon, Oxon), p. 52.

[19] Ibid.

[20] Mwenda (2006), p. 5.

[21] Burton and Brown (2014), p. 52.

[22] Mwenda (2006), p. 5.

[23] Burton and Brown (2014), p. 52.

[24] Ibid.

[25] Ibid.

The regulation of financial market players is now a priority, especially post the 2007 financial crisis. There have been varied arguments along the years on which type of regulatory system is ideal for the financial system. The trend, at least in most developed economies, has been to have independent financial regulators. This is because the financial system today encompasses all market players such as those involved with banking: insurance, securities, lending and pension. Most jurisdictions have moved to, or moved between regulatory models based on twin peaks, multiple peaks or single peak model.[26] Up to 2012, the UK's Financial Services Authority was the most notable single peak model.[27] The Financial Services Act 2012 replaced the Financial Services Authority with the Financial Conduct Authority and Prudential Regulation Authority.[28] The Act also established the Financial Policy Committee.[29] The Financial Policy Committee is a committee of the Bank of England and has not been given direct regulatory powers. It is however responsible for "macro issues affecting economic and financial stability and for responding to any threats which it identifies".[30] Since the Financial Policy Committee has not been given regulatory powers, the UK has moved from a single peak to a twin peaks system of financial service regulation; separating prudential and conduct regulation.[31] This would make the UK in line with other jurisdictions like the Netherlands, South Africa and Australia.[32]

[26] Eddy Wymeersch (2007) 'The Structure of Financial Supervision in Europe: About Single Financial Supervisors, Twin Peaks and Multiple Financial Supervisors' 8 *European Business Organization Law Review* 237.

[27] Clive Briault (1999) *The Rationale for a Single National Financial Services Regulator* (Occasional Paper Series, Financial Services Authority, London), http://citeseerx.ist.psu.edu/viewdoc/download?doi=10.1.1.468.6859&rep=rep1&type=pdf. 12 May 2018.

[28] David Blair (2013) 'The FSA Is Dead; Long Live the FCA, the PRA and the FPC', http://www.osborneclarke.com/connected-insights/publications/the-fsa-is-dead-long-live-the-fca-the-pra-and-the-fpc/#sthash.PzXxYUIX.dpuf. 3 March 2018.

[29] Section 9B, Financial Services Act, UK (United Kingdom: Chapter 21, 2012).

[30] Blair (2013).

[31] Jane Fuller (2010) 'The King Is Dead; Long Live the King' *Financial World*, http://fwarchive.ifslearning.ac.uk/financial_world/Archive/2010/2010_07July/Comment/Jane%20Fuller/pdf/18908.pdf. 28 February 2018.

[32] Bryane Michael (2014) 'The "Twin Peaks" Regulatory Model: The Future of Financial Regulation?' *Banking Today* 3, http://www.law.hku.hk/aiifl/wp-content/uploads/2014/09/Twin-Peaks.pdf. 3 October 2018.

Taylor in his seminal work laid the foundation for the adoption of a twin peaks system in the UK.[33] He later argued that the USA ought to consider adopting the twin peaks model as "prudential and conduct of business regulation don't mix".[34] However, the current existing US model has been described as a sector-based model which is also found in China and Hong Kong.[35] The twin peaks, single peak and sector model are regarded as the main regulatory models and most jurisdictions gravitate around them.[36] It must be pointed out however, that despite its name, the twin peaks model adopted in the UK is not Taylor's blueprint. While Taylor advocated for distinct peaks, there is a much closer collaboration between the Prudential Regulation Authority and Financial Conduct Authority.

Burton and Brown say, in most countries, states regulate the financial system because it "is vital to a healthy economy".[37] States regulate the financial sector for two basic reasons: consumer protection and to maintain financial stability.[38] The former is achieved by providing a framework of rules that can help prevent excess and failures of a market left entirely to its own whims and devices and the latter is seen as a clear public good that justifies a more elaborate framework of regulation and supervision.[39] Singh argues that financial stability is a key rationale for regulation.[40]

[33]Robin Hui Huang and Dirk Schoenmaker (2014) *Institutional Structure of Financial Regulation: Theories and International Experiences* (Routledge, London), p. 2 describe Taylor as the father of the twin peaks model.

Taylor however admits that the model was first mooted by Andrew Hilton (1994) *UK Financial Supervsion: A Blueprint for Change* (Centre for the Study of Financial Innovation, London)—Michael W Taylor (1995) *"Twin Peaks": A Regulatory Structure for the New Century* (Centre for the Study of Financial Innovation, London).

[34]Taylor (2011), p. 89.

[35]Huang and Schoenmaker (2014), p. 1.

[36]Ibid., pp. 1–2.

Taylor (1995), Wymeersch (2007), Jeroen Kremers and Dirk Schoenmaker (2010) 'Twin Peaks: Experiences in the Netherlands' December 2010 *LSE Financial Markets Group Paper Series*, http://www.lse.ac.uk/fmg/workingPapers/specialPapers/PDF/SP196.pdf. 4 October 2018. Taylor (2011), Michael (2014).

[37]Burton and Brown (2014), p. 5.

[38]Quintyn and Taylor (2002).

[39]Ibid.

[40]Singh (2007), p. 1.

Taylor has argued that financial stability and consumer protection lead to prudential supervision and conduct of business regulation.[41] This is the basis on which the traditional twin peaks model of regulation is based.[42] He further argues that in complex financial products, self-regulation may not work because it assumes that "participants to a transaction possess appropriately equal knowledge, information and bargaining" which is not the case.[43] Regulation can address this information imbalance in favour of the unsophisticated consumer. Kremers and Schoenmaker have expanded the two objectives into five: "monetary stability; financial stability (macro-prudential); soundness of financial institutions (micro-prudential); orderly and well-functioning markets and fair treatment of consumers (conduct of business); and competition policy".[44]

In effect, however, it seems that the first 3 objectives listed by Kremers and Schoenmaker fall under what Taylor refers to as systemic protection or prudential regulation and the last two would be in the ambit of conduct of business regulation.[45] It is however submitted that regardless of the model adopted, any regulatory framework must put in place at least the following:

a. Authorisation of their operation;
b. Rules of operation;
c. Supervision and compliance processes;
d. Rules or principles of conduct of financial services business;
e. Investigation of breaches;
f. Cooperation and exchange of information with other regulators.[46]

As was discussed in Chapter 2, Goodhart says at the time of their creation, "there was … little, or no, consideration, or attention, given to the possibility of [central] banks playing a supervisory role in relation to other banks".[47] However, when central banks assumed the role of

[41] Taylor (1995), p. 3.

[42] Ibid.

[43] Ibid., p. 8.

[44] Kremers and Schoenmaker (2010), p. 2.

[45] Taylor (1995), p. 3.

[46] Mwenda (2006), p. 7.

[47] Goodhart (1988), p. 4.

lender of last resort, they had to exercise prudence, which meant evaluating the soundness of their counterparties.[48] This served a dual purpose. It ensured that central banks only lent out to counterparts that had the capacity to repay and it provided confidence in the financial system that all the market players were financially sound.[49] Even without a formal supervisory mandate, Padoa-Schioppa says this placed the "central bank in a natural position to address financial stability concerns".[50]

According to Padoa-Schioppa, being a lender of last resort through which the central bank provides "final liquidity remains a most powerful rationale for the role of central banks in promoting and providing for financial stability".[51] Taylor has argued that the roles of lender of last resort are in fact two, giving rise to different regulatory concerns. He says, the first is a direct result of Bagehot's theory of the central bank "as a provider of general liquidity to the market".[52] The second relates to the central bank providing liquidity to financial institutions in distress.[53] Padoa-Schioppa argues, "the role of the central banks in financial stability is part of their genetic code … as an inseparable component of their role as the banker's banks and of their monopoly on ultimate liquidity".[54] This raises an interesting issue of whether the role of the central bank is principally an economical one or as an agent of the state? It is submitted that with the modern central bank the roles have become subsumed and are virtually identical and any distinction is largely superficial.

However, the restriction of who could issue money and how is arguably one of the earlier efforts to start regulating money and the financial services. Fear of contagion within the financial system has been a key driving force behind the involvement of central banks in regulating the sector. The G-10 defines systemic financial risk as:

> The risk that an event will trigger a loss of economic value or confidence in, and attendant increases in uncertainty about, a substantial portion of

[48] Padoa-Schioppa (2003), p. 273.

[49] Ibid.

[50] Ibid.

[51] Ibid., p. 274.

[52] Taylor (1995), p. 14.

[53] Ibid.

[54] Padoa-Schioppa (2003), p. 274.

the financial system that is serious enough to quite probably have significant adverse effects on the real economy.[55]

Contagion may also arise when the market perceives risk, also referred to as psychological contagion.[56] This may arise despite ring fencing or firewalls created as long as the perceived risk relates to subsidiary or counterparty.[57] This is common with conglomerates or interlinked businesses.[58] Therefore, financial stability is not so much about avoiding financial crises but rather also about managing systemic financial risk.[59] Schinasi suggests that managing the following functions is key in avoiding systemic financial crises:

a. Market participants through their private risk management (first line of defence)
b. The authorities through banking supervision
c. Market surveillance
d. Systemic risk management.[60]

In most countries, the central bank is charged with prudential regulation.[61] However, there are always debates for and against the separation of the central bank from this role on the argument that "conflicts of

[55] G-10 (2001) *Chapter III: Effects of Consolidation on Financial Risk in Report on Consolidation in the Financial Sector* (Group of 10, IMF, Washington, DC), p. 126, https://www.imf.org/external/np/g10/2001/01/Eng/pdf/file3.pdf. 1 June 2018.

[56] Tom de Swaan and Others (1995) *The Supervision of Financial Conglomerates* (Tripartite Group of Bank, Securities and Insurance Regulators, Mardrid), p. 18, https://www.iosco.org/library/pubdocs/pdf/IOSCOPD47.pdf. 3 October 2018.

[57] Taylor (1995), p. 5.

[58] Ibid.

[59] Garry J Schinasi (2003) *Responsibility of Central Banks for Stability in Financial Markets* (IMF Working Paper, Washington, DC), p. 4, https://www.imf.org/external/pubs/ft/wp/2003/wp03121.pdf. 1 June 2018.

[60] Ibid., p. 4.

[61] ECB (2002) *The Role of Central Banks in Prudential Supervision* (European Central Bank), p. 1, https://www.ecb.europa.eu/pub/pdf/other/prudentialsupcbrole_en.pdf. 1 May 2018.

'Prudential Regulation Authority' (2017) *Bank of England*, http://www.bankofengland.co.uk/pra/Pages/default.aspx. 1 May 2018.

Section 10, Financial Services Act (Malaŵi, 2010).

Daniel K Tarullo (2016) 'Financial Regulation Since the Crisis' (*Federal Reserve Bank of Cleveland and Office of Financial Research 2016 Financial Stability Conference*)

interest may arise when combining the two responsibilities of monitory policy and supervision".[62] Goodhart and Schoenmaker observed a trend indicating the separation between monetary policy and supervision, whereby the central bank was left to concentrate on monetary policy and independent regulators were tasked with regulation and supervision.[63] Padoa-Schioppa says, this may have been necessitated by a fear of "excessive concentration of power in a central bank endowed with a highly independent status".[64] Even with prudential regulation, there seems to be a separation of functionalities with the central bank in charge of the macro and the micro being overseen by supervisory agents.[65] Padoa-Schioppa has cautioned against the "danger of a hard separation" between micro and macro as it may lead "to a situation in which neither central banks nor supervisory agencies would be able to perform their functions satisfactorily".[66] Goodhart agrees that there are no "advantages

Washington, DC. 2 December 2016, https://www.federalreserve.gov/newsevents/speech/tarullo20161202a.htm. 1 May 2018.

Rose Cunningham and Christian Friedrich (2016) *The Role of Central Banks in Promoting Financial Stability: An International Perspective* (Bank of Canada Staff Discussion Paper 2016–15, Bank of Canada, Ottawa, Ontario), p. 4, http://www.bankofcanada.ca/wp-content/uploads/2016/07/sdp2016-15.pdf. 1 May 2018.

Chris Hunt (2016) *A Short History of Prudential Regulation and Supervision at the Reserve Bank* (Bulletin, Reserve Bank of New Zealand, Wellington), http://www.rbnz.govt.nz/-/media/ReserveBank/Files/Publications/Bulletins/2016/2016aug79-14.pdf. 1 May 2018.

[62] Padoa-Schioppa (2003), p. 277.

[63] Charles Goodhart and Dirk Schoenmaker (1995) 'Should the Functions of Monetary Policy and Banking Supervision Be Separated?' 47 (4) *Oxford Economic Papers* 539, p. 539, http://oep.oxfordjournals.org/content/47/4/539.extract. 12 February 2018.

[64] Padoa-Schioppa (2003), p. 277.

[65] Ibid., p. 294. A discussion of "macro" and "micro" prudential regulation is outside the scope of this work but the reader may wish to consult:

'Macro-Prudential and Micro-Prudential Regulation' (Chapter 2) The Warwick Commission (2009) in *The Warwick Commission on International Financial Reform: In Praise of Unlevel Playing Fields* (University of Warwick), https://www2.warwick.ac.uk/research/warwickcommission/financialreform/report/uw_warcomm_intfinreform_09.pdf. 2 June 2018.

[66] Padoa-Schioppa (2003), p. 294.

[to] be obtained from separating these functions, and hiving off certain micro supervisory and insurance functions to other official institutions (separate and distinct from the central bank)".[67]

While prudential regulation and supervision may have started out as unified undertaking, together with monetary policy and financial stability, under the early central banks, it is now increasingly becoming clear that there has been an unbundling of activities.[68] Even where the central bank may still be involved in prudential regulation, as is the case of the UK, this is done through an independent body and not the central bank itself. There is, therefore, a distinct division of functions even if all 3 functions are within the same agency. However, even where the central bank is not the lead financial regulator, its involvement is still paramount, especially post-financial crisis. Schinasi lists 3 key elements of resolving a financial crisis. First there must be a vibrant insolvency and bankruptcy legal framework and closeout procedures.[69] Secondly, there must exist strategies that allow insolvent institutions to exit the system; and lastly the availability of the central bank as lender of last resort.[70] Regardless of the regulatory framework or model adopted, there is a need for clarity between the roles and responsibilities of the various regulatory agencies.[71] Ideally, the regulatory framework needs to be embedded in positive law and the autonomy and independence of the agencies clearly spelt out.[72]

### 5.1.2 *The Regulatory Issues Involving the Financial Services*

Goodhart says the rationale for the evolution of the role of regulation involving money "is to assure stable and smoothly functioning financial and payment systems".[73] Since money is the oil that lubricates the financial and payment systems, then regulating money is key. The central

[67] Goodhart (1988), p. 10. Worth pointing out is Goodhart worked from 1968 to 1985 for the Bank of England.

[68] Padoa-Schioppa (2003), p. 286.

[69] Schinasi (2003), p. 11.

[70] Ibid.

[71] V Sundararajan and others (2005) *Financial Sector Assessment* (World Bank & International Monetary Fund, Washington, DC), p. 102.

[72] Ibid.

[73] Goodhart (1988), p. 6.

bank's role in regulation is not only because of its monopoly of currency issue, but also in arresting moral hazard.[74]

#### *5.1.2.1 Genuineness of Money and Stability Value*

Central bank money is legal tender in most countries. This typically comprises notes and coins. While the coins may have metallic value, the notes usually have no intrinsic value. The role of the central bank is, therefore, to determine what will serve as legal tender as well as set its value. The central bank must ensure that the only money circulating is that it has issued or authorised. An example of a currency that is legal currency but not legal tender is the Scottish Pound. Interestingly although widely accepted in Scotland, it is not even legal tender in Scotland.[75] Ostensibly, there is a direct correlation between genuine currency and value. The corollary is that influx of counterfeit money will dilute the value of money and destabilise the currency. The combined effect of designating a currency as legal tender as well as fixing its value in terms usually based on some other asset such as gold or indeed the currency of another is central to regulation and helps to stabilise its value.[76]

#### *5.1.2.2 Maintaining Financial Stability*

Financial institutions play a central role, which is different from other institutions. Goodhart puts it like this:

> [T]he failure of banks causes people to seek to hold their liquid assets in currency, thereby precipitating a general run on bank reserves. The failure of an engineering company, for example, though it may embarrass its creditors, is unlikely to have secondary, "contagion," effects of the same order as a bank failure could and did, at least until some form of insurance was thought to be in operation.[77]

In the ideal world, the supply of money is supposed to be fixed and controlled by the central bank. However, in practice, this is not the case.

[74] Ibid., p. 7.

[75] The Committee of Scottish Bankers (2016) 'Scottish Banknotes Legal Position' (*The Committee of Scottish Bankers*, Edinburgh), http://www.scotbanks.org.uk/legal_position.php. 13 September 2018.

[76] Goodhart (1988), p. 21.

[77] Ibid., pp. 61–2.

With commercial banks creating money based on deposits and derivative and other security instruments, it may mean that on occasions when financial institutions are in distress, they may face a liquidity risk. In the worst-case scenario, the central bank will pump in final liquidity as lender of last resort.[78] The central bank usually does this to avoid panic in the financial system as well as contagion. Panic in one bank, for example, can quickly spread. The case of Northern Rock is a testimony of a bank run that occurred, despite the Bank of England's assistance of liquidity leading which developed into a full financial crisis and its nationalisation.[79] Campbell and Lastra have wondered, though, whether the "stigma" associated with this type of assistance, following a premature disclosure in the press that Northern Rock was in financial distress may have played a role.[80]

Central banks have the vital role of ensuring that they supply liquidity to banks in distress to avoid shock or contagion. However, they must guard against moral hazard by putting in place systems that discourage banks from risky lending.[81] Moral hazard may arise because of the assurance that the central banks will rescue a financial institution in distress.[82] At times, the central bank must provide this liquidity to save the financial system. This is common in relation to the so-called *too big to fail*.[83] In times of financial distress, if one financial institution is likely to draw in other financial institution into its death-spin, the central bank has a choice whether to save it, by injecting in extra liquidity or depriving it of liquidity and allowing it to close shop. There will, therefore, be cases where the central banks must withhold final liquidity and allow an institution to go under to protect the market. Where this is the case, the central bank still has a role to provide a wall and protect the other institutions. Provision of extra liquidity to other financial institutions during such a time may also in a way calm the market and ease panic.[84]

[78] Schooner and Taylor (2010), pp. 53–6.

[79] Hyun Song Shin (2009) 'Reflections on Northern Rock: The Bank Run That Heralded the Global Financial Crisis' 23 (1) *The Journal of Economic Perspectives* 101, http://dx.doi.org/10.1257/089533009797614045. 4 October 2018.

[80] Campbell and Lastra (2009), p. 487.

[81] Schooner and Taylor (2010), pp. 60–3.

[82] Ibid., p. 60.

[83] Ibid., pp. 63–4.

[84] Ibid., pp. 59–60.

Provision of a deposit insurance scheme may also be a policy tool that can be employed to protect financial institutions.[85] However, is the *too big to fail* concept in itself morally hazardous? In the USA, the intervention by the Federal Deposit Insurance Corporation, while breaking up some firms, led to the creation of even larger firms, which are themselves now declared *too big to fail.*[86]

As a trust-based system, a central bank has to ensure the soundness of counterparts.[87] Participants of the financial system have trust in it because they trust that the central bank will supervise compliance and ensure all the other players play by the rules to the benefit of all.[88] Put in another way, to ensure there is no free rider, it is in the interest of all other players to have regulation in place.[89] This also includes any entry restrictions on who can and cannot be allowed to become a member.

#### *5.1.2.3 Consumer Protection*

With the evolution of financial services and complex financial products, there is information asymmetry between providers and consumers of these services. Mwenda says regulation needs to address such things as unauthorised disclosure of information, insider dealing and illicit financing and money laundering to boost consumer and investor confidence.[90] Taylor says consumer protection is premised on protecting "individual investors, depositors and policyholders to the extent that they cannot reasonably be expected to protect their own interests".[91] While this may sound harsh, in relation to developing countries, where financial literacy is still relatively low, this may very well be a more pressing need and the burden that is placed on the regulator to address the information imbalance is greater. Where a regulator realises that there is information asymmetry, especially to the disadvantage of consumers, the regulator can put

[85] Ibid., pp. 56–9.

[86] FCIC (2011) *The Financial Crisis Inquiry Report: Final Report of the National Commission on the Causes of the Financial and Economic Crisis in the United States* (The Financial Crisis Inquiry Commission, Washington, DC), https://www.gpo.gov/fdsys/pkg/GPO-FCIC/pdf/GPO-FCIC.pdf. 1 May 2018.

[87] Padoa-Schioppa (2003), p. 305.

[88] Goodhart (1988), p. 69.

[89] Ibid., pp. 69, 73.

[90] Mwenda (2006), p. 3.

[91] Taylor (1995), p. 9.

in place regulations that are aimed to deliberately even up the scales in favour of consumers such as imposing minimum standards on the sector of business conduct or requiring the disclosure of certain information mandatory.[92] Where the regulator is seen to be enforcing compliance by the market players, consumer and investor confidence is promoted and maintained.[93] It also instils trust in the system.

Setting up deposit insurance schemes and mandatory adequate capital reserves are important in protecting consumer funds.[94] Ultimately, though, it may also require a speedy resolution framework. Unfortunately, in some developing countries like Malaŵi, this is not the case. For example, the Finance Bank of Malaŵi started winding-up procedures in 2005, but the processes have not been finalised to date.[95] In fact the owners of the bank, which has not truly been finally wound up, have opened a new bank, New Finance Bank of Malaŵi.

### 5.1.3 *The Regulatory Issues Involving Globalised Money*

Most global currencies are now no longer restricted within the jurisdiction of the issuing authority.[96] Cohen calls it the de-territorialisation of currencies.[97] The development of the Eurodollar market is an excellent example of this. A Eurodollar is created when a deposit is dominated

[92] Mwenda (2006), p. 4.

[93] Ibid.

[94] Goodhart (1988), p. 85.

[95] Frank Phiri (2005) 'Finance Bank Closure: Precursor to Return of Forfeiture Act?' (*Malawiana*), https://groups.yahoo.com/neo/groups/MALAWIANA/conversations/topics/3175. 23 February 2018.

*Finance Bank of Malaŵi Ltd (In Voluntary Liquidation) v Reserve Bank of Malawi and and Attorney General* Constitutional Cause No. 5 of 2010 High Court (Constitutional Division), http://www.malawilii.org/mw/judgment/high-court-general-division/2013/451. 9 March 2018.

Adam Phiri (2016) 'Finance Bank in K3 billion case' *The Times* (3 February 2016), http://www.times.mw/finance-bank-in-k3-billion-case/. 9 March 2018.

[96] Benjamin J Cohen (2008) 'The International Monetary System: Diffusion and Ambiguity' *International Affairs* 455, pp. 17–8, http://escholarship.org/uc/item/97r5n8jx. 4 October 2018.

[97] Ibid., p. 18.

in US Dollars but outside the USA.[98] The challenge that emerges with such globalised money is which regulator has jurisdiction over such Eurodollars. Traditionally, where the deposit is situated will determine who the regulator will be. The host regulator's laws will determine the regulatory framework of the Eurodollars.[99] So in effect, the US Federal Reserve has no control over the Eurodollar market. Eurodollars represent an obligation to pay actual Dollars.[100] This presents an immediate problem as the host regulator may not have the state sanction over the currency. However, do Eurodollars actually exist or are they just a bookkeeper's creation? The Eurodollar market is a good illustration that money is now no more than an accounting exercise of balancing the books. There are in fact no actual Dollars being shipped across the continents to satisfy the demand of the Eurodollar market.[101] With an increased interdependence of global finance, the Eurodollar deposit account represents an international mirror of domestic deposits.

The Eurodollar is however, not the only Eurocurrency, but it is by far the dominant one.[102] To be traded as a Eurocurrency, a currency must be easily convertible.[103] To be convertible, a currency must be freely interchangeable with other currencies, used in global trade, and must be relatively stable.[104] It is therefore not unsurprising that the Eurocurrency market is associated with currencies of developed nations. The advent of Eurocurrencies together with derivatives and other financial instruments as well as the expansion of debt has transformed the stability otherwise associated with money. The question then becomes whether new forms of money exacerbate this problem.

[98] Milton Friedman (1971) 'The EuroDollar Market: Some First Principles' *Review (Federal Bank of St Louis)* 16, p. 17, https://research.stlouisfed.org/publications/review/71/07/Principles_Jul1971.pdf. 13 September 2018.

[99] Ibid.

[100] Ibid., p. 18.

[101] Ibid.

[102] Reed Jr (1998), 94–5.

[103] Ibid., p. 14.

[104] Ibid.

## 5.2 Regulatory Approaches to Mobile Money

The regulatory dilemma that mobile money presents are well summarised by Maurer:

> [T]he evolution of mobile money has led regulators and industry professionals to turn once more back to the original infrastructural question that animated mobile money in the first place: do mobile telecommunications networks represent a new set of rails for payments? What else can ride on those rails?[105]

The rapid growth of mobile money presents evidence that the telecommunications service is now a multidisciplinary one, embracing finance and commerce. This is a result of the communications revolution, which leads to convergence of technologies and processes. This in effect is the argument that this book makes. With this comes unique challenges, different from those faced by regulators of the telecommunication or financial services. One challenge has been identified by Maurer who wonders how regulators will regulate "cross-boundary airtime top-up services, which have the potential to offer a truly transnational remittance service riding whole separate rails from the traditional payment systems"?[106]

Financial regulation has traditionally worked in an evolutionary and innovative manner. It allows the regulator to be an enabler and embraces other forms of financial services to come under its supervision. With the advent of new alternative forms of money, such as mobile money, the issue is whether this traditional regulatory architecture can adequately supervise these alternative forms of payment. Does the regulatory space require a regulator to alter the approach as alternative forms of payments come into the market? Is it a regulatory dilemma or is it the provision of financial services in a new way? Or is it both? The main argument being advanced is therefore that the traditional architecture of regulation which has predominantly been used in banking and allied services does not fit the new alternative forms of payment.

According to Córdova-Novion and Hanlon, since "financial markets are characterised by high levels of systemic risk, regulation of financial

[105] Maurer (2011).

[106] Ibid.

services is highly influenced by prudential considerations".[107] This results in regulatory emphasis being placed on financial stability and integrity as opposed to consumer protection or competition.[108] However, because of its low risk, mobile money regulation is predominantly one that is based on conduct of business, as opposed to prudential regulation.

### 5.2.1 *Business Conduct Regulation*

This looks at how the institution conducts its business. Issues such as consumer protection and money laundering are therefore topical.[109] Other than systemic risk, consumer protection ranks second as a "fundamental rationale for financial regulation".[110] Consumer protection includes having a system that ensures the integrity of any data stored and transferred.[111] Klein and Mayer say with business conduct, regulators have two choices; they can allow commercial law to govern the relationship between the consumers and the institutions, or deliberately "set standards for the integrity of system operations and to review their practice".[112] Issues like mandatory disclosure may help to address this.[113] The problem with relying on commercial law is that mobile money involves a complex layer of actors. Apart from the mobile network operators, there are the mobile money issuer, agents, customers and those relying on the mobile money service for procuring and selling of goods and services. Commercial law would therefore be ill-equipped to resolve all the possible issues that may arise and special regulations may need to be promulgated to address these.[114]

[107] Córdova-Novion and Hanlon (2002), p. 59.

[108] Ibid.

[109] Klein and Mayer (2011), p. 10.

[110] Richard J Herring and Anthony M Santomero (2000) 'What Is Optimal Financial Regulation?' in Benton E Gup (ed) *The New Financial Architecture* (Quorum Books, Westport, Connecticut), p. 54.

[111] Klein and Mayer (2011), p. 15.

[112] Ibid., pp. 10, 11.

[113] Ibid., p. 11.

[114] Ibid., p. 25.

### 5.2.2 *Prudential Regulation*

This is more concerned with the operational soundness of financial institutions.[115] It delimits the area within which banks and other prudentially regulated institutions can operate.[116] It deals with issues such as capital adequacy reserves as well as liquidity requirements.[117] It also includes the fit and proper test requirement for senior management.[118] It is mainly concerned with the risk taken by institutions regarding their investments and assets.[119] In 2015, a Directive for the "fit and proper test" was issued under the Financial Services Act (Malaŵi) 2010.[120] Under the Directive, the Registrar of financial institutions has to approve a list of shareholders and management of firms dealing with securities markets.[121] The test itself is twofold. The person must have proper qualifications and must meet eligible criteria which include, not being declared bankrupt, convicted of a financial-related offence or otherwise disqualified on grounds of professional misconduct.[122] In prudential regulation, the essential issue is whether the client's money is available should the client wish to withdraw it.[123] Fear of systemic risk and contagion are therefore at the heart of prudential regulation.[124] Such risks may be endogenous or exogenous.[125] The system must be able to contain risk from within and keep out risk from outside.

As will be discussed later, how mobile money is used will determine whether it falls under prudential regulation. Mobile money is fully

[115] Vincent P Polizatto (1992) 'Prudential Regulation and Banking Supervision' in Dimitri Vittas (ed) *Financial Regulation: Changing the Rules of the Game* (The World Bank, Washington, DC), p. 286.

[116] Ibid.

[117] Klein and Mayer (2011), p. 11.

[118] Quintyn and Taylor (2002), p. 15.

[119] Klein and Mayer (2011), p. 11.

[120] Financial Services (Fit and Proper Requirement for Persons Associated with Ownership and Management of Securities Market Players) Directive 2015 (Malaŵi), https://www.rbm.mw/Supervision/GetContentFile/?ContentID=6457. 20 July 2018.

[121] Part II Financial Services Directive (2015).

[122] Part IV Financial Services Directive (2015).

[123] Di Castri (2013), p. 15.

[124] Polizatto (1992), p. 286.
Herring and Santomero (2000), p. 52.

[125] Herring and Santomero (2000), p. 52.

backed up by deposits in a commercial bank. Compared to rules under which banks are only required to keep a fraction of deposits, the requirement to have full liquidity means mobile money is subject to more onerous regulations.[126] Should the regulator have a say on how the banks can invest deposits from mobile money accounts? The current position in Malaŵi is that banks are free to use such deposits as they would with any other deposits.[127] The crucial issue to realise is that mobile network operators do not create money by issuing electronic value in the form of mobile money. In this regard, mobile money operates as prepaid value.[128] The only thing mobile money can answer for is that because it does not require physical transmissions, it affects the velocity of money, but it does not pose a risk to the money supply.[129]

Understandably therefore, most of the regulation of mobile money will cover conduct of business. Unless the mobile money issuer starts to invest funds deposited by customers, or starts offering credit to its customers, prudential regulation will only apply to the commercial banks where the money is deposited.

## 5.3 Regulatory Issues Around Mobile Money

Mobile money is a recent entrant in the financial market and usually there is no pre-existing regulatory framework in place to supervise the service. In their report on regulating mobile money in Malaŵi, Buckley et al. recommend a proportionate and risk-based approach.[130] According

[126] Michael Tarazi and Paul Breloff (2010) *Nonbank Electronic Money Issuers: Regulatory Approaches to Protecting Customer Funds* (Focus Note, CGAP, Washington, DC), p. 3, https://www.cgap.org/sites/default/files/CGAP-Focus-Note-Nonbank-Electronic-money-Issuers-Regulatory-Approaches-to-Protecting-Customer-Funds-Jul-2010.pdf. 3 February 2018.

[127] Interview at Reserve Bank of Malaŵi Headquarters (RBM HQ) on 6 August 2015.

[128] Lee and Longe-Akindemowo (1999), p. 63.

[129] Alaxander P Reed Jr (1998) *Money and the Global Economy* (Woodhead Publishing, Cambridge), p. 27.

Klein and Mayer (2011), p. 12.

[130] Ross Buckley, Jonathan Greenacre and Louise Malady (2015) 'The Regulation of Mobile Money in Malawi' 14 (3) *Washington University Global Studies Law Review* 435, p. 480, http://openscholarship.wustl.edu/cgi/viewcontent.cgi?article=1536&context=law_globalstudies. 3 February 2018.

See also Webb and others (2014), p. 1.

to Laurer and Tarazi, this is when "the costs to the regulator, the institutions, and the consumers are proportionate to the risks being addressed, taking into consideration as well the anticipated benefits".[131] The regulatory approach chosen can either be an enabler or act as a constraint and barrier.[132] The approach adopted in regulating most mobile money schemes has been described by Skinner as "an innovative mixture of 'light touch' and caution".[133] Heyer and Mas say this allows the operator a degree "of freedom in structuring the business model, service proposition and distribution channels".[134] It is however submitted, this approach only deals with the pre-financial inclusion phase of mobile money. In a regulatory environment where the financial sector is supervised by an approach other than light touch, once financial inclusion is achieved, light touch may no longer be adequate to safeguard the interest of the consumers and the financial integrity of the market.

There is also the risk posed by an increase in money circulation in the financial system. According to Jack and Suri, as mobile money "becomes more widely acceptable as an easily transferable store of value", it adopts and mimics the features of fiat money.[135] This then means mobile money could increase the effective money supply, and may have inflationary effects.[136] Mobile money services have the effect of increasing "the pace of monetary transactions" because of an increase in cash circulation, "looping more people into the financial sector and leading to demand goods and services outstripping supply".[137] Inflation is not caused by the injection of mobile money into a local economy, but by the lack of an equivalent injection in the amount of goods and services, resulting in

[131] Tarazi and Breloff (2010), p. 1.

[132] Amrik Heyer and Ignacio Mas (2009) *Seeking Fertile Grounds for Mobile Money* (Mobile Money for the Unbanked, GSMA, London), p. 12, http://www.gsma.com/mobilefordevelopment/wp-content/uploads/2012/03/fertile_grounds_mobile_money55.pdf. 14 February 2018.

[133] Chris Skinner (2015) 'When Everyone on the Planet Has a Mobile Money Account, Things Will Change' (24 Jun 2015), http://thefinanser.com/2015/06/when-everyone-on-the-planet-has-a-mobilelectronic-money-account-things-will-change.html/. 9 February 2018.

[134] Heyer and Mas (2009), p. 12.

[135] Jack and Suri (2011), p. 11.

[136] Ibid.

[137] Ngigi (2012).
See also Mutua (2012).

money chasing too few goods. Regulating mobile money so that there is an equilibrium in the circulation of money is therefore crucial for the stability and integrity of the financial system.

For the mobile money services to grow, it needs an enabling environment, or at least a non-hindering one.[138] Such an environment entails openness and certainty at the early stage.[139] The former imports an attraction that allows and encourages new entrants into the market so as not to stifle innovation while for the latter, the regulatory and policy framework much not be susceptible to arbitrary changes, which may prejudice prospects for new entrants.[140] The regulator has to balance between avoiding "over-reacting and stifling market development" and "under-reacting to potential large scale risks until it is too late".[141] An enabling environment must also delicately balance between being an enabler and offering stability. Mobile money targets low-income people who usually fall outside the formal financial sector.[142] Regulators therefore have a challenge not to come up with barriers that will prevent the emergence of cost-lowering business models to assist those outside the formal financial system.[143] At the same time, they must define the role of mobile network operators and their agents, as these were not previously subject to financial regulation and supervision.[144] The regulatory framework needs to have a built-in mechanism that allows for responsiveness of both the industry and the regulator, taking into consideration the various regulatory issues at play.

Maurer refers to the concept of "regulation as retrospective ethnography" and argues that instead of looking at regulation as proscriptive or restrictive, there is a need for the regulators to "look backwards, learning from the past problems, ranging from small inconveniences to systemic

[138] Flores-Roux and Mariscal (2010), p. 59.

[139] Porteous (2006), p. 15.

[140] Ibid.

[141] Ibid., p. 39.

[142] Olga Morawczynski and Mark Pickens (2009) *Poor People Using Mobile Financial Services: Observations on Customer Usage and Impact from M-PESA* (CGAP Brief, August, CGAP, Washington, DC), pp. 3–4, http://www.cgap.org/publications/poor-people-using-mobile-financial-services. 29 April 2018.

[143] Timothy Lyman (2016) 'Regulation and Supervision' (*CGAP*), http://www.cgap.org/topics/regulation-and-supervision. 21 May 2018.

[144] Ibid.

failures" and prevent such issues in the future.[145] Regulators are not soothsayers so instead of being prescriptive, they should instead "take a relaxed, mature approach and let the channels emerge".[146] It is submitted that such a regulatory approach is essentially what responsive and reflexive regulation calls for, inward reflection and response while appreciating limits of regulatory influence

In providing an enabling environment, the regulator must also bear in mind the need for flexibility in creating mobile money ecosystems. The regulatory environment must be one that enables the growth and flourishing of such an ecosystem. However, the regulator needs to recognise that even ecosystems have a built-in mechanism to protect themselves up to a point. The challenge, without engaging in futurology, is to balance flexibility against external hazards. For an effective mobile money ecosystem, there is need to rope in a cross section and a wide range of players such as mobile network operators, banks, agents, shops, service and utility providers.[147] Generally, the mobile network operators have been the ones interconnecting the nodes of the ecosystem. Therefore, although the regulation has evolved this way, the regulator has to provide an enabling environment under which a mobile money ecosystem may develop and take root, grow and flourish.[148] This can be achieved by providing some regulatory latitude that allows for innovation.[149] Regulation may act as a constraint in the development of the mobile money service if it is too restrictive.[150] For a service that is just starting up, less regulation (light touch) or much more self-regulation may spur the growth of the service. The task of the regulator is to check when the critical mass has been achieved to ensure that the system is not only financially inclusive but also stable and does not pose a risk to the financial system and consumers.

145 Maurer (2012), p. 302.

146 Ibid.

147 Ibid., p. 7.

148 Ibid., pp. 11, 12.

149 Ibid.

150 Ignacio Mas and Daniel Radcliffe (2011) 'Mobile Payments Go Viral: M-PESA in Kenya' 32 *The Capco Institute Journal of Financial Transformation* 169, p. 170, http://www.capco.com/sites/all/files/journal-32_article-16.pdf. 15 December 2018.

To prevent mobile network operators from creating money and causing runaway inflation,[151] regulators must ensure that mobile money is fully backed up. In Malaŵi, the balance on pool accounts must always be equal to the outstanding balance of all holders of the mobile money.[152] This ensures there is an equilibrium of money supply. There is also another reason to be cautious with mobile money. Although it was never intended to be used as a bank (storage), it has had this unintended consequence in that customers may sometimes store their mobile money in it.[153] In Malaŵi, where distances are far and travel is not always safe, it would certainly be attractive to buy mobile money from an agent and redeem it at the destination for a minimal transactional fee. The service could also become a useful vehicle to canvass savings,[154] a direct challenge to the banking system.

Currently mobile money is regulated through a light-touch approach, allowing the service to grow and gain traction. The regulation is currently a two-way arrangement between the regulator and the regulatees. Although light touch describes the approach, the relationship between the parties seems to be still premised on command and control, with the regulator issuing guidelines that govern the mobile money service. Stakeholders are currently not included in the regulator arena. As discussed in Chapter 4, really responsive regulation must evolve continuously and embrace change. It must be able to employ a combination of instruments depending on the developments and need of the industry. Light touch seems to be ideal to allow the service to grow and contribute to the financial inclusion agenda. However, the regulation will have to constantly evolve as financial inclusion is achieved, the service has matured and its risk portfolio has changed. In considering this, it is important to take into consideration the local context. Setting up too fine and sophisticated a system will not work if there are not enough

[151] A reported joke by a former Safaricom CEO to the governor of the Kenyan central bank that the latter does not need to print any more money as M-PESA was taking over underscores this—Donovan (2012), p. 2653.

[152] Section 8.10 Guidelines for Mobile Payment Systems (Malaŵi, 2011).

[153] Donovan (2012), p. 2647

Ignacio Mas and Olga Morawczynski (2009) 'Designing Mobile Money Services Lessons from M-PESA' 4 (2), p. 89 *Innovations* 77, http://www.mitpressjournals.org/doi/pdf/10.1162/itgg.2009.4.2.77. 20 May 2018.

[154] Mas and Morawczynski (2009), p. 89.

resources to implement it. On the other hand, there is a danger that letting things loose may lead to a crisis. The balance is to achieve the appropriate regulatory fit applicable to each country. The needs are clear. The system must extend the consumers' engagement with the medium of mobile money but at the same time, there is need to safeguard both the consumer and the national interest. It must consider the culture, economic and sociopolitical context.

Mobile money needs to be regulated as a unique service combining elements of the financial and communications services. While it is definitely a financial service, it does not fit the bill as a banking service, as some key ingredients are missing such as interest on savings. Some literature says that for lack of a better word, mobile money is at least a quasi-banking project.[155] If the law can appreciate and recognise this unique and complex nature of mobile money, then the law can formulate a regulatory strategy acceptable by the mobile money service and one, which essentially allows for the self-reproduction of the service. Really responsive regulation is therefore an approach that embraces this plurality and flexibility.

The departure point in formulating a regulatory strategy for mobile money is to access the risks that clients and consumers may be exposed to as well as risks that the service poses to the financial system.[156]

### 5.3.1 *Genuineness of Money and Stability Value*

As an electronic form of value, the genuineness of the mobile money is tied to the integrity of the whole financial system. Trust in the system is of paramount importance.[157] If the mobile money is within the ecosystem, and the integrity of the ecosystem and payment system are secure, issues of genuineness do not arise. It is at the point of cashing out that problems could arise. These problems would relate to either fraud or corruption in the data (discussed below). Since mobile money is directly

155 Hughes and Lonie (2007), p. 64.

156 Porteous (2006), p. 31.

157 Olga Morawczynski and Gianluca Miscione (2008) 'Examining Trust in Mobile Banking Transactions: The Case of M-PESA in Kenya' in Chrisanthi Avgerou, Matthew L Smith and Peter van den Basselaar (eds) *Social Dimensions of Information and Communication Technology Policy* (Springer, Boston), p. 289.

tied to cash, the only risk of stability of value would be that of cash itself. Mobile money does not suffer from fluctuations in value on its own.

### 5.3.2 *Maintaining Financial Stability and Integrity*

Mobile money is private money issued by private entities. However, it is issued on the backbone of central bank money. The issue that would arise would be if it was issued without deposits backing it up. If this were to happen, then mobile money issuers would in effect be creating and injecting new money into the system and this would affect supply and financial stability. It may be argued that this would be no different from what the old bankers used to do, issuing gold certificates as credit without any gold deposits to match. One would also argue that it is the same as what the central bank does, issuing fiat money against no liabilities. However, therein lies the difference. Mobile money issuers are not banks and are not authorised to issue money unless it is backed on a one-to-one ratio with money in a pool account. They are prevented from intermediating the funds that they have.

Mobile money works on the principle of full liquidity of deposits in a commercial bank. However, the bank holding this money is at liberty to use it as part of its loan portfolio.[158] Since the funds in a pool account are not demand deposits, there is a risk that banks may engage in moral hazard. The risk is that banks may not exercise the same prudence compared to other deposits and investments. This potentially exposes the system to a liquidity risk if a bank has lent out most of the money deposited against the mobile money and for whatever reason mobile money users want to cash out en masse. There is no restriction in how banks lend mobile money deposits. However, this risk may be balanced by the fact that mobile money comprises a small fraction of bank deposits.[159] Increases in mobile money deposits, however, may change the risk profile.

The values of transactions in mobile money are naturally small, reflective of its main clientele, the rural population. However, because the mobile money system is connected to the main financial system via the pool account, any risks that the service may potentially pose on

[158] RBM HQ (2015).

[159] Di Castri (2013), p. 8.

the financial stability and integrity of the financial system need to be addressed. As stated earlier, the ability by the central bank to timely assess the risk posed by a financial institution is crucial to maintaining financial stability and integrity.[160]

#### 5.3.2.1 *Assessing Risk*

Due to non-stringent identification requirements for mobile money accounts, there is a potential risk of mobile money being used for illicit means. Even though the amounts transferred are relatively small and restricted, both in value and daily transaction, mobile money may act as a laundry or mixer of funds in such a manner that what comes in cannot be connected to what comes out. Furthermore, the fact that the units of value can be subdivided would make it easy for funds to be channelled to several sources as well as to have funds channelled from several sources and consolidated into one account. The ultimate recipient may get cash out.

As a global response to money laundering and terrorism financing concerns, the Financial Action Task Force (FATF), an intergovernmental body was established in 1989.[161] Issues of proceeds of money laundering and terrorism financing have been on the international agenda for some time but the 9/11 terrorist attacks on the USA[162] may have accelerated the need to ensure that the financial sector is not used a conduit for illicit purposes. The FATF sets standards and promotes "effective implementation of legal, regulatory and operational measures for combating money laundering, terrorist financing and other related threats to the integrity of the international financial system".[163] The FATF has been behind the enactment of municipal anti-money laundering and combating the financing of terrorism legislation as well as many regulatory reforms.[164]

The setting of Financial Intelligence Units (FIUs) is one of the successes of the FATF. The FATF issues recommendations, also referred to

[160] Singh (2007).

[161] FATF (2016) 'Financial Action Task Force' (FATF), http://www.fatf-gafi.org/. 15 December 2018.

[162] This refers to the attack organised by international terrorist organisation *Al Qaeda* on the USA using planes as simultaneous "bombs" that took place in a coordinated manner on 9 September 2001 (9/11/01 or simply '9/11').

[163] FATF (2016).

[164] Ibid.

in international law as soft law, which are now recognised as an international standard.[165] The first guidelines were issued in 1990 and there have been four revisions with the latest one done in 2012.[166] The reason mobile money has been earmarked is that since it was not initially taken to be part of the formal financial sector (and therefore not regulated), it poses a risk as a potential conduit for money laundering and terrorism financing. De Koker says Recommendation 14 of the FATF (2012) now requires that money or value transfer service providers, which includes mobile money, "be licensed or registered and subject to effective systems for monitoring and ensuring compliance with the relevant FATF measures".[167]

In Malaŵi, the FIU was established as the lead operating agency under the Money Laundering, Proceeds of Serious Crime and Terrorist Financing Act (2006) [Money Laundering Act].[168] Although autonomous, it works closely with law enforcement agencies[169] and may enter into cooperative "agreements or arrangements with any domestic government institution regarding exchange of information".[170] The FIU may also have cooperative agreements and arrangements with similar bodies in other jurisdictions.[171] All financial institutions are now obliged to conduct a customer due diligence before entering into any business transactions with a potential customer.[172] The FIU may apply for a search warrant if it reasonably believes that an offence may have been committed.[173] A new Financial Crimes Act 2017 has since been passed.[174] It renames the FIU to the Financial Intelligence Authority (FIA).

[165] As well as in the controversial issue of proliferation of weapons of mass destruction.

[166] FATF (2016).

[167] Louis de Koker (2013) 'The 2012 Revised FATF Recommendations: Assessing and Mitigating Mobile Money Integrity Risks Within the New Standards Framework' 8 *Wash JL Tech & Arts* 165, p. 14.

[168] Section 11(1) Money Laundering Act (Malaŵi, 2006).
The Money Laundering Act has been replaced with the Financial Crimes Act (2017).

[169] Section 11(2)(*d*), ibid.

[170] Section 11(2)(*q*), ibid.

[171] Section 12, ibid.

[172] Section 24(1), ibid.

[173] Section 41, ibid.

[174] February 2017.

Apart from enhancing the powers of the FIA, the new Act also has enhanced penalties for financial crimes.

In relation to operations of the pool account, the FIU/FIA is not involved in its oversight. The FIU's Director, Atuweni Phiri, who now heads the FIA, says her institution views this as "a prudential matter that falls under the Reserve Bank of Malaŵi".[175] Therefore, mobile money operators are not required to make reports to the FIU/FIA regarding the operation of the pool account.[176] However, the operators are under an obligation to submit reports to the FIU/FIA on transactions involving amounts from K1,000,000.00 (£1 = K947.09)[177] and above as well as suspicious transactions.[178] In practice, though, this does not happen because mobile money has a ceiling of K500,000.00 which means such transactions will not be reported to the FIU unless they are deemed suspicious. It would seem that K1 million threshold did not envisage low-value services like mobile money. The FIA is negotiating with operators to lower the threshold for the purposes of mobile money.[179] It is however aware that such an arrangement would not have the sanction of the law and would largely depend on the goodwill of the operators to keep their end of the agreement.[180] The biggest challenge that the FIA faces is to get operators who are competitors to sign up to such an agreement, as they are under no obligation legally to do so. Under the Financial Crimes Act, there is no framework to regulate mobile money.[181] When the new Act was being formulated, the then FIU Director had indicated a hope that the formulation of a new legal framework would include new forms of money and payment, including mobile money.[182] A review of the new Act and the regulations made under it discloses that mobile

[175] Interview with Atuweni Tupochire Phiri, Director, Financial Intelligence Unit (FIU) (7 August 2015).

[176] Ibid.

[177] XE (2018) 'XE Currency Converter' (XE), https://www.xe.com/currencyconverter/convert/?Amount=1&From=GBP&To=MWK. 10 November 2018.

[178] Phiri (2015).

[179] Ibid.

[180] Ibid.

[181] Ibid.

[182] Ibid.

money has not been explicitly included other than as a general subset of electronic funds.[183]

Unlike the central bank, the FIA does not have any authority to issue regulations.[184] However, Phiri says, when the central bank was coming up with its guidelines for mobile payments, the FIU provided input.[185] This does not mean that the FIU/FIA is not involved at all. For example, at the point when the central bank gives an operator the go-ahead to do a pilot, Phiri says, the FIU will undertake a know your customer (KYC) audit.[186] The audit is, however, limited to money laundering issues.[187] The FIA issues guidelines on minimal KYC requirements.[188] At the heart of this is the requirement for any financial institution to undertake a customer due diligence or conduct a KYC audit before such customer can have access to financial services.[189] This extends to mobile money services and the central bank requires that one must satisfy the KYC requirements laid out in the law.[190]

The KYC requirement is for all financial institutions, such that for one to register for the mobile money service, one needs to produce some form of identification.[191] The central bank requires that one must satisfy the KYC requirements laid out in the law.[192] The author's own

[183] Financial Crimes Act (Malaŵi, 2017).

Financial Crimes (Suppression of Terrorist Financing and Proliiferation) Regulations, 2017, Government Notice No. 11 of 2017 (Malaŵi).

[184] Phiri (2015). The new Act has not provided these powers either. Regulations can only be issued by the Minister of Finance—Section 144 Financial Crimes Act (Malaŵi, 2017).

[185] Phiri (2015).

[186] Ibid.

[187] Ibid.

[188] Ibid.

[189] Jennifer Isern and Louis De Koker (2012) *AML/CFT: Strengthening Financial Inclusion and Integrity* (CGAP Focus Notes, CGAP, Washington, DC), http://dro.deakin.edu.au/eserv/DU:30020790/dekoker-amlcft-2009.pdf. 14 November 2018.

[190] Ibid.

[191] What exactly this comprises in a country without a formal national identity system is an area requiring more research. This is because it may be prone to misrepresentation and can easily be taken advantage of by people with money laundering and terrorism financing motives.

[192] Guidelines for Mobile Payment Systems (Malaŵi, 2011), p. 12 referred to the reopealed Money Laundering Act, but should now be read as to refer to the Financial Crimes Act (2017).

experience shows that registering with *Mpamba* is more onerous and cumbersome as compared to Airtel Money. The reasons provided for the myriad of information sought were to ensure regulatory compliance. It can be concluded that both mobile network operators are conducting some *sort of* KYC, although the information sought and demanded seems to vary.[193] Although the KYC requirements of *Mpamba* were more demanding, it can be said that both mobile operators are not strictly following the KYC requirements provided by the FIU/FIA. This can be seen as a good sign that shows that the mobile money issuers are using a risk-based approach in their assessment. Being an entry point, it is important that this process is user-friendly. It should not pose as a barrier to financial inclusion.

It has been argued that a possible solution lies in the introduction of a national identity system, which Malaŵi has done in the last year, after the passing of the legislative framework for its implementation.[194] The FIU believes that a system similar to the South Africa's Regulation of Interception of Communications and Provision of Communication-Related Information Act (RICA) would best serve the FIU but this can only work after a national ID system is fully in place.[195] Under the RICA, every mobile phone user must register their phone number.[196] It is seen as one of the initiatives to prevent crime and money laundering as well as combat terrorism financing.[197] Under the RICA:

> Users must provide their name and surname, and bring proof of identity in the form of an identity document or passport, as well as a proof of a physical address in the form of either a bank statement or utility bill. Persons

[193] Whether this is due to a difference of interpretation of the Money Laundering, Proceeds of Serious Crimes and Terrorist Financing Act's 'know your customer requirements' or not is yet to be researched.

[194] Malaŵi_Government (2015) 'Commencement of Universal and Compulsory Birth & Death registration and Issuance of Certificates' (Government of Malaŵi), https://www.facebook.com/malawigovernment/posts/439708072882359. 21 July 2018.

National Registration Act (Malaŵi, 2010), https://www.globalintegrity.org/wp-content/uploads/2016/01/Malawi-NATIONAL-REGISTRATION-ACT.pdf. 21 July 2018.

[195] Phiri (2015).

[196] Nicola Jentzsch (2012) 'Implications of Mandatory Registration of Mobile Phone Users in Africa' 36 (8) *Telecommunications Policy* 608, p. 611, http://doi.org/10.1016/j.telpol.2012.04.002. 14 November 2018.

[197] Ibid., p. 608.

> living in informal settlements may bring a letter/affidavit from a school, church, or nearby retail store. The registration has to be done face-to-face with RICA agents.[198]

In Malaŵi, the communications regulator Malaŵi Communications Regulatory Authority (MACRA) has also decided to go the RICA way. MACRA initially set 31 March 2018 as the deadline for registration. This was extended to 30 September 2018. Indeed after 30 September 2018, social media was awash with complaints of people who claimed to have registered but had been disconnected from their network. The framework governing registration of mobile phone users is the Communications Act 2016. Users must provide their full names, gender, date of birth address and their national ID number. Considering that this programme and the national ID registration were being rolled almost at similar times, this may explain the decision to extend the deadline to 30 September 2018. While advantages for registering accrue to the mobile phone industry as a whole, for mobile money, it removes anonymity and makes mobile money transactions traceable as they can be matched with a unique subscriber number, time and date of transaction and location.[199] Cash on the other hand is for most parts the perfect mask.[200] The challenge is that until recently, the country did not have a national ID system in place.[201] So even at present, not every Malaŵian has a national ID yet. It must however be pointed that national IDs are issued for citizens as well as non-citizens who have resident status. The FIU/FIA encourages a KYC regime based on risk-based assessment.[202] The FATF provides the model and requires countries to use a risk-based assessment to formulate local regulations.[203] However, Phiri says:

> The problem with FATF guidelines is that they are rule based. They require that financial institutions be treated the same way. For example,

[198] Ibid., p. 611.

[199] Di Castri (2013), p. 18.

[200] Ibid.

[201] Yvonnie Sundu (2016) 'APM Says National IDs Will Transform Malawi' *The Nation* (28 October 2016), http://mwnation.com/apm-says-national-ids-will-transform-malawi/. 14 November 2018.

[202] Phiri (2015).

[203] Ibid.

> *Mpamba* must be treated similarly to Standard Bank, which is not practically possible.[204]

Therefore, the onus has shifted to institutions to show the FIU/FIA that they have done a risk-based assessment on their customers as well as a KYC.[205] However, even where there is no national ID system in place, opening mobile money accounts still requires some form of identification. This allows mobile money transactions to be matched over time. The uniqueness of subscriber numbers to which the mobile money accounts are tied also means over time; the service can develop a user profile of its customers.[206] Unlike cash, even where the KYC system is imperfect, the mobile money system is not as elusive.[207]

#### 5.3.2.2 *Balancing the Risk*

Between financial inclusion and financial stability/integrity, which then should drive the regulatory agenda for mobile money? There are two divergent schools of thought over this. The first argues that there is need to ensure that the rules of financial inclusion are such that they ensure financial stability and financial integrity. An extension to this is that financial inclusion inevitably leads to financial stability and integrity since all covered under one roof. The other argues that the rules that ensure financial stability and integrity should not lead to financial exclusion. The FATF President Bjørn Aamo summarised the relationship between financial inclusion and its work in this way:

> Financial exclusion represents a real risk to achieving effective implementation of the Anti-money laundering and counter terrorism financing. [AML/CTF] recommendations… Financial inclusion and AML/CTF pursue mutually supportive and complimentary objectives: the application of measures which enable more citizens to use formal financial services will increase the reach and the effectiveness of AML/CTF regimes.[208]

[204] Ibid.

[205] Ibid.

[206] Interview with Webster Mbekeani Head, Mobile Money Division, TNM (20 August 2015).

[207] Di Castri (2013), p. 19.

[208] Bjørn S. Aamo (2012) 'FATF's Focus on Financial Inclusion Protecting the Integrity of the Global Financial System' (*Global Partnership for Financial Inclusion Conference on Standard-Setting Bodies and Financial Inclusion: Promoting Financial Inclusion Through Proportionate Standards and Guidance*) Basel, 29 October 2012, http://www.fatf-gafi.org/

Stringent KYC requirements, which may be necessary for financial stability and financial integrity may however, be a barrier to financial inclusion. This in turn harms the anti-money laundering and counterterrorism financing efforts. There is therefore a need to strike a balance in assessing this risk,[209] especially in countries where asking for too much biometric data may prove a barrier. The FATF now calls for a risk-based approach where a country must "identify, assess and understand" their money laundering and terrorism financing risks.[210]

Viable KYC procedures need to consider the circumstances surrounding most African households. The Universal Postal Union estimates that only 21% of African households receive mail at home, 49% have mail access and 30% have no access at all.[211] Isern et al. argue that even verification of address is not easy and they commend South Africa for adopting a flexible approach to identification and verification.[212] South Africa has introduced "a compliance exemption that relaxes requirements for a category of clients known as 'mass banking clients': those clients with small balances and small size transactions".[213] Maurer refers to this approach as *proportionate KYC* which allows mobile banking customers online registration without the need to physically appear before a person or produce proof of identification.[214] He argues that since KYC requires the production of acceptable identity documents, lack of these

publications/fatfgeneral/documents/fatfsfocusonfinancialinclusionprotectingtheintegrityoftheglobalfinancialsystem.html. 20 February 2018.

[209] Porteous (2006), p. 31.

[210] de Koker (2013), p. 9.

[211] *Development of postal services in 2011: A Few Key Figures* (2011) (Universal Postal Union), http://www.alejandrobarros.com/media/users/1/50369/files/4363/Statistics_2011_UPU.pdf. 10 May 2018.

[212] Jennifer Isern and Others (2005) 'AML/CFT Regulation: Implications for Financial Service Providers That Serve Low-Income People' 29 *CGAP Focus Note*, https://www.cgap.org/sites/default/files/CGAP-Focus-Note-AML-CFT-Regulation-Implications-for-Financial-Service-Providers-That-Serve-Low-Income-People-Jul-2005.pdf. 10 May 2018.

[213] Ibid.

[214] Maurer (2012), p. 309, citing South Africa's Guidance No. 6 on Mobile banking and Exemption 17 to the Financial Intelligence Centre Act (FICA). However, Maurer argues that the RICA has reintroduced some of the classic financial inclusion barriers that made South Africa be hailed by linking the heavy ID requirements of RICA to the right to use a mobile phone, essentially negating the benefits of Guidance Note 6 and Exemption 17.

"documents is often one of the most powerful barriers to financial inclusion".[215] Porteous argues that transformational models such as mobile money whose target is people less likely to have a formal address require flexibility in their application of KYC requirements.[216]

In Malaŵi, there is no system of marked physical addresses. A small percentage has access to postal addresses but with the advent of the mobile phone, most Malaŵians are less likely to use the postal services for personal mail deliveries. It is therefore not possible to produce traceable physical addresses. In Nigeria, a country with similar identification problems to Malaŵi, recognition has been made of the potential barrier that a stringent KYC regime may prove and has adopted a strategy to restructure the KYC regulation to a risk-based tiered framework.[217]

However, the need to recognise the risk associated with a systemic failure of the financial system must be appreciated. Mwenda has argued that a key institutional aspect of financial regulation and supervision is reducing contagion and maintaining consumer confidence in the financial system.[218] Indeed once the informal sector grows, the distinction between the formal, the informal sector is blurred, and a point is then reached where the morphed system may potentially pose a systemic financial risk. For financial regulators, it is the maintenance of sound banking and payment systems that occupy their focus.[219] Since the financial regulator usually focuses on the banking industry, the danger is therefore from exogenous risk, such as an improperly regulated mobile money service.[220] In reality however, the low ceiling in transaction value means that the risk of mobile money being used for such illicit purposes is very low.[221] Looked at from this perspective, because of its low limit, and the fact that transactions leave a digital trail, mobile money is a key

215 Maurer (2011).

216 Porteous (2006), p. 34. See also generally Di Castri (2013).

217 Francis N Ngwu (2014) 'Promoting Formal Financial Inclusion in Africa: As Institutional Re-examination of the Policies with a Case Study of Nigeria' *Journal of Banking Regulation* 9.

218 Mwenda (2006), p. 3.

219 Porteous (2006), p. 32.

220 Maurer (2012), p. 306.

221 Di Castri (2013), p. 9.

anti-money laundering and counterterrorism financing tool.[222] The FATF also recommends that each country assesses its own risk:

> There are circumstances where the risk of money laundering or terrorist financing may be lower. In such circumstances, and provided there has been an adequate analysis of the risk by the country or by the financial institution, it could be reasonable for a country to allow its financial institutions to apply simplified customer due diligence measures.[223]

### *5.3.3 Consumer Protection*

The mobile money system operates on trust.[224] First is the trust consumers have in their own phone. Then is the trust they have of the mobile network operator. It is argued that the trust consumers have in the mobile money service is premised on the trust they have in the mobile network operator. The fact that they can also transact in mobile money leads to a growth in confidence. A growing mobile money ecosystem is key to building trust and increasing financial inclusiveness.[225] There is a direct correlation between the unbanked, the rural poor and the financially excluded. Protection of consumers of mobile money becomes not only an economic or legal function but a social function as well. Consumer protection in relation to banks usually aims to address information asymmetries. It is therefore argued that the differences between consumers and service providers in the mobile money industry are even bigger.

Most mobile network operators in developing countries seem to be flourishing thereby giving an assurance that they are here to stay. However, insolvency on the part of the mobile money issuer, the mobile network operator or the commercial bank hosting the pool account may leave customers with worthless values of mobile money. As noted earlier, mobile money is private money. Although there are two mobile money issuers in

[222] Ibid.

[223] FATF (2012) *International Standards on Combating Money Laundering and the Financing of Terrorism & Proliferation (updated October 2016)* (Financial Action Task Force), http://www.fatf-gafi.org/media/fatf/documents/recommendations/pdfs/FATF_Recommendations.pdf. 20 February 2018.

[224] See generally Morawczynski and Miscione (2008).

[225] Di Castri (2013), p. 7.

Malaŵi, even with the recent developments of sending money across the services, one cannot just exchange the two monies. There is in fact a privatisation of money at play.[226] They can only be exchangeable using cash as an intermediary or if it has been credited in one mobile money account, and debited in another, even though the send and recipient maybe on different mobile money platforms. However, it must be pointed out that this leads subsequently to loss of value due to transactional costs.

Currently, mobile money issuers are not regulated on the same level as banks and other prudentially regulated institutions.[227] Would an increase in the regulatory threshold result in greater consumer protection? Alternatively, is it likely to harm the very consumer it is trying to protect? Would a deposit insurance scheme be the answer? Alternatively, should the central bank require mobile money issuers to have similar capital reserves requirements like banks? Or would such a requirement end up hurting the very consumer it aims to protect? While these may appear academic at this point, they may have to be answered in earnest once financial inclusion has been achieved, as the post-financial inclusion era is likely to pose a new set of challenges.

### 5.3.4 *Operational Risk*

This is a risk associated with failure of operations including cessation of business of the mobile network operator, mobile money issuer, the bank or any combination of these. Even a temporary loss of service can adversely affect the service.[228] Mobile money operates using a telecommunications backbone. Any failures in the backbone invariably affect mobile money transactions. In addition, any failure in the chain of operations can pose a risk. This includes the risk posed by mobile money agents, the bank that holds the pooled funds, the mobile money issuer and the mobile network operator. If any link were to cease function or derail, it would affect the whole chain and pose an operational risk.

[226] Maurer (2012), p. 307.

[227] AFI (2010) *Enabling Mobile Money Transfer: The Central Bank of Kenya's Treatment of M-Pesa* (Alliance for Financial Inclusion), http://www.gsma.com/mobilefordevelopment/wp-content/uploads/2013/09/enablingmobilemoneytransfer92.pdf. 15 December 2018.

Greenacre et al. (2014).

[228] Porteous (2006), p. 31.

### 5.3.5 *Fraud*

So far, there have been no reported cases of fraud involving mobile money. If fraud was perpetrated on the service, it may have catastrophic results for the entire system. This is because the system is built on trust. People trust that the mobile money value they have is directly tied to cash. People trust that when they have exchanged their cash with mobile money, it will indeed be worth the value. There is trust that no one will interfere with what they have acquired. There is also an implicit trust that if one approaches a mobile money agent to cash out, the mobile money in one's phones constitutes good value. If someone were to break down the encryption system of mobile money, it would lead to many customers losing out on their funds. The system must protect "information in transit" from third party attempts to steal or interfere with it.[229] It must also be able to identify the parties. A breakdown of trust would be irreparable. This is more so, when it is now possible to send money from one mobile money service to another.

### 5.3.6 *Data Security and Integrity*

As a digital form of money, mobile money faces risks associated with the security of its data. This may be interference by third parties like in the case of theft or fraud described above or failure or corruption in the system. Mobile network operators keep data about their customers. Apart from their names and numbers, this may also include when and where transactions are conducted, and what has been purchased and its value.[230] Having system backups is one way of mitigating against data loss, which can occur.[231] Airtel Money, for example, claims that their product "is safe, secure and reliable. It runs on a dependable network with little or no breakdowns".[232] The author's experience, however, is that this may not be entirely correct. Malaŵi has for some time now been experiencing intermittent power supply which affects not only the quality

[229] Klein and Mayer (2011), p. 15.

[230] Di Castri (2013), p. 30.

[231] Klein and Mayer (2011), p. 13.

[232] Airtel (2013c) 'About Airtel Money' (*Airtel Malaŵi*), http://africa.airtel.com/wps/wcm/connect/AfricaRevamp/Malawi/Airtel_Money/Home/Personal/About_airtel_money. 23 March 2018.

but also availability of telecommunication services.[233] There may also be a system failure. How to protect the system as well as ensure recovery is, therefore, vital. Redundancy of equipment and databases may be a solution but duplication has a cost.[234] Physically separating data of mobile money accounts from mobile phone users would be one way of ensuring data integrity of both in case there is a problem with either.[235] Hopefully, for a company like Airtel, which experienced system failure due to fire that destroyed its equipment,[236] some lessons would have been learnt about ensuring the integrity and safety of data. Problems of power supply however are beyond individual mobile network operators and something that the whole Southern Africa is grappling with.[237]

The second issue is related to the integrity of the data. Unlike most other transactions, electronic transactions rely on electronic verification. This is usually in a form of electronic signature which is evidenced by either a unique subscriber number, a personal identification number (PIN) or biometric identification.[238] A well-designed system should reject any data that does not meet the specified thresholds.[239] If the system wrongly rejects or accepts data, this can leave agents and others in the ecosystem open to possible legal challenges.[240] The system should therefore be designed to minimise interference and to operate on the highest level of accuracy.

Another issue that may affect data security and privacy is customer literacy. Mistakes by customers may lead to data rejection. Customers also need to be advised to secure any passwords and PINs.[241] Therefore, although customers are ultimately responsible for keeping their PINs

[233] Anon (2003) 'Power Failure Rocks Malawi's Telecoms' (*PANA Press*), http://www.panapress.com/Power-Failure-Rocks-Malawi-s-Telecoms--13-475501-18-lang1-index.html. 29 June 2018.

[234] Author's experience in designing a database system for monitoring the electricity grid.

[235] Klein and Mayer (2011), p. 13.

[236] Anon (2007) 'Malawi Mobile Phone Network Goes off the Air' (*ClickAfrique*), http://www.clickafrique.com/Magazine/ST010/CP0000002372.aspx. 29 June 2018.

[237] Michael Malakata (2015) 'Power Problems Disrupt Africa's Telecom Sector' (*PCWorld*), http://www.pcworld.com/article/2926892/power-problems-disrupt-africas-telecom-sector.html. 29 June 2018.

[238] Porteous (2006), p. 31.

[239] Ibid.

[240] Ibid.

[241] Di Castri (2013), p. 30.

and passwords private, customer education is one way of ensuring PIN and password security.[242] Because of the sensitivity of the data stored by mobile network operators, regulators may require them to implement enhanced data protection measures to prevent theft or fraud.[243] In doing so, however, regulators need to be aware of what is feasible in the Malaŵian context.

### *5.3.7 Resolution Risk*

In the case of resolution, the question that arises is how protected is the pool account to ensure that consumers can redeem their mobile money in the event of a failure of either the mobile network operator or the mobile money issuer? The trust account needs to be ring-fenced against creditors not only of the bank but also of the parent mobile network operator.[244] However, as the funds are comingled within the bank, this leads to two problems. If the bank were to become insolvent, the trust account is likely to be part of the pool of resources, which creditors may have access. If the mobile service provider were to become insolvent, it is unclear if the pool account would not be available to creditors. In fact, it is unclear whether this pool account operates under Trust law, where there is a fiduciary duty to hold the funds for the benefit of customers.[245] In practice, the customers are not the true beneficiaries of the pool account. Unknown charities are. Trustees appointed by the mobile network operators decide who should benefit from the proceeds.[246] At this point, it is unclear if ring fencing of the account alone would protect it in the event of a failure of the bank. It is argued that ring fencing would only be of use in the event of a failure of the mobile network operator or the mobile money issuer.

The failure of the parent mobile network operator may *prima facie* not affect the trust account as the mobile money issuer is a separate company. However, since mobile money rides on the rail of the

[242] Ibid.

[243] Ibid.

[244] Klein and Mayer (2011), p. 5.

[245] Di Castri (2013), p. 15.

[246] Mbekeani (2015).

Interview with Bigboy Mkoloma Product and Development Manager, Airtel Money (7 August 2015).

telecommunications backbone, failure of the parent company would also lead to the failure of the mobile money service. Ring fencing the pool account is therefore a key regulatory issue to be considered. Another would be a system guaranteeing depositors' funds. However, there would be a need to balance this with placing onerous financial obligations on the mobile money issuers which may end up making the service more expensive and unaffordable to its target group. The issue may be complicated where a catastrophic failure in the system results in failure of the mobile network operator itself. In such a case, even if the customers were to have protection, how would their interest be protected where there is unreliable data to back up their claims? It is submitted that having a separate database housed physically away from the servers of the mobile money issuer would help in the event of such a catastrophe.

### *5.3.8 Investment Risk*

Mobile network operators are precluded from investing mobile money deposits.[247] Therefore, any investment risk is at the hands of the bank where the pool account is domiciled. Where there are no specific rules to regulate how such deposits may be invested, the bank is at liberty to intermediate the funds as it would any other deposits. It is only restricted by the general prudential rules that govern deposits in general.[248] To mitigate against this, regulators may limit investment of such deposits to those considered safe and highly liquid.[249] Regulators could also direct that deposits be diversified and spread over several banks to minimise any impact that a single investment failure may have.[250] Since mobile money is fully backed by deposits in a pool account, any investment failure by the bank would affect the supply of mobile money. In the event of a major investment failure affecting a pool account, two things would immediately result. The first would be that if this were not made known, the mobile money would be circulated without a full backing of fiat money. This would mean that money has been created which cannot be backed up by any deposits or reserves. The second would be a scenario

[247] Di Castri (2013), p. 15.
[248] Klein and Mayer (2011), p. 16.
[249] Ibid.
[250] Ibid., p. 26.

where the mobile money essentially loses its value because it cannot be redeemed at par value. This would lead to a collapse of the mobile money system.

### 5.3.9 *Systemic Risk*

Systemic risk has to do more with the banking system than mobile money itself. Since mobile money is created on the back of deposits, the stability of the banking system is vital for the operation of mobile money. There is no risk in the issuance of the mobile money itself and no fear that this would affect money supply.[251] Prudential requirements put in place for the banking service are therefore sufficient to mitigate any liquidity risks.[252] Although the mobile network operator issues mobile money, this issuance is not the creation of money in the banking sense.[253] This is because the mobile money is not issued against fractional reserves.[254] Traditionally the intermediation of deposits into loans is the basis of money multiplication or creation.[255] Mobile money is issued against full liquidity on a one-to-one ratio of funds deposited in a pool account.[256] Money manifests itself in different forms and the term money is used to collectively define these monetary aggregates.[257] Money can be broadly separated into money for making daily payments and money for settling obligations but the latter is not readily available in the near future.[258] The first category referred to as M1 or narrow money includes fiat money, demand posits and other forms that can be easily converted to cash.[259] Mobile money forms part of M1.[260] Therefore, to

[251] Porteous (2006), p. 37.

[252] Di Castri (2013), p. 8.

[253] Porteous (2006), p. 37.

[254] Schooner and Taylor (2010), pp. 3–7.

[255] Di Castri (2013), p. 10.

[256] Porteous (2006), p. 37.

[257] Reed Jr (1998), p. 4.

[258] Ibid.

[259] Roger E Backhouse (1991) 'Money' in *Applied UK Macroeconomics* (Basil Blackwell, Oxford), p. 205.

[260] Di Castri (2013), p. 10. The designation of other forms of money will depend on countries and can be from M2 to M4—Reed Jr (1998), p. 10.

**Table 5.1** Risk analysis of mobile money

| *Risk* | *Conduct of business regulation* | *Prudential regulation* |
|---|---|---|
| Consumer protection | Yes | No |
| Operational | Yes | No |
| Fraud | Yes | No |
| Data security/Integrity | Yes | No |
| Resolution | Yes | No |
| Investment | Yes | Yes |
| Systemic | Yes | Yes |

mitigate the risk to mobile money customers the following 3 steps need to be followed:

a. Backing up the mobile money with 100% liquidity deposited in a prudentially regulated bank
b. Non-intermediation by the mobile money issuer
c. Ring fencing the pool account and isolating it from creditors of the issuer or its parent mobile network operator.[261]

In theory, a run on mobile money could lead to an indirect bank run. This would occur if enough mobile money customers decided to cash out at the same time. Since the deposits on which the mobile money is created are intermediated, the bank would face a liquidity squeeze. Fear and panic may easily spread within the financial system causing contagion. However, because the aggregate value of mobile money transactions is very low,[262] such a run would most likely have little impact on the bank. Any fears of a bank run caused by mobile money are therefore misplaced. However, although not highly likely, systemic risk is one that still needs to be considered with the mobile money service. Weakness in security and liability may pose a risk to the financial system. The table below summarises the risks associated with mobile money (Table 5.1).

[261] Di Castri (2013), p. 15.

[262] Ali and others (2014b), p. 8.

## 5.4 Conclusion

In Malaŵi, there has not been any meaningful analysis of regulation, especially in the financial sector. This is not surprising because although regulatory theory and regulation have been around for some time, it is a relatively new field of study in Malaŵi. The only work that has been published is a project report by Beckley et al.[263] While this report is useful in providing some nuanced insights, it does not adopt the same conceptual and analytical framework as this book. The report is primarily a project report and does not delve into the theoretical and conceptual underpinnings of mobile money. Therefore, while a lack of literature was a handicap, it provides an opportunity to start filling in this gap and lay a foundation for future research in this field.

So, which regulatory approach would be ideal for Malaŵi in relation to mobile money and its contemporary culture? Looking at the situation in Malaŵi, it would seem that because of the level of development of the legal system and its limited "regulatory experience", the country's legal system is still largely stuck in what Teubner describes as the "classical model of law as a body of rules enforceable through adjudication".[264] It therefore needs to move on from this, especially in the financial sector, so that the law can largely play a facilitative role.[265] One individual theory or approach, it is submitted, cannot provide the perfect solution. Real responsive regulation, it is submitted, would embrace the evolution of mobile money through the various financial inclusion phases. The ecosystem of mobile money with several stakeholders makes this approach ideal in regulating the service. The fact that the approach evolves with changes in the environment and time also means that it can keep up with changes in the mobile money service. In the greater scheme of things, a shift of the whole financial regulatory framework to really responsive would be recommended. However, this is outside the scope of this book.

[263] Jonathan Greenacre, Louise Malady and Ross Buckley (2014) *The Regulation of Mobile Money in Malawi* (Centre for International Finance and Regulation, New South Wales), http://www.uncdf.org/sites/default/files/Documents/the_regulation_of_mobile_money_in_malawi_project_report_final_version.pdf. 30 June 2018.
Buckley et al. (2015).

[264] Teubner (1983), p. 271.

[265] Ibid., p. 273.

## References

Adam Phiri (2016) 'Finance Bank in K3 billion case' *The Times* (3 February 2016), http://www.times.mw/finance-bank-in-k3-billion-case/. 9 March 2018.

AFI (2010) *Enabling Mobile Money Transfer: The Central Bank of Kenya's Treatment of M-Pesa* (Alliance for Financial Inclusion), http://www.gsma.com/mobilefordevelopment/wp-content/uploads/2013/09/enablingmobilemoneytransfer92.pdf. 15 December 2018.

Airtel (2013c) 'About Airtel Money' (*Airtel Malaŵi*), http://africa.airtel.com/wps/wcm/connect/AfricaRevamp/Malawi/Airtel_Money/Home/Personal/About_airtel_money. 23 March 2018.

Alexander P Reed Jr (1998) *Money and the Global Economy* (Woodhead Publishing, Cambridge).

Amrik Heyer and Ignacio Mas (2009) *Seeking Fertile Grounds for Mobile Money* (Mobile Money for the Unbanked, GSMA, London), http://www.gsma.com/mobilefordevelopment/wp-content/uploads/2012/03/fertile_grounds_mobile_money55.pdf. 14 February 2018.

Andrew Campbell and Rosa Lastra (2009) 'Revisiting the Lender of Last Resort' 24 (3) *Banking and Finance Law Review* 453, http://0-search.proquest.com.pugwash.lib.warwick.ac.uk/docview/218867839?accountid=14888. 10 December 2018.

Andrew England (2016) 'Zimbabwe to Print "Bond Notes" to Tackle Cash Shortage' *Financial Times* (5 May 2016), http://www.ft.com/cms/s/0/90a66462-12da-11e6-91da-096d89bd2173.html#axzz4AKE4BM9k. 1 June 2018.

Andrew Hilton (1994) *UK Financial Supervision: A Blueprint for Change* (Centre for the Study of Financial Innovation (CSFI), London).

Anon (2003) 'Power Failure Rocks Malawi's Telecoms' (*PANA Press*), http://www.panapress.com/Power-Failure-Rocks-Malawi-s-Telecoms--13-475501-18-lang1-index.html. 29 June 2018.

Anon (2007) 'Malawi Mobile Phone Network Goes off the Air' (*Click Afrique*), http://www.clickafrique.com/Magazine/ST010/CP0000002372.aspx. 29 June 2018.

Anon (2016) 'What Is the Bristol Pound?' (*Bristol City*), http://bristolpound.org/what. 13 September 2018.

Benjamin J Cohen (2008) 'The International Monetary System: Diffusion and Ambiguity' *International Affairs* 455, http://escholarship.org/uc/item/97r5n8jx. 4 October 2018.

Bill Maurer (2011) 'Mobile Money Regulation: A Story Arc of Best Practices and Emerging Realizations' *Notes from the Field* (December 2011), http://faculty.sites.uci.edu/wmmaurer/files/2011/12/Note_Dec2011_IMTFI.pdf. 15 December 2018.

Bill Maurer (2012) 'Payment: Forms and Functions of Value Transfer in Contemporary Society' 30 *Cambridge Anthropology* 15.

Bjørn S Aamo (2012) 'FATF's Focus on Financial Inclusion: Protecting the Integrity of the Global Financial System' (*Global Partnership for Financial Inclusion Conference on Standard-Setting Bodies and Financial Inclusion: Promoting Financial Inclusion Through Proportionate Standards and Guidance*) Basel. 29 October 2012, http://www.fatf-gafi.org/publications/fatfgeneral/documents/fatfsfocusonfinancialinclusionprotectingtheintegrity-oftheglobalfinancialsystem.html. 20 February 2018.

Boon-Chye Lee and Olujoke Longe-Akindemowo (1999) 'Regulatory Issues in Electronic Money: A Legal-Economics Analysis' 1 (1) *Netnomics* 53.

Bryane Michael (2014) 'The "Twin Peaks" Regulatory Model: The Future of Financial Regulation?' *Banking Today*, http://www.law.hku.hk/aiifl/wp-content/uploads/2014/09/Twin-Peaks.pdf. 3 October 2018.

*Case Concerning the Payment of Various Serbian Loans Issued in France (France v. Serbia) and Payment in Gold of the Brazilian Federal Loans Contracted in France (France v. Brazil)* PCIJ Rep Series A Nos 20–21 Permanent Court of international Justice, http://legal.un.org/PCIJsummaries/documents/english/PCIJ_FinalText.pdf. 7 November 2018.

César Córdova-Novion and Deirdre Hanlon (2002) 'Regulatory Governance: Improving the Institutional Basis for Sectoral Regulators' 2 (3) *OECD Journal on Budgeting*, https://www.oecd.org/gov/budgeting/43505850.pdf. 15 February 2018.

Charles Goodhart (1988) *The Evolution of Central Banks* (MIT Press Books, Cambridge).

Charles Goodhart and Dirk Schoenmaker (1995) 'Should the Functions of Monetary Policy and Banking Supervision Be Separated?' 47 (4) *Oxford Economic Papers* 539, http://oep.oxfordjournals.org/content/47/4/539.extract. 12 February 2018.

Chris Hunt (2016) *A Short History of Prudential Regulation and Supervision at the Reserve Bank* (Bulletin, Reserve Bank of New Zealand, Wellington), http://www.rbnz.govt.nz/-/media/ReserveBank/Files/Publications/Bulletins/2016/2016aug79-14.pdf. 1 May 2018.

Chris Skinner (2015) 'When Everyone on the Planet Has a Mobile Money Account, Things Will Change' (24 June 2015), http://thefinanser.com/2015/06/when-everyone-on-the-planet-has-a-mobilelectronic-money-account-things-will-change.html/. 9 February 2018.

Clive Briault (1999) *The Rationale for a Single National Financial Services Regulator* (Occasional Paper Series, Financial Services Authority, London), http://citeseerx.ist.psu.edu/viewdoc/download?doi=10.1.1.468.6859&rep=rep1&type=pdf. 12 May 2018.

Dalvinder Singh (2007) *Banking Regulation of UK and US Financial Markets* (Ashgate Publishing, Aldershot, Hampshire).
Daniel K Tarullo (2016) 'Financial Regulation Since the Crisis' (Federal Reserve Bank of Cleveland and Office of Financial Research 2016 Financial Stability Conference) Washington, DC. 2 December 2016, https://www.federalreserve.gov/newsevents/speech/tarullo20161202a.htm. 1 May 2018.
David Blair (2013) 'The FSA Is Dead; Long Live the FCA, the PRA and the FPC', http://www.osborneclarke.com/connected-insights/publications/the-fsa-is-dead-long-live-the-fca-the-pra-and-the-fpc/#sthash.PzXxYUIX.dpuf. 3 March 2018.
David Porteous (2006) *The Enabling Environment for Mobile Banking in Africa* (Report Commissioned by Department for International Development [DFID], Boston), http://bankablefrontier.com/wp-ontent/uploads/documents/ee.mobil_.banking.report.v3.1.pdf. 14 September 2018.
*Development of Postal Services in 2011: A Few Key Figures* (2011) (Universal Postal Union), http://www.alejandrobarros.com/media/users/1/50369/files/4363/Statistics_2011_UPU.pdf. 10 May 2018.
ECB (2002) *The Role of Central Banks in Prudential Supervision* (European Central Bank), https://www.ecb.europa.eu/pub/pdf/other/prudentialsupcbrole_en.pdf. 1 May 2018.
Eddy Wymeersch (2007) 'The Structure of Financial Supervision in Europe: About Single Financial Supervisors, Twin Peaks and Multiple Financial Supervisors' 8 *European Business Organization Law Review* 237.
Ernesto M Flores-Roux and Judith Mariscal (2010) 'The Enigma of Mobile Money Systems' (79) *Communications & Strategies*, ftp://ftp.repec.org/opt/ReDIF/RePEc/idt/journl/CS7903/CS79_MARISCAM_FLORES-ROUX.pdf. 14 February 2018.
FATF (2012) *International Standards on Combating Money Laundering and the Financing of Terrorism & Proliferation (updated October 2016)* (Financial Action Task Force), http://www.fatf-gafi.org/media/fatf/documents/recommendations/pdfs/FATF_Recommendations.pdf. 20 February 2018.
FATF (2016) 'Financial Action Task Force' (FATF), http://www.fatf-gafi.org/. 15 December 2018.
FCIC (2011) *The Financial Crisis Inquiry Report: Final Report of the National Commission on the Causes of the Financial and Economic Crisis in the United States* (The Financial Crisis Inquiry Commission, Washington, DC), https://www.gpo.gov/fdsys/pkg/GPO-FCIC/pdf/GPO-FCIC.pdf. 1 May 2018.
*Finance Bank of Malaŵi Ltd (In Voluntary Liquidation) v Reserve Bank of Malawi and Attorney General* Constitutional Cause No. 5 of 2010 High Court (Constitutional Division), http://www.malawilii.org/mw/judgment/high-court-general-division/2013/451. 9 March 2018.
Financial Crimes Act (2017).

Financial Crimes (Suppression of Terrorist Financing and Proliferation) Regulations, 2017, Government Notice No. 11 of 2017 (Malaŵi).

Financial Services Act (Malaŵi, 2010).

Financial Services Act, UK (United Kingdom, 2012).

Financial Services (Fit and Proper Requirement for Persons Associated with Ownership and Management of Securities Market Players) Directive 2015 (Malaŵi), https://www.rbm.mw/Supervision/GetContentFile/?ContentID=6457. 20 July 2018.

Francis N Ngwu (2014) 'Promoting Formal Financial Inclusion in Africa: As Institutional Re-examination of the Policies with a Case Study of Nigeria' 16 (14) 306 *Journal of Banking Regulation*, http://link.springer.com/article/10.1057/jbr.2014.13. 15 December 2018.

Frank Phiri (2005) 'Finance Bank Closure: Precursor to Return of Forfeiture Act?' (*Malawiana*), https://groups.yahoo.com/neo/groups/MALAWIANA/conversations/topics/3175. 23 February 2018.

Friedrich August v Hayek (1990) *Denationalisation of Money—The Argument Refined: An Analysis of the Theory and Practice of Concurrent Currencies* (3rd Ed) (Institute of Economic Affairs, London) Chapter III.

G-10 (2001) *Chapter III: Effects of Consolidation on Financial Risk in Report on Consolidation in the Financial Sector* (Group of 10, IMF, Washington, DC), https://www.imf.org/external/np/g10/2001/01/Eng/pdf/file3.pdf. 1 June 2018.

Garry J Schinasi (2003) *Responsibility of Central Banks for Stability in Financial Markets* (IMF Working Paper, Washington, DC), https://www.imf.org/external/pubs/ft/wp/2003/wp03121.pdf. 1 June 2018.

George Ngigi 'M-Pesa Linked to Rise in Inflation' *Business Daily* (14 February 2012), http://www.businessdailyafrica.com/M-Pesa-linked-to-rise-in-inflation/-/539552/1327538/-/13rogmr/-/index.html. 28 March 2018.

Guidelines for Mobile Payment Systems (Malaŵi, 2011).

Gunther Teubner (1983) 'Substantive and Reflexive Elements in Modern Law' *Law and Society Review* 239, http://www.jstor.org/stable/3053348. 18 November 2018.

Heidi Mandanis Schooner and Mark W Taylor (2010) *Global Bank Regulation: Principles and Policies* (Academic Press, Burlington, MA).

Hyun Song Shin (2009) 'Reflections on Northern Rock: The Bank Run That Heralded the Global Financial Crisis' 23 (1) *The Journal of Economic Perspectives* 101, http://dx.doi.org/10.1257/089533009797614045. 4 October 2018.

Ignacio Mas and Daniel Radcliffe (2011) 'Mobile Payments Go Viral: M-PESA in Kenya' 32 *The Capco Institute Journal of Financial Transformation* 169, http://www.capco.com/sites/all/files/journal-32_article-16.pdf. 15 December 2018.

Ignacio Mas and Olga Morawczynski (2009) 'Designing Mobile Money Services Lessons from M-PESA' 4 (2) *Innovations* 77, http://www.mitpressjournals.org/doi/pdf/10.1162/itgg.2009.4.2.77. 20 May 2018.

Interview at Reserve Bank of Malaŵi Headquarters (RBM HQ) on 6 August 2015.

Interview with Webster Mbekeani Head, Mobile Money Division, TNM (20 August 2015).

Jane Fuller (2010) 'The King Is Dead; Long Live the King' *Financial World*, http://fwarchive.ifslearning.ac.uk/financial_world/Archive/2010/2010_07July/Comment/Jane%20Fuller/pdf/18908.pdf. 28 February 2018.

Jennifer Isern and Louis De Koker (2012) *AML/CFT: Strengthening Financial Inclusion and Integrity* (CGAP Focus Notes, CGAP, Washington, DC), http://dro.deakin.edu.au/eserv/DU:30020790/dekoker-amlcft-2009.pdf. 14 November 2018.

Jennifer Isern and others (2005) 'AML/CFT Regulation: Implications for Financial Service Providers That Serve Low-Income People' 29 *CGAP Focus Note*, https://www.cgap.org/sites/default/files/CGAP-Focus-Note-AML-CFT-Regulation-Implications-for-Financial-Service-Providers-That-Serve-Low-Income-People-Jul-2005.pdf. 10 May 2018.

Jeroen Kremers and Dirk Schoenmaker (2010) 'Twin Peaks: Experiences in the Netherlands' December 2010 *LSE Financial Markets Group Paper Series*, http://www.lse.ac.uk/fmg/workingPapers/specialPapers/PDF/SP196.pdf. 4 October 2018.

Jonathan Greenacre, Louise Malady and Ross Buckley (2014) *The Regulation of Mobile Money in Malawi* (Centre for International Finance and Regulation, New South Wales), http://www.uncdf.org/sites/default/files/Documents/the_regulation_of_mobile_money_in_malawi_project_report_final_version.pdf. 30 June 2018.

Joseph Noko (2011) 'Dollarization: The Case of Zimbabwe' 31 (2) *Cato Journal*, https://www.ciaonet.org/attachments/18686/uploads. 14 September 2018.

Kenneth Kaoma Mwenda (2006) *Legal Aspects of Financial Services Regulation and the Concept of a Unified Regulator* (World Bank, Washington, DC).

Kevin P Donovan (2012) 'Mobile Money, More Freedom? The Impact of M-PESA's Network Power on Development as Freedom' 6 *International Journal of Communication* 2647, http://ijoc.org/index.php/ijoc/article/view/1575. 20 May 2018.

Louis de Koker (2013) 'The 2012 Revised FATF Recommendations: Assessing and Mitigating Mobile Money Integrity Risks Within the New Standards Framework' 8 *Wash JL Tech & Arts* 165.

Macro-Prudential and Micro-Prudential Regulation (Chapter 2) The Warwick Commission (2009) in *The Warwick Commission on International Financial Reform: In Praise of Unlevel Playing Fields* (University of Warwick), https://

www2.warwick.ac.uk/research/warwickcommission/financialreform/report/uw_warcomm_intfinreform_09.pdf. 2 June 2018.

Malaŵi Government (2015) 'Commencement of Universal and Compulsory Birth & Death Registration and Issuance of Certificates' (Government of Malaŵi), https://www.facebook.com/malawigovernment/posts/439708072882359. 21 July 2018.

Malcom Webb and others (2014) *Mobile Money Regulation* (WebbHenderson, Sydney), http://webbhenderson.com/wp-content/uploads/2015/06/Mobilelectronic-money-Regulation-April-2014.pdf. 9 February 2018.

Marc Quintyn and Michael W Taylor (2002) *Regulatory and Supervisory Independence and Financial Stability* (International Monetary Fund, Washington, DC), https://www.imf.org/external/pubs/ft/wp/2002/wp0246.pdf. 1 February 2018.

Maureen Burton and Bruce Brown (2014) *The Financial System and the Economy: Principles of Money and Banking* (Routledge, Abingdon, Oxon).

Michael Malakata (2015) 'Power Problems Disrupt Africa's Telecom Sector' (*PCWorld*), http://www.pcworld.com/article/2926892/power-problems-disrupt-africas-telecom-sector.html. 29 June 2018.

Michael Tarazi and Paul Breloff (2010) *Nonbank Electronic Money Issuers: Regulatory Approaches to Protecting Customer Funds* (Focus Note, CGAP, Washington, DC), https://www.cgap.org/sites/default/files/CGAP-Focus-Note-Nonbank-Electronic-money-Issuers-Regulatory-Approaches-to-Protecting-Customer-Funds-Jul-2010.pdf. 3 February 2018.

Michael U Klein and Colin Mayer (2011) *Mobile Banking and Financial Inclusion: The Regulatory Lessons* (Policy Research Working Paper, The World Bank), http://documents.worldbank.org/curated/en/docsearch/document-type/620265. 14 February 2018.

Michael W Taylor (1995) "Twin Peaks": A Regulatory Structure for the New Century (Centre for the Study of Financial Innovation, London).

Michael W Taylor (2011) 'The Road from "Twin peaks"—And the Way Back' 16 (1) *Connecticut Insurance Law Journal* 61, http://insurancejournal.org/wp-content/uploads/2011/07/Abstract-21.pdf. 3 October 2018.

Milton Friedman (1971) 'The EuroDollar Market: Some First Principles' *Review (Federal Bank of St Louis)* 16, https://research.stlouisfed.org/publications/review/71/07/Principles_Jul1971.pdf. 13 September 2018.

Mona Naqvi and James Southgate (2013) 'Banknotes, Local Currencies and Central Bank Objectives' *Bank of England Quarterly Bulletin* Q4, http://www.bankofengland.co.uk/publications/Documents/quarterlybulletin/2013/qb130403.pdf. 4 October 2018.

Money Laundering and Proceeds of Terrorism Act (Malaŵi, 2006).

National Registration Act (Malaŵi, 2010), https://www.globalintegrity.org/wp-content/uploads/2016/01/Malawi-NATIONAL-REGISTRATION-ACT.pdf. 21 July 2018.

Nick Hughes and Susie Lonie (2007) 'M-PESA: Mobile Money for the "Unbanked" Turning Cellphones into 24-Hour Tellers in Kenya' 2 (1–2) *Innovations* 63, http://www.mitpressjournals.org/doi/pdf/10.1162/itgg.2007.2.1-2.63. 15 December 2018.

Nicola Jentzsch (2012) 'Implications of Mandatory Registration of Mobile Phone Users in Africa' 36 (8) *Telecommunications Policy* 608, http://doi.org/10.1016/j.telpol.2012.04.002. 14 November 2018.

Olga Morawczynski and Gianluca Miscione (2008) 'Examining Trust in Mobile Banking Transactions: The Case of M-PESA in Kenya' in Chrisanthi Avgerou, Matthew L Smith and Peter van den Basselaar (eds) *Social Dimensions of Information and Communication Technology Policy* (Springer, Boston).

Olga Morawczynski and Mark Pickens (2009) *Poor People Using Mobile Financial Services: Observations on Customer Usage and Impact from M-PESA* (CGAP Brief, August, CGAP, Washington, DC), http://www.cgap.org/publications/poor-people-using-mobile-financial-services. 29 April 2018.

'Prudential Regulation Authority' (2017) *Bank of England*, http://www.bankofengland.co.uk/pra/Pages/default.aspx. 1 May 2018.

Richard J Herring and Anthony M Santomero (2000) 'What Is Optimal Financial Regulation?' in Benton E Gup (ed) *The New Financial Architecture* (Quorum Books, Westport, Connecticut).

Robin Hui Huang and Dirk Schoenmaker (2014) *Institutional Structure of Financial Regulation: Theories and International Experiences* (Routledge, London).

Robleh Ali and others (2014b) 'The Economics of Digital Currencies' 54 *Quarterly Bulletin* (Bank of England), http://www.bankofengland.co.uk/publications/Documents/quarterlybulletin/2014/qb14q3digitalcurrenciesbitcoin2.pdf. 14 September 2018.

Rose Cunningham and Christian Friedrich (2016) *The Role of Central Banks in Promoting Financial Stability: An International Perspective* (Bank of Canada Staff Discussion Paper 2016–15, Bank of Canada, Ottawa, Ontario), http://www.bankofcanada.ca/wp-content/uploads/2016/07/sdp2016-15.pdf. 1 May 2018.

Roger E Backhouse (1991) 'Money' in *Applied UK Macroeconomics* (Basil Blackwell, Oxford).

Ross Buckley, Jonathan Greenacre and Louise Malady (2015) 'The Regulation of Mobile Money in Malawi' 14 (3) *Washington University Global Studies Law Review* 435, http://openscholarship.wustl.edu/cgi/viewcontent.cgi?article=1536&context=law_globalstudies. 3 February 2018.

Ruby Szarowicz (2016) 'Bringing Bristol Pound to Massive Attack at the Downs' *Bristol Pond Our City Our Money* (Bristol, 6 September 2016), http://bristolpound.org/blog/. 13 September 2016.

Simone Di Castri (2013) *Mobile Money: Enabling Regulatory Solutions* (GSMA, London), http://www.gsma.com/publicpolicy/wp-content/uploads/2013/02/GSMA2013_Report_Mobilelectronic-money-EnablingRegulatorySolutions.pdf. 20 February 2018.

The Committee of Scottish Bankers (2016) 'Scottish Banknotes Legal Position' *The Committee of Scottish Bankers* (Edinburgh), http://www.scotbanks.org.uk/legal_position.php. 13 September 2018.

Timothy Lyman (2016) 'Regulation and Supervision' (*CGAP*), http://www.cgap.org/topics/regulation-and-supervision. 21 May, 2018.

Tom de Swaan and Others (1995) *The Supervision of Financial Conglomerates* (Tripartite Group of Bank, Securities and Insurance Regulators, Madrid), https://www.iosco.org/library/pubdocs/pdf/IOSCOPD47.pdf. 3 October 2018.

Tommaso Padoa-Schioppa (2003) 'Central Banks and Financial Stability: Exploring the Land in Between' in Vitor Gaspar, Philipp Hartmann and Olaf Sleijpen (eds) *Second ECB Central Banking Conference: The Transformation of the European Financial System* (European Central Bank).

V Sundararajan and Others (2005) *Financial Sector Assessment* (World Bank & International Monetary Fund, Washington, DC).

Vincent P Polizatto (1992) 'Prudential Regulation and Banking Supervision' in Dimitri Vittas (ed) *Financial Regulation: Changing the Rules of the Game* (The World Bank, Washington, DC).

Will Mutua (3 June 2012) 'How M-Pesa Disrupts Entire Economies', http://memeburn.com/2012/03/how-m-pesa-disrupts-entire-economies/. 28 March 2018.

William Jack and Tavneet Suri (2011) 'Mobile Money: The Economics of M-PESA' (National Bureau of Economic Research), http://www.nber.org/papers/w16721. 15 December 2018.

William Stanley Jevons (1875) 'Barter' in *Money and the Mechanism of Exchange* (D. Appleton and Company, New York).

XE (2018) 'XE Currency Converter' (*XE*), https://www.xe.com/currencyconverter/convert/?Amount=1&From=GBP&To=MWK. 10 November 2018.

Yvonnie Sundu (2016) 'APM Says National IDs Will Transform Malawi' *The Nation* (28 October 2016), http://mwnation.com/apm-says-national-ids-will-transform-malawi/. 14 November 2018.

CHAPTER 6

# The Concept of Financial Inclusion

## 6.1 Introduction

Financial inclusion or exclusion usually affects people on the margins of society, the so-called vulnerable groups.[1] Sarma and Pais say financial exclusion is "a manifestation of social exclusion".[2] According to Donovan, "poverty is more than just a lack of money".[3] People who are socially excluded may have money, but their exclusion from the social system exacerbates their poverty.[4] Mobile money has by its nature the potential of getting on board such people who would otherwise not be covered by services providers within the formal financial system. In solving the remittance dilemma, mobile money has also introduced an alternative payment system, which is virtually unlimited in scope. While traditional models of financial inclusion have been credit-led or savings-led, mobile money "suggests a third approach – focussing on building the payment rails on which a broader set of financial services can

[1] Mandira Sarma and Jesim Pais (2011) 'Financial Inclusion and Development' 23 *Journal of International Development* 613, p. 614, http://onlinelibrary.wiley.com/doi/10.1002/jid.1698/pdf. 20 April 2018.

[2] Ibid., p. 626.

[3] Kevin Donovan (2012) 'Mobile Money for Financial Inclusion' in *Information and Communications for Development 2012* (World Bank, Washington, DC), p. 62.

[4] Ibid.



S. Madise, *The Regulation of Mobile Money*, Palgrave Macmillan Studies in Banking and Financial Institutions, https://doi.org/10.1007/978-3-030-13831-8_6

ride".[5] Chibba found a nexus connecting financial inclusion, poverty reduction and millennium development goals.[6] He argues that financial inclusion "offers incremental and complementary solutions to tackle poverty, to promote inclusive development and to address the millennium development goals".[7]

With mobile money, the fundamental question is, what should regulation be like pre and post-financial inclusion? Currently, Malaŵi is dealing with the pre-financial inclusion stage. However, what happens when financial inclusion has been achieved? Lessons from Kenya, where mobile money has been successful, may help in shaping the future regulatory framework post-financial inclusion. As this chapter will show, the formal financial system has left a vacuum. Mobile money, as an alternative form, provides an essential financial service to the unbanked. Mobile money is not just filling in a vacuum left by the formal financial services providers but is becoming a desirable service. The introduction of mobile money has been hailed as a key step towards attaining financial inclusion.[8] However, lack of access to formal financial services should never be equated with a lack to possess the necessary financial expertise. Demirguc-Kunt and Klapper argue that despite most people in rural areas being outside the formal financial system, they "juggle complex financial transactions every day and use sophisticated techniques to manage their finances".[9] Globally, lack of money itself has been cited as the key barrier to financial inclusion.[10] In this regard, mobile money opens an avenue where people, especially in rural areas of developing countries can have access to money, largely through remittances. Mobile money also has the advantage of being convenient, cheap, secure and reliable.[11]

[5] Mas and Radcliffe (2011), p. 172.

[6] Michael Chibba (2009) 'Financial Inclusion, Poverty Reduction and the Millennium Development Goals' 21 (2) *The European Journal of Development Research* 213, pp. 214–6, https://doi.org/10.1057/ejdr.2008.17. 20 April 2018.

[7] Ibid., p. 213.

[8] Asli Demirguc-Kunt and Leora Klapper (2012) *Measuring Financial Inclusion: The Global Findex Database* (Policy Research Working Papers, The World Bank), p. 2, https://laomfa.org/wp-content/uploads/formidable/7/Measuring-Financial-Inclusion_The-World-Bank-2010.pdf. 20 April 2018.

[9] Ibid., p. 3.

[10] Ibid.

[11] Ibid., p. 26.

This chapter provides a critical analysis of the concept of financial inclusion using Malaŵi's financial inclusion agenda as the baseline. It argues that financial inclusion cannot be achieved without contextualising the institutional and infrastructural problems that have led to many being unbanked. The case of local village banks is given as a way in which local communities overcome challenges associated with access to formal financial services. It calls for a redefinition of the concept of financial inclusion to suit the local context. It further argues that although many people in the developing world remain unbanked and outside the formal financial system, they are nonetheless not financially excluded. This chapter is divided into three sections. The first section presents an overview of the concept of financial inclusion. The second section uses a case study to analyse the concept of village "banking". The third section examines mobile money as a possible solution to the needs of rural people.

## 6.2 Financial Inclusion in the Malaŵian Context

The problem that rural people face is that banks and other financial service providers do not extend their services to them because they "do not present an attractive business case".[12] Most providers understandably target cities and towns. Cities and towns not only have well-built infrastructure, but are also hubs for people looking for financial services. If people in the rural areas wish to access banking or financial services, they must travel to the cities and towns. Banks also require a minimum credit balance to open and operate a savings account and impose restrictions on withdrawals. The third hurdle is the lack of a formalised national identity system, which makes it difficult for people in rural areas to open bank accounts, as banks demand a form of identification from potential customers. A common problem identified with most financial products is a mismatch between service provision and the demand.[13] Mahendra Dev argues that financial service providers need "to be friendly to small and marginal farmers and other vulnerable groups. It requires a specific type of organisational ethos, culture and attitude".[14] In regulation language, one would say it requires a really responsive approach to this specific group of consumers. Therefore,

[12] CPSS (2012), p. 33.

[13] Donovan (2012), p. 71.

[14] S Mahendra Dev (2006) 'Financial Inclusion: Issues and Challenges' 41 (41) *Economic and Political Weekly* 4310, p. 4310, http://www.jstor.org/stable/4418799. 20 April 2018.

it is not that the people in the rural areas are incapable of banking per se but rather the service providers are not servicing them.[15] The result is that people in these areas remain unbanked and under-banked.[16] The Reserve Bank of Malaŵi has identified the following initiatives to achieve financial inclusion:

- Microfinance
- Agent banking
- Mobile money
- Consumer protection.[17]

Dev defines financial inclusion as the "delivery of banking services at an affordable cost to the vast sections of disadvantaged and low-income groups".[18] According to Mohan, it denotes access "to appropriate, low cost, fair and safe financial products and services from mainstream providers".[19] Use of formal accounts seems to be the indicative measure of financial inclusion.[20] Financial inclusion is not only beneficial to the vulnerable groups, but also avails to the formal system greater resources, which can be intermediated for higher returns.[21] As such, while fulfilling a developmental agenda, financial inclusion also simultaneously fulfils a capitalist one, without the two agendas being mutually exclusive. Financial inclusion also leads to empowerment brought about by a greater awareness of financial products as well as increased financial literacy.[22] Sarma and Pais found that there is a direct correlation between the index of financial inclusion (IFI) and the human development index

[15] Interview at Reserve Bank of Malaŵi (RBM) MicroFinance Division on 19 August 2015.

[16] Ibid.

[17] Ibid.

[18] Dev (2006), p. 4310.

[19] Rakesh Mohan (2008) 'Economic Growth, Financial Deepening and Financial Inclusion' in Manoranjan Sharma (ed) *Dynamics of Indian Banking: Views and Vistas* (Atlantic Publishers, New Delhi), p. 100.

[20] Franklin Allen and others (2012) *The Foundations of Financial Inclusion* (Policy Research Working Papers, The World Bank), http://documents.worldbank.org/curated/en/348241468329061640/pdf/wps6290.pdf. 20 April 2018.

[21] Mohan (2008), pp. 101–2.

[22] Ibid., p. 116.

(HDI) although a high HDI does not correlate with a high IFI.[23] Allen et al. argue that this provides "both an economic and a political rationale for policies that promote financial inclusion".[24]

Provision of microfinance loans was initially seen as one way of not only alleviating poverty but also contributing to financial inclusiveness. However, a recent study has challenged this approach, while acknowledging its usefulness as a financial tool in that it allows for greater financial freedom among the poor.[25] In other words, the argument is that the bar must not be set unrealistically high.[26] While mobile money and other innovations have been hailed as better alternative, commentators have warned against any euphoric embrace of these alternative services without thorough research.[27]

Lack of availability of financial services, however, does not mean the poor have no sense of finance.[28] The growth of mobile money and its impact on financial inclusion across sub-Saharan Africa is testimony that poor people can embrace new products, once they gain trust in them.[29] Di Castri says mobile money has seen "millions of households, mostly low-income, from a cash only economy into the formal financial system".[30] A year after mobile money was launched in Malaŵi, the country's central bank in its 2014 Payment Systems Annual Report said:

> Mobile network operator-led mobile payments services have grown at a very significant rate, in fact at a much faster rate than the mobile banking services offered by the commercial banks, in terms of both transactions (volumes and value) and number of subscribers. This development confirms the potential for mobile network operator-led microfinance[31]

[23] Sarma and Pais (2011), p. 619.

[24] Allen and others (2012), p. 1.

[25] Claire Luke (2015) 'Critique of Microfinance Raises Questions about Efficacy, Donor Support of the Industry' (*Devex Impact*), https://www.devex.com/news/critique-of-microfinance-raises-questions-about-efficacy-donor-support-of-the-industry-85617. 20 April 2018.

[26] Ibid.

[27] Ibid., referring to Esther Duflo of the Abdul Latif Jameel Poverty Action Lab.

[28] Dittus and Klein (2011), p. 3.

[29] Ibid., pp. 3–4.

[30] Di Castri (2013), p. 7.

[31] A confirmation of the misunderstanding that mobile money is a component of microfinance.

> service as a significant tool in the financial inclusion agenda, as they cater for a wider section of the population including the unbanked.[32]

Malaŵi is a rural-based economy, and the primary means of payment among individuals remain cash.[33] Even among the banked, cash is still the premier instrument used for payment.[34] In such an environment, mobile money has the potential of availing to the formal economy, cash held by the unbanked. Because of its electronic platform, mobile money not only avails to its users an array of various services, but it also plays a key role in achieving financial inclusion and reducing cash dependency.[35] In its financial inclusion matrix, the central bank looks at three aspects: availability, convenience and access.[36] The central bank had targeted to increase the adult bankable population from 19% (2008) to 40% by 2014.[37] A survey conducted in 2014 found that the target was not achieved and the figure was only 27%.[38] The percentage of those financially excluded reduced from 55 to 51.[39] The following have been singled out as challenges hindering Malaŵi's achievement of full financial inclusion:

i. Low penetration of cell phones among the unbanked population;
ii. Low penetration of mobile money agents in rural areas;
iii. Low financial literacy and awareness among the populace;
iv. Lack of interconnectivity or integrated national switch through which mobile network operators can integrate with commercial banks' payment systems; and
v. High relative cost of financial services.[40]

32 RBM (2015), p. 14.

33 RBM (2008), p. 6.

34 Dermish et al. (2012), p. 4.

35 Di Castri (2013), p. 8.

36 RBM MicroFinance Division (2015).

37 RBM (2013) *National Payment Systems Annual Report 2012* (Reserve Bank of Malawi), p. 11, http://www.rbm.mw/documents/payment_systems/payment%20systems%20annual%20report%202012.pdf. 10 February 2014. It may be argued that at the end of 2014, an evaluation can be undertaken to see if this rather ambitious target has been achieved.

38 Finscope (2014), p. 19.

39 Ibid.

40 RBM (2013), pp. 11–2.

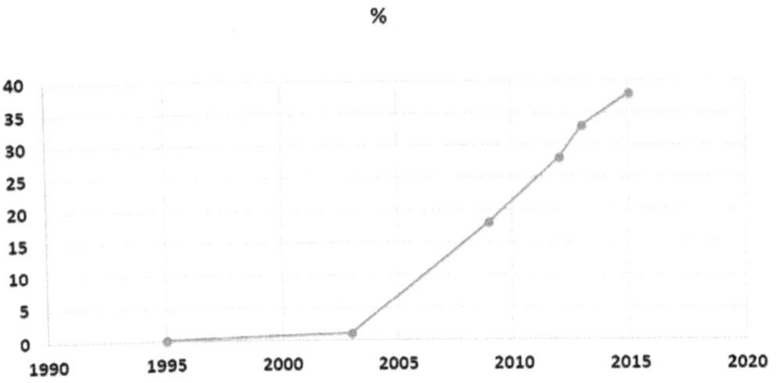


**Fig. 6.1** Growth in mobile penetration rates (*Source* Author's creation from data collected)

Figure 6.1 shows that real increase in mobile penetration has occurred in the last decade in Malaŵi. Mobile penetration grew rapidly from 1% in 2003 to 28% in 2012 and was expected to peak at 38% by the end of 2015.[41] As discussed below, there are indications that the market is saturated.

Figure 6.2 provides a split analysis of the numbers of subscribers for each of the two dominant mobile network operators.

Interestingly, the projected peak for total mobile subscribers in 2015 was 7.8 million, which is almost the figure that comprises those who are 16 years and above.[42] This would indicate that the mobile phone market in Malaŵi is saturated, a view shared by TNM's head of *Mpamba*, Webster Mbekeani:

> The market is small. Malaŵi is a country of 14 million. About 50% are adults. That gives you 7 million. Not all of them can afford a mobile phone, so that gives you 5.5 to 6 million. That is the addressable market. Airtel, and ourselves have already reached that number. Therefore, there will not be any new customers coming from anywhere.[43]

[41] Anon (2010) 'Mobile Cellular Subscriptions (per 100 People) in Malawi' (*Trading Economics*), http://www.tradingeconomics.com/malawi/mobile-cellular-subscriptions-per-100-people-wb-data.html. 11 March 2018.
Lancaster (2015).

[42] Finscope (2014), p. 2.

[43] Mbekeani (2015).

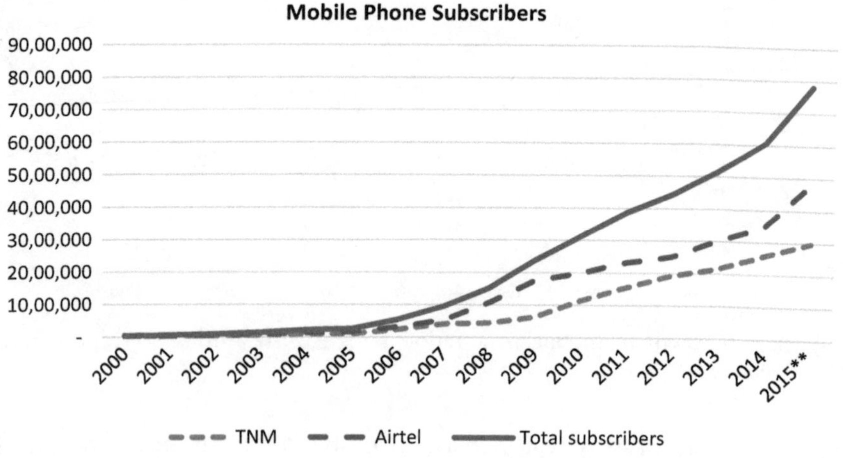


**Fig. 6.2** Subscribers growth of TNM and Airtel and the totals (*Source of data for figures* MACRA [2015] *Subscriber Trends 2000–2014* [Malaŵi Communications Regulator Authority]; *Source* Author's creation from data collected)

Figure 6.3 confirms that the growth rate has since 2013 been slow (less than 0.5%) although Airtel seems to be on the rise while TNM is flat. However, these statistics do not tell the whole story. In fact, although the mobile penetration is said to be at 7.8 million, this is not the total number of mobile users per se but rather the aggregate of Airtel (just under 5 million) and TNM (just under 3 million) customers.[44] It includes customers, like me, who are registered with both networks.

The reason why most subscribers will register with both networks is to take advantage of cheaper own-network calls and avoid, as much as possible, costly across-network calls. It is, therefore, submitted that the combined figures of subscribers are not the total number of Malaŵians using mobile phones. Andrew Nyirenda of the Malaŵi Communications Regulatory Authority says:

> The data shows Malaŵians have become aware of the exorbitant across network charges and are now using more of their own network. 93% of the traffic is comprised of own network calls. They have two SIM cards

[44] MACRA (2015).

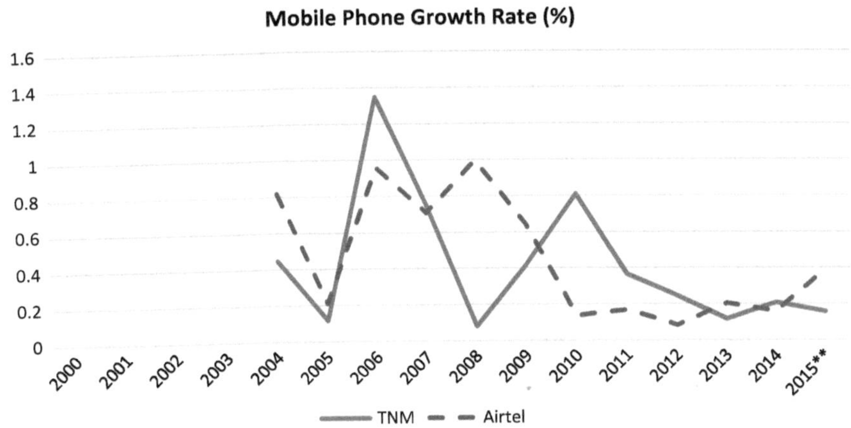


**Fig. 6.3** Showing growth rates of the two dominant mobile companies (MACRA 2015) (*Source* Author's creation from data collected)

> or phones, one for each network. That is why the mobile money network operators have introduced many promotions targeting own-network calls and services.[45]

Out of the registered subscribers across both networks, only 23% are active.[46] So Mbekeani's estimate of just under 6 million may be more accurate.

Turning mobile phone subscribers into mobile money users is the key to unlocking the potential of mobile money. TNM has converted only 30% of its customer base into registered users while Airtel has a 34% conversion rate.[47] Active, not registered, users are the lifeblood of mobile money. Active users are those that have been using the mobile money service within the preceding 30 days.[48] The latest report by the central bank shows that the combined figure for mobile money active users is 28.3 and 38% over

[45] Interview with Andrew Nyirenda Malawi Communications Regulatory Authority (3 August 2015).

[46] Ibid.

[47] Computed using the data provided by MACRA and the two mobile money service providers.

[48] Mkoloma (2015).

30-day and 90-day periods.[49] According to the central bank, the 90-day percentage is slightly higher than the global rate of 35.8.[50] In 2015, TNM had 800,000 registered users of *Mpamba* but on average, 35% were active users.[51]

Despite these statistics, *Mpamba* has a target of 80% active users of the whole TNM customer base.[52] TNM has ambitious plans to remove registration and offer the *Mpamba* service as part of the TNM bouquet.[53] This will entail that once a client registers as a customer of TNM, they will automatically also be registered for *Mpamba*. Airtel Money has a similar target, to convert all registered Airtel customers into Airtel Money customers.[54] Product and Development Manager for Airtel Money, Bigboy Mkoloma, puts it this way:

> There is a benefit to the mother business: retention of customers. The moment they open a mobile money account, the assumption is that they will rarely leave the network or search for other networks to make calls. Innovation is the way to convert the mobile phone customers into mobile money customers.[55]

However, it would appear that these targets by both mobile money service providers are rather ambitious and way above the global averages. There are currently no indications that the trajectory will change any time soon. Indeed, when one considers that most of the users of mobile phones in sub-Saharan Africa may be in the financially excluded category, it begs the question, how does mobile money fit into the financial inclusion agenda? Dittus and Klein have outlined a general framework for attaining financial inclusion:

[49] Reserve Bank of Malaŵi (2018) 'Monthly National Payment System Report, May 2018' Issue 5 Vol 6, https://www.rbm.mw/PaymentSystems/GetContentFile/?ContentID=26223. 2 December 2018.

[50] Ibid.

[51] Mbekeani (2015).

[52] Ibid.

[53] Ibid.

[54] Mkoloma (2015).

[55] Ibid.

a. Exchanging different forms of money
b. Storing money (safe-keeping)
c. Remittances (from one owner to another)
d. Investing money.[56]

It is argued that mobile money fits very well into this framework. As a form of book entry money, it is easily exchangeable though on commission with cash.[57] Although not designed as a saving, it can function as a vehicle to canvass savings. Once a person converts their cash into mobile money, the mobile money retains its face value until it is used. As noted earlier, mobile money was initially rolled out as a remittance service. In doing so, it overcomes the problem that had long existed of how to transport money, especially to rural areas. Mobile money which rides on the telecommunication backbone has removed the need for physical transfer of money.[58] In the hands of the customer, mobile money cannot be invested. The only investing that occurs is at the bank's end. The bank can invest the deposited funds in the pool account. However, even though mobile money cannot satisfy the investment category, it is submitted that the use of the service can act as a catalyst that can lead to customers trying other financial products, such as investments.

With the promise that mobile money holds, slow growth in mobile money users has been noted with concern by the Malaŵi's central bank. The central bank says the growth has been generally unsatisfactory, with the only noticeable spike in 2013 when *Mpamba* launched.[59] It would seem that both mobile money issuers are struggling to convert registered users into active users. It is also clear that the numbers of registered users of mobile money are far less than the numbers of mobile phone subscribers. This low growth may be attributable to the marketing strategy that was employed when the product was launched. Both issuers used a similar model, promising agents bonuses and commissions upon registering new customers.[60] Customers were encouraged to register with an offer of an equivalent value of mobile money purchased in airtime.[61] This was

[56] Dittus and Klein (2011), p. 7.
[57] Ibid., p. 8.
[58] Ibid., p. 11.
[59] RBM HQ (2015).
[60] Ibid.
[61] Ibid.

later reduced to 51% of mobile money purchased.[62] So most customers registered to access the free airtime credit while maintaining their electronic value, which was not the purpose of the service.[63] Both incentives were unsustainable and were soon discontinued.[64] This resulted in the low number of active users as well as a low uptake of new customers.[65] It would seem the two mobile money operators have their work cut out for them not only in converting the number of registered users to active users but also attracting those who have not yet registered.

As noted above, the country's central bank had a target to increase the adult bankable population to 40% by 2014. However, how realistic was this target? The central bank was established in 1965, a year after the country's independence from British colonial rule. By 2008, some 43 years later, only 19% of the population had been banked.[66] Malaŵi's population is young with 46% comprising those aged below the age of 15.[67] This category is unlikely to become economically active anytime soon. Most people in Malaŵi do not have regular incomes, and unemployment is very high. Although the official unemployment rate was in 2013 estimated at 6.6%, the number of people actually employed is very low.[68] The official unemployment rate is based on a measure of the number of people actively looking for a job as a percentage of the labour force as opposed to the number of people actually employed.[69] Literacy levels are very low, and 62% of the population live below the poverty

[62] Ibid.

[63] Ibid.

[64] Ibid.

[65] Ibid.

[66] RBM (2013), pp. 11–2.

[67] NSO (2009) *2008 Population and Housing Census* (Malawi Government [National Statistics Office], Zomba), http://www.mw.one.un.org/wp-content/uploads/2014/04/Malawi-Population-and-Housing-Census-Preliminary-Report-2008.pdf. 29 April 2018.

[68] Anon (2016) 'Malawi Unemployment Rate 2005–2016' (*Trading Economics*), http://www.tradingeconomics.com/malawi/unemployment-rate. 4 May 2018.

[69] In the 2008 census, 41% of women were illiterate. 36% of the population was illiterate—(2009) *2008 Population and Housing Census* (Malawi Government [National Statistics Office], Zomba), p. 14.

Anon (2014) 'Malawi Unemployment Rate' (*Trading Economics*), http://www.trading-economics.com/malawi/unemployment-rate. 28 May 2018.

line.[70] It is also unclear what data is used to compute the percentage of the banked. As cautioned earlier, if it is the number of bank accounts, then this may be erroneous as it may be due to double or triple counting where people have multiple bank accounts.

These may be some factors leading to financial exclusion. Most Malaŵians may be busy trying to make a decent living for themselves and getting on the formal financial bandwagon may be the least of their priorities or concerns. There does not seem to be anything that would suddenly propel a surge among the unbanked. This, sadly, seems an all too familiar story. In Nigeria, the central bank's plan to increase adult inclusion from 30% in 2010 to 70% in 2020 has been criticised by Ngwu for being too ambitious and reflective of adoption of neoliberal institutions which ignore Nigeria's fundamental institutional peculiarities.[71] However, the increase from 19 to 33% within 6 years illustrates that Malaŵi's central bank's strategies for financial inclusion may be bearing fruit. The reduction in the numbers that are financially excluded from 55 to 51% also shows that there is a gradual progression towards financial inclusion.

However, more still needs to be done to achieve higher rates of financial inclusion. Without addressing the basic structural bottlenecks such as electrification, feeder road infrastructure, there is no incentive that would make banks and other formal financial service providers invest in establishing their presence in the rural areas. Without the creation of jobs, urbanisation is unlikely to increase significantly any time soon. Relying on mobile money to kick-start and achieve, the set target may be taking a narrow view of the problem. This is because mobile money has also started offering added services such as paying bills and purchasing car fuel, which would show that the target, at least for these added services, may be the very population that is already banked.[72] This then raises the question whether mobile money has abandoned its initial objective as a tool aimed at financial inclusion of targeting the unbanked in favour of profit maximisation. Arguably, there are higher returns among the high-end market users. While this service may be lucrative in the short term, it is argued that it may not be so in the long term. Once banks become

[70] Anon (2013) 'Malawian Snapshot: 2013 Quarter 2' (KPMG, Malawi), p. 1, https://www.kpmg.com/Africa/en/KPMG-in-Africa/Documents/2013%20African%20Country%20Reports/KPMG_Malawi%202013Q2.pdf. 13 September 2018.

[71] Ngwu (2015), p. 313.

[72] Kihagi (2013).

organised, they may offer competition to the mobile money service. In fact, the entry of mobile money in this market segment demonstrates a lacuna, which can easily be filled by banks. The same cannot be said for the core mobile money business in the rural areas where banks are non-existent. Maybe instead of spreading themselves too thin, too early, the mobile money issuers should consider deepening their roots and holding the anchor in the core business of mobile money first.

However, can mobile money be relied on to lead to financial inclusion without addressing the issue of low penetration of mobile phones among the unbanked?[73] Ancillary to this is the issue of low penetration of mobile money agents in rural areas. As noted above, there is a slow growth in mobile money users and with an unimpressive conversion ratio of registered users to active users. These are challenges that the mobile money issuers are grappling with. The central bank on its part does not provide clear solutions as to how the identified challenges cited above will be overcome.

## 6.3 Village Banks

Any meaningful financial inclusion agenda must bring on board the rural population to have an impact. As discussed above, banks do not find a business case to establish branches in rural areas. On the other hand, the people find it expensive to travel long distances to access banking or financial services. So, is all hope lost for these people? Maybe not. Village banks seem to provide the solution to the needs of the rural people, at least in Malaŵi. It is important to clarify at the outset that despite their name, village banks are not banks per se. They are a community saving and lending initiative, which operate as a stand-alone financial system. They mimic the banking system but are modelled on the concept of saving and credit cooperatives (SACCOs).[74] Membership is usually drawn from the members of a particular village or in the rural areas. Village

[73] Although the total number of mobile phones indicates saturation, it must be borne in mind that most users have both a TNM and Airtel phone. Therefore, the actual number of people with mobile phones may be much less.

[74] Alexander Borda-Rodriguez and Sara Vicari (2014) 'Rural Co-operative Resilience: The Case of Malawi' 2 (1) *Journal of Co-operative Organization and Management* 43, p. 4, http://oro.open.ac.uk/40390/1/Rural%20co-operative%20resilience%20The%20case%20of%20Malawi.pdf. 13 December 2018.

**Fig. 6.4** *Chitemwano* Club premises

banks are therefore an example of society's innovation due to lack of provision of financial services by the formal sector. In a way, the success of village banks can be viewed in another lens as a failure of the formal financial system to service the needs of rural people. The following study is representative of the typical village bank. However, as noted above, despite what the villagers call it, it is in fact a savings and credit union (Fig. 6.4).

---

Occupants of Munthali Village have a village "bank" called *Chitemwano*[75] Club. At each weekly meeting, members contribute towards "buying of shares". Each share is valued at K200.00, and members must procure at least one share. Members take loans from the treasury proportionate to their shares up to a maximum of 100% of the shares held. Every 6 months, all the club's proceedings are shared and a new cycle starts again. The interest that accrues is not shared under a common pool. In a rather strange but interesting scheme, everyone earns their own interest.

The club has a treasurer who keeps a record of transactions. This entails that for one to be a treasurer; one must be literate and possess numeracy skills. The committee works on a pro-bono basis. The idea of accruing interest to the borrower is to encourage an entrepreneurial spirit as well as to reward those who take the risk. Those who

[75] *Chitemwano* is a *Tumbuka* name meaning Love. *Tumbuka* is a language largely spoken in north Malaŵi.

are risk averse are not rewarded. There is another type of club, which employs a different system. At this "bank", interest accrues to the whole group and is divided proportionately to the shares. It is common to have people with multiple memberships of these village banks.

Most members borrow to engage in business. Most of the business ventures involve ordering products from neighbouring villages. The consensus, however, is that the level of financing is insufficient and this prevents members from engaging in high-return businesses. Most members are unemployed and lack regular income. This prevents them from accessing high amounts of loans as they may be stranded with unsold goods. Members decided to set up the village "bank" after realising that it was not easy for each person to mobilise savings on their own as well as have access to finance. If a member is in financial distress and is unable to repay the loan, the loan is refinanced but the interest must be paid. In such a way, the loans never become delinquent. So, suppose a member borrowed K5000.00 and is unable to repay the loan after one month, the member must then pay at a minimum K1000.00 as interest and the K5000.00 is recorded in the books as a new loan. The member may also repay part of the principal if they have the means and only the balance will be re-financed. The needs of the club in relation to what the central bank can do are:

a. How can they be assisted in terms of financial advice on how to improve their village banks and make them more efficient?
b. How can the village banks be strengthened to ensure sustenance?

The members of *Chitemwano* Club assist each other because they realised that if they wait for the formal financial service providers to start offering them banking and other financial services, this may take forever.[76] The figure below is the "bank hall". The venue is an abandoned nursery school. This club is lucky to have this enclosed venue for meetings. Other clubs meet in the open.

[76]Personal observation and views from Interview with Chitemwano Club Chairperson; NyaMoyo (10 August 2015). Munthali Village is situated in an area called Madise, in the District of Mzimba, in the Northern part of Malaŵi. Madise is the author's rural home.

In the greater scheme of things, this village does not exist. When the economists and statisticians aggregate the economic performance of the country, this village and many like it are excluded. To the central bank, the residents of this village and many like it are part of the financially excluded. That in the villages, people have a deeper understanding of finances is either unknown or it is ignored. As already stated, this typically accounts for the life of 86% of the population.[77] Put another way, the formal economy represents the economic activity of the 14% who mostly stay in urban areas. Can it be said that the inhabitants of this village are really financially excluded? Do they not have access to credit; deal with each other economically on almost a daily basis? If the definition of financial exclusion or inclusion were contextualised, would they still not qualify? It is submitted they would and that it is because of the rather narrow definition adopted by the country's central bank of financial inclusion that they are not.

This does not, however, mean the central bank is unaware of the existence of such village banks. The bank concedes that the village bank concept is fast growing in Malaŵi and is not restricted to rural areas.[78] Several clubs modelled on village banks have been established in towns and cities, but the concept is the same; several people with a common bond come together to mobilise savings and access finance.[79] Protection of members' savings is, however, a big concern to the central bank.[80] Village banks also pose a regulatory challenge. As an alternative financial system, the question is what regulatory tools are available to the central bank to try to regulate them? How exactly will the bank protect members' savings? Currently, there seem to be two choices available to the bank; attempt to regulate village banks as financial institutions or leave them to their own devices. It is submitted both do not address the issue of such an alternative system. It is argued that there is a need for new regulatory tools to supervise these village banks. However, and maybe more fundamentally, is the central bank the ideal institution to do this? It would seem it may not be. This brings the issue of whether being a single regulator is healthy for the financial system. It is submitted that it

[77] Finscope (2014), p. 2.

[78] RBM MicroFinance Division (2015).

[79] Ibid.

[80] Ibid.

is not as it prevents specialisation, especially where you have new services, which do not fit the traditional banking structure.

The central bank acknowledges that regulation and supervision as employed in the formal financial system can stifle the development of these village banks.[81] The bank indicates that it is looking at mechanisms of linking village banks to the formal financial system.[82] However, this approach manifests the short-term view of the issues. The bank is desirous to link these village banks to formal financial institutions because it has leverage over the latter. The bank is looking at these village banks as agencies of banks or other financial institutions. This, it is argued, is in fact the wrong approach. However, even if this was to be realised, the biggest hurdle is that these village banks are not juridical persons. Under Malaŵian law, legal persona is a requirement as banks can only transact with legal personalities.[83]

Setting up village banks as agencies for commercial banks may therefore not be a solution. However, is there another way of circumventing the barriers presented by company law? Would a specialised law, such as the Business Groups Incorporation Act of Papua New Guinea,[84] not be used to allow these banks to incorporate while avoiding the onerous regulations of incorporating as a company? Another possibility is for these village banks to be allowed to open bank accounts as unincorporated associations. Currently, this is not the case. However, all this is premised on the presumption that these banks will be agents of commercial banks. However, is this ideal situation? Would it not amount to boxing them into a regulatory corner for the purposes of easing the work of the regulator? What if the village banks did not want to become part of the formal system? If this can be the departure point, then clearly it reinforces the argument that has been made above that there is a need to develop new regulatory tools for their operation. It is submitted that in furtherance of this, the central bank may not be the ideal body to regulate village banks.

The handicap that the central bank has is evidenced in its approach to alternative systems like village banks. Although village banks offer an avenue for people in rural areas to get on the financial bandwagon, there is a

[81] Ibid.

[82] Ibid.

[83] Ibid.

[84] Business Groups Incorporation Act (Papua New Guinea, 1974), http://www.paclii.org/pg/legis/consol_act/bgia1974365/. 21 July 2018.

reluctance by the bank to include them and other similar alternative systems as part of the financial system. This is hardly surprising as, according to the bank, financial inclusion is measured by looking at access to the formal services offered by the financial sector.[85] This includes microfinance institutions but excludes village banks and other such informal financial set-ups.[86] The central bank, however, realises the value of local informal institutions in bringing people to participate in financial services and appreciate the value of savings.[87] This may appear contradictory. In fact, it represents the perfect example of a dilemma of contemporary neoliberalism. In one breath, the central bank refuses to accept village banks as part of the financial system. In another, it looks at the same village banks as a window through which people in rural areas can start appreciating the opportunities offered by the formal financial sector. So, the central bank essentially has a problem of either servicing only for the best market players or attempt to connect with capitalism those previously unconnected.

De Soto has ably analysed the problem of transplanting capitalism to local communities in places like Africa. He argues that "even in the poorest countries, the poor save. The value of savings among the poor is, in fact, immense: forty times all the foreign aid received throughout the world since 1945"[88] De Soto, however, argues that it is the difference in property rights between rich and poor countries that determine why capitalism has triumphed in the west.[89] He argues that it is the form of property that is the determining factor.[90] He says, poor countries:

> [H]old their resources in defective forms: houses built on land whose ownership rights are not adequately recorded, unincorporated business with undefined liability, industries located where financers and investors cannot see them. Because the rights to these possessions are not adequately documented, these assets cannot readily be turned into capital, cannot be traded outside the narrow local circles where people know and trust each

[85] RBM HQ (2015).

[86] Ibid.

[87] Ibid.

[88] Hernando de Soto (2001) *The Mystery of Capital: Why Capitalism Triumphs in the West and Fails Everywhere Else* (Black Swan, London), p. 6.

[89] Ibid.

[90] Ibid.

> other, cannot be used as collateral for a loan and cannot be used as a share against an investment.[91]

De Soto may be right that "property documentation fixes the economic characteristics of assets so that they can be used to secure commercial and financial transactions, and ultimately provide the justification against which central banks issue money".[92] It is accepted that village banks demonstrate that the system is highly localised and operates on trust. Property rights hardly play any role in financial transactions. But is transplanting property rights law on to these poor communities the solution? As noted earlier, there are myriad of reasons why banks do not operate in rural areas and it is doubtful that a change in property rights on its own would make a significant impact on whether they expand their services to this sector. Ideally, the solution would lie in embracing these alternative forms of financial service provision. But therein lies the root problem, the inability of the central bank to regulate these village banks.

One issue that the central bank may need to deal with is trust. It is important to realise that people may decide not to use the formal financial system because they do not understand or trust it compared to the informal economy.[93] In Malaŵi, almost all banks communicate in written English, which is not even always easy to understand. In a population where most cannot read, this presents a problem. There is something about keeping one's money in one's bank beneath the bed that is self-assuring. Those who are slightly less risk averse will keep their money in a membership local SACCO or farmer's club. Depositing money in a bank, trusting a distant third party, requires a change of mindset.

Having a financial inclusion target, without contextualising why people may be formally excluded shows, that the central bank may be unable to attain its financial inclusion goals. The assumption that the informal sector is not regulated may not be true. It may not be formally regulated, but within its informal setup, there are self-regulatory mechanisms that ensure that it works efficiently and is transparent enough for people to trust it. The locals trust it and consider it safe. Through it, they can access credit, save, and earn interest. For most people in the village who on their own volition decide to be excluded from the formal financial sector,

[91] Ibid.

[92] Ibid.

[93] Ngwu (2015), p. 316.

the usual strategy of hoping that introducing formal financial products and services will make them want to access them may simply not work. Furthermore, while remittances provide an injection of liquidity into local economies, it is submitted that this on its own is not enough. Dev argues that success of any financial inclusion intervention will depend on the sustainability of vulnerable groups with viable economic activities.[94] This requires investment into livelihoods and means of production such as irrigation, farming and produce market infrastructures.[95]

## 6.4 Mobile Money: A Solution to Needs of the Rural People?

The fundamental issue for mobile money regarding these village banks is; how can the service tap into this market? Suppose all members of the "bank" had access to a mobile phone, it means they would potentially use the mobile money payment system to transact. This may mean reduced profits as some money would have to be paid as transaction fees. However, would the advantage of having a more secure payment system help to balance this? A case whereby robbers attacked the house of a village "bank" treasurer at night in *Chikwawa*[96] and went away with all the money illustrates the risk with keeping cash.[97] It is submitted that with rising cases of such robberies, mobile money could offer a viable alternative. Both mobile money issuers have lined up innovative services to offer to their customers, and both issuers argue that once these game-changing products roll out, banks will be caught napping.[98] This arises out of a gap that both mobile money issuers have identified in the financial market, which is not being filled in, by the banks. In the words of Airtel Money's Mkoloma:

[94] Dev (2006), p. 4313.

[95] Ibid.

[96] A town in the southern part of Malaŵi.

[97] RBM MicroFinance Division (2015).

[98] In interviews, both Airtel Money and TNM Mpamba outlined new products. However, an undertaking was made that these would not be released as they were still considered company secrets. Interestingly, both operators seem to be operating on a similar wavelength with regard to the scope of the new services.

> In the telecom business, when we go to the market. Compared to the banks, we run at a supersonic speed. The banks, they crawl.

*Mpamba*'s Mbekeani is more forthright and lays down the gauntlet:

> If the banks cannot become innovative, we will. We have approached banks to work with us in this, and most have been resistant because they think we are in competition. If they can't see that opportunity then they will realise too late that we are not afraid to compete with them.[99]

According to the central bank, mobile money is a stepping stone into the formal economy:

> Mobile money allows people to send and receive money using the formal financial platform. Through this interaction, they appreciate the importance of value, and eventually as they appreciate the services, they may open a bank account.[100]

This view by the central bank seems to be a top-down view of what is happening. It would seem the central bank has a tunnel-view, expecting the convergence of services. It may well be that divergence may be the way the financial services grow. Granted a converging sector would be easier to regulate and supervise, but forcing diverging services to converge may also not be the solution. It would be better if the central bank recognised that there are various ways of providing financial services, each with different regulatory issues.

As noted earlier, the Malaŵi Government has embarked on a financial inclusion. However, regarding mobile money, there are problems. Airtel Money's Mkoloma laments:

> The government has a social cash transfer system.[101] It never uses mobile money. We have tried to engage the government in taking over their payments points across the country using the mobile money platform. We have done our research and the major ones are:

[99] Mbekeani (2015).

[100] RBM HQ (2015).

[101] To poor families and girl-headed households.

- Chiefs who receive honoraria but who are in the remote areas
- Teachers in remote areas far from towns and banking services
- Pensioners in rural areas

> For these categories to get paid, they must travel long distances and incur great expenses to access their pay. Although we may not have agents in some of the remote areas, if the government decided to use mobile money, a business case would be made to go into that area, establish an mobile money presence, and mobilise agents. The reality is, since government remains the biggest employer, if it cannot come in, then financial inclusion may remain a song. The Ministry of Finance has a Mobile Money Acceleration Programme yet the government does not want to come to the party.[102]

Although the government has a financial inclusion agenda, it has not shown interest to become an active participant. This lack of interest by the government has a huge impact on financial inclusion. The central bank has lamented that mobile money has not had a noticeable impact on financial inclusion, but the blame may not be on the mobile money issuers alone. The government needs to come to the party. The lacklustre approach is best illustrated by the fact that in the government's Financial Sector Development Strategy for 2010–2015, mobile money was not even mentioned once despite financial inclusion being a pillar for financial development.[103]

When one considers the 3 categories of people who would benefit from if government introduced wholesale payments on the mobile money platform as cited by Mkoloma, there would be of mutual benefit to the government and to the payees. In Malaŵi, chiefs, teachers, and pensioners living in rural areas must travel or trek long distances to the nearest bank to receive their pay or honoraria. Often, the remuneration barely covers the travelling cost. The following case study illustrates this.

---

Theodose Twea is a pensioner. He lives just outside the Madise area in a village called Thela in the northern part of Malaŵi. He is a retired teacher. He is also an epileptic. He must travel to Mzuzu, the nearest

[102] Mkoloma (2015).
See similar views expressed by Di Castri (2013), p. 8.

[103] *Financial Sector Development Strategy: 2010–2015* (2015).

> town (city) which is some 22 miles[104] to get his pension from a bank. He does this every month. Since the pension pay is not enough to cover the cost of transport, he must walk some of the distance so that he has some money left to use at home. Sometimes he is not able to collect his pay and must seek refuge and spend the night in Mzuzu. If there was a way to receive money at home, that would save him the time of travelling (he spends the whole day travelling) but also ensure that he has more money at his disposal.[105]

As Mkoloma points out, mobile money has the potential to help people like Theodose Twea and much more like him living in the rural areas of Malaŵi.

## 6.5 Conclusion

This chapter has looked at the nation's financial inclusion agenda and how mobile money can positively contribute to making more Malaŵians financially included. Although localised to the Malaŵian context, it is submitted the challenges that rural communities face in accessing financial services may be universal to most developing countries, especially in sub-Saharan Africa. One thing that becomes all too clear is that the financial inclusion matrix needs to be contextualised. *Chitemwano* Club is a case in point and represents the bipolar views of financial inclusion held by the central bank on one hand and the people in the villages on the other. If access to finance is a key ingredient for financial inclusiveness, the financial inclusion matrix needs to be recomputed. Mobile money does offer hope, though. The key issue that arises in this chapter is how the mobile money platform can be used as a vehicle to put on board the formal financial system, people who are in the rural areas. The fact that mobile money suppliers are integrating with banks is a positive step but more needs to be done. A pertinent issue that has been flagged is how the lack of active participation by the government can affect

[104] That is the straight-line distance. The actually travelling distance is most likely much higher because of bad terrain and road network—'Distance from Galasi Madise to Mzuzu', http://malawi.places-in-the-world.com/929816-925475-distance-from-galasi-madise-to-mzuzu.html. 16 December 2018.

[105] Interview with Theodose Twea Pensioner (19 August 2015).

negatively the financial inclusion agenda. In Malaŵi, like most developing countries in sub-Saharan Africa, the government is a key player in the employment sector.

So, is mobile money a solution to the needs of the rural people? Mobile money has the potential of bridging the financial inclusion gap. For example, if mobile money can link to the local savings and credit unions, the so-called village banks, then money collected could be saved through a more secure system to which mobile money is connected. Regarding remittances of remuneration of people in rural areas such as chiefs, teachers or pensioners, it would seem mobile money is uniquely placed to offer a solution to the challenges faced by such groups. Using mobile money would in a way circumvent the need for special regulation of village banks. However, as an alternative form of payment, mobile money does pose its own regulatory challenges. It raises questions as to the suitability of the regulatory framework of the traditional financial architecture to regulate this new service.

## References


Ahmed Dermish, Joel Phiri and Caitlin Sanford (2012) *Mapping the Retail Payment Services Landscape Malawi* (FinMark Trust), http://www.finmark.org.za/wp-content/uploads/pubs/Rep_RPS_landscape_Malawi_2012.pdf. 10 February 2018.

Alexander Borda-Rodriguez and Sara Vicari (2014) 'Rural Co-operative Resilience: The Case of Malawi' 2 (1) *Journal of Co-operative Organization and Management* 43, http://oro.open.ac.uk/40390/1/Rural%20co-operative%20resilience%20The%20case%20of%20Malawi.pdf. 13 December 2018.

Anon (2010) 'Mobile Cellular Subscriptions (per 100 People) in Malawi' (*Trading Economics*), http://www.tradingeconomics.com/malawi/mobile-cellular-subscriptions-per-100-people-wb-data.html. 11 March 2018.

Anon (2013) 'Malawian Snapshot: 2013 Quarter 2' (KPMG, Malawi), https://www.kpmg.com/Africa/en/KPMG-in-Africa/Documents/2013%20African%20Country%20Reports/KPMG_Malawi%202013Q2.pdf. 13 September 2018.

Anon (2014) 'Malawi Unemployment Rate' (*Trading Economics*), http://www.tradingeconomics.com/malawi/unemployment-rate. 28 May 2018.

Anon (2016) 'Malawi Unemployment Rate 2005–2016' (*Trading Economics*), http://www.tradingeconomics.com/malawi/unemployment-rate. 4 May 2018.

Asli Demirguc-Kunt and Leora Klapper (2012) *Measuring Financial Inclusion: The Global Findex Database* (Policy Research Working Papers, The World Bank), https://laomfa.org/wp-content/uploads/formidable/7/Measuring-Financial-Inclusion_The-World-Bank-2010.pdf. 20 April 2018.

Business Groups Incorporation Act (Papua New Guinea, 1974), http://www.paclii.org/pg/legis/consol_act/bgia1974365/. 21 July 2018.

Claire Luke (2015) 'Critique of Microfinance Raises Questions about Efficacy, Donor Support of the Industry' *Devex Impact*, https://www.devex.com/news/critique-of-microfinance-raises-questions-about-efficacy-donor-support-of-the-industry-85617. 20 April 2018.

CPSS (2012) *Innovations in Retail Payments* (Bank for International Settlements [Committee on Payment and Settlement Systems], Basel, Switzerland), http://www.bis.org/cpmi/publ/d102.pdf. 20 February 2018.

Financial Sector Development Strategy: 2010–2015 (2015) (Government of Malaŵi), http://www.finance.gov.mw/fspu/index.php/financial-sector-laws/strategy-documents/55-malawi-financial-sector-development-strategy-2010-2015/file. 21 December 2018.

Finscope (2014) *FinScope Consumer Survey Malawi 2014* (Finmark Trust, Midrand, Johannesburg), http://www.finmark.org.za/wp-content/uploads/2016/08/FS-Malawi-2014-Launch-presentation.pdf. 5 May 2017.

Francis N. Ngwu (2015) 'Promoting Formal Financial Inclusion in Africa: As Institutional Re-examination of the Policies with a Case Study of Nigeria' 16 (4) 306 *Journal of Banking Regulation*, http://link.springer.com/article/10.1057/jbr.2014.13. 15 December 2018.

Franklin Allen and others (2012) *The Foundations of Financial Inclusion* (Policy Research Working Papers, The World Bank), http://documents.worldbank.org/curated/en/348241468329061640/pdf/wps6290.pdf. 20 April 2018.

Henry Lancaster (2015) 'Malawi—Telecoms, Mobile and Broadband—Statistics and Analyses' (Paul Budde Communication Pty Ltd), https://www.budde.com.au/Research/Malawi-Telecoms-Mobile-and-Broadband-Statistics-and-Analyses. 11 October 2018.

Hernando de Soto (2001) *The Mystery of Capital: Why Capitalism Triumphs in the West and Fails Everywhere Else* (Black Swan, London).

Ignacio Mas and Daniel Radcliffe (2011) 'Mobile Payments Go Viral: M-PESA in Kenya' 32 *The Capco Institute Journal of Financial Transformation* 169, http://www.capco.com/sites/all/files/journal-32_article-16.pdf. 15 December 2018.

Interview with Webster Mbekeani Head, Mobile Money Division, TNM (20 August 2015).

Interview with Bigboy Mkoloma Product and Development Manager, Airtel Money (7 August 2015).

Kevin Donovan (2012) 'Mobile Money for Financial Inclusion' in *Information and Communications for Development 2012* (World Bank, Washington DC).

MACRA (2015) *Subscriber Trends 2000–2014* (Malaŵi Communications Regulator Authority).

Mandira Sarma and Jesim Pais (2011) 'Financial Inclusion and Development' 23 *Journal of International Development* 613, http://onlinelibrary.wiley.com/doi/10.1002/jid.1698/pdf. 20 April 2018.

Michael Chibba (2009) 'Financial Inclusion, Poverty Reduction and the Millennium Development Goals' 21 (2) *The European Journal of Development Research* 213, https://doi.org/10.1057/ejdr.2008.17. 20 April 2018.

NSO (2009) *2008 Population and Housing Census* (Malawi Government [National Statistics Office], Zomba), http://www.mw.one.un.org/wp-content/uploads/2014/04/Malawi-Population-and-Housing-Census-Preliminary-Report-2008.pdf. 29 April 2018.

Peter Dittus and Michael Klein (2011) *On Harnessing the Potential of Financial Inclusion* (BIS Working Papers No. 347, Bank of International Settlements, Basel), http://www.bis.org/publ/work347.pdf. 20 February 2018.

Rakesh Mohan (2008) 'Economic Growth, Financial Deepening and Financial Inclusion' in Manoranjan Sharma (ed) *Dynamics of Indian Banking: Views and Vistas* (Atlantic Publishers, New Delhi).

RBM (2008) *Malawi National Payment System Vision Strategy Framework for the Period 2009–2013* (Reserve Bank of Malawi), http://www.rbm.mw/documents/payment_systems/NPS%20Vision%20%20Strategy%20Framework%20December%202008%20Final.pdf. 10 February 2018.

RBM (2013) *National Payment Systems Annual Report 2012* (Reserve Bank of Malawi), http://www.rbm.mw/documents/payment_systems/payment%20systems%20annual%20report%202012.pdf. 10 February 2014.

RBM (2015) *Financial and Economic Review* (Reserve Bank of Malawi), https://www.rbm.mw/Home/GetContentFile?ContentID=7492. 14 December 2018.

RBM (2018) 'Monthly National Payment System Report, May 2018' Issue 5 Vol 6 (Reserve Bank of Malaŵi), https://www.rbm.mw/PaymentSystems/GetContentFile/?ContentID=26223. 2 December 2018.

S Mahendra Dev (2006) 'Financial Inclusion: Issues and Challenges' 41 (41) *Economic and Political Weekly* 4310, http://www.jstor.org/stable/4418799. 20 April 2018.

Selipha Kihagi (2013) 'Malawians to Pay for Fuel Services Using Airtel Money' (*HumanIPO*), http://www.humanipo.com/news/36717/malawians-to-pay-for-fuel-services-using-airtel-money/. 12 March 2018.

Simone Di Castri (2013) *Mobile Money: Enabling Regulatory Solutions* (GSMA, London), http://www.gsma.com/publicpolicy/wp-content/uploads/2013/02/GSMA2013_Report_Mobilelectronicmoney-EnablingRegulatorySolutions.pdf. 20 February 2018.

CHAPTER 7

# Comparative Study of Mobile Money in Kenya and Malaŵi

## 7.1 Introduction

Arguably, in terms of mobile money, Kenya is the standard bearer of a successful service. This chapter compares the mobile money services in Kenya and Malaŵi. Comparison may, however, not be the right word, as in Kenya, the mobile money service has attained financial inclusivity and permeated all aspects of society while in Malaŵi, the service is still in its nascent stage. The mobile money service in Malaŵi is largely modelled on the Kenyan model, especially the *M-Pesa*. However, unlike in Malaŵi where there are two dominant mobile network operators, Airtel and Telekom Networks Malawi (TNM), Kenya essentially has one, Safaricom, now considered the biggest company in East Africa.[1] In looking at the Kenya model, the chapter also analyses why the unique conditions in Kenya have made it almost impossible to replicate the success of the Kenyan model. In this regard, the introduction of *M-Pesa* in Tanzania is used as an example to illustrate this.

[1] Bilichi Kenya (2018) 'Top Ten Companies in Kenya by Market Valuation 2018' (28 February 2018), https://bilichi.co.ke/top-10-companies-kenya-2018/. 27 December 2018.




S. Madise, *The Regulation of Mobile Money*, Palgrave Macmillan Studies in Banking and Financial Institutions,
https://doi.org/10.1007/978-3-030-13831-8_7

## 7.2 *M-Pesa* Leads the Way

Safaricom, in Kenya, a subsidiary of Vodafone UK, offers the *M-Pesa*.[2] The service was initially conceived as a DFID[3] pilot project[4] for microfinance loan disbursements and repayments.[5] The pilot project proved unsuccessful but the service demonstrated potential and Safaricom decided to develop it as a solution to the remittance dilemma.[6] *M-Pesa*'s primary target is the unbanked and financially excluded, mainly in rural areas.[7] Three years after its launch, the Economist described *M-Pesa* this way:

> IT IS like magic. By clicking a few keys on a mobile phone, money can be zapped from one part of Kenya to another in seconds. For urban migrants sending money home to their villages, and for people used to queuing at banks for hours to pay bills or school fees, the *M-Pesa* … is a godsend.[8]

Apart from the peer-to-peer transaction, *M-Pesa* also provides a savings platform for the unbanked. This in itself is revolutionary because *M-Pesa* was not conceptualised for savings. A study by Morawczynski and Miscione found that "customers would often make large deposits and several small withdrawals" implying that *M-Pesa* is "being used not just to send, but also to store money".[9] Due to the small amounts of money that are carried on from day to day, *M-Pesa* is still not considered a money-saving (deposit) scheme and therefore not regulated as such.[10] *M-Pesa*'s 4 core services are:

1. Paying bills;
2. Purchasing airtime;

[2] Mas and Ng'weno (2010).

[3] The development fund arm of the British Government.

[4] Porteous (2006), p. 26. See also Hughes and Lonie (2007).

[5] AFI (2010), p. 4.

[6] Ibid. The remittance dilemma is discussed in Chapter 4.

[7] Mas and Ng'weno (2010).

[8] Anon (2010) 'Out of Thin Air' *The Economist* (10 June 2010), http://www.economist.com/node/16319635. 15 December 2018.

[9] Morawczynski and Miscione (2008), p. 292.

[10] Ibid.

3. Transferring money to both users and non-users; and
4. Depositing and withdrawing money.[11]

Describing the simplicity and ease of using *M-Pesa*, Mas and Morawczynski say:

> The M-PESA user interface is driven by an application that runs on the user's mobile phone. The menu prompts the user to provide all the necessary information, one piece at a time, based on the type of transaction requested. Once all the information is gathered, it is sent for processing through the air interface in a single text message. This reduces messaging costs, as well as the risk of the transaction request being interrupted halfway through… The application use[s] security keys in the user's SIM card to encrypt messages end-to-end.[12]

## 7.3 Why *M-Pesa* Succeeded in Kenya

The success of *M-Pesa* can be attributed to 5 factors.

1. It targeted the unbanked, who were shunned by the banks and therefore there was a ready mass of clients waiting for such a service.
2. Low cost of transacting.
3. It has an easy intuitive service design, working on the most basic phone.
4. It built on the trust that people have in the mobile phone generally.
5. It quickly expanded to allow business transactions. This allowed the making of mass payments.[13]

*M-Pesa* also benefitted from the simplicity of registration. All that is needed is an acceptable identification (ID), and all Kenyans have a national

[11] Nathan Hedgedus (2012) 'An African Success Story Revealed' (2) *Ericsson Business Review* 10, p. 12, http://www.ericsson.com/res/thecompany/docs/publications/business-review/2012/issue2/an_african_success_story_explained.pdf. 15 December 2018.

[12] Mas and Morawczynski (2009), pp. 79–80.

[13] Sam Floy (2016) 'How and Why Mobile Money (M-Pesa) Works in Kenya' *Our Mobile World* (13 October 2016), http://samfloy.com/how-and-why-mobilelectronic-money-m-pesa-works-in-kenya/. 7 April 2018. Also see Mas and Ng'weno (2010), p. 8.

ID.[14] This has allowed Safaricom to navigate any customer due diligence concerns that the Financial Action Task Force (FATF) or others may have had.[15] In most jurisdictions, the FATF has raised concerns about customer due diligence processes in countries without national IDs.[16]

Even though these factors have all positively contributed to *M-Pesa*'s success, in effect, other key drivers ensured the success of *M-Pesa*. In summary, the success of *M-Pesa* can be attributed to 3 key drivers:

- Dominance of Safaricom;
- A permissive regulatory environment; and
- Customer demand for additional services.[17]

By the time Safaricom was launching *M-Pesa* in 2007, it was already a dominant player. It had 73% mobile market share and this increased to 84% in 2010[18] but had since dropped to 66% by the end of 2015.[19] Safaricom also tapped into the already existing high population of mobile phone users in Kenya.[20] The Kenyan Standard described the regulatory environment as a "regulatory free pass" allowing Safaricom and *M-Pesa* to pretty much have a free run by having "3+years of unregulated

[14] Jack et al. (2010), p. 87.

[15] Akin Oyebode (2014) 'M-Pesa and Beyond—Why Mobile Money Worked in Kenya and Struggles in Other Markets' *Venture Capital for Africa* (15 May 2014), http://vc4africa.biz/blog/2014/01/15/m-pesa-and-beyond-why-mobilelectronicmoney-worked-in-kenya-and-struggles-in-other-markets/. 15 December 2018.

[16] Isern and De Koker (2012).

[17] IFC (2011) 'IFC Mobile Money Study 2011—Summary Report' (International Finance Corporation), p. 18, http://www.ifc.org/wps/wcm/connect/fad057004a052eb-88b23ffdd29332b51/MobileMoneyReport-Summary.pdf?MOD=AJPERES. 15 December 2018.

[18] Ibid., p. 18.

[19] Graham Kajilwa (2015) 'Safaricom and Airtel Lose Market Share to New Comers, Regulator Report Shows' *Standard* (28 December 2015), http://www.standardmedia.co.ke/business/article/2000186415/safaricom-and-airtel-lose-market-share-to-new-comers-regulator-report-shows. 31 October 2018.

[20] Kristie Wang (2012) 'Replicating M-Pesa: Mobile and Cloud Technology Spur Innovation in Financial Inclusion' (15 December 2016), http://nextbillion.net/blogpost.aspx?blogid=2869.

growth".[21] The initial conception that *M-Pesa* was not a banking service was key to the service's initial take-off.[22] The bold decision by the central bank to adopt what Mas and Ng'weno describe as an "experiment first, then regulate" later stance was also instrumental in the initial phase that laid the foundations for the success of the service.[23] This light-touch regulation facilitated the initial pilot phase in the development of the service.[24]

Safaricom's dominance may be due to its marketing and business strategy but how the company came into being may have had an influence. Safaricom resulted out of the unbundling of the state-owned Kenya Posts and Telecommunications Corporation.[25] From this process emerged Kenya Telkom, which was initially the fixed-line telephone provider.[26] Kenya Telkom then created Safaricom when the telecommunication market was liberalised, with the government, through Kenya Telkom, owning 60% shares.[27] Vodafone UK bought the remaining shares.[28] Eventually, the government sold 25% of its shares to the public through a public issue.[29] Safaricom itself maybe said to be the omnipresent operator.[30]

For most Kenyans, Safaricom is still perceived as a government or at least a Kenyan company, notwithstanding Vodafone's controlling stake. It has been argued that the fact that the government owns a stake in

[21] Matt Krueger (2011) 'Four Reasons M-Pesa Succeeded in Kenya' *Mobile Money Exchange* (9 May 2011), https://mobilemoneyexchange.wordpress.com/2011/05/09/four-reasons-m-pesa-succeeded-in-kenya/. 10 March 2018.

[22] Wolgang Fengler (2012) 'How Kenya Became a World Leader for Mobile Money' (Africa Can End Poverty, The World Bank, 16 July 2012), http://blogs.worldbank.org/africacan/how-kenya-became-a-world-leader-for-mobilelectronicmoney. 7 April 2018.

[23] Mas and Ng'weno (2010), p. 24.

[24] Heeks (2012).

[25] Idongesit Williams and Benjamin Kwofie (2014) 'The Impact of Liberalization on the Mobile Telephony Market in Africa' in Knud Erik Skouby and Williams Idongesit (eds) *The African Mobile Story* (River Publishers, Copenhagen), p. 37.

[26] Ibid.

[27] Ibid.

[28] Sean Kane (2002) 'Telecom Reform and Poverty Alleviation in Kenya' (3) *African Journal of Information and Communication* 31, p. 38.

[29] Williams and Kwofie (2014), p. 38.

[30] Fengler (2012).

Safaricom, and therefore has a financial incentive to ensure it succeeds, may account for the regulatory free pass granted to it by the central bank.[31] It has been further argued that the same latitude was not provided to competitors like Airtel.[32] Safaricom may, therefore, have benefited from the first-mover advantage as it has had the opportunity to lock down its consumers and easily wade off any competition.[33] Oyebode says, unlike most jurisdictions where regulation precedes any rollout or development lags behind regulation, in Kenya, development-led regulation[34] or regulation followed innovation.[35]

From the day it was launched, Safaricom made an effort to emphasise that *M-Pesa* was not a banking service.[36] This emphasis was obviously to avoid prudential regulation by Central Bank of Kenya.[37] The central bank agreed went along with this but it was not smooth sailing for Safaricom. A year after its launch, the Minister of Finance "publicly - and suddenly – requested the [central bank] to conduct an immediate risk assessment audit of the service".[38] The Minister was quoted to have said: "I don't know whether *M-Pesa* will end well".[39] The request to the central bank followed discussions in the Kenyan Parliament on the implications of an unregulated money transfer service.[40] This was after the central bank had already conducted an internal audit that led to a conclusion that *M-Pesa* was not a banking business and could safely be issued a Letter of No Objection to commence operations.[41]

Kenya's central bank then engaged on a three-pronged approach to the *M-Pesa* question:

[31] Krueger (2011).

[32] Ibid.

[33] Oyebode (2014).

[34] Ibid.

[35] Fengler (2012).

[36] Jack and Suri (2011), p. 7.

[37] Ibid.

[38] AFI (2010), p. 1.

[39] Ibid., p. 2. The Standard carried an article described it as disaster waiting to happen—John Njiraini and James Anyanzwa (2008) 'Unmasking the Storm Behind M-Pesa' *The Standard* (30 December 2008), http://www.standardmedia.co.ke/?articleID=1144002826&story_title=. 13 March 2018.

[40] AFI (2010), p. 3.

[41] Ibid., p. 1.

1. *Legal status*: was *M-Pesa* a banking business or not?
2. *Money laundering*: could the system be used illicitly for money laundering?
3. *Operational risk*: what risk could arise from the use of the new technology?[42]

In the end, the due diligence conducted by the central bank demonstrated that *M-Pesa* did not pose a systemic risk to the financial sector and that it was not a banking business.[43] In its report, the Alliance for Financial Inclusion found that as a company, Safaricom also may have positively affected this because it had engaged in self-regulating.[44] In 2009, mainly due to the fact that the Minister had made a public request to the central bank regarding *M-Pesa*, the central bank gave out a public notification essentially clearing *M-Pesa*.[45]

Since *M-Pesa* was conceived as an added service, it meant that it benefitted from the relationship that already was in existence between Safaricom and its customers. It may also have helped that in the initial start off, Safaricom "did not expect an immediate return on its investment", seeing *M-Pesa* "as a pure value-added service, a way to cement its bond with its customers".[46]

### 7.3.1 A Good Agent Network

Even before the inception of *M-Pesa*, Safaricom already had an extensive network of agents across the country. However, with the launch of the service, this network further expanded such that by 2015 it had grown to 55,000 agents compared to 1000 bank branches.[47] Unlike banks, which have buildings representing branches, *M-Pesa* uses real people agents as

[42] Ibid., p. 4.

[43] Ibid., pp. 4–5.

[44] Ibid., p. 3.

[45] Ibid., p. 12.

[46] Hedgedus (2012), p. 15.

[47] Anon (2016a) 'Mobile Money—M-Pesa in Kenya, 7 Things Worth Knowing' *SEPA Mobile Payments* (20 November 2015), http://www.sepaforcorporates.com/sepa-mobile-payments/mobilelectronicmoney-m-pesa-kenya-7-things-didnt-know/. 31 October 2018.

branches and "not faceless banks".[48] Having an effective and efficient distribution system has therefore been central to the success of *M-Pesa*.[49]

When *M-Pesa* customers go to the agent, this does not mean that they trust the agent. A study has found out that actually, they trust Safaricom, the organisation behind the agents.[50] Customers feel as if they are actually dealing with Safaricom in their transactions, and much of this trust arises from the fact that the company has been in existence since 1997 with a massive share of the mobile market.[51] Since, *M-Pesa* relies on the small messaging system (SMS), it is susceptible to congestion during peak texting times resulting in transactions failures.[52] Even where the transaction goes through, the confirmation SMS may not be sent.[53] The customer does not blame *M-Pesa* for the failure but instead accuses the agent of stealing their money.[54]

#### *7.3.1.1 The Dual System*

Most Kenyans maintain a strong link to their ancestral homes, even though they are working or engaged in business in the cities and towns. Mas and Morawczynski say one reason, unique to sub-Saharan Africa is "their wish to retire to and be buried on their ancestral land".[55] Krueger says, like most African urban dwellers, most Kenyans migrated from the rural areas and therefore "domestic remittances, especially from Nairobi, the country's capital, represent a huge flow of money in Kenya".[56] Remittances do not only serve an economic function, but they also serve a sociological one as they serve as they maintain familial ties.[57]

[48] Hilton Tarrant (2011) 'Why Kenya's M-Pesa Won't Work Anywhere Else' (Moneyweb, 13 March 2015), http://www.moneyweb.co.za/archive/why-kenyas-mpesa-wont-work-anywhere-else/.

[49] Ibid.

[50] Morawczynski and Miscione (2008), p. 293.

[51] Ibid., p. 295.

[52] Ibid., p. 293.

[53] Ibid.

[54] Ibid.

[55] Mas and Morawczynski (2009), p. 78.

[56] Krueger (2011).

[57] Camner and Sjöblom (2009), p. 7.

Tragic events during the 2007 elections may also have contributed to the success of *M-Pesa*. The elections saw widespread violence and instability, effectively putting the country on lockdown.[58] This meant that urban dwellers had even more reason to remit funds to "relatives trapped in the villages and slums".[59] The Economist wrote that *M-Pesa* was perceived as a safer platform to use for remittance as well as save money compared to the commercial banks "which were entangled in ethnic disputes".[60] Most of the commercial banks were seen as providing electoral money funding to politicians based on tribal affiliations of their leaders.[61] Safaricom was, on the other hand, deemed to be above tribal politics because, in the words of Morawczynski and Miscione, "Michael Joseph [then chief executive] did not belong to any of Kenya's tribes".[62] Being political neutral, therefore, played a great role in the trust that the average Kenyan reposed in *M-Pesa*. Maybe, unsurprisingly, after Joseph left his position in 2010, another non-Kenyan, Bob Collymore, who had been working at Vodafone's South African affiliate, Vodacom, filled it.[63]

Within the urban dwellers, especially in the capital Nairobi, one slum notably stands out and may have played a key role in the early adoption of *M-Pesa*. *Kibera* is a slum in the outskirts of Nairobi. It is the biggest slum in Africa, and one of the biggest in the world, with about a million people from the total Nairobi population of 2.5 million.[64] It is also one of the most impoverished in Kenya.[65] At 83%, it has one of the highest

[58] Heeks (2012).

[59] Oyebode (2014).

[60] Anon (2013b) 'Why Does Kenya Lead the World in Mobile Money?' *The Economist* (27 May 2013), http://www.economist.com/blogs/economist-explains/2013/05/economist-explains-18. 15 December 2018.

[61] Morawczynski and Miscione (2008), p. 296.

[62] Ibid.

[63] Eric Ombok (2010) 'Safaricom Names Collymore as Chief Executive Officer' *Bloomberg Business* (22 July 2010), http://www.bloomberg.com/news/articles/2010-07-22/kenya-s-safaricom-appoints-bob-collymore-as-ceo-replacing-michael-joseph. 16 March 2018.

[64] Anon (2007a) 'Kibera UK—The Gap Year Company' (Kibera UK Charity), http://www.kibera.org.uk/Facts.html. 16 March 2018. Others have *Khayelitsha*, the South African slum in Cape Town as the biggest in Africa—Daniel Tovrov (2011) '5 Biggest Slums in the World' *International Business Times* (9 December 2011), http://www.ibtimes.com/5-biggest-slums-world-381338. 16 March 2018.

[65] Morawczynski and Miscione (2008), p. 289.

unemployment rates in Kenya.[66] *Kibera* boasts no financial institutions and was, therefore, ripe for the emergence of a financially empowering service such as *M-Pesa*.[67] *M-Pesa* benefitted from the demand for banking services as well as money transfer services and the fact that the population in *Kibera* did not have anywhere safe to put their money.[68] The latter was due to high insecurity in the slum.[69] These factors propelled *M-Pesa* as the solution to their problems and needs.[70] *Kibera* is mostly populated by migrants looking for work.[71] When they get money, they mostly remit it back home.[72]

### 7.3.2 Strong Brand, Clear Message and Optimised Pricing

*M-Pesa* obviously benefited from the dominant position of Safaricom in building a strong brand. The catchphrase that was used to champion the service by Safaricom was simple but effective: *Send money home*.[73] Once the initial takers had established a critical mass, there was a multiplier or rub-off effect. The Economist says, the service "benefitted from network effects: the more people who used it, the more it made sense for others to sign up for it",[74] thereby growing exponentially.[75] A strong brand and marketing strategy also ensured that the service could overcome the chicken-and-egg trap in that "in order to grow, *M-Pesa* had to attract both customers and stores in tandem".[76] For two years after the launch of *M-Pesa*, Safaricom also used the same television advert to promote the service but also inculcate the service in peoples' minds.[77] To ensure the

[66] Ibid.
[67] Ibid., p. 290.
[68] Ibid.
[69] Ibid.
[70] Ibid.
[71] Ibid.
[72] Ibid.
[73] Anon (2013b).
[74] Ibid.
[75] Tarrant (2011).
[76] Mas and Ng'weno (2010), p. 2.
[77] Ibid., p. 6.

brand's omnipresence, retail outlets or agent shops were boldly "painted Safaricom green with a prominent *M-Pesa* logo".[78]

The design of the service, which provided customers with instant confirmation of their transaction, proved instrumental in helping customers to learn to use and trust the system through their own personal experience.[79] One thing that may have eased the acceptance of *M-Pesa* was the pricing scheme that Safaricom adopted. The scheme was designed so that it provided incentives for both customers and providers of services and goods to join.[80] Customers are only charged for doing something with their money, such as making a transfer, withdrawal or buying airtime, but not depositing.[81] To prevent customers from avoiding to pay transaction fees, deposits into another user's account are prohibited.[82] The pricing scheme is such that if an *M-Pesa* customer is sending money to a customer without an *M-Pesa* account, the cost is much higher.[83] It is submitted that this is deliberate to entice *M-Pesa* customers to encourage others to join since it is cheaper to send if both are on *M-Pesa*.

## 7.4 Why *M-Pesa* Did Not Do as Well in Tanzania

The success of *M-Pesa* in Kenya seems not to have yielded the same results when the model has been replicated.[84] Of the 200 or so experiments that have been made based on the *M-Pesa* model around the world, only a handful have been successful.[85] There is nothing extraordinary in the concept of *M-Pesa* itself and the concept of remitting funds using a mobile platform is not particularly difficult.[86] Therefore, there

[78] Ibid., p. 7.

[79] Ibid., p. 8.

[80] Ibid., p. 3.

[81] Mas and Morawczynski (2009), p. 86.

[82] Safaricom (2016a) 'M-PESA Rates' (Safaricom), https://www.safaricom.co.ke/personal/m-pesa/get-started-with-m-pesa/m-pesa-tariffs. 9 May 2018.

[83] Ibid.

[84] IFC (2011), p. 19.

[85] James Crabtree (2012) 'M-Pesa's Cautious Start in India' *Financial Times* (New York, 27 December 2012), http://www.ft.com/cms/s/0/a09c0f68-4a9a-11e2-9650-00144feab49a.html#axzz3UGBgLWPj. 15 December 2018.

[86] Tarrant (2011).

must be other factors that make the service successful in Kenya as compared to other markets.

*M-Pesa* has been replicated in India, Afghanistan, South Africa, and Tanzania but in all these markets it has not achieved the same level of success as in Kenya.[87] The problems in India and South Africa have largely been regulatory in nature.[88] The central banks in these countries see *M-Pesa* as part of the banking sector and therefore attempt to regulate it as such.[89] This section looks at why *M-Pesa* has not succeeded in Tanzania, which shares a common language, border and population size with Kenya.

Tanzania was perceived as a market ready for the picking because while as in Kenya domestic remittances were at 17% at the start of the *M-Pesa* launch, the comparable rate in Tanzania was 28%.[90] Added to this, Tanzania had far fewer banks and branches meaning that it had a "greater need for a financial service such as *M-Pesa*".[91] However, when the service was launched, the market take-up was lukewarm at best and nowhere to the speed of growth in Kenya.[92] So why was a product based on the same killer slogan, *Send money home* and launched by a Vodafone affiliate on the same marketing strategy not as successful? What were some of the factors that may have been ignored by simply transplanting the Kenya's *M-Pesa* model into the Tanzanian market?

### *7.4.1 Economic, Political and Social Factors*

Although Tanzania and Kenya have a similar population, Kenya boasts a stronger economy with twice the gross domestic product (GDP) of Tanzania.[93] At independence, Kenya embraced a capitalist agenda and encouraged urban economic growth while Tanzania, led by Julius Nyerere

[87] Crabtree (2012) and Wang (2012).

[88] Oyebode (2014) and James Crabtree (2012).

[89] Ibid.

[90] Camner and Sjöblom (2009), p. 3.

[91] Ibid., p. 4.

[92] Ibid.

[93] Emil Sjöblom, Gunnar Camner and Caroline Pulver (2009) *What Makes a Successful Mobile Money Implementation? Learnings from M-PESA in Kenya and Tanzania* (GSMA), p. 4, http://www.gsma.com/mobilefordevelopment/wp-content/uploads/2012/03/What-makes-a-successful-mobilelectronicmoney-implementation.pdf. 1 March 2018.

pursued a socialist agenda.[94] Nyerere's socialist vision was embodied in what became known as the Arusha Declaration where he conceived the concept of *Ujamaa*.[95] *Ujamaa* was a programme of villagization which moved "peasant families into cooperative villages where they [could] expressly work together more productively".[96] By the early 1970s, 80% of the population were living in registered *Ujamaa* villages.[97]

Because of this, the population in Tanzania is more evenly distributed than that in Kenya leading to a reduced general density.[98] By 2006, Kenya had achieved 41% urban population while Tanzania was at 30%, although the mobile penetration was comparable, at 34 and 30%, respectively.[99] Therefore, although Swahili is spoken in both countries, the Swahili slogan *Send money home* did not communicate quite the same message in Tanzania.[100] It also meant that unlike Safaricom, which could concentrate in the pockets with high population density, Vodacom, the local Vodafone affiliate, had logistical and marketing challenges to cover Tanzania.[101] Safaricom also had another advantage in that although both it and Vodacom are dominant players in both countries, Safaricom has almost twice the size of market share, with three times as much revenue.[102] This meant that Safaricom had more funds available for its market budget as compared to Vodacom.[103] Vodacom also had to contend with the logistical fact that Tanzania is twice the size of Kenya.

[94] Camner and Sjöblom (2009), p. 7.

[95] Julius Nyerere (1967) 'The Arusha Declaration' (Tanganyika African National Union), https://www.marxists.org/subject/africa/nyerere/1967/arusha-declaration.htm. 15 December 2018.

[96] Camner and Sjöblom (2009), p. 7.

[97] Ibid., p. 7.

[98] Ibid., p. 2.

Population density of 66.2 per square km for Kenya and 43.9 for Tanzania.

[99] Camner and Sjöblom (2009), p. 6.

[100] Ibid., p. 2.

[101] Ibid.

[102] Ibid.

[103] Ibid., p. 4.

As already noted above, most Kenyans treat Safaricom as a Kenyan company. On the other hand, 65% of Vodacom's stake is Vodacom (South Africa), which is itself technically owned, by Vodafone UK.[104] It is, therefore, understandable that although Vodacom was one of the first mobile operators in Tanzania, it is not treated as a home-grown company in the same way Safaricom is. Vodacom also suffered from a trust issue in that its products and services were viewed as somewhat expensive, leading to further reduction in its market share.[105] It, however, remains the largest company in Tanzania.[106]

The even population distribution in Tanzania may also have played a role in how the message of *Send money home* was perceived in Tanzania. Unlike Kenya where the bulk of remittance are ***urban to rural***, in Tanzania, there are other corridors of money transfer such as ***urban to rural***, ***rural to urban***, ***urban to urban*** and ***rural to rural***. Therefore, while to the ***urban to rural*** corridor, the slogan was a hit, it was a dud to the other corridors.[107]

### 7.4.2 *Other Local Factors*

While Safaricom built up a large base of agents, Vodacom was unable to achieve the same success. For example, as opposed to 1000 super dealers for airtime for Safaricom, Vodacom only had 6.[108] Super dealers are the ones that provide wholesale services on behalf of the service provider to retailers. While Safaricom boasted of some 40,000 agents, Vodacom only had 1000 in 2009.[109] Agents not only facilitate cash deposits and withdrawals, but they also register customers, conduct customer due diligence and customer education, especially to new users. It must be pointed out, as the Table 7.1 illustrates, Vodacom has over the years increased the number of agents considerably. After a year of operation,

[104] Camner and Sjöblom (2009), p. 4.

[105] Ibid.

[106] Ibid.

[107] Camner and Sjöblom (2009), p. 7.

[108] Ibid., p. 2.

[109] Ibid., p. 3.

Vodacom's *M-Pesa* had only 280,000,[110] compared to 2.5 million for Safaricom after the same timeline, and only reached 4.5 million by the end of 2008.[111]

Although *M-Pesa* uses its own payment platform, it still requires the availability of cash to convert mobile money. The presence of bank branches is, therefore, crucial. In 2006, Kenya had 1.38 branches per 10,000 people compared to 0.57 for the same number of people in Tanzania.[112] Unlike Kenya, Tanzania has no national ID for its citizens. This presents a problem to people who want to register on *M-Pesa*. To overcome this, voter registration cards are accepted instead.[113] Generally, the numbers of mobile phone and *M-Pesa* users in Kenya still trump those in Tanzania. The Table 7.1 provides a comparison of the different mobile phone statistics in the two countries in 2016. From the Table 7.1, the dominance of Safaricom over Vodacom becomes evident. Safaricom has twice the number of subscribers with almost 95% of these as *M-Pesa* users. It may also be pointed that Kenya now has almost double the mobile penetration rate than Tanzania.

Camner and Sjöblom have cautioned that although *M-Pesa* is capable of being replicated, future models of mobile money services are more likely to take the trajectory of the development of *M-Pesa* in Tanzania with "things happening more slowly but still moving in the right direction and picking up pace over time".[114] In 2016, Vodacom announced that it would discontinue its *M-Pesa* service in South Africa.[115] The service launched in 2010, targeted 10 million users but after 6 years only managed 1 million users, out of which a mere 76,000 were active users.[116]

[110] Camner and Sjöblom (2009), p. 3.

[111] AFI (2010), p. 1.

[112] Camner and Sjöblom (2009), p. 2.

[113] Ibid.

[114] Camner and Sjöblom (2009), p. 9.

[115] Lynsey Chutel (2016) 'Vodacom Has Given Up on Revolutionary Mobile Money Service M-Pesa, in South Africa' *Quartz Africa Weekly Brief* (9 May 2016), https://qz.com/679059/vodacom-has-given-up-on-revolutionary-mobilelectronicmoney-service-m-pesa-in-south-africa/. 10 January 2018.

[116] Ibid.

**Table 7.1** Contrasting mobile phone statistics in Kenya and Tanzania[a]

| | *M-Pesa users* | *M-Pesa agents* | *Safaricom Vodacom users* | *Safaricom/Vodacom airtime outlets* | *Unique mobile subscribers* | *Mobile penetration (%)* |
|---|---|---|---|---|---|---|
| Kenya | 24 million | 100,744 | 25.2 million | 252,000 | 38.2 million | 89.2 |
| Tanzania | 7 million | 86,943 | 12.4 million | Data unavailable | 25.3 million | 47.37 |

[a]Table compiled from data from
Safaricom (2016b) *SAFARICOM LIMITED Annual Report 2016* (Nairobi), https://www.safaricom.co.ke/annualreport_2016/downloads/Safaricom%20Annual%20Report%202016.pdf. 10 May 2018
Vodacom (2016a) *Vodacom Integrated Report for the Year Ended* (31 March 2016), http://www.vodacom-reports.co.za/integrated-reports/ir-2016/pdf/full-integrated.pdf. 10 May 2018
Lara Gilman (2016) *The Impact of Mobile Money Interoperability in Tanzania*, http://www.gsma.com/mobilefordevelopment/wp-content/uploads/2016/10/2016_GSMA_The-impact-of-mobilelectronicmoney-interoperability-in-Tanzania.pdf. 10 May 2018
Philemon Matoi (2016) *M-Pesa in Tanzania: The Journey So Far* (Vodacom, Mlimani), https://www.udbs.udsm.ac.tz/images/ICAESB2016/M-Pesa_in_Tanzania.pdf. 10 May 2018

The pricing of *M-Pesa* in Tanzania is similar to that of Kenya *M-Pesa*. It costs more to send money to an unregistered user.[117] The rationale it would seem is the same, to encourage the circulation of mobile money within the *M-Pesa* ecosystem.

## 7.5 In the Footsteps of *M-Pesa*: Airtel Money and *Mpamba*

Following the popularity of *M-Pesa*, Airtel and TNM, the two dominant mobile network operators in Malaŵi launched their own mobile money services: Airtel, Money and *Mpamba*.[118] The two services are modelled on *M-Pesa* such that in terms of how the services work, the description of the operation for *M-Pesa* made above generally applies. However, although the mobile money service in Malaŵi is modelled on the Kenyan

[117]Vodacom (2016b) 'Ada za M-Pesa' (Vodacom Tanzania PLC), https://vodacom.co.tz/mpesa/consumers/mpesa_tarrifs. 9 May 2018.

[118]Airtel (2013a). Anon (2013a) 'TNM Launches Mobile Money Mpamba to Build Great Malawi Nation' *Nyasa Times*, http://www.nyasatimes.com/tnm-launches-mobilelectronicmoney-mpamba-to-build-great-malawi-nation/. 28 December 2018.

model, in reality, the countries have little in common. Apart from having a similar legal system as a result of being former British colonies,[119] the economic situation in the two countries is very different. In its report, the African Development Bank categorised Kenya as one of Africa's largest economies while Malaŵi was in the "medium to small" economy category.[120] Kenya has more than three times the GDP of Malaŵi,[121] and just under three times the population size[122] with almost five times the land mass.[123] These differences may explain why the service reception may different in the two countries.

### 7.5.1 *Airtel Money*

Airtel Money was launched in February 2012.[124] Initiated in 2009 as an add-on service; Airtel soon realised that the service had financial underpinnings so it engaged the central bank for regulatory clearance.[125] Being a new service, the central bank suggested a pilot phase before rolling out.[126] After a successful pilot, Airtel received a "Letter of No Objection" in February 2010.[127] The "Letter of No Object" approach seems to be one that was adopted from Kenya. Airtel also soon enough realised that there was no regulatory framework to guide operations of mobile money. Airtel Money's Bigboy Mkoloma says:

119 Although in truth Malaŵi was never a colony but a protectorate.

120 ADB (2014) 'Comparing the Real Size of African Economies' (African Development Bank), p. 16, https://www.afdb.org/fileadmin/uploads/afdb/Documents/Project-and-Operations/Highlights_-_Comparing_the_Real_Size_of_Africa_Economies_%E2%80%93_Main_results_of_the_2011_round_of_the_International_Comparison_Program__ICP_.pdf. 20 July 2018.

121 ADB (2014), p. 24.

122 Anon (2017) 'African Countries by Population' (Worldometers), http://www.worldometers.info/population/countries-in-africa-by-population/. 20 July 2018.

123 CIA (2014) 'The World Factbook' (Central Intelligence Agency), https://www.cia.gov/library/publications/the-world-factbook/rankorder/2147rank.html. 20 July 2018.

124 Airtel is owned by the Barhti Group of India. The company (in Malaŵi) was previously known as Zain after Zain had bought the company from Celtel.

125 Mkoloma (2015).

126 Ibid.

127 Ibid.

> Initially, we were tossed around; not knowing which department or section of the Reserve Bank of Malaŵi is supposed to have control. However, later after several engagements, we found that we were pushed to the National Payment System. It is there that we got guidance on how to roll out the product.[128]

Mkoloma says it took two years before the service was officially launched because Airtel was unsure whether it would be given permission to roll out.[129] Therefore, when Airtel run the pilot phase, they used test equipment and only started procuring the main equipment after being given permission.[130] The lack of a clear regulatory and institutional framework at the time was a huge contributing factor in delaying the project.[131] Being the first to roll out had its challenges. Many initiatives had to be put in place to achieve a good adoption rate.[132] Most customers and potential customers were sceptical with the new service, regardless of the literacy levels.[133] Mkoloma says:

> Even the literate could not understand how they can use mobile money to transact as most are used to dealing in cash. For them to understand that the same phone, which they use for talking, can be used to send and receive money, required a shift in the mindset. There was, therefore, a low uptake initially.[134]

Airtel also soon realised they had a problem at the hands:

> With mobile money, you must ensure that you have the right ecosystem otherwise you have a challenge. More specially, you must have the customers. However, for you to have the customers, you must make sure that you have the agents. You can have the agents but if you don't have the customers, the agents will disappear. If you have the customers but don't have the agents, the customers will disappear. It is an egg and chicken type of a game. The key is to achieve the right balance. It must make a business case for all players.[135]

[128] Ibid.

[129] Ibid.

[130] Ibid.

[131] Ibid.

[132] Ibid.

[133] Ibid.

[134] Ibid.

[135] Ibid.

Airtel has had a bit of luck that provided them valuable lessons during their pilot phase. The first place to be rolled out was in Karonga, the most northern district in Malaŵi. According to Mkoloma:

> There was an earthquake in Karonga. Red Cross wanted to give money to the victims so they could rebuild their houses and was looking for the right channel of sending this money. We provided free phones and opened accounts for the beneficiaries. We then had to ensure that most of the key merchants of building materials were on board and that they should also open Airtel Money accounts to necessitate the payments to happen. We also recruited some agents so that those who wanted to cash out to buy something somewhere else could do so.[136]

It would seem this proved to be a good experience for Airtel, merchants, and the community, although most did not fully understand the service.[137] Similar to *M-Pesa*, tragic events may have acted as a catalyst to get the service rolling. Airtel admits that building up the ecosystem was not easy. Sometimes people would have mobile money in the phones but could not find the products they required.[138] On the other hand, some agents ended up tying their capital waiting for customers who never turned up.[139] The teething problems, it is submitted, gave Airtel the first-mover advantage as it had an almost three-year head start over its competitor, TNM. Airtel characterises the period between 2010 and March 2015 as the introduction of Airtel Money in terms of product development.[140] This allowed the service to start growing with more organisations getting on board.[141] Airtel says that from then on the service has witnessed a growth period with increased rate of growth.[142] Even the customer complaints are also different:

[136] Ibid.

[137] Ibid.

[138] Ibid.

[139] Ibid.

[140] Ibid.

[141] Ibid.

[142] Ibid.

> Initially it was, I have my money, I am going around but I can't find an agent. The story this time is different. It is not about I can't find an agent, but I can't buy electricity units; I can't buy ABCD.[143]

Registering for Airtel Money is not difficult. The author's experience was that it was less onerous than for *Mpamba*. It uses its offices and agents for registration. Airtel boasts of having over mobile money 5000 agents.[144] These agents do similar tasks to the *M-Pesa* agents. Airtel, however, has onerous requirements for one to become an agent such as proof of registration of a partnership, business or company and business permits or trading licences.[145] It is submitted that though it would make sense if these requirements were for super agents but not for agents who are mainly street vendors or hawkers.

Airtel Money uses a series of interactive steps to transact as well as password encryption.[146] Airtel boasts that "every transaction uses encryption and password that adheres to the highest banking security standards".[147] What this statement exactly means is unclear since Airtel Money is surely not a banking service and no independent verification has been made on the robustness of the security features of its SMS. Like *M-Pesa*, a confirmation message of the transaction is sent to the customer upon completion.[148] All the information on Airtel's website is in English although the author is aware from personal experience that there is a Chew̑a (widely spoken local language) menu. Airtel Money's menu is more interactive, utilising a menu resident in the phone that Airtel has developed and added mobile money service on to it. All the user needs to do is to access the Airtel Money menu to transact. Although the product was launched as *Khusa M'manja*, it is notable that on the menu, the service is called Airtel Money. It is argued this is a result of the internationalisation and uniformity of the Airtel brand and service. The Airtel menu is, therefore, a standard menu, although there is a Chew̑a version, which one can choose. Airtel boasts that customers can withdraw money

[143] Ibid.

[144] Airtel (2013e) 'Agents' (Airtel Malaŵi), http://africa.airtel.com/wps/wcm/connect/AfricaRevamp/Malawi/Airtel_Money/Home/Agents. 23 March 2018.

[145] Ibid.

[146] Airtel (2013a).

[147] Ibid.

[148] Ibid.

from automated teller machines (ATMs).[149] This, however, presupposes that the customer has a bank account and an ATM card.

Airtel also explicitly explains that once their network is down, customers will not be able to transact on the mobile money platform because it relies on the network for its operation.[150] This also invariably implies that one can only use the mobile money service where a network is present. Mkoloma says:

> When the network is down on the part of the service or utility provider, to the customer, the blame on failure to transact is put on Airtel Money since what they have is e-value provided by the service. To them, it does not matter whatever happens on the other side of the interconnectivity setup.[151]

Congestion in the network or poor network quality will also have an adverse effect on the service. With *M-Pesa*, it was found that problems in the network and lack of a confirmation could be a cause of tension. Airtel has explained that there may be cases where a message is not delivered, varying from a full inbox or delays in the network.[152] Importantly, it has provided a number to call in case twenty minutes elapse without a confirmation of the transaction having been processed.[153] The service also uses the interactive steps platform, which allows the complete transaction[154] to be sent as one message, therefore, saving cost and minimising network congestion.

Airtel has created a growing ecosystem collaborating with service providers, merchants and fuel stations across the country.[155] Airtel has also started making inroads into cross-borders remittances. Airtel says market research revealed that costs of existing cross-border remittances were

149 Airtel (2013c).

150 Ibid.

151 Mkoloma (2015).

152 Airtel (2013a).

153 Ibid.

154 Airtel (2013d) 'Airtel—How It Works: Send Money' (Airtel Malaŵi), http://africa.airtel.com/wps/wcm/connect/africarevamp/malawi/airtel_money/home/personal/how_it_works/send_money. 23 March 2018.

155 Airtel (2013b) 'Airtel—Merchants and Utilities' (Airtel Malaŵi), http://africa.airtel.com/wps/wcm/connect/AfricaRevamp/Malawi/Airtel_Money/Home/Merchants_and_utilities. 23 March 2018.

enormous due to stringent foreign exchange requirements of the central bank.[156] After being satisfied with the low risk involved in the low-value cross-border remittance, Airtel was given the green light by the central bank.[157] To ensure compliance with foreign exchange regulations, Airtel collaborated with a local bank, FDH Bank.[158] This collaboration takes care of any financial security issues regarding these cross-border remittances. It also means that although the central bank gave a go-ahead for the service, the central bank prudentially regulates the actual remittances. Transactions are denominated in US Dollars.[159] The service is, however, restricted to countries where Airtel Money is operational, which ostensibly are also countries where Airtel as a mobile network operator has network presence.[160]

### *7.5.2* Mpamba

*Mpamba* was launched by TNM in May 2013.[161] In a way, both the regulator and TNM may have benefited from regulatory lessons learnt from the pilot phase of Airtel Money. During *Mpamba*'s pilot phase, the system had to demonstrate that it can keep an audit trail.[162] Apart from the central bank's own assessment, an external auditing firm submitted a report to the central bank.[163] Although TNM found that the mobile money market already had an existing player, it still faced similar teething problems to what Airtel faced. Mbekeani highlights the challenges:

> Mobile money is a new concept. Therefore, there has been a lot of hand-holding of people, to help them to understand it. We had few early adopters. However, most seemed to adopt a wait-and-see attitude. Others did not just want to be bothered. Others were afraid of leaving an audit trail. Now to roll out a service such as *Mpamba* needs agents. That is the

[156] Mkoloma (2015).

[157] Ibid.

[158] Ibid.

[159] Ibid.

[160] Ibid.

[161] Formerly Telekom Networks Malaysia, it was the first player in the mobile phone business in Malaŵi.

[162] Mbekeani (2015).

[163] Ibid.

> only way customers will access the service. Some agents do not understand the business very well. For those that understand, the return is not as big, so it's been a problem.[164]

Mbekeani says within the ecosystem, smaller merchants have been difficult:

> When you buy from a merchant, there is no fee charged to the customer or to the merchant. So, this opened us up to certain transactions where a merchant would cash in a customer. When they cash in a customer, they get value and a commission paid to them. Instead of cashing out so that the customer is charged, they would do a merchant purchase with the customer. So, they accept a payment from the same customer as if they have bought goods and send the money back to the customer as cash in, get a commission, receive the money back from the customer as if they have bought goods, continuously like that.[165]

With a cash-out ratio of less than 30%, more than 70% of the electronic value is used within the *Mpamba* ecosystem.[166] The goal of *Mpamba* is to help in offering financial services especially to the unbanked by utilising the network presence of TNM.[167] The service also aims to link those customers who have bank accounts so they can seamlessly transact between accounts.[168] Apart from peer-to-peer transactions and buying airtime, one can also pay electricity and water bills and television subscription using *Mpamba*.[169] TNM touts the following as the advantages of using *Mpamba*:

- *Safety*—it is safer to transfer funds through mobile money than carrying physical cash;
- *Convenience*—make payments anywhere, anytime;
- *Cost-effectiveness*—cut travel costs and time to make payments;

[164] Ibid.

[165] Ibid.

[166] Ibid.

[167] TNM (2014a) 'What Is Mpamba' (Telekom Networks Malawi), https://www.tnmmpamba.co.mw/index.php/what-is-mpamba. 20 March 2018.

[168] Ibid.

[169] Ibid.

- *Efficiency and Reliability*—make real-time transactions at less cost;
- *Innovative*—have an enhanced profile and a part of innovative users.[170]

*Mpamba*'s user interface is also like *M-Pesa*'s. The customer is taken through a series of interactive steps until the transaction is almost complete and a single message is sent, after which a confirmation that the transaction has been processed appears.[171] *Mpamba* has also adopted the super agent and agent structure that *M-Pesa* developed. The main duty of super agents is to serve fellow agents and act as a direct link with *Mpamba*.[172] Nationalistic sentiments that endeared Safaricom to Kenyans have not rubbed off TNM. Granted that *Mpamba* did not pioneer the mobile money revolution, but even when *Mpamba* was launched, there was no euphoria of embracing a national brand, as it were. This is despite that TNM was a company born out of the unbundling of the Department of Posts and Telecommunications.[173] Unlike Safaricom, Malawians have never fondly regarded TNM as a government or national company.

### *7.5.3 Airtel Money and* Mpamba *Tariffs Compared*

Tables 7.2 and 7.3 show the tariffs for Airtel Money and *Mpamba*.

Just like *M-Pesa*, the cost of sending money to unregistered users for both services is generally higher. Research still needs to be conducted on the effects of having a different fee structure for sending money for the two services on service uptake since there are only two known mobile service money issuers. While Airtel Money has a flat rate for utility bill, *Mpamba* has a graduated scale with payments above K10,000.00

[170] Ibid.

[171] TNM (2014b) 'How to Use Mpamba: Customers' (Telekom Networks Malawi), https://www.tnmmpamba.co.mw/index.php/user-guide. 20 March 2018.

[172] TNM (2014c) 'How to Use Mpamba: Agents' (Telekom Networks Malawi), https://www.tnmmpamba.co.mw/index.php/user-guide/agent-user-guide. 20 March 2018.

[173] The author worked for the telecommunications sector (1991–1999).

**Table 7.2** Airtel money 2018 tariffs[a]

| *Airtel money tariffs* | | | | |
|---|---|---|---|---|
| *Transaction rage (K)* | | *Transaction type and customer charge (K)* | | |
| *Minimum* | *Maximum* | *Transfer to other Airtel Money users* | *Transfer to unregistered customer* | *Withdrawal from Airtel Money agent* |
| 50 | 500 | 10.00 | 95.00 | 20.00 |
| 501 | 1000 | 20.00 | 115.00 | 40.00 |
| 1001 | 2500 | 50.00 | 175.00 | 100.00 |
| 2501 | 5000 | 60.00 | 275.00 | 200.00 |
| 5001 | 10,000 | 80.00 | 455.00 | 380.00 |
| 10,001 | 20,000 | 150.00 | 830.00 | 755.00 |
| 20,001 | 50,000 | 200.00 | 1975.00 | 1900.00 |
| 50,001 | 100,000 | 400.00 | 3825.00 | 3750.00 |
| 100,001 | 200,000 | 500.00 | 6575.00 | 6500.00 |
| 200,001 | 350,000 | 1000.00 | 10,575.00 | 10,500.00 |
| 350,001 | 500,000 | 2000.00 | 15,075.00 | 15,000.00 |
| *Other transactions* | | *Fee (K)* | | |
| Merchant payments | | Free | | |
| Utility bill payments | | 200.00 | | |
| Balance check | | 100.00 | | |
| Bank information | | 100.00 | | |
| Airtel Money balance check | | Free | | |
| Airtime top-up | | Free | | |
| Change PIN | | 1.00 | | |
| *Allowed transaction limits* | | *K* | | |
| Minimum transfer | | 50.00 | | |
| Maximum transfer per transaction | | 500,000.00 | | |
| Maximum current balance | | 750,000.00 | | |

[a]Airtel (2018) 'Airtel Malawi Tariffs' (Airtel), http://africa.airtel.com/wps/wcm/connect/AfricaRevamp/Malawi/Airtel_Money/Home/Personal/tariffs. 27 December 2018

*Key* K=Malaŵian Kwacha | £1=K947.09 (XE [2018] 'XE Currency Converter' [XE], https://www.xe.com/currencyconverter/convert/?Amount=1&From=GBP&To=MWK. 10 November 2018)

attracting a fee of 1% of the transaction value. The differences in the pricing structure are a good sign and indicate lack of collusion or a desire to create a cartel. It is still early days to conclude whether the mobile money service is a success. For now, the indications are that it is growing

**Table 7.3** *Mpamba* 2018 tariffs[a]

| *Mpamba tariffs* | | | | |
|---|---|---|---|---|
| *Transaction rage (K)* | | *Transaction type and customer charge (K)* | | |
| *Minimum* | *Maximum* | *Transfer to other* Mpamba *users* | *Transfer to unregistered customer* | *Withdrawal from* Mpamba *agent* |
| 100 | 500 | 10.00 | 25.00 | 20.00 |
| 501 | 1000 | 20.00 | 50.00 | 40.00 |
| 1001 | 2000 | 30.00 | 100.00 | 85.00 |
| 2001 | 3000 | 60.00 | 170.00 | 150.00 |
| 3001 | 5000 | 40.00 | 250.00 | 200.00 |
| 5001 | 10,000 | 50.00 | 450.00 | 380.00 |
| 10,001 | 20,000 | 100.00 | 880.00 | 750.00 |
| 20,001 | 40,000 | 200.00 | 1750.00 | 1700.00 |
| 40,001 | 60,000 | 300.00 | 2750.00 | 2500.00 |
| 60,001 | 100,000 | 500.00 | 4500.00 | 3750.00 |
| 100,001 | 200,000 | 500.00 | 6800.00 | 6500.00 |
| 200,001 | 300,000 | 500.00 | 10,500.00 | 9000.00 |
| 300,001 | 400,000 | 500.00 | 14,500.00 | 11,000.00 |
| 400,001 | 500,000 | 500.00 | 16,500.00 | 12,500.00 |
| *Other transactions* | | *Fee (K)* | | |
| Merchant payments | | Free | | |
| Utility bill payments ≤ K10,000 | | 200.00 | | |
| Utility bill payments > K10,000 | | 1% | | |
| Information service (Balance enquiry and mini statement) | | First 5 balance checks per month—free K15.00 per transaction from the 6th onwards | | |
| Balance check | | Free | | |
| Airtime top-up | | Free | | |
| *Allowed transaction limits* | | *K* | | |
| Minimum transfer | | 100.00 | | |
| Maximum transfer per transaction | | 500,000.00 | | |
| Maximum current balance | | Variable[b] | | |

[a]TNM (2018) 'Mpamba Customer Fees' (Telekom Networks Malawi), https://www.tnmmpamba.co.mw/index.php/customer-fees. 20 December 2018

[b]Mpamba has several categories with different maximum limits. The entry level requires the minimal KYC requirements but to graduate to higher thresholds requires extras identification checks

steadily. Local banker Daud Suleman captures the growth very well when he said in 2015 that:

> Since banking started in Malawi, all the banks combined have managed a total base of 1.2 million customers, yet in its two, short years, mobile money has already registered 1.5 million users.[174]

By mid-2016, the total number of mobile money account holders had jumped to 2.6 million with annual growth of 96 and 127% in volume and value over the previous year.[175] It would, therefore, seem that the two mobile money services are on the rise with an increase not only in the subscriber base but also in revenue. TNM in 2016 reported a revenue growth for *Mpamba* of 378%.[176] This was the highest among TNM's revenue streams, but nowhere compared in value to any of the others.[177] Data from Airtel could not be sourced.[178] In terms of mobile phone use, Airtel has just under 56% share of the market while TNM has just under 44%.[179] Interestingly, this share is not evenly spread across the country's three regions. TNM has a major share in the North and the South.[180] Airtel has three-quarters of the market share in the Central Region.[181]

The distribution between the two mobile network operators and their mobile money services can be summarised in the Tables 7.4 and 7.5.

[174] Charles Simango (2015) 'Mobile Money Is New Fashion in Malawi' *The Nation* (3 February 2015), http://mwnation.com/mobilelectronicmoney-newfashion-malawi/. 11 May 2018.

[175] RBM (2016) *Monthly National Payments System Report: July 2016* (Reserve Bank of Malaŵi), p. 1, https://www.rbm.mw/PaymentSystems/GetContentFile/?ContentID=7870. 12 May 2018.

[176] TNM (2016) *Annual Report 2015* (Telekom Networks Malaŵi Limited), p. 10, https://drive.google.com/file/d/0B9DwraK-rABVQUlRYnoyTlo0Znc/view. 11 March 2018.

[177] Ibid., p. 10.

[178] Unlike TNM which is a publicly listed company, Airtel is a private company.

[179] MACRA (2016) *National Survey on Access to and Usage of ICT Services in Malawi* (Malaŵi Communications Regulatory Authority Blantyre), p. 12, http://www.macra.org.mw/wp-content/uploads/2016/01/MACRA-Survey-Report-National-Household-and-Individual-access-to-and-usage-of-ICT.pdf. 11 March 2018.

[180] Ibid.

[181] Ibid.

**Table 7.4** Mobile and mobile money market share distribution[a]

| | *Mobile phone users (%)* | *Mobile money users (%)* |
|---|---|---|
| Airtel | 55.9 | 62.2 |
| TNM | 43.7 | 31.1 |

[a] *Source of data* MACRA (2016), pp. 12–3

**Table 7.5** Mobile and mobile money statistics[a]

| | *Mobile phone users* | *Mobile money users* | *Mobile money agents* |
|---|---|---|---|
| Airtel | 3.5 million[b] | 1.9 million | 5000 |
| TNM | 3 million[c] | 1.6 million | 3800 |

[a] *Source of data*
Akossa Mphepo (2017) Senior Public Relations Manager (Telekom Networks Malaŵi, 30 January 2017)
TNM (2016), p. 4
Anon (2016b) 'Airtel Leads the Way' *The Times* (Blantyre, 28 January 2016), http://www.times.mw/airtel-malawi-leads-the-way/. 11 March 2018
Luke Bisani (2016) 'Airtel Proud of Airtel Money' *Malawi24* (27 June 2018), https://malawi24.com/2016/06/27/airtel-proud-airtel-money/. 11 March 2018
RBM (2017) *Monthly National Payments System Report: January 2017* (Reserve Bank of Malaŵi), p. 1, https://www.rbm.mw/PaymentSystems/GetContentFile/?ContentID=12203. 10 March 2018
[b] 2015 figures
[c] 2015 figures

Statics indicate that the premier use of mobile money in Malaŵi is airtime procurement, which in 2015 accounted for just under 65% of mobile money revenue.[182] Remittances only amounted to slightly over 27%.[183] This shows that mobile money is beneficial to the mobile network operators as it provides a steady stream of revenue through airtime purchases. However, when looked at from an urban/rural viewpoint, the picture changes. In rural areas, remittances form most of the transactions, at slightly over 45% compared to just under 43% for airtime purchases.[184] For the rural areas, mobile money is delivering on its premier goal and may already have started positively to affect the attainment of financial inclusion.

[182] MACRA (2016), p. 14.
[183] Ibid.
[184] Ibid.

Although they started out as competitors, to benefit from economies of scale, *Mpamba* disclosed that it has engaged Airtel Money on developing a joint mobile money payment system.[185] With customers of each service now able to send money across networks, it would seem the last hurdle that was preventing seamless connectivity between the two mobile money services has been overcome. The two service providers are also working closely towards achieving financial inclusion.[186] Head of *Mpamba*, Webster Mbekeani says:

> Unlike the telco side, where there is a rivalry, with mobile money, things are different. It's not the time to compete. I do not even have 50% of my client base, why should I be thinking about grabbing Airtel Money customers? It's time to convert the mindset of the people to begin to accept mobile money as an acceptable way of transacting. There and then can we begin to compete. For now, I believe we should vest our energies, efforts, and monies into that mindset changing, behavioural changing, making people understand. Moving from people from becoming aware to becoming active.[187]

## 7.6 Telco-Led Versus Banking-Led Model

*M-Pesa*, Airtel Money and *Mpamba* are all issued based on deposits in a pool account of a bank. There is no requirement for individual customs who hold the mobile money accounts to have bank accounts. As the telecommunications network is the carrier of the service, this model is called a telco-led.[188] This is the main factor distinguishing the telco-led model of mobile money from the bank-led model where one links their mobile phone to their pre-existing account. For the bank-led model, the mobile phone works as an extension of the bank account, and in many ways, bears similarities to mobile banking offered by banks. Examples of bank-led mobile money services are WIZZIT and MTN Mobile Money, both offered in South Africa, which are briefly discussed below.

[185] Mbekeani (2015).

[186] Ibid.

[187] Ibid.

[188] Maurer (2011).

The end of apartheid in South Africa saw a positive movement in the number of the banked from 29 to 39% in by 1994.[189] At the time the mobile money revolution began in earnest, more than half of the population in South Africa was still unbanked.[190] However, despite South Africa having many people unbanked, the conditions seeming right and having arguably one of the biggest slums in Africa, *Khayelitsha*,[191] the service seems not to have picked up as expected. WIZZIT was launched in 2005 with links to Bank of Athens SA.[192] The bank provides account holders with access to other e-payments systems including use of ATM machines.[193] The opening of WIZZIT accounts was done remotely through agents called WIZZkids.[194] WIZZIT targeted 300,000 accounts in the medium term,[195] but it only attracted 250,000 in more than 4 years of operation.[196] Apart from using the mobile banking platform, the service also offers a debit card by MasterCard.[197]

WIZZIT adopted a similar but somewhat modified slogan to that of *M-Pesa: Send money home to family and friends.*[198] Although it is linked to a bank, WIZZIT is a virtual branchless banking platform and does not require customers to physically visit bank branches.[199] WIZZIT has now

[189] Alan Gibson (2006) *Developing Financial Services Markets for the Poor: FinMark in South Africa* (Making Markets Work for the Poor: Case Studies Series, Schweizerische Eidgenossenschaft, Bern), p. 5, http://www.value-chains.org/dyn/bds/docs/614/M4P_case_study_FinMark_april2007.pdf. 19 March 2018.

[190] Ibid., p. 11.

[191] Tovrov (2011).

[192] Porteous (2006), p. 27.

[193] By use of a Maestro branded debit card which is part of the account—ibid., p. 27.

[194] Ibid.

[195] Rabecca Harrison (2005) 'Cell Phones Plug Africa's Poor into Mobile Banking' *Reuters South Africa* (1 November 2005), https://www.mail-archive.com/telecom-cities@forums.nyu.edu/msg00327.html. 21 Janaury 2018.

[196] Mas and Morawczynski (2009), p. 77.

[197] WIZZIT (2016a) 'History' (WIZZIT), http://www.wizzit.co.za/?q=node/197. 14 May 2018.

[198] WIZZIT (2016b) 'Cellphone Banking' (WIZZIT), http://www.wizzit.co.za/?q=node/68. 14 May 2018.

[199] WIZZIT (2016c) 'Who We Are' (WIZZIT International), http://wizzit-int.com.dedi89.cpt1.host-h.net/who-we-are/. 14 May 2018.

been deployed in 9 countries[200] and boasts of over 6 million customers through partner banks.[201] However, details of the number of customers that it has in South Africa could not be obtained. It is also unclear whether these 6 million customers were recruited by WIZZIT or have become customers by its association with partner banks. WIZZIT is built to operate across networks and not linked to any one operator.[202]

MTN (Mobile) Money started as a venture between the telecommunications company MTN and Standard Bank in 2005.[203] Customers are required to provide biometric identifiers when opening accounts through an interactive process, which takes place remotely.[204] In 2014, MTN launched MTN Mobile Money and its catchphrase is clear in what type of service it is offering: "Mobile money is a safe, secure and affordable way to do your *banking*, and is available to customers on all cell phone network" (emphasis supplied).[205] MTN says, customers are given Mobile Money Visa Cards, which they can use for "everyday purchases at any point-of-sale machine".[206] The cards can also be used to withdraw money from any ATM.[207] Customers, however, need to purchase the Visa Card separately.[208]

Both WIZZIT and MTN Mobile Money are premised on the notion of branchless banking. In sub-Saharan Africa, one of the greatest

[200] South Africa, Zambia, Tanzania, Romania, Rwanda, Namibia, Botswana, Honduras, and Nigeria.

[201] WIZZIT (2016c). Anon (2014) 'WIZZIT CEO: Reflections & Predictions for the Future of Mobile Money' (Mondato Insight, Mondato, 14 January 2016), http://mondato.com/blog/wizzit-founder/. 14 May 2018.

[202] WIZZIT (2016c).

[203] An entity called MTN Mobile Money South Africa was formed—Cisco (2012) *MTN Mobile Money Service* (Mobile Connected Life Experiences, Cisco), http://www.cisco.com/en/US/solutions/collateral/ns341/ns525/ns537/ns705/ns1058/Cisco_MTN_CS.pdf. 19 March 2018.

[204] Porteous (2006), p. 26.

[205] MTN (2016) 'MTN Mobile Money' (Mobile Telephone Network, South Africa), https://www.mtn.co.za/everyday_services/useful_extras/Banking/Pages/mobile_banking.aspx. 19 March 2018.

[206] Ibid.

[207] Ibid.

[208] Ibid.

challenges faced by banks is the establishment of branches in rural and far-flung areas. In 2007, Brian Richardson founder of WIZZIT said:

> If you talk to any bank anywhere in the world, banking equals branches, and as long as you have that mindset, it becomes expensive to bring affordable banking to the mass market. It is estimated in South Africa that 30 million people have a cell phone 11 million people have a bank account. So, the option is to utilise technology. The challenge we had, was to have technology that worked on the lowest common denominator, that could work on any phone, any SIM and across all the networks.[209]

Looking at the bank-led and telco-led models, what comes out clearly is that the two models function on different rails. Since WIZZIT and MTN Mobile Money are bank-led, it is only natural that they are subjected to the more stringent prudential regulatory framework for banks. It is submitted this is what may have led to the differences in uptake. The fact that WIZZIT and MTN Mobile Money are regarded as banking services may be a hindrance. There is a good reason why the telco-led models are at pains to emphasise that they are not banking services. Bank-led models, by their nature, are within the clutches of the banking regulator. This leaves them little or no room for innovative manoeuvre unless sanctioned by the regulator, a process that may be laborious. Heeks argues that tighter regulation is one of the factors that negatively affected the roll-out and expansion of mobile money services in South Africa.[210] As noted earlier, *M-Pesa*, which was introduced by Vodacom (South Africa), was withdrawn for failure to gain traction.[211] The uptake of mobile money in South Africa has generally stalled over the years.[212]

The Table 7.6 offers a comparison between the telco-led and bank-led models of mobile money and the services offered within each model.

[209] Anon (2007b) 'WIZZIT: Banking the Unbanked in South Africa' (World Bank) (Audio Visual), https://www.youtube.com/watch?v=2SKhCYoF0Lg. 1 March 2018.

[210] Heeks (2012).

[211] Chutel (2016).

[212] Rabelani Dagada (2015) 'Mobile Money Stalls in SA' *ITWeb in Banking* (10 February 2018), http://www.itweb.co.za/index.php?option=com_content&view=article&id=141012. 19 March 2018.

**Table 7.6** Comparisons of the mobile money services[a]

| *Criteria* | *M-Pesa* | *Airtel Money* | *Mpamba* | *MTN Money* | *WIZZIT* |
|---|---|---|---|---|---|
| Targets unbanked customers | Yes | Not specifically but as part of offering | Not specifically but as part of offering | Not specifically but as part of offering | Yes |
| Safety | Funds in a pool account held at a bank | Funds in a pool account held at a bank | Funds in a pool account held at a bank | Account held at a bank | Account held at a bank |
| Easy access to cash | Yes—through agents | Yes—through agents | Yes—through agents | Card access to existing ATMs/Bank branch | Card access to existing ATMs/Bank branch |
| Ability to transfer | Yes | Yes | Yes | Yes, to a bank account | Yes, to a bank account |
| Linked to one operator | Yes | Yes | Yes | Yes | No |
| Model | Telco-led | Telco-led | Telco-led | Bank-led | Bank-led |

[a]This figure has been adapted from Proteus Tables 3 and 4, Porteous (2006), p. 27 and 29
Aker and Mbiti (2010), p. 20 say despite *M-Pesa* being touted as targeting the low income and poor and "banking the unbanked", M-Pesa "users are wealthier, better educated, urban and already banked"

## 7.7 Conclusion

This chapter has provided an operational overview of how mobile money operates. Using the *M-Pesa* as the standard, the chapter looked at the factors that contributed to its success and how attempts to replicate it in other jurisdictions failed to achieve the same results. The chapter then looked at the two mobile money services provided by Airtel and TNM and it became clear that these services are largely modelled on the *M-Pesa*. The chapter also undertook a brief comparative analysis of the telco-led and bank-led models of mobile money. It was found that the bank-led models have not fared well compared to the telco-led model, and one possible reason advanced is a regulatory restriction of the former as they are treated as banking services, and therefore subject to more stringent regulation. Now, because of the inclusiveness of its risk-based know your customer requirements, it can be concluded that the telco-led is the most ideal in achieving financial inclusion goals.

The main issues that arise in this chapter are how a service like *M-Pesa* can be successfully replicated and what is the best way of regulating it? It was suggested that future replications of *M-Pesa* are more likely to follow the Tanzanian model: slow but steady. For Malaŵi, this is a valuable lesson for Airtel Money and *Mpamba*. It is imperative, therefore, that the model is not simply replicated without factoring in some of the unique and distinguishing factors present in Malaŵi. In fact, it begs the question whether the research was first done or the service was introduced in a niche market, having seen the success in Kenya, and has had to be adapted along the way. As has been highlighted, the economic situation in Kenya is very different from that of Malaŵi. For now, both Airtel Money and *Mpamba* seem to be gaining traction. The basic mobile money ecosystem infrastructure has been laid down and only time will tell how the services grow.

## References


ADB (2014) 'Comparing the Real Size of African Economies' (African Development Bank), https://www.afdb.org/fileadmin/uploads/afdb/Documents/Project-and-Operations/Highlights_-_Comparing_the_Real_Size_of_Africa_Economies_%E2%80%93_Main_results_of_the_2011_round_of_the_International_Comparison_Program__ICP_.pdf. 20 July 2018.

AFI (2010) *Enabling Mobile Money Transfer: The Central Bank of Kenya's Treatment of M-Pesa* (Alliance for Financial Inclusion), http://www.gsma.com/mobilefordevelopment/wp-content/uploads/2013/09/enablingmobilemoneytransfer92.pdf. 15 December 2018.

Airtel (2013a) 'Airtel Money Launch in Malawi' (Airtel), http://africa.airtel.com/wps/wcm/connect/africarevamp/malawi/home/personal/airtel-money. 15 December 2018.

Airtel (2013b) 'Airtel—Merchants and Utilities' (Airtel Malaŵi), http://africa.airtel.com/wps/wcm/connect/AfricaRevamp/Malawi/Airtel_Money/Home/Merchants_and_utilities. 23 March 2018.

Airtel (2013c) 'About Airtel Money' (Airtel Malaŵi), http://africa.airtel.com/wps/wcm/connect/AfricaRevamp/Malawi/Airtel_Money/Home/Personal/About_airtel_money. 23 March 2018.

Airtel (2013d) 'Airtel—How It Works: Send Money' (Airtel Malaŵi), http://africa.airtel.com/wps/wcm/connect/africarevamp/malawi/airtel_money/home/personal/how_it_works/send_money. 23 March 2018.

Airtel (2013e) 'Agents' (Airtel Malaŵi), http://africa.airtel.com/wps/wcm/connect/AfricaRevamp/Malawi/Airtel_Money/Home/Agents. 23 March 2018.

Airtel (2018) 'Airtel Malawi Tariffs' (Airtel), http://africa.airtel.com/wps/wcm/connect/AfricaRevamp/Malawi/Airtel_Money/Home/Personal/tariffs. 27 December 2018.

Akin Oyebode (2014) 'M-Pesa and Beyond—Why Mobile Money Worked in Kenya and Struggles in Other Markets' *Venture Capital for Africa* (15 May 2014), http://vc4africa.biz/blog/2014/01/15/m-pesa-and-beyond-why-mobilelectronicmoney-worked-in-kenya-and-struggles-in-other-markets/. 15 December 2018.

Alan Gibson (2006) *Developing Financial Services Markets for the Poor: FinMark in South Africa* (Making Markets Work for the Poor: Case Studies Series, Schweizerische Eidgenossenschaft, Bern), http://www.value-chains.org/dyn/bds/docs/614/M4P_case_study_FinMark_april2007.pdf. 19 March 2018.

Anon (2007a) 'Kibera UK—The Gap Year Company' (Kibera UK Charity), http://www.kibera.org.uk/Facts.html. 16 March 2018.

Anon (2007b) 'WIZZIT: Banking the Unbanked in South Africa' (World Bank) (Audio Visual), https://www.youtube.com/watch?v=2SKhCYoF0Lg. 1 March 2018.

Anon (2010) 'Out of Thin Air' *The Economist* (10 June 2010), http://www.economist.com/node/16319635. 15 December 2018.

Anon (2013a) 'TNM Launches Mobile Money Mpamba to Build Great Malawi Nation' *Nyasa Times*, http://www.nyasatimes.com/tnm-launches-mobilelectronicmoney-mpamba-to-build-great-malawi-nation/. 28 December 2018.

Anon (2013b) 'Why Does Kenya Lead the World in Mobile Money?' *The Economist* (27 May 2013), http://www.economist.com/blogs/economist-explains/2013/05/economist-explains-18. 15 December 2018.

Anon (2014) 'WIZZIT CEO: Reflections & Predictions for the Future of Mobile Money' (Mondato Insight, Mondato, 14 January 2016), http://mondato.com/blog/wizzit-founder/. 14 May 2018.

Anon (2016a) 'Mobile Money—M-Pesa in Kenya, 7 Things Worth Knowing' *SEPA Mobile Payments* (20 November 2015), http://www.sepaforcorporates.com/sepa-mobile-payments/mobilelectronicmoney-m-pesa-kenya-7-things-didnt-know/. 31 October 2018.

Anon (2016b) 'Airtel Leads the Way' *The Times* (Blantyre, 28 January 2016), http://www.times.mw/airtel-malawi-leads-the-way/. 11 March 2018.

Anon (2017) 'African Countries by Population' (Worldometers), http://www.worldometers.info/population/countries-in-africa-by-population/. 20 July 2018.

Bilichi Kenya (2018) 'Top Ten Companies in Kenya by Market Valuation 2018' (28 February 2018), https://bilichi.co.ke/top-10-companies-kenya-2018/. 27 December 2018.

Bill Maurer (2011) 'Mobile Money Regulation: A Story Arc of Best Practices and Emerging Realizations' *Notes from the Field* (December 2011), http://faculty.sites.uci.edu/wmmaurer/files/2011/12/Note_Dec2011_IMTFI.pdf. 15 December 2018.

Charles Simango (2015) 'Mobile Money Is New Fashion in Malawi' *The Nation* (3 February 2015), http://mwnation.com/mobilelectronicmoney-newfashion-malawi/. 11 May 2018.

CIA (2014) 'The World Factbook' (Central Intelligence Agency), https://www.cia.gov/library/publications/the-world-factbook/rankorder/2147rank.html. 20 July 2018.

Cisco (2012) *MTN Mobile Money Service* (Mobile Connected Life Experiences), http://www.cisco.com/en/US/solutions/collateral/ns341/ns525/ns537/ns705/ns1058/Cisco_MTN_CS.pdf. 19 March 2018.

Daniel Tovrov (2011) '5 Biggest Slums in the World' *International Business Times* (9 December 2011), http://www.ibtimes.com/5-biggest-slums-world-381338. 16 March 2018.

David Porteous (2006) *The Enabling Environment for Mobile Banking in Africa* (Report Commissioned by Department for International Development [DFID], Boston), http://bankablefrontier.com/wp-ontent/uploads/documents/ee.mobil_.banking.report.v3.1.pdf. 14 September 2018.

Emil Sjöblom, Gunnar Camner and Caroline Pulver (2009) *What Makes a Successful Mobile Money Implementation? Learnings from M-PESA in Kenya and Tanzania* (GSMA), http://www.gsma.com/mobilefordevelopment/wp-content/uploads/2012/03/What-makes-a-successful-mobilelectronicmoney-implementation.pdf. 1 March 2018.

Eric Ombok (2010) 'Safaricom Names Collymore as Chief Executive Officer' *Bloomberg Business* (22 July 2010), http://www.bloomberg.com/news/articles/2010-07-22/kenya-s-safaricom-appoints-bob-collymore-as-ceo-replacing-michael-joseph. 16 March 2018.

Graham Kajilwa (2015) 'Safaricom and Airtel Lose Market Share to New Comers, Regulator Report Shows' *Standard* (28 December 2015), http://www.standardmedia.co.ke/business/article/2000186415/safaricom-and-airtel-lose-market-share-to-new-comers-regulator-report-shows. 31 October 2018.

Gunnar Camner and Emil Sjöblom (2009) *Can the Success of M-PESA Be Repeated?—A Review of the Implementations in Kenya and Tanzania*, http://emil.sjoblom.com/pdf/M-Pesa_implementations_Ke_Tz.pdf. 15 December 2018.

Hilton Tarrant (2011) 'Why Kenya's M-Pesa Won't Work Anywhere Else' (Moneyweb, 13 March 2015), http://www.moneyweb.co.za/archive/why-kenyas-mpesa-wont-work-anywhere-else/.

Idongesit Williams and Benjamin Kwofie (2014) 'The Impact of Liberalization on the Mobile Telephony Market in Africa' in Knud Erik Skouby and Williams Idongesit (eds) *The African Mobile Story* (River Publishers, Copenhagen).

IFC (2011) 'IFC Mobile Money Study 2011—Summary Report' (International Finance Corporation), http://www.ifc.org/wps/wcm/connect/fad057004a052eb88b23ffdd29332b51/MobileMoneyReport-Summary.pdf?MOD=AJPERES. 15 December 2018.

Ignacio Mas and Amolo Ng'weno (2010) *Three Keys to M-PESA's Success: Branding, Channel Management and Pricing* (GSMA), http://www.www.oneapigw.gsma.com/mobilefordevelopment/wp-content/uploads/2012/06/keystompesassuccess4jan69.pdf. 15 December 2018.

Ignacio Mas and Olga Morawczynski (2009) 'Designing Mobile Money Services Lessons from M-PESA' 4 (2) *Innovations* 77.

Interview with Webster Mbekeani Head, Mobile Money Division, TNM (20 August 2015).

Interview with Bigboy Mkoloma Product and Development Manager, Airtel Money (7 August 2015).

James Crabtree (2012) 'M-Pesa's Cautious Start in India' *Financial Times* (New York, 27 December 2012), http://www.ft.com/cms/s/0/a09c0f68-4a9a-11e2-9650-00144feab49a.html#axzz3UGBgLWPj. 15 December 2018.

Jennifer Isern and Louis De Koker (2012) *AML/CFT: Strengthening Financial Inclusion and Integrity* (CGAP Focus Notes, CGAP, Washington, DC), http://dro.deakin.edu.au/eserv/DU:30020790/dekoker-amlcft-2009.pdf. 14 November 2018.

Jenny Aker and Isaac Mbiti (2010) 'Mobile Phones and Economic Development in Africa' 24 (3) *Journal of Economic Perspectives* 207, https://www.aeaweb.org/atypon.php?doi=10.1257/jep.24.3.207. 13 December 2018.

John Njiraini and James Anyanzwa (2008) 'Unmasking the Storm Behind M-Pesa' *The Standard* (30 December 2008), http://www.standardmedia.co.ke/?articleID=1144002826&story_title=. 13 March 2018.

Julius Nyerere (1967) 'The Arusha Declaration' (Tanganyika African National Union), https://www.marxists.org/subject/africa/nyerere/1967/arusha-declaration.htm. 15 December 2018.

Kristie Wang (2012) 'Replicating M-Pesa: Mobile and Cloud Technology Spur Innovation in Financial Inclusion' (15 December 2016), http://nextbillion.net/blogpost.aspx?blogid=2869.

Lara Gilman (2016) *The Impact of Mobile Money Interoperability in Tanzania*, http://www.gsma.com/mobilefordevelopment/wp-content/uploads/2016/10/2016_GSMA_The-impact-of-mobilelectronicmoney-interoperability-in-Tanzania.pdf. 10 May 2018.

Luke Bisani (2016) 'Airtel Proud of Airtel Money' *Malawi24* (27 June 2018), https://malawi24.com/2016/06/27/airtel-proud-airtel-money/. 11 March 2018.

Lynsey Chutel (2016) 'Vodacom Has Given Up on Revolutionary Mobile Money Service M-Pesa, in South Africa' *Quartz Africa Weekly Brief* (9 May 2016), https://qz.com/679059/vodacom-has-given-up-on-revolutionary-mobilelectronicmoney-service-m-pesa-in-south-africa/. 10 January 2018.

MACRA (2016) *National Survey on Access to and Usage of ICT Services in Malawi* (Malaŵi Communications Regulatory Authority Blantyre), http://www.macra.org.mw/wp-content/uploads/2016/01/MACRA-Survey-Report-National-Household-and-Individual-access-to-and-usage-of-ICT.pdf. 11 March 2018.

Matt Krueger (2011) 'Four Reasons M-Pesa Succeeded in Kenya' *Mobile Money Exchange* (9 May 2011), https://mobilemoneyexchange.wordpress.com/2011/05/09/four-reasons-m-pesa-succeeded-in-kenya/. 10 March 2018.

MTN (2016) 'Mobile Money' (Mobile Telephone Network, South Africa), https://www.mtn.co.za/everyday_services/useful_extras/Banking/Pages/mobile_banking.aspx. 20 May 2018.

Nathan Hedgedus (2012) 'An African Success Story Revealed' (2) *Ericsson Business Review* 10, http://www.ericsson.com/res/thecompany/docs/publications/business-review/2012/issue2/an_african_success_story_explained.pdf. 15 December 2018.

Nick Hughes and Susie Lonie (2007) 'M-PESA: Mobile Money for the "Unbanked" Turning Cellphones into 24-Hour Tellers in Kenya' 2 (1–2) *Innovations* 63, http://www.mitpressjournals.org/doi/pdf/10.1162/itgg.2007.2.1-2.63. 15 December 2018.

Olga Morawczynski and Gianluca Miscione (2008) 'Examining Trust in Mobile Banking Transactions: The Case of M-PESA in Kenya' in Chrisanthi Avgerou, Matthew L. Smith and Peter van den Basselaar (eds) *Social Dimensions of Information and Communication Technology Policy* (Springer, Boston).

Philemon Matoi (2016) *M-Pesa in Tanzania: The Journey So Far* (Vodacom, Mlimani), https://www.udbs.udsm.ac.tz/images/ICAESB2016/M-Pesa_in_Tanzania.pdf. 10 May 2018.

Rabecca Harrison (2005) 'Cell Phones Plug Africa's Poor into Mobile Banking' *Reuters South Africa* (1 November 2005), https://www.mail-archive.com/telecom-cities@forums.nyu.edu/msg00327.html. 21 January 2018.

Rabelani Dagada (2015) 'Mobile Money Stalls in SA' *ITWeb in Banking* (10 February 2018), http://www.itweb.co.za/index.php?option=com_content&view=article&id=141012. 19 March 2018.

RBM (2016) *Monthly National Payments System Report: July 2016* (Reserve Bank of Malaŵi), https://www.rbm.mw/PaymentSystems/GetContentFile/?ContentID=7870. 12 May 2018.

RBM (2017) *Monthly National Payments System Report: January 2017* (Reserve Bank of Malaŵi), https://www.rbm.mw/PaymentSystems/GetContentFile/?ContentID=12203. 10 March 2018.

Richard Heeks (2012) 'Why M-Pesa Outperforms Other Developing Country Mobile Money Schemes' *ICTs for Development*, http://ict4dblog.wordpress.com/2012/11/24/why-m-pesa-outperforms-other-developing-country-mobilelectronicmoney-schemes/. 8 May 2018.

Safaricom (2016a) 'M-PESA Rates' (Safaricom), https://www.safaricom.co.ke/personal/m-pesa/get-started-with-m-pesa/m-pesa-tariffs. 9 May 2018.

Safaricom (2016b) *SAFARICOM LIMITED Annual Report 2016* (Nairobi), https://www.safaricom.co.ke/annualreport_2016/downloads/Safaricom%20Annual%20Report%202016.pdf. 10 May 2018.

Sam Floy (2016) 'How and Why Mobile Money (M-Pesa) Works in Kenya' *Our Mobile World* (13 October 2016), http://samfloy.com/how-and-why-mobilelectronicmoney-m-pesa-works-in-kenya/. 7 April 2018. Also see Mas and Ng'weno (2010).

Sean Kane (2002) 'Telecom Reform and Poverty Alleviation in Kenya' (3) *African Journal of Information and Communication* 31.

TNM (2014a) 'What Is Mpamba' (Telekom Networks Malawi), https://www.tnmmpamba.co.mw/index.php/what-is-mpamba. 20 March 2018.

TNM (2014b) 'How to Use Mpamba: Customers' (Telekom Networks Malawi), https://www.tnmmpamba.co.mw/index.php/user-guide. 20 March 2018.

TNM (2014c) 'How to Use Mpamba: Agents' (Telekom Networks Malawi), https://www.tnmmpamba.co.mw/index.php/user-guide/agent-user-guide. 20 March 2018.

TNM (2016) *Annual Report 2015* (Telekom Networks Malaŵi Limited), https://drive.google.com/file/d/0B9DwraK-rABVQUlRYnoyTlo0Znc/view. 11 March 2018.

TNM (2018) 'Mpamba Customer Fees' (Telekom Networks Malawi), https://www.tnmmpamba.co.mw/index.php/customer-fees. 20 December 2018.

Vodacom (2016a) *Vodacom Integrated Report for the Year Ended* (31 March 2016), http://www.vodacom-reports.co.za/integrated-reports/ir-2016/pdf/full-integrated.pdf. 10 May 2018.

Vodacom (2016b) 'Ada za M-Pesa' (Vodacom Tanzania PLC), https://vodacom.co.tz/mpesa/consumers/mpesa_tarrifs. 9 May 2018.

William Jack and Tavneet Suri (2011) 'Mobile Money: The Economics of M-PESA' (National Bureau of Economic Research), http://www.nber.org/papers/w16721. 15 December 2018.

William Jack, Tavneet Suri and Robert M Townsend (2010) 'Monetary Theory and Electronic Money: Reflections on the Kenyan Experience' 96 (1) *Federal Reserve Bank of Richmond Economic Quarterly* 83, https://www.richmondfed.org/publications/research/economic_quarterly/2010/q1/townsend. 15 December 2018.

WIZZIT (2016a) 'History' (WIZZIT), http://www.wizzit.co.za/?q=node/197. 14 May 2018.

WIZZIT (2016b) 'Cellphone Banking' (WIZZIT), http://www.wizzit.co.za/?q=node/68. 14 May 2018.

WIZZIT (2016c) 'Who We Are' (WIZZIT International), http://wizzit-int.com.dedi89.cpt1.host-h.net/who-we-are/. 14 May 2018.

Wolgang Fengler (2012) 'How Kenya Became a World Leader for Mobile Money' (Africa Can End Poverty, The World Bank, 16 July 2012), http://blogs.worldbank.org/africacan/how-kenya-became-a-world-leader-for-mobilelectronicmoney. 7 April 2018.

XE (2018) 'XE Currency Converter' (XE), https://www.xe.com/currencyconverter/convert/?Amount=1&From=GBP&To=MWK. 10 November 2018.

CHAPTER 8

# Malaŵi's Existing Regulatory Framework of Mobile Money

## 8.1 Introduction

So far, mobile money has been analyses as a commodity, a financial service and a payment system. This chapter focuses on the existing regulatory framework of mobile money in Malaŵi. Although the discussion is restricted to the regulatory environment in Malaŵi, it is submitted that the framework is broadly representative of the telco-led model in most parts of sub-Saharan Africa. As has been discussed, mobile money is an emerging service that straddles between the telecommunication and financial services and it is regulated in parts by several agencies. Malaŵi's current regulatory framework comprises five regulators, each having different roles. The lead regulator is the central bank. The other key regulator is the communications regulator. The other ones are the financial intelligence unit, the Consumers Protection Council and the Competition and Fair Trading Commission. The multiplicity of regulators has the potential to lead to the problems associated with cross-sanctioning between regulatory regimes.[1] Although attempts have been made to achieve regulatory coordination, what comes out confirms Teubner's theory of autopoiesis.[2] Each of the regulators operates in its own cocoon and although there are cooperating agreements; they

[1] Scott (2001), p. 346.

[2] Teubner (1993), generally.



S. Madise, *The Regulation of Mobile Money*, Palgrave Macmillan Studies in Banking and Financial Institutions, https://doi.org/10.1007/978-3-030-13831-8_8

usually talk past each other because of the different communication language they employ. Apart from being distinct sector regulators, they also employ different regulatory approaches. As has been argued in Chapters 3 and 4, really responsive regulation, which continuously responds to the mobile money environment holistically, is the preferred approach throughout the various phases of financial inclusion. To achieve this however requires a paradigm shift in the regulatory model. In presenting the current framework, this chapter hopes to lay a foundation for the justification for a different regulatory approach.

This chapter is divided into three broad sections. The first discusses Malaŵi's regulatory framework while the second analyses the regulatory issues that arise from this framework. The discussion of the regulatory framework includes the financial, communication, consumer protection and fair-trading regimes. The financial intelligence unit is not included because it has already been discussed in Chapter 4. Incoherencies of the framework, technical issues and the regulatory space contestations form up the discussion of the regulatory issues posed. The last section provides a brief overview of the existing regulatory framework of mobile money in Kenya. The comparison with Kenya is for learning purposes. Kenya has navigated the pre-financial inclusions hurdles and is now in the post-financial inclusion phase. It therefore offers countries like Malaŵi a looking glass on what potentially may lie on the other side.

## 8.2 Regulatory Framework

### *8.2.1 Financial Regulatory Structure*

The country's central bank, Reserve Bank of Malaŵi, is the single regulator operating as a perfect "monolith".[3] One advantage of having a single regulator is that it makes it easier for market participants as they only have to deal with one single regulator.[4] It also means that there is a single approach to regulation and supervision compared with a situation

[3]Monolith is used deliberately instead of peak. A monolith is a massive rock and it aptly describes a unified regulator laden with many responsibilities. The term 'monolith' was used interchangeably with 'peak' by Richard Parlour (2014) *Strategic Issues in Financial Markets Regulation* (2014) Post-Graduate Seminar, University of Warwick, 5 March 2018.

[4]Singh (2007), p. 25.

where you have a myriad of regulators.[5] The central bank governor is registrar of the financial services.[6] As noted earlier, the governor and the board of the central bank are appointed by the country's president. There is, therefore, the serious question of whether such appointees can be truly independent. Furthermore, by making the governor the registrar, and the central bank the regulator of the financial sector, it is submitted, this has led to a situation where both are overburdened. Apart from regulating, the governor or his appointee is responsible for running any financial institution placed under statutory management.[7]

So far, there have been three cases of statutory management, one involving a bank and two involving insurance companies.[8] In all three cases, the matters ended up in court where the governor was the defendant. In the *Re: Citizen Insurance Company*, the High Court ordered the governor to reimburse expenses on the basis that there was no cause for statutory management in the first place.[9] The governor was further ordered to account for all transactions undertaken.[10] Although the Malaŵi Supreme Court of Appeal later ruled that the company should be wound up, the matter still had to be litigated for several years. The governor or his appointee is also the statutory liquidator of all prudentially regulated financial institutions.[11]

The central bank employs a *silo* regulatory structure. It has directorates in charge of specific institutions such as banks, insurance, pensions.[12] The directors are the de facto registrars of the sectors falling under their silo, and the directorates are the de facto regulators. The bank's head office is in the capital, Lilongwe with a branch in Blantyre, the principal commercial city.[13] The main function of the branch in

[5] Ibid., p. 26.

[6] Section 8(2) Financial Services Act (Malaŵi, 2010).

[7] Section 68, ibid.

[8] Finance Bank of Malaŵi, Prime Insurance Limited and Citizen Insurance Limited.

[9] *In the Matter of Citizen Insurance Company Limited Exparte the Registrar of Financial Services*, Commercial Case No. 55 of 2011 HC (Malaŵi), http://www.malawilii.org/mw/judgment/high-court-commercial-division/2012/5/. 27 February 2018.

[10] Ibid.

[11] Section 73(6) Financial Services Act (Malaŵi, 2010).

[12] RBM (2017).

[13] The country has only 4 cities, Blantyre, Zomba, Lilongwe and Mzuzu. Zomba was the old capital.

Blantyre is currency issue and supervision of financial institutions.[14] The central bank has recently set up a financial services regulation directorate in Blantyre. Most banks and financial institutions are headquartered in Blantyre.[15] This may explain vesting supervisory and regulatory powers with the Blantyre branch.

Malaŵi recently enacted the Payment Systems Act 2016[16] and the Electronic Transactions Act 2016.[17] These Acts and the Mobile Payment Systems Guidelines 2011[18] have attempted to bring some clarity to electronic payments. However, none of these Acts was drafted with mobile money as the focal point. In terms of approach, all the financial service laws seem to adopt an approach that is closer to the command and control model of regulation.

#### *8.2.1.1 Payment Systems Act 2016*

The Act is the overarching legal framework for the operation, regulation and supervision of payment systems in Malaŵi.[19] As a regulator, the central bank has been given expansive powers to ensure that there is an efficient payment system in place and that the various players abide by the rules.[20] These powers may be delegated,[21] and it is submitted the operation of the national switch by the bankers' association (discussed in Chapters 1 and 2) is one such case. The Act defines the mobile money payment system as "a system that enables the process of money transfer and exchange of money for goods and services between two parties using a mobile phone or an electronic mobile device".[22] While previously mobile money operators were allowed to operate with a "Letter of No

[14] SADC (2011) *SADC Bankers: Reserve Bank of Malawi* (Committee of Central Bank Governors in Southern Africa Development Community), http://www.sadcbankers.org/SADC/SADC.nsf/LADV/E4E3EF0D1F5967B8422576740044D454/$File/Malawi-.pdf. 10 October 2018.

[15] Among the big banks, only Standard Bank has its headquarters in Lilongwe. About a decade or so ago, NBS Bank moved from Lilongwe to Blantyre.

[16] Payment Systems Act (Malaŵi, 2016).

[17] Electronic Transactions Act (Malaŵi, 2016).

[18] Guidelines for Mobile Payment Systems (Malaŵi, 2011).

[19] Memorandum to the Payment Systems Bill 22 of 2015 (Malaŵi), http://www.parliament.gov.mw/docs/bills/BILL22_2015.pdf. 19 July 2018.

[20] Section 4 Payment Systems Act (Malaŵi, 2016).

[21] Section 5, ibid.

[22] Section 2, ibid.

Objection", the law now requires them to be licensed and authorised by the central bank.[23] Mobile money issuers that were operating under the mobile payment guidelines[24] now have to apply to be licensed or authorised.[25]

To avoid contagion, the central bank is empowered to issues directions to any participant of the payment system.[26] Where there is non-compliance, criminal proceedings may be brought or the central bank may compel compliance through a court order.[27] The law also empowers the bank to issue a prohibition order where it feels the "safety, efficient and smooth operation of the payment system" is at stake.[28] Ultimately, where there is deemed a major risk posed to the payment system, the central bank may suspend or even revoke authorisation or a licence.[29] Although the law has all the hallmarks of command and control, it seems to encourage self-regulation on the part of system operators. It requires them to "implement and operate a payment system in a manner that promotes secure, efficient and coordinated execution of payment services".[30] However, any rules promulgated by such system operators need to be vetted and approved by the central bank.[31] The move towards a more self-regulatory framework is new, having started with the Financial Services Act 2010. However, even in that Financial Services Act, this is limited to self-regulatory organisations.[32] Although there is a sense that self-regulation is encouraged, the central bank retains regulatory oversight[33] as well as investigative powers.[34] The central bank therefore still holds the veto power in any self-regulation.

[23] Sections 4(*d*) and 12(1), ibid.

[24] Guidelines for Mobile Payment Systems (Malaŵi, 2011).

[25] Section 44(1) Payment Systems Act (Malaŵi, 2016).

[26] Section 10, ibid.

[27] Section 11, ibid.

[28] Section 12(2), ibid.

[29] Section 15(1), ibid.

[30] Section 16(1), ibid.

[31] Section 16(3), ibid.

[32] Part V Financial Services Act (Malaŵi, 2010).

[33] Section 16(2) Payment Systems Act (Malaŵi, 2016).

[34] Section 18, ibid.

All settlements between participants in the payment system must be final, unconditional and irrevocable.[35] Parties may not reverse a settlement instruction, which has been processed. It also implies that where a mistake has been made, then a new settlement instruction must be issued and processed to correct the mistake. The new law requires system participants to retain records of transactions for a minimum period of 7 years.[36] While such a requirement may be normal for banks, it may require greater investment in data storage systems for those who wish to enter a non-bank payment system such as mobile money.

#### *8.2.1.2 The Electronic Transactions and Cybersecurity Act 2016*

This Act not only regulates electronic commerce but also includes broader issues of electronic communications.[37] There is an acceptance that hitherto; the legal framework has not provided "economic actors and citizens with a secure and reliable legal environment despite their importance to the development of electronic transactions".[38] The Act is complimentary to the Communications Act 2016 in regulating the information and communication technology (ICT) Sector.[39]

The law has clarified message transmission in e-commerce. An electronic message will be deemed sent by the sender, if it was sent personally or through an agent or programmed system.[40] Since mobile money uses the small messaging service (SMS), it can easily be verified as to the source of the message because of the uniqueness of the mobile phone number to which the mobile money account is tied. With the new law, an electronic message will now "be admissible as evidence in court proceedings".[41] Until now, courts have generally been reluctant or inconsistent in their acceptance of such messages because of a lack of legal framework to guide them and any acceptance of such evidence has been ad hoc and dependent on an individual judicial officer.

[35] Section 21, ibid.

[36] Section 40(1), ibid.

[37] Memorandum to the Electronic Transactions Bill, No. 11 of 2015 (Malaŵi), http://www.parliament.gov.mw/docs/bills/BILL11_2015.pdf. 19 July 2018.

[38] Ibid.

[39] Ibid.

[40] Section 26(1) Electronic Transactions Act (Malaŵi, 2016).

[41] Section 20(1), ibid.

For purposes of electronic commerce, the new law provides that in the default case, a message is deemed sent once it has left the sender's gadget or information system.[42] Receipt is also deemed to have occurred when the message has been received by the receiver's gadget or system, even though the message may not have been seen.[43] This has huge implications. One area that rapidly comes to mind is in cases of offer and acceptance or rejection in relation to contracts. The law also has provisions for disclosure in electronic commerce transactions. A vendor is required to disclose all material facts such as full name, address and legal personality.[44] The address must include telephone number, web and email address.[45] Considering that online transactions are not physical, this is of paramount importance. Consumers need to make a value judgement on whether they can deal with the supplier based on the information provided online.

The Act has introduced verification of electronic signatures for use in electronic transactions. An electronic signature is defined as "data attached to, incorporated in, or logically associated with, other data and which is intended by the user to serve as a signature".[46] A digital signature is defined as "an electronic signature consisting of a transformation of an electronic message using an asymmetric cryptosystem and a hash function".[47] Legally, there is therefore, a distinction between electronic and digital signatures. Digital signatures can be said to be the means through which electronic signatures are implemented. Hitherto, the position was that only handwritten signatures could validate transactions. The law now requires that electronic signatures be treated as if they were handwritten if the requirements of their authentication are met.[48]

The law also requires that such signatures be verified otherwise legal consequences may befall on the person relying on such signatures.[49] Verification is on two levels. The first level is to ensure the electronic signature's authenticity. The signature must be exclusive to the

[42] Section 24(1), ibid.

[43] Section 24(2), ibid.

[44] Section 37(1), ibid.

[45] Section 37(1), ibid.

[46] Section 2, ibid.

[47] Ibid.

[48] Section 9, ibid.

[49] Section 14, ibid.

signatory or the signatory must have exclusive control of means of creating the electronic signature.[50] The second level is to ensure that the signature satisfies the authentication system designated by the Malaŵi Communications Regulator Authority (MACRA).[51] MACRA is the authority, which has the mandate to approve digital signatures.[52] Any such authentication mechanism must comply with international standards.[53] Verification is therefore dependent on being connected to specific verification systems. That is where things may become tricky. How does one verify an electronic signature since it can be copied by a third party? How does one verify that the electronic signature has come from the owner and not a fraudster? This is where businesses need to invest in their ICT systems and beef up cyber security expertise. Consumer and awareness education is also paramount. Consumers need to be careful how to use the Internet and online including mobile communications. For those using electronic signatures, they need to be fully aware of who else has access to them.

The law also introduces something relatively new in commerce in Malawi: a cooling off period.[54] Goods or services procured online can be returned at no penalty if this is done within 7 days of receipt of goods or formation of the contract of services.[55] Therefore, those who want to go into e-commerce must factor in returns. They must be slow to celebrate sales done until the cooling off period has expired. The law provides that the supplier must reimburse the consumer within 14 days all sums paid otherwise interest starts accruing.[56] In Western economies, this has been lauded by consumers but scoffed at by suppliers as the returned goods end up being sold at rock bottom products as rejects. Schmidt et al. have coined the term *deshopping* as the term to refer to the propensity to return goods even though they may not have defects.[57]

[50] Section 8, ibid.

[51] Section 12(1), ibid.

[52] Section 12(2), ibid.

[53] Section 12(3), ibid.

[54] Section 39(1), ibid.

[55] Section 39(1)(*a*), ibid.

[56] Section 39(2), ibid.

[57] Ruth A Schmidt and others (1999) 'Deshopping—The Art of Illicit Consumption' 27 (8) *International Journal of Retail & Distribution Management* 290, p. 292, http://www.emeraldinsight.com/doi/pdfplus/10.1108/09590559910288569. 4 November 2018.

The law has also provided some consumer protection mechanisms. The first is a consumer's right to demand cancellation, where there has been fraudulent use of his payment and the supplier.[58] The second relates to data security. The law has introduced a provision that is the closest the country will have to a data protection regime. All entities that keep consumer data obtained via electronic means now have an obligation to the consumer concerning the use of such data.[59] However, this only relates to electronic data. The country does not have a general data protection regime.

#### *8.2.1.3 Guidelines for Mobile Payment Systems 2011*

These guidelines, issued by the central bank, are the only framework drawn with mobile payments in mind. Granted, the guidelines cover all mobile payments, but there is no doubt that the focus is on mobile money. However, in reference to the issuer of electronic value, the generic term electronic money is used in discussing these guidelines. As guidelines, they are soft law and not binding. However, since the central bank has the powers to grant and revoke authorisation for operation of a mobile payment system under them, in truth they are much more than mere soft law. In doing so, although on the surface the regulatory approach seems to be light touch, the regulator still uses the benign big gun[60] approach to ensure compliance. In effect therefore, the central bank may be said to be using a new mode of regulation, which combines the two approaches.

To be allowed to participate in the mobile payment system, an applicant must present at least the following to the central bank:

- A copy of a licence issued by MACRA or another regulator in the relevant sector.
- A generic agency agreement.
- Proof of ICT policies and proposed disaster recovery plans.
- Description of customer protection procedures.
- Identity and qualifications of directors and senior managers.[61]

[58] Section 42, Electronic Transactions Act (Malaŵi, 2016).

[59] Part VII, ibid.

[60] Ayres and Braithwaite (1992), Chapter 2.

[61] Section 5 Guidelines for Mobile Payment Systems (Malaŵi, 2011).

Although there is no requirement to register agents separately with the central bank, the electronic money issuer must "obtain verifiable name, address, signature and/or bio-data" for individual agents.[62] In a country where the national registration system has just commenced, this raises the question; how does one verify name and signature? The problem of addresses was already highlighted in Chapter 4. It is submitted that for individual agents, mobile network operators will most likely fall back on airtime agents. Under the guidelines, the issuer is prohibited from setting up exclusive agreements with agents.[63] On their part, agents have a duty to report suspicious transactions to the issuer.[64]

Each applicant must undergo a pilot phase during which a system audit by an independent auditor shall be carried out.[65] Under the guidelines, a "Letter of No Objection" was to be granted upon the completion of a successful pilot phase.[66] However, this provision has now been overtaken with events. The Payment Systems Act 2016 now requires licensing and authorisation. The Letter of No Objection has been dispensed with. Apart from the issues highlighted above, the mobile money issuer[67] is expected to have in place measures to ensure system integrity. This includes having a system that can leave an audit trail, having a risk management framework and maintaining a pool[68] account with restricted usage to settling mobile payment obligations.[69] The issuer must also ensure interoperability of its system.[70] The operator or issuer of electronic money is restricted on the use of any interest earned. The mobile network operators have set up trusts, and the trustees have been giving interest earned on the pool account to charities.[71] This however

[62] Section 11.2, ibid.

[63] Section 11.10, ibid.

[64] Section 11.8, ibid.

[65] Section 6.0, ibid.

[66] Section 6.0, ibid.

[67] Called Mobile Payment Service Provider.

[68] Called Trust Account in the Guidelines.

[69] Section 8 Guidelines for Mobile Payment Systems (Malaŵi, 2011).

[70] Section 8.6, ibid.

[71] Anon (2016) 'TNM Mpamba Builds K11m School Block in Chileka' *Nyasa Times* (19 December 2016), http://www.nyasatimes.com/tnm-mpamba-builds-k11m-school-block-chileka/. 12 March 2018.

Blessings Kamanga (2016) 'Malawi Junior Queens Gets K10mil Airtel Money for Africa Games' (19 July 2016), http://www.nyasatimes.com/malawi-junior-queens-gets-k10mil-airtel-money-africa-games/#sthash.CdRa3jCd.dpuf. 12 March 2018.

is not enshrined in the guidelines. The guidelines only state that any such interest earned shall not benefit the issuer.[72] Interestingly, they do not also expressly state that it cannot be paid to the mobile money customers. However, the traditional view is that for now, customers do not earn interest on mobile money. Or put different, once a customer has exchanged his fiat money with electronic value, he has no proprietary interest in the fiat money so exchanged.

The guidelines also state that there must be a one-to-one ratio between deposits in the pool account and any electronic money issued. As such that no electronic money can be issued more than the credit balances in the pool account.[73] As part of the regulatory oversight, issuers are required to submit monthly reports to the central bank indicated among other things, subscriber numbers and volume of payments.[74] This does not preclude the bank from asking for any ad hoc information or data.[75]

Before enrolling customers, issuers must ensure that they satisfy know your customer (KYC) requirements as laid down in the Money Laundering Act (2006) [MLA].[76] However, as noted in Chapter 4, the Financial Intelligence Authority has adopted a risk-based assessment for KYC and does not strictly follow the tough regime in the Act for small value transactions such as mobile money. All transactions must contain the following information about each transaction:

- amount,
- type,
- date,
- time, and
- agent identification details.[77]

[72] Section 8.8 Guidelines for Mobile Payment Systems (Malaŵi, 2011).

[73] Section 8.10–2, ibid.

[74] Section 8.1, ibid.

[75] Section 8.15, ibid.

[76] Section 9.1.4, ibid. However, this Act has been repealed and replaced by the Financial Crimes Act 2017.

[77] Section 9.3.2, ibid.

For a transaction to be completed, it requires a valid payer and payee.[78] However, what does valid payee mean when mobile money can be sent to a non-registered user? Would the same KYC requirements for registration be required for cashing out by such a user? Looked at from an anti-money laundering view, it would be argued that similar requirements should be applied. From a financial inclusion viewpoint however, it may well mean certain sections being unable to cash out for not possessing acceptable identification. It is submitted, this is where agents exercise daily their own risk assessment of the customer before them.

All settlements within the ecosystem of the mobile money issuer must be settled in real time.[79] This is what gives the mobile payment system an advantage over other payment systems. Although the central bank does not deal with technological issues, as this is the domain of MACRA, in so far as electronic money systems are concerned, it must "secure and ensure confidentiality, integrity, authenticity, and non repudiation".[80] Where SMS technology is used, it must be encrypted, end to end.[81] The system should not allow customer details to be saved on the handset.[82] I am however aware that the phone I use does save my details on the handset and I do not have to re-enter them every time I want to transact.

The guidelines also require that only secure channels be used for electronic money payments.[83] This would ideally require mobile network operators to have at least two separate firewalled channels; one for the normal SMS data and one for mobile payments. The mobile network operators could however just decide to have one encrypted channel for both. The system should have at a minimum a two-step validation based on both the mobile number and the personal identification number (PIN).[84] All electronic money accounts must be linked to a mobile number.[85] To protect the system from third-party interaction, it must have a firewall that ensures that there is no direct connection between

[78] Section 9.3.3, ibid.

[79] Section 9.4.1, ibid.

[80] Section 10, ibid.

[81] Section 10.1.4 and 10.2, ibid.

[82] Section 10.4.5, ibid.

[83] Section 10.1.5, ibid.

[84] Section 10.4.4, ibid.

[85] Section 10.4.6, ibid.

the system and the Internet.[86] The issuer must periodically conduct penetration tests to ensure that the integrity of the system remains intact.[87] Issuers are also required to work with the Finance Intelligence Authority and adhere to the anti-money laundering regime and regulations issued by the Authority.[88] Crucially, they must furnish the Authority within 3 days, any suspicious transaction.[89] This means each operator now needs to have a fully functioning compliance unit.

The guidelines also have a provision that encourages switchovers by users from one issuer to another without any bottlenecks.[90] However, where the mobile money is tied to one particular mobile network operator, it is difficult to see how this can be achieved, unless the regulator expressly provides a regulatory regime that allows for this. Chapter 9 discusses this as a recommendation. These guidelines are however set to be replaced. Draft Electronic Money Regulations 2015, as subsidiary legislation under the Reserve Bank of Malaŵi Act 1989 were supposed to supersede them. However, this was overtaken by events with the enacting of the Payment Systems Act 2016. The draft regulations were withdrawn and are being reworked to be in line with the new Act.[91] The draft regulations had two notable changes. First was a prohibition of payment of interest. This the raises the question as to whether banks will still be allowed to intermediate on the pool funds or that they will be strictly ring-fenced from the rest of the bank's lending portfolio. If banks cannot make money from the deposits, then what will be the motivation for them to keep the funds? The other is provision for levies to be collected by the central bank. This is a welcome inclusion as it allows for the cost of regulation to be internalised by the market participants.

[86] Section 10.4.10, ibid.

[87] Section 10.4.11, ibid.

[88] Section 13.2, ibid.

[89] Section 13.1, ibid.

[90] Section 10.3.3, ibid.

[91] Mbane Ngwira (2017) Spokesperson, Reserve Bank of Malaŵi (10 March 2017) (personal communication).

### 8.2.2 Communication Regulation Structure

The establishment of MACRA as a regulator[92] came on the heels of a World Bank-led privatisation programme of the communications sector. Before the establishment of MACRA, the Department of Posts and Telecommunications was the communications regulator.[93] The department was later commercialised and became the Malaŵi Posts and Telecommunications Corporation.[94] The corporation was then unbundled into the Malaŵi Telecommunications Limited and Malaŵi Post Corporation.[95] The discussion that follows in this section is limited to MACRA's role in regulating the telecommunications sector, which forms the backbone of not only mobile money but also the banking system.

Under the law, the country's president appoints the board of director of MACRA[96] while the director general is appointed by the board.[97] The appointment of the board is however subject to the approval of the Public Appointments Committee of Parliament.[98] There have, however, been cases where the president has appointed the director general. For example, in 2014, the president appointed Andrew Kumbatira as director general and replaced him as post master general with Godfrey Itaye.[99] A year later, the two were swapped in another presidential appointment with Kumbatira going back as post master general and Itaye heading MACRA.[100] This would ordinarily be ultra vires the powers of the president under the law and it is submitted both appointments were

[92] Section 4 Communications Act (Malaŵi, 2016).

[93] Author's personal experience of working with the Department of Posts and Telecommunications: 1991–1993.

[94] George RG Clarke, Frew A Gebreab and Henry R Mgombelo (2003) *Telecommunications Reform in Malawi* (Policy Research Working Papers, The World Bank), p. 3, http://dx.doi.org/10.1596/1813-9450-3036. 2 December 2018.

[95] Section 8(1) Communications Act (Malaŵi, 2016).

[96] Section 7(1), ibid.

[97] Section 91(1), ibid.

[98] Section 8(1), ibid.

[99] Lucky Mkandawire (2014) 'Kumbatira Appointed New Macra Boss' *The Nation* (2 September 2014), http://mwnation.com/kumbatira-appointed-new-macra-boss/. 8 February 2018.

[100] Lucky Mkandawire (2015) 'Macra, MPC Bosses Swap Posts' *The Nation* (6 August 2015), http://mwnation.com/macra-mpc-bosses-swap-posts/. 8 February 2018.

illegally made as the wrong appointing authority made them. The reason MACRA and the position of director general are considered politically sensitive is MACRA's control of broadcasting rights, especially radio and television. The national and state broadcaster, Malaŵi Broadcasting Corporation is monopolised by the *ruling party* for political mileage.[101] In an election, this can play a decisive factor and although there have been calls for reform; each succeeding *ruling party* has upheld the status quo for its own benefit. The term *ruling party* is loosely used here as the country is a presidential system and not a parliamentary one. Therefore regardless of how many legislators the president's party has, it is still termed a *ruling party* by most political commentators. Like the central bank discussed earlier, although the law stipulates its independence,[102] MACRA suffers from a serious lack of regulatory independence, especially from political forces.

Although initially MACRA separated providers of telecom services, the regulator has embraced a unified licence regime.[103] One telecommunication operator can operate fixed and mobile telephone services under one licence.[104] In terms of regulation, MACRA use the following instruments:

1. Communications Sector Policy Statement 2013[105];
2. Communications Act 2016;
3. Operator licences.[106]

[101] Mustafa Kennedy Hussein (2009) 'Opposition Politics in Malawi: Hopeful Signs Amid the Warnings' 16 (3) *South African Journal of International Affairs*, p. 362.

[102] Section 5(3) Communications Act (Malaŵi, 2016).

[103] MACRA (2014) 'Strategic Plan 2015–2020', p. 7 (Malaŵi Communications Regulatory Authority), http://www.macra.org.mw/wp-content/uploads/2014/09/MACRA-Strategic-Plan-2015-2020.pdf. 12 March 2018.

[104] Ibid., p. 7.

[105] Malaŵi Government (2013) 'National ICT Policy' (Malaŵi Government), http://www.macra.org.mw/wp-content/uploads/2014/07/Malawi-ICT-Policy-2013.pdf. 4 November 2018.

[106] MACRA (2016) 'Telecommunications' (Malaŵi Communication Regulatory Authority), http://www.macra.org.mw/?cat=7. 8 February 2018.

Unless expressly exempted, it is illegal to operate a telecommunication network within the country without a licence.[107] As part of its regulatory mandate, MACRA is charged with consumer protection,[108] promoting competition and promoting open and universal access.[109] It also has the power to investigate and deal with complaints.[110] As a regulator, MACRA has the power to suspend a licence or revoke it.[111] All these powers are subject to oversight by the High Court under judicial review proceedings.[112] MACRA is principally financed through licence fees and levies.[113] It may also issue fines.[114] Clarke et al. say, although MACRA has attained financial independence from its parent ministry, it still is subject to interference from the minister who can "issue written direction to MACRA on how the Authority should carry out its duties".[115]

MACRA is concerned only with the communication part of the mobile money service.[116] Therefore, if a customer fails to transact because of a network problem, that is within the regulatory ambit of MACRA but if it is to do with financial issues then the central bank takes control.[117] To the consumer, this can be frustrating. It entails that the consumer is expected to have discerning skills to isolate which aspect is to blame when something goes wrong with the system. This seems like pushing the burden from the operators onto consumers.

Although MACRA regulates the communication part, it is not concerned with the technology of the services being used by the issuers.[118] MACRA operates under a model it terms "service and technological neutrality".[119] However, MACRA and the central bank in 2013 entered

[107] Section 31 Communications Act (Malaŵi, 2016).

[108] Part XVII, ibid.

[109] Part XVIII, ibid.

[110] Part XX, ibid.

[111] Section 43(1), ibid.

[112] Section 174, ibid.

[113] Section 28(1)(a), ibid.

[114] Section 28(1)(b), ibid.

[115] Clarke et al. (2003), p. 21.

[116] Interview with Thokozani Chimbe Deputy Director—Legal (Consumer Affairs); Malaŵi Communications Regulatory Authority (3 August 2015).

[117] Ibid.

[118] Ibid.

[119] Ibid.

into a memorandum of understanding (MOU) so that they can try to co-regulate the mobile money service.[120] Under the MOU, MACRA retains the regulation of the telecommunications platform.[121] Since MACRA only comes in when it is a mobile network operator driving the business, the MOU is not concerned with money transfer services of banks or other financial institutions.[122] However, where an operator wishes to provide an mobile money or similar service before they can be granted an operating licence by MACRA, they need to get the central bank's prior approval.[123] In practice, before the central bank grants any approval to such a service, it consults MACRA, essentially asking the question: *Does MACRA have any issues?*[124]

In assessing the regulatory framework, MACRA's Thokozani Chimbe admits that the MOU has exposed a gap in the law and regulatory framework of mobile money.[125] She states that the situation where two regulators regulate the same service, with one looking only at the aspects that they are interested in cannot continue.[126] Chimbe sums it up like this:

> Ideally, if there were one law and regulatory framework to regulate mobile money, it would make everyone's life easier. There is a need to develop specific laws on how mobile money should be regulated.[127]

The current mobile money regulatory framework therefore resembles the twin peaks model. However, unlike the traditional twin peaks model, which has conduct of business and prudential regulation as peaks, this model has financial and communication regulation as peaks. Because of the involvement of other regulators, discussed below, the model may be rightly considered as multiple peaks.

The Communications Act 2016 replaced the Communications Act of 1998. Maybe one of the fundamental features of the new act is that it has embraced developments in the digital and electronic arena. The Act

[120] Ibid.

[121] Ibid.

[122] Ibid.

[123] Ibid.

[124] Ibid.

[125] Ibid.

[126] Ibid.

[127] Ibid.

has also introduced mandatory registration of generic numbers and SIM cards.[128]

### 8.2.3 Consumer Protection

The Consumer Protection Act 2003 is the overall legal framework regulating consumer protection.[129] However, since its enactment in 2003, the Consumer Protection Council, which is mandated to administer the Act, is yet to be appointed.[130] The result has been that an otherwise useful legal instrument has been rendered useless. With this gap, the task of protecting consumer rights has been taken up by a local non-government organisation, the Consumers Association of Malaŵi (CAMA).[131] This development is in itself perplexing as the Act categorically states, "the Government shall in its policies, laws and administrative measures ensure that consumers draw maximum benefit from national, economic, environmental, social and other resources".[132] This does not, however, negate any rights that the consumer has, only that the consumer is now forced to use the courts to enforce those rights or remedy any wrong.[133] In the same way, suppliers are not absolved from their obligation to provide safe and correct goods and services, which meet the country's standards.[134] However, as noted above, in the absence of the Consumer Protection Council, the consumer has to go to court in the event that suppliers have reneged on their obligations. This may not only be costly to the consumer financially but may also be time-consuming and energy draining.

[128] Part XI, Communications Act (Malawi, 2016).

[129] Consumer Protection Act (Malaŵi, 2003), https://www.rbm.mw/Home/GetContentFile/?ContentID=3752. 14 November 2018.

[130] Section 10, ibid.

[131] CAMA (2016) 'Consumers Association of Malawi', https://www.facebook.com/Consumers-Association-of-Malawi-104178233025786/. 20 December 2018.

Grace Khombe (2014) 'CAMA to Name and Shame Traders on Receipt Guarantee and Warranty' *Zodiak Online* (Lilongwe), http://zodiakmalawi.com/top-stories/cama-to-name-and-shame-traders-on-receipt-guarantee-and-waranty. 14 November 2018.

[132] Section 4(1) Consumer Protection Act (Malaŵi, 2003).

[133] Section 3, ibid.

[134] Section 6, ibid.

The law also seems to have a claw-back clause. It calls on the consumer to "take initiative to acquire the necessary knowledge of consumer life and endeavour to behave self-reliantly and rationally".[135] What this exactly means is unclear. What does *knowledge of consumer life* mean? Do rationality and self-reliance impose a negative obligation on the consumer to act as the reasonable consumer? There is a presumption under the Act to construe an ambiguous contract in favour of the consumer.[136]

In relation to financial transactions, the law states, "a consumer shall have access to banking and financial services at affordable or lowest possible rates".[137] Once again, this provision seems more like a wish. To start with, banks and other financial institutions as private entities are not obliged to offer access to consumers. As to offering services at affordable or lowest possible rates, this seems again an expression of a mere ambition since Malaŵi is known for its expensive banking services.[138] Unlike other jurisdictions, in Malaŵi there is no capping of the interest payable on loans.[139] An interest to introduce an interest capping bill in Parliament under the Private Member's Motion was thwarted and the bill referred to a committee.[140]

The law also enshrines the right of retraction within a period of 7 days provided the contract was "entered into a place other than the ordinary premises of the supplier or trader".[141] In the case of defective goods or services, a consumer "may request cancellation of an agreement or a reduction of the price, without prejudice to being indemnified for injury,

[135] Section 7, ibid.

[136] Section 8(1), ibid.

[137] Section 28(1), ibid.

[138] Chinyamata Chipeta and Esmie Kanyumbu (2015) *Improving Access to Banking Services in Malawi* (Southern African Institute for Economic Research), p. 11, http://aercafricaevents.org/wp-content/uploads/2015%20December/Group%20C/C3-Improving-access-to-banking-services-in-Malawi-Chinyamata-Chipeta-and-Esmie-Kanyumbu-FR.pdf. 14 November 2018.

[139] Hanna Ziady (2016) 'Interest Rate Caps Are Now Effective' *The Citizen* (10 May 2016), http://citizen.co.za/business/business-news/1109479/interest-rate-caps-are-now-effective/. 5 December 2018.

[140] Gladys Nthenda (2018) 'Parliament Refers Interest Cap Bill to Joint Committee' *Kulinji.com* (13 December 2018), https://www.kulinji.com/article/news/2018/parliament-refers-interest-cap-bill-joint-committee. 28 December 2018.

[141] Section 30(1) Consumer Protection Act (Malaŵi, 2003).

or loss".[142] A consumer may also opt for a replacement without paying a fee, or repair of the faulty goods or an adjustment of the technology.[143] Consumers are entitled to compensation for misleading advertising.[144] It would seem the Electronic Transactions and Cybersecurity Act 2016 has reinforced these provisions, albeit for commerce involving electronic transactions. Subordinate courts[145] have primary jurisdiction of consumer claims.[146]

### *8.2.4 Fair-Trading*

The Competition and Fair Trading Act 1998 regulates competitions and fair-trading in Malaŵi through the Competition and Fair Trading Commission.[147] The commission has quasi-judicial powers of investigation, which include summoning and examining witnesses as well as administering oaths.[148] The law requires that unless the circumstances warrant it, all hearings conducted by the commission be held in public.[149] A party dissatisfied with any findings of the commission may appeal to a judge in chambers.[150] An appeal, however, does not stay the decision of the commission in itself.[151] The Act prohibits anti-competitive trade practices which are defined as "any category of agreements, decisions and concerted practices which are likely to result in the prevention, restriction or distortion of competition to an appreciable extent".[152] Rival market players who collude in any way in their trade agreements face the penalty of an offence.[153]

[142] Section 32(1), ibid.

[143] Section 32(2), ibid.

[144] Section 47(1), ibid.

[145] Courts which are below the rank of High Court.

[146] Section 50 Consumer Protection Act (Malaŵi, 2003).

[147] Section 8(1) Competition and Fair Trading Act, Act No. 43 of 1998 (Malaŵi, 1998), http://www.itu.int/ITU-D/treg/Legislation/Malawi/act43.pdf. 18 November 2018.

[148] Section 10(1), ibid.

[149] Section 11, ibid.

[150] Section 48(1), ibid.

[151] Section 49, ibid.

[152] Section 32(1), ibid.

[153] Section 33, ibid.

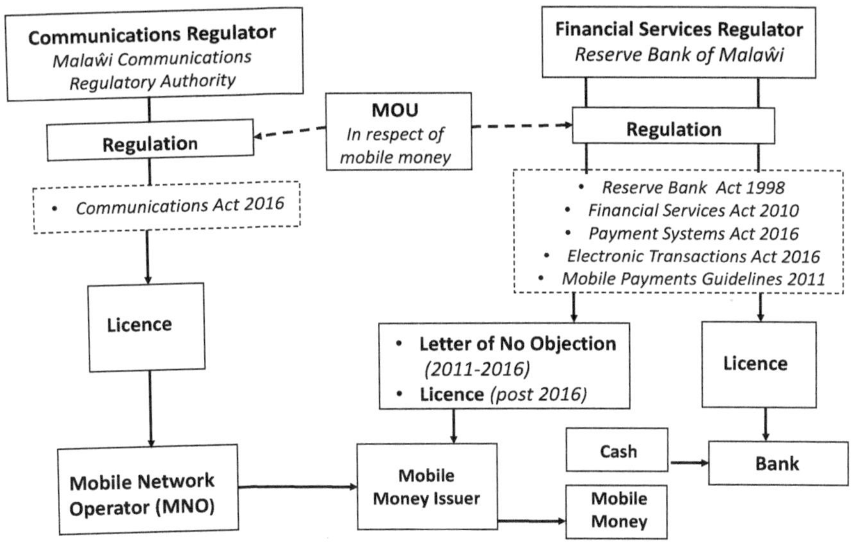


**Fig. 8.1** Regulatory and operating structure of mobile money (*Source* Author)

Under the law, before any merger or acquisition can be done, the commission must give its prior authorisation.[154] However, when the Malaŵi Savings Bank (MSB Bank) and IndeBank, hitherto state companies, were acquired by FDH Holdings and National Bank of Malaŵi, respectively, the authorisation was only sought after the deal was already signed. The state house issued a statement in July 2015 that government had sold its stake in MSB Bank and IndeBank.[155] That the statement came from state house was the first sign that something was amiss. Sale of state assets should not be announced from state house but ordinarily by the relevant line minister, in this case, minister of finance. The commission, however, only approved the merger of MSB Bank and FDH on 12 February 2016[156] and that of IndeBank with National Bank on 3

[154] Section 36, ibid.

[155] Kondwani Nankhumwa MP (Minister of Information) (2015) *Statement on the Sale of MSB and IndeBank* (State House Residences Malaŵi, 2015).

[156] Charlotte Wezi Malonda (2016) *Approval of the Merger Between FDH Financial Holdings and Malaŵi Savings Bank (MSB)* (Competition and Fair Trading Commission, 2016).

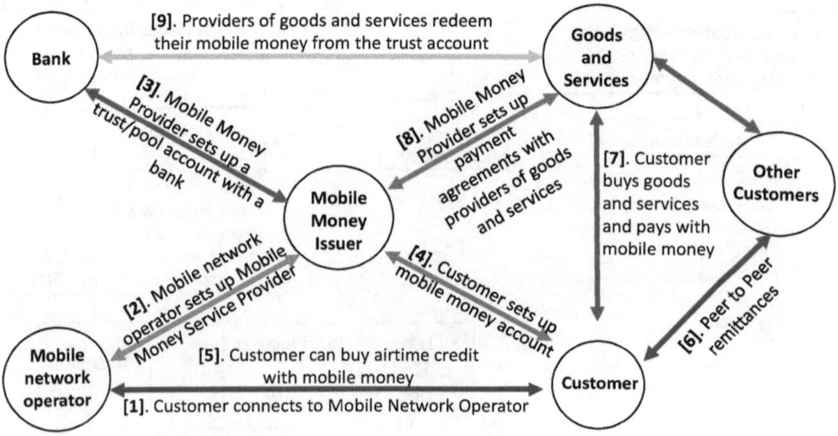


**Fig. 8.2** Mobile money ecosystem (*Source* Author)

June 2016.[157] This was against a legal provision that renders any merger or acquisition without prior authorisation from the commission a nullity.[158] The fact that the commission adopted a merger and an acquisition that flouted the law and gave it its blessings retrospectively is worrisome, and of concern considering the crucial role that the commission plays in antitrust law. There is no retrospective authorisation under the Act. Commentators attributed this to political pressure due to the political sensitivity that surrounded the acquisition.[159]

[157] CFTC (2016) 'Competition and Fair Trading Commission (Malaŵi)—History' (Competition and Fair Trading Commission), http://www.cftc.mw/index.php/about-us/history.html. 29 December 2018.

[158] Section 35(2), Competition and Fair Trading Act, Act No. 43 of 1998 (Malaŵi, 1998).

[159] Lameck Masina (2015) 'Controversy as Government Sells Malawi Savings Bank' *African Business* (7 August 2015), http://africanbusinessmagazine.com/african-banker/controversy-as-government-sells-malawi-savings-bank/. 18 November 2018.

Happy Soko (2015) 'Malaŵi Government Drilled Over MSB Sale' *Malaŵi24* (18 March 2015), http://allafrica.com/stories/201503190408.html. 18 November 2018.

Suzgo Khunga (2015) 'MSB Sale Fallout, Goes at K9.5 Billion' *The Nation* (3 July 2015), http://mwnation.com/msb-sale-fallout-goes-at-k9-5-billion/. 18 November 2018.

The Act expressly prevents anyone with a dominant position of market power from using that power to eliminate or damage competitors, prevent new entrants or deter or prevent anyone from engaging in competitive conduct.[160] Employees of the commission, acting as investigating officers have powers of entry and search but these can only be exercised upon obtaining a search warrant from a court of law.[161]

## 8.3 Regulatory Issues Posed by the Infrastructure

An empirical study done by Evans and Pirchio found that "heavy regulation is usually fatal to igniting mobile money schemes in a country".[162] On the other hand, light-touch regulation is directly proportional to an ignition in the scheme.[163] Ignition occurs when there is explosive growth of a service after it has "obtained enough participants (critical mass)".[164] A service such as mobile money will either ignite or fail to attain critical mass and implode or fizzle.[165] Almost like a zero-sum game, a service will both ignite and explode quickly or not at all.[166] Evans and Pirchio's research also found that a poor country lacking basic infrastructure is likely to have a successful mobile money service as the service is deemed to create more value.[167] Would it therefore be argued that a poor country is likely to adopt light-touch regulation out of desperation?[168]

Lessons can be learnt from the light-touch approach by the central bank in relation to *M-Pesa* in Kenya. However, it must be noted that this did not mean that *M-Pesa* was not subject to any regulation at all. As noted in the last chapter, an exhaustive due diligence was conducted before *M-Pesa* could be given a go-ahead to operate. Countries that do

160 Section 41 Competition and Fair Trading Act, Act No. 43 of 1998 (Malaŵi, 1998).

161 Section 46, ibid.

162 David S Evans and Alexis Pirchio (2014) 'An Empirical Examination of Why Mobile Money Schemes Ignite in Some Developing Countries but Flounder in Most' 13 (4) *Review of Network Economics* 397, p. 401, https://www.degruyter.com/view/j/rne.2014.13.issue-4/rne-2015-0020/rne-2015-0020.xml. 12 May 2018.

163 Ibid., p. 401.

164 Ibid., pp. 398–9.

165 Ibid., p. 399.

166 Ibid., p. 401.

167 Ibid., p. 400.

168 Ibid., p. 400.

not adopt a hard KYC regime and impose "minimal restrictions on who [can] serve as an agent" are likely to ignite while those adopting a contrary position are likely to implode.[169] The success of mobile money services is directly dependent on a developed agency network and "there is a positive correlation between the density of the [agent] networks and mobile money use".[170]

### 8.3.1 *Incoherent Regulatory Framework*

The first problem posed is legal and institutional in nature. Mobile money is a recent entrant in the financial market and usually, there is no separate legislation regulating it. TNM and Airtel are regulated by MACRA. Airtel Money and *Mpamba* are principally regulated by the central bank.[171] MACRA and the central bank have sought to co-regulate mobile money through an MOU. This ambiguity leads to the conclusion that the regulation of mobile money is incoherent. So far, the only framework that deals with mobile money is the central bank guidelines, which unfortunately lack the authority of positive law. The figure illustrates the current regulatory framework as well as the structural operations of the mobile money system. The figure does not include the whole ecosystem and excludes other regulators such as Financial Intelligence Authority, Consumer Protection Council and Competition and Fair Trading Commission (Fig. 8.1).

To ensure that there is a separation between the operations (and assets) of mobile network operators, between their telecommunication side of the business and mobile money, the operators are required to set up separate companies. These special purpose vehicles (SPVs) are the ones that are subject to regulatory oversight by the central bank. Although legally separate, these SPVs are however currently housed within the mobile network operators' buildings. As SPVs, it may take time for them to evolve into their own distinct brands. As seen with the case of *M-Pesa* and Safaricom in Kenya, it may be argued that there is value in associating with the well-established, recognised and known brand of the parent mobile network operator. As noted with TNM, the

[169] Ibid., p. 400.

[170] Ibid., p. 435.

[171] Section 2 Financial Services Act (Malaŵi, 2010).

contribution of *Mpamba* to its total revenues is still very small, although it is the fastest growing revenue stream.[172]

As indicated earlier, the various regulators involved with regulating aspects of mobile money are at different levels and the system would therefore be aptly named multiple peaks model. Despite not written down, each of the five regulators has its own regulatory approach. Figure 8.2 offers an insight of the various players within the mobile money ecosystem. The next chapter discusses the composition of the participants in the regulatory arena. For now, a holistic approach is needed and in this approach, regulation that really responds to the true needs and demands of the ecosystem seems the right approach.

### *8.3.2 Technical Issues*

Apart from the issues discussed above, mobile money also faces unique regulatory issues because it is a hybrid service and relies on other services to operate. For a start, because of the ability of wireless networks to reach far-flung off areas, population density is no longer of systemic importance. By 2013, the mobile network operators had already achieved 80% mobile coverage.[173] Mobile coverage is a measure of the geographical spread as opposed to population spread. The main issues that arise from the technical side are mainly concerned with the reliability of the network. Service disruption and contingency planning are therefore key regulatory issues. The mobile money service is a service that has two service strata: the telecommunication service as the backbone and the financial service on top. Disruption in either or both will directly affect the overall service.

It is because of this reliability on the technical backbone, that separating the service into two or several parts for purposes of regulation may be problematic. From a service viewpoint, the services offered by the mobile network operators and that offered by the mobile money issuers may be different. From a function viewpoint, one is an extension of the other. Problems such as interruption of transmission or congestion ought to be looked at not only as disruptive to the communication service, but also to the financial service as well. In 2015, the performance of

[172] TNM (2016), p. 10.
[173] MACRA (2014), p. 8.

telecom services, especially by the mobile network operators, was generally dubbed poor.[174] There seems not to have been much improvement over the years, and social media is always awash with various complaints related to the telecommunications sector in general, but the mobile network platform in particular.

As was discussed in Chapters 1 and 2, another issue unique with mobile money is that it is digital money. This presents a few issues. The first is the possibility of double spending. To avoid this, the system needs to have a validation process whereby once a transaction has been authorised, it is given a unique code, which prevents double spending.[175] The second is fraud perpetuated by third parties such as flooding the ecosystem with fake mobile money. In such a situation, the issuer could face a liquidity squeeze if the system failed to distinguish between forgeries and genuine electronic money.[176] Ultimately, the integrity of the pool account would be compromised as there would have been created e-value which cannot be backed by deposits. Setting up regulatory guidelines to preserve the integrity of the system are therefore key regulator issues.

Regulatory arbitrage may also arise because of the dual nature of the mobile money service. Arbitrage as used here does not refer to the choice between similar regulators in different countries, but between different regulators within the same country. Initially, mobile network operators tried to pass off the service as an add-on service to their core business as telecom operators.[177] Why they did this can only be explained by regulatory arbitrage. The mobile network operators were already being regulated by the communications regulator. They did not want to be further regulated by the financial regulator. It is common knowledge that among most regulations, financial regulation is the most onerous. In economic terms, it is a cost. Looked at as a cost, it is only natural that the rational institution would wish to avoid it unless the cost of non-compliance was greater.[178] In the end, however, the financial

[174]Grace Phiri (2015) 'Telecom Operators' Performance Poor' *The Nation* (18 December 2015), http://mwnation.com/telecom-operators-perfomance-still-poor/. 12 March 2018.

[175]Lee and Longe-Akindemowo (1999), p. 55.

[176]Ibid.

[177]Discussion with a top executive of Airtel Malaŵi in 2012.

[178]Dumez and Jeunemaitre (1997), p. 5.

regulator caught up with them and introduced guidelines to regulate their participation. That said, there is still regulatory arbitrage at play. This is so because; various parts of the service are still regulated by different regulators. Unlike the mobile network operator or the commercial bank, the mobile money issuer still must negotiate regulatory compliance between the two lead regulators; MACRA and the central bank.

### *8.3.3 Regulatory Space Contestation*

With mobile money, the regulation is not only concerned with market participants but also the entire ecosystem. The regulatory issues affecting mobile money are therefore best looked at by analysing the ecosystem. As was noted in Fig. 3.5 (reproduced as Fig. 8.2), the ecosystem is comprised of several nodes. Each of these nodes is also a subsystem in its own rights and presents its own regulatory challenges. For example, the bank node represents a whole subsystem. As was discussed in Chapter 1, this includes the inter-bank payment and settlement system. The mobile network operator also has its own subsystem, which includes its agency and distribution network. The same applies to the mobile money issuer. As for the customers, once the mobile money is created, customers can circulate the electronic value within their own subsystem with much ease. The peer to peer system on which the SMS technology is based makes this possible.[179] The suppliers of goods and services can also create their own subsystem where mobile money can circulate. However, as can be noted from the figure, mobile money issuer is the central node within the ecosystem.

The regulation of the ecosystem is however not as interconnected. That is why in the discussion above, it was presented as an incoherent regulatory framework. What emerges is a service that does not quite fit into the perfect mould of each of the regulators. The therefore needs to appreciate and recognise this unique and complex nature of mobile money. If that is achieved, a regulatory strategy can be formulated that is responsive to the needs of the service. As the above discussion illustrates, the regulatory space of mobile money is heavily contested and under constant re-negotiation.[180]

[179] Mas and Radcliffe (2011), p. 171.

[180] See Hancher and Moran (1998) and Scott (2001).

Another issue to consider is what Scott describes as *cross-sanctioning*.[181] In an arena where there are multiple regulators trying to regulate the same industry, albeit over different issues, it begs the question whether a more powerful regulator may not impose sanction even though the breach is under a different regime?[182] Where the issues are common or interrelated, this may be a welcome thing. However, there is a danger of one regulator usurping the powers and authorities of other regulators and clouding up the regulatory space. The other danger that would naturally result from this assumption of authority would be that the other regulators might start deferring their authority to the one that is more resourceful or has greater power.[183] While it may be argued that this may have beneficial consequences to those regulated, in that, they are essentially dealing with one super-regulator, its lack of expertise in the other regimes may have a negative impact on the regulatory framework.

## 8.4 Overview of the Mobile Money Regulatory Framework in Kenya

It is important to state that although *M-Pesa* is by far the dominant mobile money service, it is by no means the only one in Kenya. Others mobile money platforms are Airtel Money, Orange Money, MTN Mobile Money and *Pesa* Point.[184] Like Malaŵi, Kenya also has a dual regulatory framework of mobile money. The Communications Authority of Kenya (CAK) regulates the communications sector while the Central Bank of Kenya, apart from being given statutory powers of a central bank[185] regulates the financial services.[186]

181 Scott (2001), p. 346.

182 Ibid.

183 Ibid.

184 Joseph Tiampati Ole Musuni (2015) 'Mobile Money: The Kenyan Experience' (Government of Kenya), http://www.cto.int/media/events/pst-ev/2015/Broadband%20 2015/Presentations/Mobile%20Money%20Service%20Joseph%20Tiampati%20Ole%20 Musuni.pdf. 28 December 2018.

185 Section 3(3), Central Bank of Kenya Act (Kenya, 1966), https://centralbank.go.ke/ images/docs/The_Central_Bank_of_Kenya_Act_1st_January_2014.pdf. 28 December 2018.

186 Section 4A(1)(d), ibid.

### *8.4.1 The Communications Sector*

The CAK licences telecommunications operators and service providers and supervises their performance.[187] The CAK is established under the Kenya Information and Communications Act 1998.[188] While in Malaŵi the Communications Act 1998 was wholly repealed and replaced with a new Act, in Kenya the Information and Communications Act has not been replaced but undergone several revisions to keep it up to date with modern developments in the communications sector. The Act clearly spells that the CAK is an independent authority free of control by government, political or commercial interests in the exercise of its powers and performance of its functions.[189] The board chairperson of CAK is appointed by the country's president and other appointed members are appointed by the cabinet secretary (minister).[190] However, the appointment of the board chairperson is by way of a public invitation upon a vacancy arising and the convening a selection panel drawn from a list of organisations.[191] This therefore provides an opportunity for qualified members of the public to apply as well as some form of transparency in the selection system.

### *8.4.2 The Financial Sector*

Unlike in Malaŵi, in Kenya, the functions of chairperson of the board of the central bank and governor have been separated and are not subsumed in one person.[192] Kenya also has a safeguard mechanism in that although the board of the central bank is appointed by the country's president, it is subject to parliamentary approval.[193] The same applies to the appointment of the governor.[194] The Central Bank of Kenya Act has

[187] CAK (2018) 'Telecommunications Overviews' (Communications Authority of Kenya), https://ca.go.ke/industry/telecommunication/overview/. 28 December 2018.

[188] Kenya Information and Communications Act (1998), http://kfcb.co.ke/wp-content/uploads/2016/07/Kenya_Information_and_Communications_Act.pdf. 28 December 2018.

[189] Section 5A(1), ibid.

[190] Section 6(1), ibid.

[191] Section 6B, ibid.

[192] Section 11(1), ibid.

[193] Section 11(2), ibid.

[194] Section 13(1), ibid.

also introduced a fit and proper test for persons who hold the post of governor and deputy governor.[195]

### *8.4.3 E-Money[196] Regulation 2013*

The Central Bank of Kenya issued E-Money Regulation in 2013.[197] The Regulation is issued under powers of statute given to the minister (Central Bank of Kenya Act 1966 and National Payment System Act 2011). The Regulation defines e-money as monetary value as represented by a claim on its issuer, that is

1. Electronically, including magnetically, stored;
2. Issued against receipt of currency of Kenya; and
3. Accepted as a means of payment by persons other than the issuer.[198]

The Regulation empowers the central bank to authorise e-money issuers, regulate their conduct of business and ensure protections of clients.[199] It also regulates the engagement of agents by the e-money issuers.[200] The Regulation is restricted to e-money issuers who are not licensed as banks or financial institutions and those banks who conduct the business of an e-money issuer in addition to their core banking business.[201] To be authorised, an applicant must demonstrate several requirements including incorporation, minimal capitalisation of 60 million Shillings (£1 = KES 129.09),[202] financial soundness and the managers must be fit and proper persons.[203] The Kenyan regime also has provisions for a

[195] Section 13C, ibid.

[196] Electronic money.

[197] CBK (2013) 'E-Money Regulation' (Central Bank of Kenya), https://www.centralbank.go.ke/images/docs/NPS/Regulations%20and%20Guidelines/Regulations%20-%20E-%20Money%20regulations%202013.pdf. 28 December 2018.

[198] Clause 4, ibid.

[199] Clause 3.1, ibid.

[200] Clause 9, ibid.

[201] Clause 3.2, ibid.

[202] XE (2018) 'XE Currency Converter' (XE), https://www.xe.com/currencyconverter/convert/?Amount=1&From=GBP&To=KES. 28 December 2018.

[203] Clause 5.2, ibid.

category termed "small e-money issuers", whose authorisation requirements are less onerous.[204]

The Regulation has set up transaction limit of 75,000 Shillings and an aggregate monthly load limit of 1 million Shillings.[205] E-Money issuers are also required to comply with the Proceeds of Crime and Anti-Money Laundering Act and regulations made under it.[206] All e-money accounts are required to be under written agreement, and the agreement must clearly identify the client.[207] The Regulation prohibits the earning of interest on e-money, and e-money must be redeemed at par value.[208] The Regulation also restricts e-money issuers from intermediating (lending and investing).[209]

E-Money issuers are required to retain records of transactions for a period of 7 years.[210] Prior notification to the central bank needs to be made, at least thirty days before implement, before any outsourcing agreement of the e-money service can be implemented.[211] To protect consumers, the Regulation has placed onerous disclosure requirements on e-money issuers as well as provided for redress mechanisms.[212]

A review of the Kenyan regulatory framework reveals that the mobile money service is now intricately connected with the banking service. There are more cross-links between mobile money service providers and providers of other financial services. The diversity of the mobile money service has seen links in provision of e-banking services including saving and loan services.[213] The service has truly matured and the issues that the regulation aims to address are those most associated with post-financial inclusion.

[204] Clause 6, ibid.
[205] Clause 7.1, ibid.
[206] Clause 7.3, ibid.
[207] Clause 7.4, ibid.
[208] Clause 7.5, ibid.
[209] Clause 7.6, ibid.
[210] Clause 10, ibid.
[211] Clause 11.1, ibid.
[212] Clause 12, ibid.
[213] Musuni (2015).

## 8.5 Conclusion

The main issue that arises from the analysis of the existing regulatory framework of mobile money is that it is disjointed and not well suited to coherently regulate such a complex service. It is also clearly that even with the best intentions, its disjointed nature makes it hard to have a unified regulatory approach for mobile money. In many ways, countries like Malaŵi have an added advantage in that they can learn from what Kenya has gone through. The regulatory framework in Malaŵi is similar to what was obtaining in Kenya, during the pre-financial inclusion phase, allowing regulation to follow invention. This light-touch approach is meant to spur growth and ignite the service. In an era where financial inclusion is the goal, it may even be encouraged. However, what happens when the services take root and attain critical mass? Can the current regulatory framework, which is largely based on the traditional financial infrastructure, still work? Can it tame a service that has attained a life of its own? It is submitted it cannot.

In Malaŵi, the evidence so far points to mobile money as a service that has been warmly embraced by the people and has come to stay. It may not have ignited with the same flame as the Kenyan *M-Pesa*, but it has not fizzled out either. With growth in customer base, transaction values and the aggregate value of the pool account, the risks posed by mobile money are constantly changing. While light touch was essential to ignite, with financial inclusion in mind, the same approach may prove fatal should the service become systemically important, especially in a post-financial inclusion phase. This is where a more stringent regime like the one in Kenya needs to be adopted. As a service that combines elements of telecommunications and finance, mobile money requires a different approach which suits its uniqueness. Having an approach on its own is however not sufficient. There is also a need to have a structure, which can embrace this approach.

## References

Anon (2016) 'TNM Mpamba Builds K11m School Block in Chileka' *Nyasa Times* (19 December 2016), http://www.nyasatimes.com/tnm-mpamba-builds-k11m-school-block-chileka/. 12 March 2018.

Blessings Kamanga (2016) 'Malawi Junior Queens Gets K10mil Airtel Money for Africa Games' (19 July 2016), http://www.nyasatimes.com/

malawi-junior-queens-gets-k10mil-airtel-money-africa-games/#sthash.CdRa3jCd.dpuf. 12 March 2018.

Boon-Chye Lee and Olujoke Longe-Akindemowo (1999) 'Regulatory Issues in Electronic Money: A Legal-Economics Analysis' 1 (1) *Netnomics* 53.

CAK (2018) 'Telecommunications Overviews' (Communications Authority of Kenya), https://ca.go.ke/industry/telecommunication/overview/. 28 December 2018.

CAMA (2016) 'Consumers Association of Malawi', https://www.facebook.com/Consumers-Association-of-Malawi-104178233025786/. 20 December 2018.

CBK (2013) 'E-Money Regulation' (Central Bank of Kenya), https://www.centralbank.go.ke/images/docs/NPS/Regulations%20and%20Guidelines/Regulations%20-%20E-%20Money%20regulations%202013.pdf. 28 December 2018.

Central Bank of Kenya Act (Kenya, 1966), https://centralbank.go.ke/images/docs/The_Central_Bank_of_Kenya_Act_1st_January_2014.pdf. 28 December 2018.

CFTC (2016) 'Competition and Fair Trading Commission (Malaŵi)—History' (Competition and Fair Trading Commission), http://www.cftc.mw/index.php/about-us/history.html. 29 December 2018.

Charlotte Wezi Malonda (2016) *Approval of the Merger Between FDH Financial Holdings and Malaŵi Savings Bank (MSB)* (Competition and Fair Trading Commission, 2016).

Chinyamata Chipeta and Esmie Kanyumbu (2015) *Improving Access to Banking Services in Malawi* (Southern African Institute for Economic Research), http://aercafricaevents.org/wp-content/uploads/2015%20December/Group%20C/C3-Improving-access-to-banking-services-in-Malawi-Chinyamata-Chipeta-and-Esmie-Kanyumbu-FR.pdf. 14 November 2018.

Colin Scott (2001) 'Analysing Regulatory Space: Fragmented Resources and Institutional Design' *Public Law* 329, http://researchrepository.ucd.ie/bitstream/handle/10197/6785/AnalysingRegSpace.pdf?sequence=2. 1 December 2018.

Communications Act (Malaŵi, 2016).

Competition and Fair Trading Act, Act No. 43 of 1998 (Malaŵi, 1998), http://www.itu.int/ITU-D/treg/Legislation/Malawi/act43.pdf. 18 November 2018.

Consumer Protection Act (Malaŵi, 2003), https://www.rbm.mw/Home/GetContentFile/?ContentID=3752. 14 November 2018.

Dalvinder Singh (2007) *Banking Regulation of UK and US Financial Markets* (Ashgate, Aldershot, Hampshire).

David S Evans and Alexis Pirchio (2014) 'An Empirical Examination of Why Mobile Money Schemes Ignite in Some Developing Countries but Flounder in Most' 13 (4) *Review of Network Economics* 397, https://www.degruyter.

com/view/j/rne.2014.13.issue-4/rne-2015-0020/rne-2015-0020.xml. 12 May 2018.

Electronic Transactions and Cybersecurity Act (Malaŵi, 2016).

Electronic Transactions and Cybersecurity Bill, No. 11 of 2015 (Malaŵi), http://www.parliament.gov.mw/docs/bills/BILL11_2015.pdf. 19 July 2018.

Financial Crimes Act (Malaŵi, 2017). Financial Services Act (Malaŵi, 2010).

George RG Clarke, Frew A Gebreab and Henry R Mgombelo (2003) *Telecommunications Reform in Malawi* (Policy Research Working Papers, The World Bank), http://dx.doi.org/10.1596/1813-9450-3036. 2 December 2018.

Gladys Nthenda (2018) 'Parliament Refers Interest Cap Bill to Joint Committee' *Kulinji.com* (13 December 2018), https://www.kulinji.com/article/news/2018/parliament-refers-interest-cap-bill-joint-committee. 28 December 2018.

Grace Khombe (2014) 'CAMA to Name and Shame Traders on Receipt Guarantee and Warranty' *Zodiak Online* (Lilongwe), http://zodiakmalawi.com/top-stories/cama-to-name-and-shame-traders-on-receipt-guarantee-and-waranty. 14 November 2018.

Grace Phiri (2015) 'Telecom Operators' Performance Poor' *The Nation* (18 December 2015), http://mwnation.com/telecom-operators-perfomance-still-poor/. 12 March 2018.

Guidelines for Mobile Payment Systems (Malaŵi, 2011).

Gunther Teubner (1993) *Law as an Autopoietic System* (Blackwell, Oxford/Cambridge).

Hanna Ziady (2016) 'Interest Rate Caps Are Now Effective' *The Citizen* (10 May 2016), http://citizen.co.za/business/business-news/1109479/interest-rate-caps-are-now-effective/. 5 December 2018.

Happy Soko (2015) 'Malaŵi Government Drilled Over MSB Sale' *Malaŵi24* (18 March 2015), http://allafrica.com/stories/201503190408.html. 18 November 2018.

Herve Dumez and Alain Jeunemaitre (1997) 'Financial Regulation: From Economic Analysis to Practical Experience' in Alain Jeunemaitre (ed) *Financial Markets Regulation* (MacMillan, Basingstoke).

Ian Ayres and John Braithwaite (1992) *Responsive Regulation: Transcending the Deregulation Debate* (Oxford University Press, Oxford) Chapter 2.

Ignacio Mas and Daniel Radcliffe (2011) 'Mobile Payments Go Viral: M-PESA in Kenya' 32 *The Capco Institute Journal of Financial Transformation* 169, http://www.capco.com/sites/all/files/journal-32_article-16.pdf. 15 December 2018.

*In the Matter of Citizen Insurance Company Limited Exparte the Registrar of Financial Services*, Commercial Case No. 55 of 2011 HC (Malaŵi), http://www.malawilii.org/mw/judgment/high-court-commercial-division/2012/5/. 27 February 2018.

Joseph Tiampati Ole Musuni (2015) 'Mobile Money: The Kenyan Experience' (Government of Kenya), http://www.cto.int/media/events/pst-ev/2015/Broadband%202015/Presentations/Mobile%20Money%20Service%20Joseph%20Tiampati%20Ole%20Musuni.pdf. 28 December 2018.

Kenya Information and Communications Act (1998), http://kfcb.co.ke/wp-content/uploads/2016/07/Kenya_Information_and_Communications_Act.pdf. 28 December 2018.

Kondwani Nankhumwa MP (Minister of Information) (2015) *Statement on the Sale of MSB and IndeBank* (State House Residences Malaŵi, 2015).

Lameck Masina (2015) 'Controversy as Government Sells Malawi Savings Bank' *African Business* (7 August 2015), http://africanbusinessmagazine.com/african-banker/controversy-as-government-sells-malawi-savings-bank/. 18 November 2018.

Leigh Hancher and Michael Moran (1998) 'Organizing Regulatory Space' in Robert Baldwin, Colin Scott and Christopher Hood (eds) *A Reader in Regulation* (Oxford University Press, Oxford).

Lucky Mkandawire (2014) 'Kumbatira Appointed New Macra Boss' *The Nation* (2 September 2014), http://mwnation.com/kumbatira-appointed-new-macra-boss/. 8 February 2018.

Lucky Mkandawire (2015) 'Macra, MPC Bosses Swap Posts' *The Nation* (6 August 2015), http://mwnation.com/macra-mpc-bosses-swap-posts/. 8 February 2018.

MACRA (2014) 'Strategic Plan 2015–2020' (Malaŵi Communications Regulatory Authority), http://www.macra.org.mw/wp-content/uploads/2014/09/MACRA-Strategic-Plan-2015-2020.pdf. 12 March 2018.

MACRA (2016) 'Telecommunications' (Malaŵi Communication Regulatory Authority), http://www.macra.org.mw/?cat=7. 8 February 2018.

Malaŵi Government (2013) 'National ICT Policy' (Malaŵi Government), http://www.macra.org.mw/wp-content/uploads/2014/07/Malawi-ICT-Policy-2013.pdf. 4 November 2018.

Mbane Ngwira (2017) Spokesperson, Reserve Bank of Malaŵi (10 March 2017) (personal communication).

Mustafa Kennedy Hussein (2009) 'Opposition Politics in Malawi: Hopeful Signs Amid the Warnings' 16 (3) *South African Journal of International Affairs.*

Payment Systems Act (Malaŵi, 2016).

Payment Systems Bill 22 of 2015 (Malaŵi), http://www.parliament.gov.mw/docs/bills/BILL22_2015.pdf. 19 July 2018.

RBM (2017) *Monthly National Payments System Report: January 2017* (Reserve Bank of Malaŵi), https://www.rbm.mw/PaymentSystems/GetContentFile/?ContentID=12203. 10 March 2018.

Ruth A Schmidt and others (1999) 'Deshopping—The Art of Illicit Consumption' 27 (8) *International Journal of Retail & Distribution Management* 290, http://www.emeraldinsight.com/doi/pdfplus/10.1108/09590559910288569. 4 November 2018.

SADC (2011) *SADC Bankers: Reserve Bank of Malawi* (Committee of Central Bank Governors in Southern Africa Development Community), http://www.sadcbankers.org/SADC/SADC.nsf/LADV/E4E3EF0D1F5967B8422576740044D454/$File/Malawi-.pdf. 10 October 2018.

Suzgo Khunga (2015) 'MSB Sale Fallout, Goes at K9.5 Billion' *The Nation* (3 July 2015), http://mwnation.com/msb-sale-fallout-goes-at-k9-5-billion/. 18 November 2018.

TNM (2016) *Annual Report 2015* (Telekom Networks Malaŵi Limited), https://drive.google.com/file/d/0B9DwraK-rABVQUlRYnoyTlo0Znc/view. 11 March 2018.

XE (2018) 'XE Currency Converter' (XE), https://www.xe.com/currencyconverter/convert/?Amount=1&From=GBP&To=KES. 28 December 2018.

CHAPTER 9

# An Alternative Regulatory Framework for Mobile Money

## 9.1 Introduction

The discussion on regulation of mobile money has been based on the pre-financial inclusion and the regulatory issues it poses. The question that inevitably must be asked is what happens when financial inclusion has been achieved? The question whether regulatory intervention is required ought to be answered in the affirmative.[1] Fundamentally, it is the type of intervention that needs to be considered. It has already been argued that the regulatory approach of the pre-financial inclusion phase where there are a plethora of regulators is not ideal to achieve financial inclusion as well as regulate a post-financial inclusion era. This chapter argues that having a coherent regulatory framework is important in this financial inclusion journey. It further argues in favour of a regulator that is focused, has stability and has a strong research arm to collect information from stakeholders. As posited in Chapter 3, really responsive regulation is the preferred approach that embraces this evolution. Ultimately, it is not the form of regulation that needs to change, but the culture. The regulator needs to sufficiently understand the context of the regulated industry and the regulatory space dynamics. As already stated, the regulatory space is contested. In such a contested space, resources are the key to power, authority and influence.[2]

[1] Córdova-Novion and Hanlon (2002), p. 62

[2] Scott (2001), p. 330.



S. Madise, *The Regulation of Mobile Money*, Palgrave Macmillan Studies in Banking and Financial Institutions,
https://doi.org/10.1007/978-3-030-13831-8_9

The various participants within the regulatory space have varying degrees of resources with those who are well resourced standing at an advantage.[3] Therefore, where a regulator is poorly resourced, its ability to regulate will be limited and may lead to power shifting towards the regulated or other actors within the regulatory space.

As has been noted, mobile money is principally a financial service and one of the developmental tools to achieve financial inclusion. Regulation can be an enabler to achieve financial inclusion as well as define the post-financial inclusion phase of mobile money.[4] An enabling regulatory environment must be delicately balanced to attract and retain business entrants as well as customers. Porteous defines this as "a set of conditions which promote a sustainable trajectory of market development in such a way as to promote socially desirable outcomes".[5] Creating such an environment in the face of a high number of regulators can be a challenge. However, an enabling regulatory environment should not be construed as leaving the service to its own devices. There is a need to be cautious as an over-liquid and under-regulated financial market is a recipe for financial crisis.[6] Regulation has a task to provide an enabling environment under which the mobile money ecosystem may develop and take root.[7]

Regulating a new service is a challenge for all the actors within the regulatory space. The problem with mobile money is that everyone seems to be in unchartered territory. The potential benefits associated with mobile money seem to be so great that the regulator may be under pressure not to be perceived as appearing to frustrate it.[8] There is a need to define the role of various actors such as the mobile network operators,

[3] Ibid.

[4] Venkatesen Mauree and Gaurav Kohli (2013) *The Mobile Money Revolution—Part 2: Financial Inclusion Enabler* (ITUT Technology Watch, International Telecommunications Union), p. 19, https://www.itu.int/dms_pub/itu-t/oth/23/01/T23010000200002PDFE.pdf. 1 May 2018.

[5] Porteous (2006), p. 13.

[6] José Gabriel Palma (2012) *How the Full Opening of the Capital Account to Highly Liquid Financial Markets Led Latin America to Two and a Half Cycles of 'Mania, Panic and Crash'* (Cambridge Working Papers in Economics 1201), p. 2, http://www.econ.cam.ac.uk/dae/repec/cam/pdf/cwpe1201.pdf. 19 May 2014.

[7] Jenkins (2008), p. 11.

[8] Omwansa (2009), p. 121.

the mobile money issuers and their agents. Agents were not previously subject to financial regulation and supervision.[9] The main question that this chapter attempts to answer is what would be an effective post-financial inclusion regulatory framework for mobile money for Malaŵi? Hopefully, such a framework can also be used by other jurisdiction who are in the same development phase like Malaŵi. It starts by considering how the regulatory space would be configured, and it then looks at whether regulatory homogeneity can be achieved. It presents two options: an agency model and one, which consists of streamlining the status quo. This chapter essentially argues that from a development perspective, an independent agency would best suit the post-financial inclusion framework. However, because of the local sociopolitical context, instead of the agency being a stand-alone one, the chapter advocates for an autonomous agency within the central bank.

## 9.2 The Regulatory Arena

The first step towards proposing an alternative regulatory framework based on a really responsive approach is to delimit the regulatory arena. The reality is that resources such as "information, wealth and organisational capacities … relevant to holding of regulatory power and exercising of capacities are dispersed or fragmented".[10] Power is no longer monopolised by the regulator. Although there is contestation for advantage, the "dispersal of regulatory authority creates relationships of interdependence negotiated between the actors within the regulatory space".[11] Therefore, the race is not to the bottom, but rather one which is characterised by a need to have a competitive edge while maintaining relationships within the regulatory space.

By its nature, space is rarely unoccupied. The task therefore is to demarcate its boundary and decide which actors should be allowed in and which ones should be kept out. Since it is the issues that define what constitutes the regulatory space,[12] then with mobile money, the actors

[9] Lyman (2016).
[10] Scott (2001), p. 330.
[11] Ibid., p. 337.
[12] Ibid., p. 332.

can be determined by looking at the issues. In a way, using the mobile money ecosystem helps to identify the key actors within the regulatory arena.[13] This section analyses the various actors and institutions and their motivation for their inclusion of within mobile money's regulatory arena to achieve a really responsive framework. To allow for meaningful stakeholder participation, the framework must provide deliberate space whereby the actors can contribute and take a part in shaping the regulation. A really responsive framework must have the process agreed to by the stakeholders from time to time. This requires a different approach on the part of the regulator and deliberate mechanisms to solicit feedback and information from the ecosystem stakeholders. It is submitted that to achieve this, the process must embrace:

- Different stakeholders including user groups
- Have an information gathering system
- Be based on mutual and experiential learning.

### *9.2.1 Mobile Network Operators and Mobile Money Issuers*

Although mobile network operators are not providing the mobile money service, since they are the ones that set up the mobile money issuers as a special purpose vehicle and provide the backbone for the service, these give them a stake within the regulatory space. Mobile network operators have a further stake on the basis that a reliable and effective telecommunication service is a key regulatory issue for both services. Conversely, where the telecommunication backbone is unreliable, the mobile money service operations will be severely disrupted. Currently, the central bank's approach is to exclude mobile network operators from its financial regulatory arena. In reality, the two services cannot be truly separated and any regulatory framework must provide space for both. Mobile money issuers are at the centre of issues within the regulatory space. The whole regulatory framework is built around mobile money and its ecosystem. Although the service may have links with other services or ride on other rails, its inclusion within the regulatory arena is, therefore, a foregone conclusion.

[13] Jenkins (2008), p. 7.

### 9.2.2 *Banks*

Banks belong to the banking regulatory arena; however, their role as the ultimate recipient of deposits from mobile money customers makes them central to the regulation of mobile money. Mobile money can only be generated on the strength of deposits in a pool account.[14] Of course, there is debate whether the banks are operating the pool accounts following trust law requirements. It is submitted they are not. There may be a body of trustees created by the issuers,[15] but strictly speaking, to the bank, the pool account is just another deposit account. Interest is payable to the trustees whose only restriction is to use it for charitable purposes.[16] Operations of banks holding pool accounts are, therefore, a regulatory issue. Any crisis that would affect the bank would have a domino effect and affect mobile money, including bank resolution. This may not only affect funds in the pool account, but could affect the stability of the mobile money ecosystem. For a meaningful engagement, banks are a key actor to be included within the regulatory arena.

### 9.2.3 *Regulators*

As noted, the mobile money regulatory arena has several regulators, but they do not all regulate the service in unison. Where there emerges a new service such as mobile money, which interconnects several regulatory nodes, the question is who among the sector regulators should regulate it or be the lead regulator?[17] Sometimes these sector regulators collaborate depending on the issues.[18] Sometimes their work overlaps especially where they must deal with consumer protection or competition issues affecting their sector.[19]

Regardless of the structural model adopted, these regulators need to be included within the regulatory arena. Currently, the Reserve Bank of

[14] Maurer (2012), p. 306.

[15] Mkoloma (2015).
Mbekeani (2015).

[16] Mkoloma (2015).
Mbekeani (2015).

[17] Klein and Mayer (2011), p. 27.

[18] Ibid.

[19] Ibid.

Malaŵi is the lead regulator overseeing mobile money operations. In its work, it mostly collaborates the communication regulator. The Financial Intelligence Authority (FIA) seems to have only one foot in, as its main concern is monitoring suspicious transactions. However, the low values of mobile money transactions are below the minimum mandatory reporting threshold set up by the FIA, unless they are suspicious.[20] The Competition and Fair Trading Commission is mainly concerned with competition and fair-trading. As noted earlier, the Consumers Protection Council is not operative. Within themselves, the regulators are already cooperating and having memoranda of understanding (MOU) guiding their cooperation. The following are the MOU already in operation:

- Reserve Bank of Malaŵi and Malaŵi Communications Regulatory Authority[21]
- Reserve Bank of Malaŵi and Financial Intelligence Authority[22]
- Malaŵi Communications Regulatory Authority and Competition and Fair Trading Commission.[23]

The basic rudiments of inter-agency cooperation are, therefore, already in place. The MOUs can be used as a stepping stone towards a more formalised cooperation arrangement between the regulators. By their nature, regulators are central in any regulatory reformulation.

### 9.2.4 *Consumers*

The mobile money service thrives on having an active body of consumers who regularly transact. Transactional fees finance the mobile money service. The central bank has already highlighted low financial literacy and awareness among the populace as one of the challenges hindering Malaŵi's achievement of full financial inclusion.[24] As was noted earlier, literacy levels in Malaŵi are generally very low, especially among

[20] Phiri (2015).
[21] Chimbe (2015).
RBM HQ (RBM 2015).
[22] Phiri (2015).
[23] Chimbe (2015).
[24] RBM (2013), pp. 11–2.

women.[25] Most of the population is under the so-called $1.25 a day poverty line.[26] Considering that this is the target for the mobile money service, it is a rather peculiar clientele. Mobile money, as a financial service, requires some level of financial literacy or awareness among its users. Low literacy levels, especially on financial issues, are therefore an issue of concern. It may be for this reason, consumer awareness bodies, such as the Consumers Association of Malaŵi (CAMA),[27] may prove useful. However, although CAMA regularly speaks for consumers on topical issues,[28] it may be incapable of fully representing all consumer interests. There is a need to engage the actual users of the mobile money service. Setting up user groups and providing them with a platform may be one such way of getting users on board as a stakeholder with a voice within the regulatory arena.

### 9.2.5 *The Legal Structure*

The current law regulating the various aspects of mobile money is fragmented. Apart from the financial service laws,[29] all the other pieces of legislation are concerned with the ancillary aspects of the mobile money service.[30] This fragmentation is not conducive to achieving a really responsive regulatory approach. While it may be argued that codification may be an easier route, considering the diversity of the legislation

[25] In the 2008 census, 41% of women were illiterate. 36% of the population was illiterate—NSO (2009), p. 14.

[26] Anon (2013), p. 1.

[27] CAMA (2016).

[28] Anon (2010) 'Consumers Demonstrate Over High Bank Rates in Malawi' (21 April 2010), http://maravi.blogspot.co.uk/2010/04/nyasatimes-consumers-demonstrate-over.html. 11 March 2014.
Khombe (2014).

[29] Such as:
Financial Services Act (Malaŵi, 2010).
Payment Systems Act (2016).
Electronic Transactions Act (Malaŵi, 2016).

[30] Communications Act (Malaŵi, 2016).
Financial Crimes Act (Malaŵi, 2017).
Consumer Protection Act (Malaŵi, 2003).
Competition and Fair Trading Act (Malaŵi, 1998).

concerned, this is discouraged. By embarking on this route, there is an acknowledgement that the regulatory flux will continue. This would be overcome if the legislature passed a law that specifically governs the operation of mobile money. The legislature has revised and enacted a new law to replace the Communications Act 1998 with a 2016 version and the Money Laundering Act 2006 with the Financial Crimes Act 2017. It is submitted the Consumer Protection Act 2003, the Competitions and Fair Trading Act 1998 may also need to be reviewed.

The enactment of the Payment Systems Act 2016 and the Electronic Transactions Act 2016 has helped to start bringing some regulatory clarity in electronic payments systems.[31] However, apart from the Mobile Payment Guidelines 2011,[32] there is no law or regulations that have been enacted or promulgated specifically to address regulation of mobile money. Furthermore, the guidelines lack the authority of positive law. To its credit, the central bank in 2015 drafted electronic money regulations, but these regulations have been withdrawn so that they can be realigned with the Payment Systems Act 2016.[33] However, some two years after the Act was enacted, the regulations are yet to see the light of day.

### 9.2.6 *The Executive and the Political Establishment*

The power that the executive arm of the government holds in regulatory issues is manifested in the power to appoint boards and senior management of the regulatory bodies. Furthermore, although the executive holds no express legislative powers, under most statutes, ministers can promulgate subsidiary legislation. Malaŵi is a constitutional democracy.[34] It is governed through an elected 5-year political cycle.[35] The executive has the constitutional duty to initiate legislation.[36] In fact, while consumers, mobile money issuers, banks and regulators may be the key actors, it is the political establishment that may make all the

[31] Payment Systems Act (Malaŵi, 2016).
Electronic Transactions Act (Malaŵi, 2016).

[32] Guidelines for Mobile Payment Systems (Malaŵi, 2011).

[33] Ngwira (2017).

[34] Section 12 Constitution of the Republic of Malaŵi (1994), http://www.malawi.gov.mw/images/Publications/act/Constitution%20of%20Malawi.pdf. 21 December 2016.

[35] Section 67, ibid.

[36] Section 7, ibid.

difference. Politics also comes to the fore when consumer issues are at play. After all, consumers crucially compose the electorate. In the case of Malaŵi, the majority of the electorate are in rural areas.

Politicians are rational beings after all, and the theory of *homo economicus* says that all things being equal, a rational being will try to maximise for their personal benefit.[37] Of course, it could be argued that politicians are also *homo politicus* and will attempt to consider what is best for society.[38] Although *homo politicus* normally stands in contrast to *homo economicus*, where politicians are concerned it is possible to have the two fused in the same personality. Politicians are likely to consider what will best benefit them, and if it will benefit the society as well, it is more likely to become a priority. Therefore, in a country like Malaŵi, where the majority of the electorate are unbanked, financially excluded and living in the rural areas, a service such as mobile money which targets this very same demographic group may all of a sudden attain political priority. In a country where resources are scarce, allocation of resources becomes subject to political interests and power play. Although most politicians have the economic good of the country as a priority, ultimately the question the politician will ask is; will allocating resources to a regulatory agency result in a greater chance of being re-elected? It is for these reasons that the mobile money regulatory arena must include the executive and the political establishment.

## 9.3 Towards Regulatory Homogeneity

The regulatory overlap for mobile money arises because it is a hybrid service.[39] However, is there a danger of this overlap resulting in the risk of coordination and regulatory failure?[40] As noted, for the mobile money services to grow, it needs an enabling environment. It needs to attract and encourage new entrants into the market so as not to stifle innovation while ensuring the regulatory and policy framework is not susceptible

[37] Karine Nyborg (2000) 'Homo economicus and homo politicus: Interpretation and Aggregation of Environmental Values' 42 (3) *Journal of Economic Behavior & Organization* 305, p. 309, http://www.sciencedirect.com/science/article/pii/S0167268100000913. 21 December 2018.

[38] Ibid., p. 310.

[39] Porteous (2006), p. 5.

[40] Ibid.

to arbitrary changes, which may prejudice prospects of new entrants.[41] However, what happens when growth has been attained? The issue that needs to be considered next is what would be the right regulatory fit as the service evolves?

### 9.3.1 An Independent Agency?

The problems posed by the emergence of electronic and other new forms of money to pre-existing regulatory architectures are not new. When faced with a new financial service such as mobile money, regulators fail to respond because they struggle to understand that they are dealing with a different species of payment platform.[42] So how would an independent agency be structured to really respond to its environment and what would be its function?

#### *9.3.1.1 Independent Agency*

The notion of setting up independent agencies to regulate business or some aspects of social life comes from the movement away from the welfare state to the regulatory state.[43] The assumption is that such agencies operate at arm's length from their principles.[44] Under the welfare state, there is a direct relationship between the state and the citizens through legislative intervention.[45] Under the regulatory state, the state, as the principal, sets up agencies to oversee the needs of citizens, referred to as consumers[46]; McCubbins et al. have argued that reduced to its lowest common denominator, the principal-agent relationship is premised on the distribution of costs.[47] The agent takes on a cost on behalf of the

[41] Ibid.

[42] Lelieveldt (1996), pp. 1165–6.

[43] Colin Scott (2017) 'The Regulatory State and Beyond' in Peter Drahos (ed) *Regulatory Theory: Foundations and Applications* (Australian National University Press, Canberra), p. 269.

[44] Ibid., p. 267.

[45] Ibid., p. 269.

[46] Ibid.

[47] Matthew D McCubbins, Roger G Noll and Barry R Weingast (1989) 'Structure and Process, Politics and Policy: Administrative Arrangements and the Political Control of Agencies' 75 *Virginia Law Review* 431, p. 433, http://scholarship.law.duke.edu/cgi/viewcontent.cgi?article=5950&context=faculty_scholarship. 20 February 2018.

principle in return for some benefit authorised or provided by the principal.[48] The agency has delegated power from a principal, typically the legislature or executive branches of government, and is accountable for how it uses those powers.[49] The principals typically comprise elected officials, and the agencies are a creature of statute.[50] The oversight provided by the independent agencies is therefore at the core of regulatory state governance.[51] Scott says such agencies utilise a combination of public and private law instruments, like licences and contracts to "enforce regulatory norms".[52] The regulatory state provides a monitoring mechanism in a market environment.[53]

Quintyn and Taylor argue that such agencies "potentially shield market intervention from political interference and improve transparency, stability, and expertise of the regulatory and supervisory process".[54] Apart from political interference, technical complexity in regulatory issues is deemed to be best managed by independent experts than government departments.[55] Over time, the consensus seems to converge that independence regulatory agencies, which are accountable to stakeholders, are more likely to lead to effective regulation.[56] Independent agencies run by experts also instil confidence and trust in the regulatory system.[57] This independence is much more needed when there is a crisis or some complex issue that needs a response.[58]

Although powers to enforce are crucial, even where the agency lacks express powers, it can formulate its own enforcement pyramid and utilise tools such as education, advice, warnings with naming and shaming

[48] Ibid., pp. 433–4.

[49] Quintyn and Taylor (2002), p. 31.

Mark Thatcher (2002) 'Delegation to Independent Regulatory Agencies: Pressures, Functions and Contextual Mediation' 25 (1) *West European Politics* 125, p. 125, http://0-dx.doi.org.pugwash.lib.warwick.ac.uk/10.1080/713601588. 16 February 2018.

[50] Thatcher (2002), p. 125.

[51] Scott (2017), p. 267.

[52] Ibid., p. 268.

[53] Ibid., p. 269.

[54] Quintyn and Taylor (2002), p. 9.

[55] Córdova-Novion and Hanlon (2002), p. 71.

[56] Quintyn and Taylor (2002), pp. 4, 8.

[57] Córdova-Novion and Hanlon (2002), p. 73.

[58] Quintyn and Taylor (2002), p. 9.

as the ultimate tool.[59] Baldwin and Black have proposed a "naming and shaming league tables" noting that some may fear this more than administrative fines.[60] The ability to escalate sanctions in itself allows the agency to offer advice, which can be seriously taken because they carry a big stick.[61] Use of the big stick anyhow may result in the agency failing to effectively enforce regulations; therefore, a responsive framework must aim to strike a balance.[62] Where an agency embraces the enforcement pyramid, the enforcement must not only respond to the environment,[63] but also do so by understanding the culture and broader framework of the regulated environment.[64]

To be effective, an agency must have the autonomy to set up rules, which must be binding on the industry.[65] The agency must also have powers of oversight, including granting and revoking licences.[66] The agency must ideally be detached from the government machinery.[67] To be competitive, the agency must be able to attract competent expertise.[68] Sources of financing are therefore vital for its operation and independence. Unless its budget is directly appropriated by Parliament, the agency must go through some government ministry for financing. The only other way of avoiding this is to raise revenue from the industry through levies and fees.[69] This may not be easy in agencies that are just being set-up. It may also lead to capture.

To avoid an agency becoming too independent, mechanisms need to be put in place as a counterbalance. Transparency and accountability are the crucial countervailing measures.[70] This accountability must be to the

[59] Scott (2017), p. 271.

[60] Baldwin and Black (2008), pp. 32, 34.

[61] Scott (2017), p. 272.

[62] Ibid.

[63] Ayres and Braithwaite (1992), p. 4.

[64] Baldwin and Black (2008), pp. 18, 19.

[65] Quintyn and Taylor (2002), p. 22.

[66] Ibid., pp. 17, 19.
Polizatto (1992), pp. 303–8.

[67] Quintyn and Taylor (2002), p. 20.

[68] Ibid., p. 21.
Polizatto (1992), p. 310.

[69] Quintyn and Taylor (2002), p. 21.

[70] Córdova-Novion and Hanlon (2002), pp. 89–97.

stakeholders such as the regulated industry, consumers, the citizenry, the principals, the legislature and the judiciary.[71] According to Freeman's stakeholder theory, each organisation has a constituency.[72] The theory argues that unlike the traditional business model where managers owed a duty to the business owners, under the stakeholder theory, they also owe a fiduciary duty to stakeholders.[73] This constituency rarely comprises homogeneous interests, but all stakeholders must be considered.[74]

The stakeholder theory is not without its distractors. Argenti says, as a concept, its time has long passed.[75] He argues that unlike shareholders who are a homogenous set, there is a lack of certainty with stakeholders.[76] Although Argenti's criticism is based on the theory's application to companies, the criticism would apply to all corporations. He criticises the theory for treating all stakeholders as if they are equal. However, it is submitted that the theory does not make this argument and Argenti's criticism may be misplaced. In fact, as noted by Phillips, the diversity of stakeholders is embraced.[77] The theory advocates for consultation or involvement of all stakeholders. How this will be undertaken will depend on a myriad of factors, including the type of business the corporation is in as well as the array of stakeholders involved.[78] His argument that "an organization designed to serve more than one set of people will fail to satisfy any" seems to be a narrow view and premised much on the profit motive.[79] In response, Campbell has rightly observed that Argenti seems to miss the fact that organisations do not exist in an empty vacuum, but

[71] Ibid., p. 89.

[72] Robert Phillips (2003) 'Stakeholder Theory and Organizational Dogma' in Robert Phillips (ed) *Stakeholder Theory and Organizational Ethics* (Berrett-Koehler Publishers, San Francisco, CA), p. 3.

[73] Edward R Freeman (1984) 'Stakeholder Theory of the Modern Corporation' in *General Issues in Business Ethics* (HarperCollins, New York), p. 39.

[74] Phillips (2003), p. 3.

[75] John Argenti (1997) 'Stakeholders: The Case Against' 30 (3) *Long Range Planning* 442, p. 445, http://www.sciencedirect.com/science/article/pii/S0024630197000046. 16 February 2018.

[76] Ibid., p. 442.

[77] Phillips (2003), p. 3.

[78] Andrew Campbell (1997) 'Stakeholders: The Case in Favour' 30 (3) *Long Range Planning* 446, p. 448, http://www.sciencedirect.com/science/article/pii/S0024630197000034. 16 February 2018.

[79] Ibid., p. 445.

are part of a space which is highly contested.[80] Campbell argues that organisations that survive are those that give all stakeholders a good deal.[81] He argues that the theory actually takes cognizance that organisations "cannot survive unless they deliver value to their stakeholders".[82]

It is submitted that in relation to corporate bodies that are charged with regulatory supervision, embracing the stakeholder theory is the only way they can truly manage to regulate the market they are in. Stakeholder involvement does not only make the regulator more responsive to the environment but also entrenches accountability. Accountability is fundamental to ensure effective agency independence.[83] The reason why regulatory independence must have accountability, as a countervailing force, is to prevent capture, avoid rigidities and minimise over-regulation.[84] As Stigler argued, institutions naturally are aligned with the best-organised and resourced entities.[85] Apart from industry or state capture, there is also the fear of self-capture, where the agency implements its own agenda.[86] Such agencies become a law unto themselves, essentially becoming the fourth estate.[87] This is much more so, since unelected officials usually run the agencies. This risk can, however, be mitigated with deliberate oversight, which while not interfering with the operations of the agency makes the agency accountable to its principals.

Balancing the levels of accountability to the competing interests of stakeholders is a task that has to be incorporated in the regulatory institutional design.[88] In most common law jurisdiction, the process of judicial review is a powerful legal process through which administrative actions and decisions of public bodies can be brought under judicial

[80] Ibid., p. 446.

[81] Ibid.

[82] Ibid., p. 449.

[83] Quintyn and Taylor (2002), p. 5.

[84] Ibid., pp. 3, 5.

[85] Stigler (1971).

[86] Córdova-Novion and Hanlon (2002), p. 82.

[87] Quintyn and Taylor (2002), pp. 9–10.
Eva Hüpkes, Marc Quintyn and Michael W Taylor (2006) 'Accountability Arrangements for Financial Sector Regulators' 39, p. 1 *IMF Economic Issues*, https://www.imf.org/external/pubs/ft/issues/issues39/ei39.pdf. 27 February 2018.

[88] Córdova-Novion and Hanlon (2002), p. 89.

scrutiny.[89] Allowing appeals to the courts is an effective means of ensuring that the agency operates within the law.[90] Judicial oversight further helps to ensure consistency in the interpretation and application of rules.[91] When formulating boundaries of jurisdiction, it is necessary to specify when the agency's mandate can be overridden and if so by whom and in what manner.[92]

Having a financial ombudsman scheme,[93] as is the case with the Financial Ombudsman Service (FOS) in the UK, is one way of entrenching this accountability.[94] According to Singh, such a scheme provides an avenue "for consumers to seek redress against financial firms once all procedures at a firm level to deal with the complainant have been exhausted".[95] Although Malaŵi does not have such a scheme, it has an office of the Ombudsman, mandated to investigate abuse of power of unfair treatment by public officials or bodies.[96] Another way of ensuring accountability is to remove statutory immunity against such an agency or its staff through the common law tort of misfeasance in public office.[97] This acts as a strong motivation for public officers to act in good faith or at least not to act in bad faith.[98] Immunity or indemnity is found in most legislation, which creates independent regulatory agencies.[99] It has now

89 Public Law Project (2013) *An Introduction to Judicial Review* (Public Law Project, London).

90 Córdova-Novion and Hanlon (2002), p. 96.

91 Quintyn and Taylor (2002), p. 32.

92 Ibid., p. 32 and Thatcher (2002), p. 144.

93 FOSL (2017) 'Financial Ombudsman Service' (Financial Ombudsman Service Limited), http://www.financial-ombudsman.org.uk/. 13 March 2018.

94 Singh (2007), p. 196.

95 Ibid.

96 Section 5 Ombudsman Act, Act No. 17 of 1996, Chpater 3:07 of the Laws of Malaŵi (Malaŵi, 1996), http://www.africanchildforum.org/clr/Legislation%20Per%20Country/Malawi/malawi_ombudsman_1996_en.pdf. 27 February 2018.

97 Singh (2007), p. 199.

98 Ibid., pp. 199–200.

99 Section 98 Financial Services Act (Malaŵi, 2010).

Singh (2007), pp. 186–90.

been held in both the UK and Malawi that regulators may be sued for how they have exercised their regulatory powers.[100] Judicial accountability is, therefore, a powerful way of checking the use of agency power without corroding on its independence.[101]

The principal-agent relationship is not static. Over time, agencies start wielding power, sometimes more than their principals.[102] The danger of an unelected body amassing policy-making, and sometimes legislating power needs to be considered.[103] Although autonomy is a hallmark of institutional independence, one way of making agencies accountable is to retain the power to appoint senior staff with elected principals either directly or through appointed boards.[104] However, this may cause problems where such appointments are politicised. Having the agencies account to the legislature through annual reports and attending parliamentary committee sessions would be one way of minimising political interference and ensuring accountability.[105] Accountability can also extend to other stakeholders such as consumers and players in the regulated industry.[106] This can include mandatory consultations and publication of reports before rules or policies are promulgated.[107] Stakeholder meetings where the regulator accounts to stakeholders are one of the ways of ensuring this autonomy as well as making it accountable. They are also the best forum for supporting a framework that really responds to stakeholder concerns.

Setting up an agency does not provide the permanent regulatory solution. The regulatory framework must constantly respond to dynamics of the environment. Increasingly, where the industry converges through mergers and acquisitions or through offering services across the board,

[100] *Three Rivers DC v Bank of England* (2001) 2 All ER 513 HOL, https://www.publications.parliament.uk/pa/ld199900/ldjudgmt/jd000518/rivers-1.htm. 27 February 2018.
*In the Matter of Citizen Insurance Company Limited Exparte the Registrar of Financial Services.*

[101] Hüpkes et al. (2006), p. 9.

[102] Thatcher (2002), p. 140.

[103] Ibid.

[104] Ibid., p. 143.

[105] Ibid.

[106] Ibid.

[107] Ibid.

regulators also need to respond, by either merging or evolving from sector to industry regulators.[108] A bank may start offering insurance services and an insurance company may start offering banking services. An mobile money issuer may cross the Rubicon and start offering loans. A mobile network operator can decide to acquire a bank, set up an insurance company and offer mobile money and a horde of other services.[109] In such a scenario, the regulation would have to evolve and respond in real time to these developments.

Ideally with a highly complex and technical service such as mobile money, some level of self-regulation is required especially as mobile network operators tend to know more about the market than the regulators. The problem, however, is that where you have a few dominant players, as is the case in Malaŵi, there is a tendency for these players to undertake oligopolistic behaviour and dominate the market to the detriment of consumer welfare and competition.[110] In such an environment, addressing information asymmetry becomes a crucial regulatory objective and dominates the regulatory focus.[111] While some degree of self-regulation may be allowed, it is submitted that at least in its early stages, the agency must attempt to balance the various regulatory objectives. Really responsive or smart regulation, which combines various regulatory approaches, would therefore be ideally suited for such an agency.

The prime design feature of the agency is that it must have clear regulatory objectives.[112] This is important as it delineates the boundaries of regulatory authority but also defines the working relationship with other stakeholders. To ensure that independence is entrenched, such an agency should ideally be instituted by law, with its independence enshrined in statute.[113] Organisationally, the agency would need to have horizontal and vertical structures. The horizontal structure would allow for cooperation with existing sector regulators and within units while the vertical node would ensure streaming of regulatory roles within the agency.

[108] Córdova-Novion and Hanlon (2002), p. 97.

[109] Airtel had contemplated buying or setting up a bank during the exploratory phase of its mobile money service—Mkoloma (2015).

[110] Córdova-Novion and Hanlon (2002), pp. 78, 79.

[111] Ibid.

[112] Ibid., p. 72.

[113] Ibid., p. 81.

#### *9.3.1.2 The Argument for an Independent Agency*

As a financial service, mobile money needs to meet some basic minimum prudential standards notwithstanding that it is not a banking service. As a service riding on the telecommunication backbone, mobile money's operation is always dependent on the operation of the latter. Therefore, although legally the mobile money issuers and the mobile network operators may be distinct, operationally they are intertwined. The current arrangement where the communications regulator only looks at the operations of the mobile network operators and not beyond illustrates the lack of appreciation of complex operations of the mobile money service. Setting up an agency to oversee all aspects of mobile money seems the ideal situation.

One thing that has been evident in the analysis of the current legal framework, in the last chapter, is that it does not provide for adequate protection of consumers' rights and interests. This is not just through a lack of comprehensive operational consumer protection scheme, but also a weak competition framework. Considering that mobile money is one of the central bank's initiatives to achieve financial inclusion,[114] protection of this vulnerable group is vital. There is a need to ensure that once the consumers are locked in, the duopoly held by Airtel Money and *Mpamba* is not exploited to the disadvantage of consumers. According to Simon's theory of bounded rationality, people or organisations will always behave in a way that attempts to obtain a result that best suits their interests.[115] Within the regulatory space, there is a contest to gain a competitive advantage. Those already in the business are keen to monopolise and enlarge their market share while new entrants seek to do so at the least cost.[116] Consumers are, on the other hand, usually only interested in affordability, quality and reliability of service.[117] The government is interested in a stable business environment and tax revenue.[118]

[114] RBM MicroFinance Division (2015).

[115] Herbert A Simon (1972) 'Theories of Bound Rationality' in C B McGuire and Roy Radner (eds) *Decision and Organization: A Volume in Honor of Jacob Marschak* (North-Holland Publishing Company, Amsterdam).

[116] Córdova-Novion and Hanlon (2002), p. 76.

[117] Ibid.

[118] Ibid.

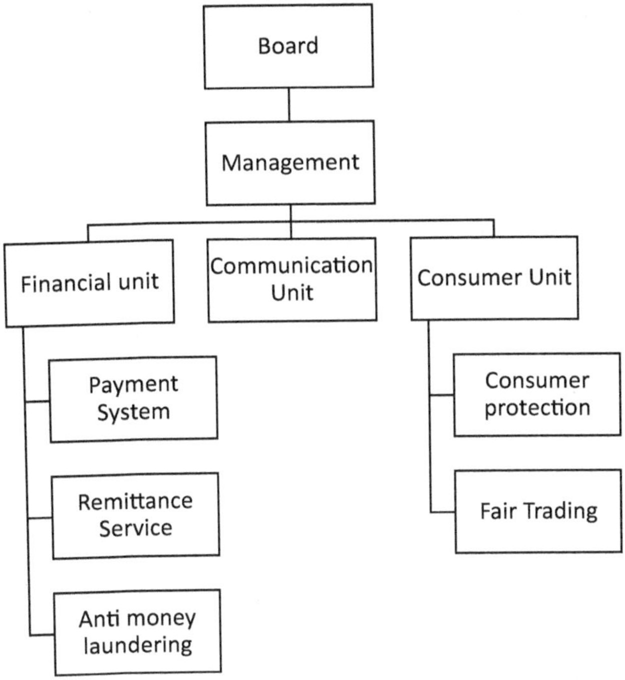


**Fig. 9.1** Organisation structure of single regulator for mobile money (*Source* Author)

An agency that embraces the really responsive regulation approach seems to be best suited to address these competing issues as it can develop coping mechanisms faster and in a much more focused manner. The figure below gives an overview of the organisation structure of how the agency would be structured and how the various units and sub-units would be connected to each other (Fig. 9.1).

Bearing in mind the independence issues highlighted regarding current regulators, the design of the agency ought to deliberately ensure its independence for it to effectively discharge its functions. This would have to start with the board. It is proposed that the board should not be appointed by the country's president. Or if appointed by the president, then it should be via a competitive selection as is the case in Kenya. The board of the agency, as well as the staff contingent, should have, at a minimum, expertise in at least the following:

a. Telecommunications
b. Law
c. Economics
d. Business
e. Finance
f. Anti-money laundering
g. Consumer rights
h. Competition policy

To ensure independence and professionalism, industrial or sector associations should be requested to nominate names of individuals to sit on the board.[119] To avoid changing the process of appointment willy-nilly, this should be entrenched in positive law.[120] The law should ideally provide the framework, which defines the powers, functions and objectives of the agency. This would help the agency to avoid conflicts with the government and guide courts when exercising any review proceedings.[121] In fact, it is submitted, such an independent agency would need the sanction of law to be able to operate within a regulatory environment, which is already populated and which has some regulatory overlaps.[122]

For key staff, where there is a separate board appointed, this may also help in hiring staff based on their expertise. However, to ensure that key staff are shielded from political pressures, it is submitted that the ideal situation would be to stagger their appointments so that they do not coincide with those of politicians.[123] This staggering of appointments or having asymmetric tenures of offices could also apply to the board. Staggered appointments do not only ensure continuity but also minimise interference from politicians. Another way of ensuring the security of tenure of staff would be to have in-built protections so that staff cannot be removed without due process.[124] Entrenching removal procedures in positive law and allowing the legislature to have a say are some of the

[119] Ibid., p. 83.

[120] Quintyn and Taylor (2002), p. 31.

[121] Ibid.

[122] Córdova-Novion and Hanlon (2002), p. 81.

[123] Ibid.

[124] Ibid., p. 82.

ways of ensuring the security of tenure which has a direct correlation with regulatory independence.[125]

### 9.3.2 *Streamlining the Existing Regulators?*

The alternative option is to stay with the status quo but streamline the operational framework of the existing regulators so that they can adequately supervise mobile money. As already seen, most of the current regulators involved with the mobile money either do not enjoy independence have operation inefficiencies or lack enforcement mechanisms. Apart from strengthening the inter-organisational cooperation, there would be a need to streamline each regulator to meet the challenges that a post-financial inclusion regulatory framework would need. Independence and autonomy are crucial elements towards this streamlining.

#### *9.3.2.1 Reserve Bank of Malaŵi*

It has been suggested that instead of setting up an independent agency, the simplest way to achieve independence is to have regulatory authority housed within the central bank.[126] The agency could piggyback on the autonomy that most central banks already possess.[127] Having all financial regulation within one organisation is cost-effective and benefits from economies of scale.[128] Furthermore, central banks usually have within their ranks a range of expertise.[129] However, therein lie the problems. The problems of regulatory independence of the central bank in view of the political context of the country have already been discussed. Apart from the manner of appointment of the governor, there is the real question of just how much can one institution handle and how much can be laid on the shoulders of the governor. The trend has been to merely expand the powers and regulatory field of the central bank with each emerging service. This expansion has not considered that the bank may

[125] Ibid., pp. 84–85.

[126] Quintyn and Taylor (2002), p. 23.

[127] Ibid.

[128] Ibid., p. 25.

[129] Ibid.

not have the expertise to regulate the new sectors that are evolving.[130] The current regulatory structure has 3 divisions[131]:

i. Banks and other financial institutions
ii. Microfinance and Securities Markets
iii. Pension and Insurance Industry.

The bank has recently introduced the financial services regulation directorate, but the main silos remain the 3 blocks listed above. Restructuring of the current financial regulatory structure may involve any one of these 3 possible routes:

a. Stand-alone unified regulator.
b. Triple peaks structure.
c. Imbedded triple peaks structure.

A stand-alone unified regulator implies leaving the regulatory structure as it is but uprooting it out of the central bank and setting it up as a separate agency. It would be akin to setting up one independent unified agency for the whole financial system similar to the defunct Financial Services Authority (FSA) in the UK. Such a unified regulator would oversee the entire financial system, including mobile money. The triple peaks structure would require setting up 3 different regulators based on the existing 3 divisions within the central bank. Such an arrangement would be similar to the post-FSA regulatory environment in the UK, only that there would be triple peaks instead of twin peaks. An imbedded triple peaks structure would be similar in set-up to the triple peaks, but the difference would be that it would remain within the central bank. The governor would cease to be registrar, and each of the functions would have a registrar heading them, but the principal regulator would remain the central bank.

Looking at these 3 options, the stand-alone unified agency is ideal but is unlikely attract political and institutional support to be implemented. The imbedded triple peaks structure is the model that would be the least

[130] Ibid., p. 26.
[131] RBM (2017).

disruptive and least costly and the most likely to be considered. It would require legislative changes, but these would most likely be amendments other than wholesale reformulations. In such a model, mobile money would fall into either (a) banks and other financial institutions or (b) microfinance and securities markets. Although mobile money was at its inception categorised as part of microfinance,[132] it is not.[133] Its significance should require its own structure even if within the central bank. The linkage between mobile money and banks as evidenced by the trust account, which triggers the creation of electronic value, would further support such a proposal. The fourth option, maintaining the status quo, has deliberately not been discussed as it simply perpetuates the current regulatory incoherence.

#### *9.3.2.2 Malaŵi Communications Regulatory Authority (MACRA)*

As noted in the last chapter, the establishment of MACRA followed a World Bank privatisation programme of the communications sector. It was therefore an externally driven process. At the time the governing Act[134] was being enacted, the focus was on the regulation of the companies established after the break-up of the vertically integrated Department of Posts and Telecommunications and reconstitution of the state broadcaster.[135] Regarding mobile network operators, the Act was loud in its silence, not mentioning them at all. The Act's focus was on regulating communication networks and services.[136] Appreciably, at the time the Act was being passed, the mobile industry was still in its infant stage. The result is that by the time the mobile industry had taken root, the Act was generally outdated. The Act has since been repealed and replaced with a 2016 version.

Looking at the repealed Act, it is obvious that in an era of an unbundled communications sector, it achieved most of its intended goals. At the same time, it was ill-suited to address the regulatory problems of a post-unbundled sector. The new Act has expanded the scope of the

[132] RBM (2015), p. 14.

[133] RBM MicroFinance Division (2015).

[134] Communications Act, Malaŵi (Malaŵi, 1998).

[135] Preamble, ibid.

[136] Part III, ibid.

telecommunications sector and made a distinction between the various telecommunication providers. The telecommunications sector in Malaŵi includes fixed telephone networks, mobile network operators and a combination of these.[137] The new Act encourages open access and interconnectivity.[138] It must be noted that even though there is a drive towards network neutrality, interconnectivity and open access, the regulatory issues affecting each of these is different and unique. The new Act, however, has been developed with a view to embrace the current state of developments in the communications sector. With a new law in place, what MACRA needs is to unshackle itself from its self-imposed bondage and break free from political interference. As a regulator, MACRA still suffers from a lack of independence and is not regarded as very transparent and accountable in its dealings.

#### *9.3.2.3 Financial Intelligence Authority (FIA)*

The biggest hurdle that the Financial Intelligence Unit (FIU) was that the law[139] did not give it the power of enforcement. As a regulator, the FIU's powers were reduced to issuing guidelines and recommendations, analysing financial transactions and reporting to prosecuting agencies. Some of the provisions that would have given the FIU greater regulatory powers were removed when the bill was presented in Parliament. In the end, it may be argued that the outcome was a compromised law. In many ways, this would reflect why the FIU, as the body entrusted with the operation of the Act, was not granted enough regulatory powers under it.

Following the passing of a new law, the Financial Crimes Act 2017, the FIU has been renamed to the FIA but nothing much has changed in how the FIA operates. The handicap that existed in the repealed law still haunts the FIA. Although the new Act was said to address mobile money issues,[140] it has not. The regulations that have been promulgated under it have nothing to do with mobile money.[141] Maybe with

[137] Data transmissions channels now include audio-video channels.

[138] Part XVIII, Communications Act (Malaŵi, 2016).

[139] Money Laundering Act (Malaŵi, 2006).

[140] Phiri (2015).

[141] Financial Crimes (Suppression of Terrorist Financing and Proliferation) Regulations, 2017 (Malaŵi Government, 2017).

time, new regulations will emerge. For now, the only notable changes are the change of name from Unit to Authority and enhancing penalties for financial crimes. The lack of real regulatory powers that characterised the FIU remains. The real enforcement will still done by prosecuting agencies outside the FIA. It would seem an opportunity to create special financial crimes prosecuting regime was lost. As a regulator, the FIA still lacks the necessary tools to supervise money laundering issues.

#### *9.3.2.4 Consumer Protection Council*

As noted in the last chapter, the one fundamental handicap with implementing the Consumer Protection Act 2003[142] is a lack of political evidenced by the failure to constitute the Consumer Protection Council, the agency given statutory regulatory powers.[143] Considering that the Act was passed in 2003, this failure would count as more than a mere oversight. In fact, it is submitted, it is a result of a deliberate policy of successive governments[144] to disempower the consumers.[145] The director of CAMA, John Kapito, put it this way:

> The President and the Ministry of Trade have failed to launch a Consumer Protection Council. We need to have a council that will be monitoring the prices of goods hand in hand with the Malaŵi Bureau of Standards.[146]

The rights enshrined in the Act as consumer rights[147] can only be fully realised when they are litigated. It is trite that in an adversarial common

[142] Consumer Protection Act (Malaŵi, 2003).

[143] Section 8(2), ibid.

[144] United Democratic Front (UDF) 1994–2005; Democratic Progressive Party (DPP) 2005–2012; People's Party (PP) 2012–2014; DPP 2014- present.

[145] Elijah Phimbi (2016) 'Kapito Faults APM on "Buy Malawi" Campaign: "Establish Consumer Protection Council"' *Nyasa Times* (18 April 2016), http://www.nyasatimes.com/kapito-faults-apm-on-buy-malawi-campaign-establish-consumer-protection-council/#sthash.DbigqXjh.dpuf. 28 December 2018.

[146] Ibid.

Note: The Malaŵi Bureau of Standards is not a price monitoring agency but a standard setting and regulating agency - Malaŵi Bureau of Standards Act, Act No. 17 of 2012, (Malaŵi, 2012), http://www.rbm.mw/documents/legislation/RBM%20ACT%20JUNE%20 2013.pdf. 10 February 2018.

[147] Section 3 Consumer Protection Act (Malaŵi, 2003).

law-based system as one obtaining in Malaŵi, litigation is not only an expensive undertaking but time-consuming as well. So, although the Act provides for construction of ambiguous contracts in favour of consumers,[148] the only competent authority in the absence of the Consumer Protection Council to do this is courts. Without the council acting as a watchdog, there is nothing to compel suppliers to comply with any rules. The result is that consumers who have unresolved complaints must go to the court for relief.[149] If the council was operational, it would be the one regulating consumer welfare issues.

Where goods are concerned, the Act looks at the Sales of Goods Act[150] for any undertakings such as warranties.[151] The Consumer Protection Council in regulating consumer welfare issues is supposed to work with the Competition and Fair Trading Commission over trade practices.[152] Although the Act does not specifically deal with mobile money consumer issues, the general regulatory consumer framework is still sufficient. Specific issues touching upon mobile money could be part of subsidiary legislation in the form of regulations.[153] Therefore, the main obstacle towards streamlining the Act to regulate mobile money as part of consumer protection would be the fact that the Consumer Protection Council only exists on paper. The council as a body corporate has its membership drawn from representatives of the main stakeholders in consumer welfare issues.[154] So ideally, if appointed, it should be an effective council. However, maybe that would be the reason the council has not been appointed. The fact that the Act attempts to give it independence may have been its downfall and undoing.

[148] Section 8, ibid.

[149] Section 3, ibid.

[150] Sale of Goods Act, Act No. 14 of 1967, Chapter 48:01 of the Laws of Malaŵi (Malaŵi, 1967), http://www.malawilii.org/mw/consolidatedlegislation/4801/48_2001_20sale_20of_20goods_1_docx_12176.pdf. 3 May 2018.

[151] Section 2 Consumer Protection Act (Malaŵi, 2003).

[152] Section 2, ibid.

[153] Section 56, ibid.

[154] Section 10(2), ibid.

#### *9.3.2.5 Competition and Fair Trading Commission*

Unlike the Consumer Protection Council, the Competition and Fair Trading Commission was constituted and is operational as a body corporate.[155] Establishing of the commission, however, took some 14 years after its parent Act was passed.[156] The commission oversees regulating competition and fair-trading.[157] The Consumer Protection Council and Competition and Fair Trading Commission are supposed to cooperate and coordinate with respect to consumer welfare issues, especially where trading practices are involved. Therefore, the failure to constitute the Consumer Protection Council affects both the consumer protection and the fair-trading regimes. The commission is a vibrant agency and has a presence on the Internet[158] and on social media.[159] It uses both outlets to issue press releases as well as alert consumers about fair-trading and competition issues.

Regarding mobile money, the work of the commission is crucial in ensuring that there are real competition and fair-trading practices between the two-major mobile money operators. The two operate as competitors but in what is effectively a two-horse race. As was noted earlier, there is already cooperation between the two services.[160] While cooperation may be useful in growing the service, it is important that the commission be on its guard against collision and cartel pricing. The regulating Act was passed in 1998, and like the repealed Communications Act, it was passed at a time when the country was undergoing rapid privatisation and deregulation. Unlike the latter, the former has mostly stood the test of time. It is therefore submitted that all that would be required is to promulgate regulations dealing with specific services such as mobile money as subsidiary legislation.[161]

155 Section 4 Competition and Fair Trading Act (Malaŵi, 1998).
CFTC (2016b).

156 Competition and Fair Trading Act (Malaŵi, 1998).

157 Section 8(1), ibid.

158 CFTC (2016b).

159 CFTC (2016a) 'Competition and Fair Trading Commission of Malaŵi', https://www.facebook.com/CompetitionAndFairTradingCommissionOfMalawi/. 29 December 2018.

160 Mbekeani (2015).

161 Section 53 Competition and Fair Trading Act (Malaŵi, 1998).

However, although on paper, the law gives the commission independence and autonomy, in the few years it has been operational, the commission is yet to pass the muster. For a start, government fully funds the commission.[162] This presents a problem where the commission must deal with issues where the government has a stake. As was seen in the last chapter, the commission had problems enforcing the law when the government sold the MSB Bank and IndeBank. The sale of MSB Bank was more problematic because it was sold to persons that were deemed to be politically connected or exposed. Government concluded the sale in a manner, which the local press viewed with deep suspicion.[163] The commission itself did not help matters. The law categorically provides for prior approval of mergers and takeovers.[164] The commission only ratified the mergers a year later.[165] Therefore, the first step in making the commission truly independent is to find another way of funding of its activities. This can be through industry levies.

### *9.3.3 Pros and Cons of the Two Options*

So, which option would be the most effective for regulating mobile money in Malaŵi? Thatcher has argued that whether a country adopts the independence agency model or relies on existing regulators depends on whether there exist strong and respected regulators in the first place.[166]

#### *9.3.3.1 Problems with Setting Up an Agency*

Lessons from the delayed enactment of the Payment Systems Act 2016 are that the legislative process is not always smooth. This Act took more than a decade to pass. Drafting a technical piece of legislation to set up an agency would require special expertise and consultation. If this was

[162] CFTC (2016b).

[163] Nankhumwa MP (Minister of Information, 2015).

Soko (2015).

Khunga (2015).

[164] Section 36, Competition and Fair Trading Act (Malaŵi, 1998).

[165] Malonda (2016).

[166] Thatcher (2002), p. 138.

done, resource and expertise would be the premier hurdle that the agency would face. For example, MACRA is principally financed through licence fees.[167] MACRA has been able to attain some financial independence, although it is still politically vulnerable[168] because the communication sector in Malaŵi has several active players. MACRA oversees the postal and courier sectors, the telecommunications sector as well as the broadcasting and frequency allocation sector. In contrast, the agency would rely only on the mobile money issuers. Now, there are only two notable issuers. To overcome this, the agency could expand its supervision to other remittance service providers and bring in more revenue but this would mean going outside its arena into one, which is regulated by the central bank. Considering that most remittance service providers are somewhat linked with banks, this route may be financially problematic. Without adequate funding, an agency cannot discharge its function effectively as an independent regulator.[169] Therefore, the agency would need to be initially or permanently, depending on the model chosen, funded, fully or partially by the state. Would this be a solution that would be politically attractive in a country, which is already struggling with balancing its national budget following the withdrawal of external aid in the form of budgetary support?[170]

Setting up an independent agency requires a completely new bureaucracy and staff contingent to be created which must interact with the central bank and other regulators. Short of poaching staff from competitors, this may not be easily achievable in the short to medium term. Coupled with the lack of financial resources, poaching staff becomes even more difficult. Resource availability is crucial for agency operation.[171] Regulatory expertise is often in short supply, so the agency needs to be competitive to attract such staff.[172] The other alternative would be to have staff seconded from other regulators or the government.[173]

[167] Section 12(1)(a) Communications Act, Malaŵi (Malaŵi, 1998).

[168] Clarke et al. (2003), p. 21.

[169] Córdova-Novion and Hanlon (2002), p. 85.

[170] Collins Mtika (2015) 'Malawi Struggles with End of Western donations' *African Independent* (3 December 2015), http://www.africanindy.com/business/malawi-struggles-with-end-of-western-donations-1435026. 20 December 2018.

[171] Córdova-Novion and Hanlon (2002), p. 82.

[172] Ibid., p. 86.

[173] Ibid.

Whether the agency would be able to compensate such seconded staff or rely on the regulators to pay them would be a key issue. In the case of the latter, it would bring in the question of royalty, allegiance and sustainability. Having its own resources would be key to attracting competent personnel as part of the agency's organisational structure.

Another problem with an agency relates to capture. Outside the government machinery, an agency is more likely to be captured by the industry.[174] To avoid this, the design of the agency must deliberately put in place ways of minimising capture. Transparency in its operations and being accountable to stakeholders is one way of doing this. This would also minimise another fear that an independent agency can become too powerful and too independent and a law unto itself.[175]

#### *9.3.3.2 Advantages of an Agency*

The strongest argument for a separate agency is that mobile money requires a different kind of regulation to that which is currently exercised. As it is dealing with fast-changing technology, it needs a different kind of regulatory expertise. The regulation must not only respond and keep up with these changes but also do so in real time while taking on board all stakeholder interests. The current regulatory architecture lacks this flexibility. The second argument is that it is dealing with the promotion of financial inclusion of people in rural areas. This requires a very different type of understanding and expertise. The regulation needs to involve the people in villages and the urban poor in the regulation process.

Setting up an independent agency allows the regulatory framework to be established from a clean slate and avoid the problems that are affecting other regulators. Such an agency would allow the industry to sidestep any issues related to lack of political will or lack of organisational independence. However, this does not mean that setting up a separate agency automatically grants it independence and political support. The only consolation may be that mobile money, as a service, is not yet politically charged. In fact, looked at as a financial service, it may be argued that it is in the interest of the political establishment to support it as it is a vehicle towards attaining financial inclusion, reducing poverty and

[174] Ibid., p. 87.
[175] Ibid.

fostering development.[176] As noted above, such an agency would need to cooperate with existing regulators, but the difference would be that all regulatory issues surrounding mobile money would be under one roof.

The second advantage of an agency is that it would take some burden off the central bank and its governor. As noted earlier, the central, apart from regulating the financial services,[177] also must fulfil its core duties as a central bank. Its governor is currently the statutory registrar of all financial institutions. For the central bank, and the governor, the truth is that mobile money is not a priority because of its low value and risk.[178] It is more likely to accept weaning it off on this basis. An agency would with time gain specialised expertise in the service and be able to streamline the regulatory framework in response to the industry needs. It would be ideally placed to implement a really responsive regulatory approach.

As has been noted in the discussion of regulators above and in the last chapter, funding is a crucial issue. However, self-funding does not in itself guarantee independence, as the example of MACRA shows. On the other hand, dependency on the government has been seen to affect independence, as is the case with the Competition and Fair Trading Commission. All things being equal, having a source of funding that is outside the government is preferable to ensure independence. However, this exposes the agency to industry capture. To prevent this, the agency could expand its work to cover all forms of electronic or digital money transactions, which are outside the direct supervision of the banking regulator. This would avail to the agency a much broader pool of service providers and allow it to raise enough funding through the levying of fees.

Another advantage is time. Mobile money as a service has been in operation for just a few years. While it is admitted that the existing regulators have developed some level of expertise, the period has not been unduly long to disadvantage a newcomer. Since none of the regulators was created with mobile money in mind, it would be easier for them to cede any regulator's powers they may have been allotted because of the emergence of this service. The fact that it would also be cooperating with other existing regulators would also allow it to tap on any expertise or skills that may have been internalised by these regulators.

176 Chibba (2009), pp. 214–6.

177 Section 8 Financial Services Act (Malaŵi, 2010).

178 Di Castri (2013), p. 25.

#### *9.3.3.3 Problems with Maintaining a Streamlined* Status Quo

The main problem with maintaining the status quo is that it perpetuates the existing incoherent regulatory architecture. The premier problem of not changing the regulatory framework would be that the framework is unlikely to cope or ably regulate in a post-financial inclusion era. With specialisation, divergence rather than convergence is likely to be the end product. Among the regulators, the central bank is likely to emerge as the only true regulator and may have MOUs with the other regulators. This would further amplify the problems that the current financial regulatory architecture faces. With time, 4 tiers of regulators would likely emerge:

a. Tier 1—Reserve Bank of Malaŵi
b. Tier 2—Malaŵi Communications Regulatory Authority
c. Tier 3—Financial Intelligence Authority
d. Tier 3—Competition and Fair Trading Commission FTC and Consumer Protection Council (when it becomes operational).

The second issue that may pose a problem would be that regulatory issues of mobile money are likely to be pushed aside in favour of the core regulatory issues. None of the regulators has mobile money as its core regulatory issue. It does not even feature in any subsidiary legislation yet. For the service itself, maintaining the status quo may have an adverse effect on growth. The mobile money service has been the case of innovation first and regulation later. Comparing the pace of development between legislation and the service, it is self-evident that legislation cannot keep up with innovation. Two issues immediately arise out of this. The first is that the service would promote self-regulation, but based on a model that is on the extreme end of the regulatory continuum. The other is that regulation would try to keep up by using old technology tools to regulate a fast-moving service. The result would be the stifling of growth of the mobile money service, as it gets restricted to what the regulation can address.

#### *9.3.3.4 Advantages of Streamlining the* Status Quo

The current regulatory framework already has several regulators, each regulating a specific aspect of the mobile money service. Therefore, streamlining existing regulators to make them more effective is more economical and easily achievable. For a start, it does not require the setting up of a separate agency and the long-drawn-out process to enact legislation. As has been noted with the case of the Consumer Protection Council, lack of political will can kill off an otherwise good legislative intention. Political buy-in into a new regulatory framework cannot be guaranteed. In any event, each of the existing regulators is already regulating some aspect of the mobile money service. Furthermore, the regulators are beginning to work and cooperate with each other through MOUs. Therefore, dismantling the status quo would mark a loss of any expertise that may have been acquired despite the short existence of the mobile money service.

Fundamentally, maintaining the existing regulatory framework would also save time and cost. While it is appreciated that having multiple regulators presents a regulatory dilemma, maintaining the status quo would be the most cost-effective and least disruptive solution. As was noted in the last chapter, the legislative framework governing the operations of MACRA and the FIA has been review and new Acts enacted. The reviews are meant to streamline the operations of MACRA and the FIA and make them more effective and respond to twenty-first-century needs.[179] While it is admitted that this review is not targeted at incorporating the mobile money service, any issues that the service presents can still be addressed via subsidiary legislation. Subsidiary legislation does not have to go through Parliament. It is usually presented for ratification. As has been noted, Parliament can be a nasty battleground for fighting various political battles.[180]

Mobile money is an emerging and evolving service. It is yet unknown what it will finally morph into. It has demonstrated great potential not only as a remittance service but also as a payment system. So far, the

[179] Chimbe (2015).

Phiri (2015).

[180] The cases of the Anti-Money Launderings Bills for example:

Jai Banda (2007) 'Money Laundering Developments in Malawi, 2004 to 2006' Confronting the Proceeds of Crime in Southern Africa: An Introspection (Institute for Security Studies, Pretoria), https://www.issafrica.org/chapter-1-money-laundering-developments-in-malawi-2004-to-2006. 22 December 2018.

Wisdom Gwede (2016) 'Malawi Parliament Rejects Financial Crimes Bill: Goodall Wants Committee Meet Weekend for Fast-Track Scrutiny' *Nyasa Times*, http://www.nyasatimes.com/malawi-parliament-rejects-financial-crimes-bill-goodall-wants-committee-meet-weekend-fast-track-scrutiny/#sthash.MZ5CaRjv.dpuf. 22 December 2018.

existing regulators have been able to manage the growth of the service. In so doing, they have been able to adapt and keep up with the growth of the service. Therefore, the current regulators may be best placed to understand the growth and development patterns of the service and to ably respond to it.

#### *9.3.3.5 Preferable Option: An Agency Within the Central Bank*

An analysis of the two options above indicates that the agency would be the ideal situation. However, the local context of the Malawi situation needs to be considered. It has already been noted that apart from the central bank and MACRA, the other regulators have operational or financial problems. MACRA also has serious independence problems. The central, which suffers from a lack of true independence from a corporate governance perspective, is nonetheless the one that would largely be deemed autonomous. So, would a third option that benefits from both options be a possible solution? It is submitted that an agency within the central bank may just be the solution to this regulatory quagmire. However, how would such an agency be structured and how would it fit within the existing structure of the central bank?

The proposal is to set up the agency as an autonomous unit within the central bank structure. This would entail that the agency would have its own staff allocation and governance structure. It may also be physically located outside the central bank offices. Setting up an autonomous agency under the central bank structure is not unique. As was discussed in Chapter 1, Malswitch was a unit that was set up by the central bank to operationalise the inter-bank switch. It is still housed in central bank property. Although it operates as a private entity, its shareholders are Malswitch Trust, central bank and the government.[181] Malswitch Trust itself is an entity created by the central bank.[182] Therefore, in the same way that Malswitch was associated with charging with operating inter-bank settlement switch, so would the proposed agency be associated with regulating mobile money. While it would report to the central bank governance structure, it would be autonomous in its operations.

[181] Malswitch (2015) 'About Malswitch' (*Malswitch Ltd*), http://www.malswitch.mw/malswitch/index.php?option=com_content&view=article&id=30&Itemid=140. 14 December 2015.

[182] Ibid.

How exactly this autonomy would manifest itself would depend on how much power the central bank be willing to cede. Any regulatory powers of the agency would be delegated powers, as the central bank remains the sole regulator of the financial services.[183]

The key advantage of this proposal is that it would not require too many resources to make it operational. Currently expertise in mobile money operation seems to be dispersed. The agency would need to attract staff with competent skill sets to complement the skill sets that are already available within the central bank. In Malaŵi, the central bank is still considered an attractive employer, both in terms of remuneration and as a vital training ground. An agency within the central bank does not require a buy-in from other sector regulators since there are already MOUs in operation. What would be required is to streamline these MOUs so that the agency is the point of contact within the central bank where mobile money regulation is involved. Fundamentally, such an agency would only require administrative and organisational changes other than substantive legislative changes. Having an agency with a specific focus on mobile money regulation would also help bring regulatory clarity. It would, for instance, recognise that mobile money is a service in its own right and can no longer be an appendage or riding on the rails of other services. In fact, it may well be that with time, the service may itself become the rails on which other add-on services ride on. An agency would therefore be best suited to manage the evolution of such a service, as it would pay its undivided attention to it.

The argument of creating an autonomous agency, even if within the central bank structure is that compared to in-house government departments; such an agency is generally seen as an improvement.[184] This is because an autonomous agency usually has clearer mandates, roles and objectives and is also subject to much more scrutiny from stakeholders.[185] In fact considering that normally the central bank operates as a closed entity, having the agency as an autonomous unit would allow it to engage stakeholders without the usual bureaucracy that the central bank faces. It is argued that unless the agency was given this room, it would be almost impossible to implement the really responsive regulatory

[183] Section 8 Financial Services Act (Malaŵi, 2010).

[184] Quintyn and Taylor (2002), pp. 3, 5.

[185] Ibid.

approach. Considering that so far, the mobile money regulatory framework in Malaŵi has not been in pursuit of a particular theory,[186] an agency would also help in the formulation of a well-defined theory for mobile money regulation.

Setting up an autonomous agency within the central bank would still require some extra levels of funding. However, this funding does not have to be sourced from the government and risk the agency to state capture. The central bank is by law allowed to impose levies on various regulatory services it provides to the financial service.[187] It is submitted further that instead of just regulating mobile money, the agency could regulate all electronic money transactions. The decision by the central bank to introduce electronic money regulations to repeal mobile money guidelines indicates the direction that it wishes to proceed. The proposed regulations have a provision for levy collection. Instead of the agency, being one that only regulates mobile money, it could easily expand its area of operation and regulate the whole arena of remittances that are done outside the banking framework. The World Bank has put forward the proposal of a single regulatory framework to combine remittances and mobile payments.[188] The argument is that the risks that both raise are similar and would be addressed under the same framework.[189] The World Bank argues that this approach is preferable because:

a. It is much more efficient as it reduces "un-justifiable rents in some parts of the value chain" and ensures that benefits accrue to the end-users.
b. It minimises distortion of competition by laying down a level playing field.

[186] Chimbe (2015).
RBM HQ (2015).
Phiri (2015).
RBM MicroFinance Division (2015).

[187] Section 13 Financial Services Act (Malaŵi, 2010).

[188] Massimo Cirasino and Mariachiara Malaguti (2012) *From Remittances to M-Payments: Understanding "Alternative" Means of Payment Within the Common Framework of Retail Payments System Regulation* (Financial Infrastrucre Series, The World Bank), p. 17, http://siteresources.worldbank.org/EXTPAYMENTREMMITTANCE/Resources/WB2012_Mobile_Payments.pdf. 20 February 2018.

[189] Ibid.

c. There is a uniform approached for consumer protection and regulation is based on risk-based assessment.
d. It empowers the agency as it has powers to supervise an entire payment system.[190]

As has been already stated, the central has recently set up a financial services regulation directorate. Although this directorate deals with all aspects of financial services regulation, and not just mobile money, it is submitted it is evidence that setting up an autonomous agency within the central bank is possible and the recently created directorate may provide lessons on its set-up. The directorate itself would be ill-suited to deal with mobile money in a wholesale manner since, as has been argued throughout in this book, the service is a hybrid one bringing together innovations in finance and telecommunications.

## 9.4 Conclusion

The regulatory framework in Malaŵi has not followed any laid down theory, but command and control seems the prevalent regulatory approach. The evidence, however, suggests that in most jurisdictions, light touch is one most associated with mobile money. There are also notable shifts towards elements of self-regulation based on responsive regulation. However, without a theoretical framework, the shift comes through as having no structural basis. Continuing with the status quo would mean that the regulatory framework continues to evolve without a structured underlying theoretical basis. Formulation of a coherent theory may therefore be the next plan of action in the regulatory evolution. One crucial pre-condition that comes out in this chapter is that before any regulatory framework can be proposed, it is important to delimit the regulatory space arena. In this regard, the regulatory issues, which define the regulatory space, are crucial. Which actors and participants to keep in and which ones to keep out becomes the challenge. However, the task can be depoliticised if the mobile money ecosystem is used as the analytical framework. A coherent regulatory theory would help in getting the various actors on board and ensuring that they all have the same regulatory approach. Really responsive regulation is the approach that would

[190] Ibid., pp. 18–20.

be best suited to regulate mobile money in the post-financial inclusion phase. The approach not only considers the roles of the regulator and the regulated industry, but also considers all the stakeholder interests within the regulatory arena.

This chapter has outlined two possible regulatory options as solutions to the existing incoherent structure, but proposes a third one having advantages of each of the two options as one that leads to an effective regulatory framework. Establishing an autonomous agency within the central bank to coordinate all the regulatory issues of mobile money would require a paradigm shift and different regulatory approach. However, this must be done if the mobile money is to grow into a service with established and clear rules of operation. Continuing with the status quo, it is submitted is likely to prove frustrating for all parties involved. It may appear to be the easier and less stressful route, but is hardly the most effective one in the end. The proposal to have an autonomous agency is not only one to bring clarity to the regulatory arena but also begin the conversation of having a defining regulatory theory of mobile money in Malaŵi. Changing from the status quo and moving into a new direction are bound to have its challenges. However, this chapter has argued that these challenges can be overcome. So, what does the future hold for mobile money service? Well, the truth is that no one really knows. However, having a coherent regulatory framework is a step towards a brighter future.

## References


Andrew Campbell (1997) 'Stakeholders: The Case in Favour' 30 (3) *Long Range Planning* 446, http://www.sciencedirect.com/science/article/pii/S0024630197000034. 16 February 2018.

Anon (2010) 'Consumers Demonstrate Over High Bank Rates in Malawi' (21 April 2010), http://maravi.blogspot.co.uk/2010/04/nyasatimes-consumers-demonstrate-over.html. 11 March 2014.

Anon (2013) 'Malawian Snapshot: 2013 Quarter 2' (KPMG, Malawi), https://www.kpmg.com/Africa/en/KPMG-in-Africa/Documents/2013%20African%20Country%20Reports/KPMG_Malawi%202013Q2.pdf. 13 September 2018.

Beth Jenkins (2008) 'Developing Mobile Money Ecosystems' (Washington, DC: International Finance Corporation and Harvard Kennedy School), http://ww.gsma.com/mobilefordevelopment/wp-content/uploads/2012/06/report_30_mobilemoney.pdf. 13 December 2018.

Bill Maurer (2012) 'Regulation as Retrospective Ethnography: Mobile Money and the Arts of Cash' 27 (2) *Banking and Finance Law Review* 299, http://www.imtfi.uci.edu/files/docs/2012/bankingfinance_law_review_27.2_maurer.pdf. 15 December 2018.

CAMA (2016) 'Consumers Association of Malawi', https://www.facebook.com/Consumers-Association-of-Malawi-104178233025786/. 20 December 2018.

César Córdova-Novion and Deirdre Hanlon (2002) 'Regulatory Governance: Improving the Institutional Basis for Sectoral Regulators' 2 (3) *OECD Journal on Budgeting*, https://www.oecd.org/gov/budgeting/43505850.pdf. 15 February 2018.

CFTC (2016a) 'Competition and Fair Trading Commission of Malaŵi', https://www.facebook.com/CompetitionAndFairTradingCommissionOfMalawi/. 29 December 2018.

CFTC (2016b) 'Competition and Fair Trading Commission (Malaŵi)—History' *Competition and Fair Trading Commission*, http://www.cftc.mw/index.php/about-us/history.html. 29 December 2018.

Charlotte Wezi Malonda (2016) *Approval of the Merger Between FDH Financial Holdings and Malaŵi Savings Bank (MSB)* (Competition and Fair Trading Commission 2016).

Colin Scott (2001) 'Analysing Regulatory Space: Fragmented Resources and Institutional Design' *Public Law* 329, http://researchrepository.ucd.ie/bitstream/handle/10197/6785/AnalysingRegSpace.pdf?sequence=2. 1 December 2018.

Colin Scott (2017) 'The Regulatory State and Beyond' in Peter Drahos (ed) *Regulatory Theory: Foundations and Applications* (Australian National University Press, Canberra).

Collins Mtika (2015) 'Malawi Struggles with End of Western Donations' *African Independent* (3 December 2015), http://www.africanindy.com/business/malawi-struggles-with-end-of-western-donations-1435026. 20 December 2018.

Communications Act, Malaŵi (Malaŵi, 1998).

Communications Act (Malaŵi, 2016).

Competition and Fair Trading Act (Malaŵi, 1998).

Consumer Protection Act (Malaŵi, 2003).

Constitution of the Republic of Malaŵi (1994), http://www.malawi.gov.mw/images/Publications/act/Constitution%20of%20Malawi.pdf. 21 December 2016.

Dalvinder Singh (2007) *Banking Regulation of UK and US Financial Markets* (Ashgate Publishing, Aldershot, Hampshire).

David Porteous (2006) *The Enabling Environment for Mobile Banking in Africa* (Report Commissioned by Department for International Development [DFID], Boston), http://bankablefrontier.com/wp-ontent/uploads/documents/ee.mobil_.banking.report.v3.1.pdf. 14 September 2018.

Edward R Freeman (1984) 'Stakeholder Theory of the Modern Corporation' in *General Issues in Business Ethics* (HarperCollins, New York).
Electronic Transactions and Cybersecurity Act (Malaŵi, 2016).
Elijah Phimbi (2016) 'Kapito Faults APM on "Buy Malawi" Campaign: "Establish Consumer Protection Council"' *Nyasa Times* (18 April 2016), http://www.nyasatimes.com/kapito-faults-apm-on-buy-malawi-campaign-establish-consumer-protection-council/#sthash.DbigqXjh.dpuf. 28 December 2018.
Eva Hüpkes, Marc Quintyn and Michael W Taylor (2006) 'Accountability Arrangements for Financial Sector Regulators' 39 *IMF Economic Issues*, https://www.imf.org/external/pubs/ft/issues/issues39/ei39.pdf. 27 February 2018.
Financial Crimes Act (Malaŵi, 2017).
Financial Crimes (Suppression of Terrorist Financing and Proliferation) Regulations, 2017 (Malaŵi Government, 2017).
Financial Services Act (Malaŵi, 2010).
FOSL (2017) 'Financial Ombudsman Service' (*Financial Ombudsman Service Limited*), http://www.financial-ombudsman.org.uk/. 13 March 2018.
George J Stigler (1971) 'The Theory of Economic Regulation' *The Bell Journal of Economics and Management Science* 3, http://hsecon.tripod.com/stigler-regulation.pdf. 1 February 2018.
George RG Clarke, Frew A Gebreab and Henry R Mgombelo (2003) *Telecommunications Reform in Malawi* (Policy Research Working Papers, The World Bank), http://dx.doi.org/10.1596/1813-9450-3036. 2 December 2018.
Grace Khombe (2014) 'CAMA to Name and Shame Traders on Receipt Guarantee and Warranty' *Zodiak Online* (Lilongwe), http://zodiakmalawi.com/top-stories/cama-to-name-and-shame-traders-on-receipt-guarantee-and-waranty. 14 November 2018.
Guidelines for Mobile Payment Systems (Malaŵi, 2011).
Happy Soko (2015) 'Malaŵi Government Drilled Over MSB Sale' *Malaŵi24* (18 March 2015), http://allafrica.com/stories/201503190408.html. 18 November 2018.
Herbert A Simon (1972) 'Theories of Bound Rationality' in C B McGuire and Roy Radner (eds) *Decision and Organization: A Volume in Honor of Jacob Marschak* (North-Holland Publishing Company, Amsterdam).
Ian Ayres I and John Braithwaite (1992) Responsive Regulation: Transcending the Deregulation Debate (Oxford University Press, Oxford).
*In the Matter of Citizen Insurance Company Limited Ex parte The Registrar of Financial Services* Commercial Case No. 55 of 2011 HC (Malaŵi), http://www.malawilii.org/mw/judgment/high-court-commercial-division/2012/5/. 27 February 2018.
Interview at Reserve Bank of Malaŵi (RBM) MicroFinance Division on 19 August 2015.
Interview at Reserve Bank of Malaŵi Headquarters (RBM HQ) on 6 August 2015.

Interview with Atuweni Tupochire Phiri, Director, Financial Intelligence Unit (FIU) (7 August 2015).

Interview with Bigboy Mkoloma Product and Development Manager, Airtel Money (7 August 2015).

Interview with Thokozani Chimbe Deputy Director—Legal (Consumer Affairs); Malaŵi Communications Regulatory Authority (3 August 2015).

Interview with Webster Mbekeani Head, Mobile Money Division, TNM (20 August 2015).

Jai Banda (2007) 'Money Laundering Developments in Malawi, 2004 to 2006' Confronting the Proceeds of Crime in Southern Africa: An Introspection (Institute for Security Studies, Pretoria), https://www.issafrica.org/chapter-1-money-laundering-developments-in-malawi-2004-to-2006. 22 December 2018.

John Argenti (1997) 'Stakeholders: the Case Against' 30 (3) *Long Range Planning* 442, http://www.sciencedirect.com/science/article/pii/S0024630197000046. 16 February 2018.

José Gabriel Palma (2012) 'How the Full Opening of the Capital Account to Highly Liquid Financial Markets Led Latin America to Two and a Half Cycles of "Mania, Panic and Crash"' *Cambridge Working Papers in Economics 1201*, http://www.econ.cam.ac.uk/dae/repec/cam/pdf/cwpe1201.pdf. 19 May 2014.

Karine Nyborg (2000) 'Homo economicus and homo politicus: Interpretation and Aggregation of Environmental Values' 42 (3) *Journal of Economic Behavior & Organization* 305, http://www.sciencedirect.com/science/article/pii/S0167268100000913. 21 December 2018.

Kondwani Nankhumwa MP (Minister of Information) (2015) *Statement on the Sale of MSB and IndeBank* (State House Residences Malaŵi 2015).

Malaŵi Bureau of Standards Act, Act No. 17 of 2012 (Malaŵi, 2012), http://www.rbm.mw/documents/legislation/RBM%20ACT%20JUNE%202013.pdf. 10 February 2018.

Malswitch (2015) 'About Malswitch' (Malswitch Ltd), http://www.malswitch.mw/malswitch/index.php?option=com_content&view=article&id=30&Itemid=140. 14 December 2015.

Marc Quintyn and Michael W Taylor (2002) *Regulatory and Supervisory Independence and Financial Stability* (International Monetary Fund, Washington, DC), https://www.imf.org/external/pubs/ft/wp/2002/wp0246.pdf. 1 February 2018.

Mark Thatcher (2002) 'Delegation to Independent Regulatory Agencies: Pressures, Functions and Contextual Mediation' 25 (1) *West European Politics* 125, http://0-dx.doi.org.pugwash.lib.warwick.ac.uk/10.1080/713601588. 16 February 2018.

Massimo Cirasino and Mariachiara Malaguti (2012) *From Remittances to M-Payments: Understanding "Alternative" Means of Payment Within the Common Framework of Retail Payments System Regulation* (Financial Infrastructure Series, The World

Bank), http://siteresources.worldbank.org/EXTPAYMENTREMMITTANCE/Resources/WB2012_Mobile_Payments.pdf. 20 February 2018.

Matthew D McCubbins, Roger G Noll and Barry R Weingast (1989) 'Structure and Process, Politics and Policy: Administrative Arrangements and the Political Control of Agencies' 75 *Virginia Law Review* 431, http://scholarship.law.duke.edu/cgi/viewcontent.cgi?article=5950&context=faculty_scholarship. 20 February 2018.

Mbane Ngwira (2017) Spokesperson, Reserve Bank of Malaŵi (10 March 2017) (personal communication).

Michael Chibba (2009) 'Financial Inclusion, Poverty Reduction and the Millennium Development Goals' 21 (2) *The European Journal of Development Research* 213, https://doi.org/10.1057/ejdr.2008.17. 20 April 2018.

Michael U Klein and Colin Mayer (2011) *Mobile Banking and Financial Inclusion: The Regulatory Lessons* (Policy Research Working Paper, The World Bank), http://documents.worldbank.org/curated/en/docsearch/document-type/620265. 14 February 2018.

Money Laundering Proceeds of Serious Crime and Terrorist Financing Act, Act No. 11 of 2006, http://www.rbm.mw/documents/pisu/Money%20Laundering%20Act%202006.pdf. 31 March 2018.

NSO (2009) *2008 Population and Housing Census* (Malawi Government [National Statistics Office], Zomba), http://www.mw.one.un.org/wp-content/uploads/2014/04/Malawi-Population-and-Housing-Census-Preliminary-Report-2008.pdf. 29 April 2018.

Ombudsman Act, Act No. 17 of 1996, Chapter 3:07 of the Laws of Malaŵi (Malaŵi, 1996), http://www.africanchildforum.org/clr/Legislation%20Per%20Country/Malawi/malawi_ombudsman_1996_en.pdf. 27 February 2018.

Payment Systems Act (Malaŵi, 2016).

Public Law Project (2013) *An Introduction to Judicial Review* (Public Law Project, London).

RBM (2013) *National Payment Systems Annual Report 2012* (Reserve Bank of Malawi), http://www.rbm.mw/documents/payment_systems/payment%20systems%20annual%20report%202012.pdf. 10 February 2014.

RBM (2015) *Financial and Economic Review* (Reserve Bank of Malawi), https://www.rbm.mw/Home/GetContentFile?ContentID=7492. 14 December 2018.

RBM (2017) *Monthly National Payments System Report: January 2017* (Reserve Bank of Malaŵi), https://www.rbm.mw/PaymentSystems/GetContentFile/?ContentID=12203. 10 March 2018.

Robert Phillips (2003) 'Stakeholder Theory and Organizational Dogma' in Robert Phillips (ed) *Stakeholder Theory and Organizational Ethics* (Berrett-Koehler Publishers, San Francisco, CA).

Robert Baldwin and Julia Black (2008) 'Really Responsive Regulation' 71 (1) *The Modern Law Review* 59, http://onlinelibrary.wiley.com/doi/10.1111/j.1468-2230.2008.00681.x/full. 18 November 2018.

Sale of Goods Act, Act No. 14 of 1967, Chapter 48:01 of the Laws of Malaŵi (Malaŵi, 1967), http://www.malawilii.org/mw/consolidatedlegislation/4801/48_2001_20sale_20of_20goods_1_docx_12176.pdf. 3 May 2018.

Simon L Lelieveldt (1996) 'How to Regulate Electronic Cash: An Overview of Regulatory Issues and Strategies' 46 *Am UL Rev* 1163, http://heinonline.org/hol-cgi-bin/get_pdf.cgi?handle=hein.journals/aulr46&section=39. 17 March 2018.

Simone Di Castri (2013) *Mobile Money: Enabling Regulatory Solutions* (GSMA, London), http://www.gsma.com/publicpolicy/wp-content/uploads/2013/02/GSMA2013_Report_Mobilelectronicmoney-EnablingRegulatorySolutions.pdf. 20 February 2018.

Suzgo Khunga (2015) 'MSB Sale Fallout, Goes at K9.5 Billion' *The Nation* (3 July 2015), http://mwnation.com/msb-sale-fallout-goes-at-k9-5-billion/. 18 November 2018.

*Three Rivers DC v Bank of England* (2001) 2 All ER 513 HOL, https://www.publications.parliament.uk/pa/ld199900/ldjudgmt/jd000518/rivers-1.htm. 27 February 2018.

Timothy Lyman (2016) 'Regulation and Supervision' (*CGAP*), http://www.cgap.org/topics/regulation-and-supervision. 21 May 2018.

Tonny K Omwansa (2009) 'M-PESA: Progress and Prospects' *Innovations* 107, https://profiles.uonbi.ac.ke/tomwansa/files/innov-gsma-omwansa.pdf. 1 December 2018.

Venkatesen Mauree and Gaurav Kohli (2013) *The Mobile Money Revolution—Part 2: Financial Inclusion Enabler* (ITUT Technology Watch, International Telecommunications Union), https://www.itu.int/dms_pub/itu-t/oth/23/01/T23010000200002PDFE.pdf. 1 May 2018.

Vincent P. Polizatto (1992) 'Prudential Regulation and Banking Supervision' in Dimitri Vittas (ed) *Financial Regulation: Changing the Rules of the Game* (The World Bank, Washington, DC).

Wisdom Gwede (2016) 'Malawi Parliament Rejects Financial Crimes Bill: Goodall Wants Committee Meet Weekend for Fast-Track Scrutiny' *Nyasa Times*, http://www.nyasatimes.com/malawi-parliament-rejects-financial-crimes-bill-goodall-wants-committee-meet-weekend-fast-track-scrutiny/#sthash.MZ5CaRjv.dpuf. 22 December 2018.

CHAPTER 10

# Conclusions

## 10.1 Introduction

Mobile money has a fertile ground in Africa because of the logistical challenges that the continent faces. Despite most of its population being financially excluded, there is migration of labour from the rural areas and these migrants need to regularly remit money home.[1] Mobile money, for now, has proved to be the most cost-effective and convenient service of meeting this need. Through mobile money, millions of Africans are slowly but surely moving from a cash-only economy towards one that is linked to the formal system.[2] Furthermore, its ability to operate independently and outside the banking system has given it a unique advantage.[3] Another advantage is that with mobile money, processes are instantaneous, offering real-time settlement.[4] Compared to the banking system which typically takes a days to clear an instrument, mobile money offers real-time settlement.

As it stands, the regulation of mobile money is in a state of flux. The pre-financial inclusion phase has shown that the unique and distinctive characteristics of mobile money have not been fully appreciated by the

[1] Heyer and Mas (2009), p. 18.

[2] Di Castri (2013), p. 34.

[3] Klein and Mayer (2011), p. 27.

[4] Ibid., p. 14.



S. Madise, *The Regulation of Mobile Money*, Palgrave Macmillan Studies in Banking and Financial Institutions,
https://doi.org/10.1007/978-3-030-13831-8_10

regulators.[5] Mobile money is still largely regulated first and foremost as a financial service and then secondly as a telecommunication service. Two separate regulators are charged with supervising these distinct services. While other regulators such as the Financial Intelligence Authority, Competition and Fair Trading Commission and Consumer Protection Council are ancillary to the regulation of mobile money, they nevertheless play a vital role. While the communication and financial regulation are characterised by command and control, mobile money is largely regulated through the light-touch approach.[6] However, for how long can this be sustained? What happens when mobile money becomes fully integrated into the national payment system? How sustainable would a divergent approach be? Reforms in both the telecommunications and financial sector indicate a shift towards a responsive regulatory approach.[7]

How can one sum up mobile money? From a function viewpoint, it can be said that mobile money is a financial service comprising a payment system and a remittance service. It is based on a telecommunications network but it is not a telecommunications service. It targets the unbanked and people in rural areas who require consumer protection. It currently poses a low-systemic risk but requires fairness in the business conduct of the mobile money issuers. All these elements present different regulatory issues and challenges. This book has advocated for a convergent framework based on elements of self-regulation. It is convergent because it aims to bring in both elements of telecommunications and financial regulation. In such an approach, really responsive regulation seems to be the most preferable. Having analysed available options for regulation of mobile money in a post-financial inclusion phase, the preference has been to set up an autonomous agency, which should not only regulate mobile money but also other non-bank remittances. Establishing such an agency has its challenges. This concluding chapter, therefore, looks at these challenges as well as some of the regulator issues that a post-financial inclusion phase may pose on mobile money.

[5] Di Castri (2013), p. 34.

[6] Skinner (2015).

[7] Chimbe (2015), RBM HQ (2015).

## 10.2 Challenges of Setting Up an Autonomous Agency

The book has advocated for an autonomous agency to supervise not only mobile money but all non-bank-based remittances. Fears of such an agency becoming too independent and too powerful are real. However, this can be mitigated by including in the design of the regulatory framework express provisions of transparency and accountability.[8] The biggest problem in setting up the agency would be in having the other regulators cede their power. The Reserve Bank of Malaŵi has been the main financial regulator since the country's independence.[9] Although there have been changes in the law over time, the end-effect has been the consolidation of regulatory authority in the central bank and its governor. Although mobile money and non-bank remittances are not core banking businesses, allowing a third party to supervise these would be a challenge that would need to be overcome. The biggest incentive which would allow the central bank to cede these powers is that it is already overburdened.

The same problem would also arise from the Malaŵi Communications Regulatory Authority (MACRA). Unlike the central bank, MACRA is highly politicised. As such, any decision would not only be subject to policy considerations, but may be subject to partisan political interests as well. It may well be that in such a case; it would all come down to the question of money. MACRA is perceived to be a 'cash-cow' for politicians who are in government.[10] If detaching the mobile money component would mean the loss of revenue, this may be resisted. However, if the parent telecommunication operators were still within the clutches of MACRA, it may be possible to let go. It is submitted that so far, it is the telecommunications sector that provides the major source of funding to MACRA. Therefore, there may be hope yet.

Another issue that would need to be addressed is that raised in the previous chapter, lack of enforcement mechanisms. This may require legislative amendments if the agency were to be given prosecutorial powers.

[8] Quintyn and Taylor (2002), p. 29.

[9] Section 4(*h*) Financial Crimes Act (Malaŵi, 2017).

[10] James Nthondo (2016) 'Exclusive: New Cashgate in Malawi, How Macra Funds Are Abused' *Nyasa Times* (12 September 2016), http://www.nyasatimes.com/exclusive-new-cashgate-malawi-macra-funds-abused/#sthash.efL9KDSw.dpuf. 27 February 2018.

Alternatively, the agency could establish MOUs with prosecuting agencies. However, where enforcement does not require use of penal law, this may be achieved either through administrative arrangements or through subsidiary legislation. Ensuring that the agency has powers to enforce its regulations is, therefore, of paramount importance.

Resources would also be a challenge. However, a financing model based on MACRA or the technical, entrepreneurial and vocational education and training authority (TEVETA)[11] models could be a solution. TEVETA, like MACRA, relies on levies to fund its operations without resorting to state support. It regulates quality technical, entrepreneurial and vocational education and training.[12] Apart from running the agency, the levy funds industry training programmes.[13] One way of broadening the revenue stream would be to allow greater competition and attract new players into the market. The major problem with the mobile money service is that it rides on the telecommunication backbone, and already the two dominant mobile network operators have a service each. Non-bank remittances are, however, broader and can use any telecommunication platform.

As the proposal situates the agency within the central bank, the agency may have access to seed funds to start operations from the bank. Since setting it up only requires administrative changes, legislative bottlenecks may be avoided. An agency within the central bank is best suited to handle any risk posed should m-mobile become systemically important. Establishing the agency would not mean the solution to all regulation issues and problems. New and emerging issues would still need to be resolved. However, it is submitted, an autonomous agency is best suited to address these challenges than remaining with the status quo. The agency would also take an active role in shaping the legal framework affecting mobile money. The next section highlights some regulatory issues the post-financial inclusion phase may face.

[11]Established under the Technical, Entrepreneurial and Vocational Education and Training Act, 1999 (Act No. 6 of 1999).

[12]TEVETA (2017) 'About Us' (Technical, Entrepreneurial and Vocational Education and Training [TEVET] Authority), http://www.teveta.mw/index.php/about-us. 27 February 2018.

[13]Jabulani Kamngoya (2015) 'Teveta to Harmonise Vocational Curricula and Certification' (1 June 2015), http://allafrica.com/stories/201506011690.html. 27 February 2018.

## 10.3 Post-financial Inclusion Regulatory Issues

### *10.3.1 Network and Service Interoperability*

The challenge is whether to force interoperability and interconnectivity through regulation or allow the market to define itself.[14] Interoperability, when achieved, has a way of reducing costs as well as broadening the payment system platform. As was noted in Chapter 7, the central bank through the Mobile Payment Systems Guidelines 2011 has encouraged this, and now the Communications Act encourages open access and network neutrality.[15] Interoperability is on two levels: network interoperability and mobile money service interoperability. For the former, it requires a regulatory regime that makes it easy for customers to change networks while keeping their own numbers. Despite the provisions in the Communications Act 2016 and the Mobile Payment Systems Guidelines 2011, currently in Malaŵi, the two major mobile network operators do not allow customers to retain their numbers. Airtel has numbers that are unique in that they start with 09XXX while TNM has numbers that start with 08XXX.[16] In contrast, in the UK, one can change networks while keeping their number.[17] My own experience is that I was able to change 3 different networks while retaining my number while resident in England. This meant I was not locked-in by one telco based on the telephone number. There are no plans by either network to change the status quo.[18] It would, therefore, fall upon the communications regulator to impose any interoperability rules. Interoperability between issuers should be encouraged.[19] For now, the regulator is keener to have a technology-neutral network than to implement such an interoperable regime.[20] Such standards would mainly focus on ensuring that the service operates on a single protocol for communication, authentication and

[14] Klein and Mayer (2011), p. 22.

[15] Part XVIII, Communications Act (Malaŵi, 2016).

[16] The author's experience in Malaŵi.

[17] Authors personal experience.

[18] Mkoloma (2015), Mbekeani (2015)

[19] Porteous (2006), p. 48.

[20] Chimbe (2015).

verification.[21] It is important, however, to ensure that any imposition of interoperability rules does not lead to high costs and disinvestment.[22]

Recent developments indicated that the two mobile money providers have now reached an interoperability agreement. This does not mean that users of either Airtel Money or *Mpamba* transact as if they were using one service. However, the services have provided a wallet to wallet arrangement where users can send money to each other across networks and the money can be accessed via mobile money. However, because the exchange is not between wallets per se, it is still not a seamless transfers and transactions between wallets of either mobile money service. The problem with this may be due to the very nature of the mobile money service as it is not a stand-alone service, but rides on the rail of the telecommunication service. With the telecommunications provider not providing a seamless interoperability platform yet, wallet to wallet synchronisation is likely to take time. True interoperability would require not only synergy in the bedrock services, but also uniformity in the pricing structure of not only the mobile money service, but the data charges of the telecommunication service as well. Another option would be for the regulator to develop a revenue distribution formula. But this is not as simple as it sounds. Litigation, which the two mobile network operators undertook against MACRA regarding the latter's decision to implement a sender keep all regime and cap interconnection charges is a case in point. The matter having started in 2010 was only decided by the Supreme Court in 2015.[23] Interoperability would also require that mobile network operators and mobile money issuers harmonise their know your customer requirements.[24] The Financial Intelligence Authority as the local body mandated to implement the Financial Action Task Force (FATF) Recommendations could help in formulating such rules bearing in mind the low risk posed by mobile money.[25] MACRA

[21] Klein and Mayer (2011), p. 22.

[22] Ibid., p. 26.

[23] *The State v Malaŵi Communications Regulatory Authority (MACRA) Ex Parte TNM and Airtel*, Misc. Civil Cause No. 4 of 2010.

Chikondi Chiyembekeza (2015) 'Court Rebuffs TNM, Airtel Over MACRA Decision' *The Nation* (1 April 2015), http://mwnation.com/court-rebuffs-tnm-airtel-over-macra-decision/. 22 February 2018.

[24] Di Castri (2013), p. 32.

[25] Interpretive Note to recommendation 10 (Customer Due Diligence) para 16: FATF (2012), p. 65.

implementation of the mandatory scheme for compulsory registration of mobile numbers, as is the case of RICA in South Africa,[26] is one way that could help. The implementation of the national identification project that Malaŵi is currently undertaking[27] is another tool for ensuring that once a customer satisfies the know your customer requirements; there is really no reason they cannot take their number across networks.

### *10.3.2 Allowing Competition*

Another regulatory issue that is related to the issue of interoperability is the question of consumer lock-in. Competition naturally enhances efficiency among market participants.[28] This is not only a competition but also a consumer protection issue. While the mobile money services are growing and recruiting, this may not be a problem. However, after they have attained their optimal levels, the services providers may resort to tendencies that lock-in their customer bases.[29] The regulators overseeing consumer protection and competition may, therefore, need to provide oversight to prevent this. Where there is an autonomous agency as proposed, collaboration with these regulators would be key. Arguably, the mobile network operators need to recover their investment but this must be balanced against consumer exploitation. Locking out not only affects consumers but also prevents new entrants.[30] Freedom of choice as well as the ability to change networks without great economic cost or loss is one way of preventing ensuring anti-competitive behaviour.[31] Allowing competition also means dealing with arrangements where mobile money issuers enter exclusive arrangements with third parties.[32] While such arrangements may be vital at the initial stage, they may prevent other newcomers to establish networks. It also leads to limited consumer choice.[33] It further makes it difficult for newcomers to break into

[26] Jentzsch (2012), p. 611.

[27] Malaŵi Government (2015).

[28] Herring and Santomero (2000), p. 56.

[29] Porteous (2006), p. 35.

[30] Ibid.

[31] Ibid.

[32] Di Castri (2013), p. 28.

[33] Ibid.

the market. The mobile money issuer that had the first-mover advantage, if allowed to maintain third-party exclusivity can easily dominate and monopolise the market.[34]

### *10.3.3 Collaboration*

Collaboration between mobile money issuers and other stakeholders within and outside the mobile money ecosystem is vital for the growth of the service. Airtel Money has collaborated with FDH Bank to start offering cross-border remittance services.[35] Both issuers are also looking at products that may link mobile money to provisions of microfinance loans.[36] In Kenya, *M-Pesa* teamed up with Equity Bank to provide a new product called *M-Kesho.*[37] *M-Kesho* allows payment of interest on saving accounts and provision of loans. *M-Pesa* is the channel through which the payments are made.[38] Mas referred to this collaboration as a "holy alliance".[39] *M-Kesho* not only allows the payment of interest but also interoperability between *M-Kesho* and *M-Pesa* accounts.[40] The collaboration was launched as an exclusive one in 2010 and was supposed to last for a year.[41] Eight years on, the marriage is still on.[42] Apart from *M-Kesho*, other products that have been launched in the footsteps of *M-Pesa* are:

[34] Ibid.

[35] Mkoloma (2015).

[36] Ibid., Mbekeani (2015).

[37] Klein and Mayer (2011), p. 27.

[38] Ibid.

[39] Ignacio Mas (2010) 'M-KESHO in Kenya' (GSMA) (27 May 2010), http://www.gsma.com/mobilefordevelopment/programme/mobilelectronicmoney/m-kesho-in-kenya. 23 February 2018.

[40] Robert Cull (2010) 'M-PESA: Mobile Payments, Improved Lives for Kenyans' (The World Bank), http://econ.worldbank.org/external/default/main?theSitePK=469382&contentMDK=22594763&menuPK=476752&pagePK=64165401&piPK=64165026. 23 February 2018.

[41] Ibid.

[42] EBL (2017) 'M-Kesho' (Equity Bank Limited), http://ke.equitybankgroup.com/business/products/ways-to-bank/mobile-banking/m-kesho. 23 February 2018.

- *M-Shwari*: like *M-Kesho*, offered in collaboration with the Commercial bank of Kenya.[43]
- *M-Hela*: an international remittance service for Kenyans living in Europe to send money home to either *M-Pesa* or Airtel Money accounts.[44]
- *M-Paisa*: launched in Afghanistan. It allows users to receive remittances from Western Union globally.[45] In line with the Afghan market, its market slogan is: *It's Mobile Hawala*.[46]
- Orange Money which is a collaboration between Equity Bank and the mobile network operator Orange, allowing customers to access their bank using the mobile phone platform.[47]
- Agreement between Airtel Money and Equity bank to allow customers who own both accounts to transact between accounts and withdraw cash at Equity bank's ATMs.[48]

It would seem that both *Mpamba* and Airtel Money are planning to go a similar route of collaborating with banks and other remittance services.[49] Collaboration is essential because mobile money based on the telco-model is precluded from intermediating on their funds.[50] This would be a better approach than competing with banks. However, as *Mpamba*'s Mbekeani said, there needs to be innovation on both sides to maximise on the opportunity that both services provide instead of competing.[51] In summing up the regulatory dilemma, that has faced mobile money, Hayat says,

[43] Aptantech (2013a) 'M-Pesa & Its "OffSpring"—A Look at 5 "M" Payments Solutions Developed after M-Pesa', http://aptantech.com/2013/08/m-pesa-its-offsprings-a-look-at-5-m-payments-solutions-developed-after-m-pesa/. 23 February 2018.

[44] Ibid.

[45] Ibid.

[46] Ibid.

[47] Aptantech (2013b) 'What Does Equity's Deal with Bharti's Airtel Money Mean for Orange Money and Safaricom's M-Kesho?', http://aptantech.com/2013/07/what-does-equitys-deal-with-bhartis-airtel-money-mean-for-orangelectronicmoney-and-safaricoms-m-kesho/. 23 February 2018.

[48] Ibid.

[49] Although this was not expressly said, it was inferred from the discussion: Mkoloma (2015), Mbekeani (2015).

[50] Di Castri (2013), p. 15.

[51] Mbekeani (2015).

> Mobile payments [are not] a turf war between the financial and telecommunication sectors but as a complement to existing financial services. Mobile network operators have in a very short span of time reached all parts of the countries they operate in, established strong nationwide distribution systems, and excelled in handling micro-payments worth millions.... In mobile payments, the question is not who is keeping the money but who is dealing with the customer... The choice is between taking the customer to the bank ... or taking the bank counter to the customer, wherever he is.[52]

That there is a turf war is a fact. The resistance that Airtel had from the banks to introduce a mobile money is a testimony to this.[53] However, should there be really a war? As Sultana says, maybe it is time banks got "back to basics and focus on making money through financial intermediation rather than through transaction fees".[54] This demarcation would be a huge step in diffusing tension between mobile money, which is essentially transaction-based and banking. It would also clear the way for smoother collaboration between the mobile money and banking services. The underlying phenomena behind mobile money are that of money and digital communications convergence. On the other hand, for most jurisdictions, including Malaŵi, regulation of banking, payments and telecommunications is done on a stand-alone basis.[55] While traditional banking is premised on the customer coming to the bank, mobile money has been emphatic that its approach is to take the service to the customer, and the mobile phone is the ideal conduit for achieving this. However, it would be foolhardy to ignore the real fears that bank regulators have regarding mobile money and any regulatory framework must address such fears.[56] Consumer protection, financial stability and integrity are, therefore, key regulatory cornerstones to be considered when collaborating.[57]

[52] Muhammad Aslam Hayat (2009) 'Mobile Payments: Will Colombo Keep Its Leadership in South Asia?' *Sunday Times* (Colombo, Sri Lanka), http://www.sundaytimes.lk/090712/FinancialTimes/ft323.html. 14 February 2018.

[53] Mkoloma (2015).

[54] Sultana (2009), p. 16.

[55] Ibid., p. 15.

[56] Ibid., p. 14.

[57] Ibid., p. 15.

### 10.3.4 *Paying Interest on Mobile Money Accounts?*

The creation of products like *M-Kesho* and *M-Shwari* indicate that mobile money issuers realise that providing a return on savings may be one way of ensuring the survival of the mobile money service.[58] Currently, mobile money has the capacity of offering savings products and interest in collaboration with other products, but the crucial question is why mobile money should not be allowed to go it alone.[59] In any event, the pool fund already earns interest which is required to be given to charity.[60] Why can the mobile money customers not earn this interest instead?[61] Tarazi and Breloff outline their argument:

> Regulatory authorities consider … interest a feature of a bank deposit and consequently ban interest payments on electronic money in an effort to clearly delineate between banking activity and payment services. However, this distinction … is of questionable legal merit… Collecting repayable funds from the general public is arguably a "deposit" regardless of [who collects it]. As electronic money is increasingly used as a savings vehicle, and as there is evidence that customers desire to earn interest, regulators may be forced to re-evaluate perceived risks and reconsider permitting nonbank electronic money issuers to pay interest earned on pooled accounts.[62]

Ehrbeck and Tarazi argue that paying interest has the following benefits:

- Encourages savings and instils (in low-income earners) a sense of time value for money;
- Allows low-income earners to earn a return on their investment;
- Acts as an incentive for more low-income earners to enter the formal economy thereby proving a means to monitor transactions.[63]

[58] *Mpamba* also have a spin-off called and *Mpamba Fesa*, later in the next section.

[59] Tarazi and Breloff (2010), p. 7.

[60] Guidelines for Mobile Payment Systems (Malaŵi, 2011).

[61] Tarazi and Breloff (2010), p. 7.

[62] Ibid.

[63] Tilman Ehrbeck and Michael Tarazi (2011) *Putting the Banking in Branchless Banking: Regulation and the Case for Interest-Bearing and Insured Electronic Money Savings Accounts* (Mobile Financial Services Development Report, World Economic Forum, Geneva, Switzerland), p. 38, http://www3.weforum.org/docs/WEF_MFSD_Report_2011.pdf. 20 February 2018.

Instituting an interest-paying regime would, however, be a novel thing as currently there is no jurisdiction where this is done.[64] Interest is only payable where mobile money collaborates with another product, typically a bank deposit or savings schemes, such as *M-Kesho* or *M-Shwari*. If mobile money issuers started paying interest, would this not bring them under the more onerous requirements of prudential regulation? On the face of it, it may. Would the fact that mobile money is mainly used for the retail payments negate such a need? Considering that pooled accounts are a deliberate device to protect liquidity of mobile money, it would be argued that is the higher aim, which should offset any need to pay interest to individual customers. This is an issue, which obviously needs more research.

### *10.3.5 Scaling Up*

The mobile money service is currently in its growing phase. However, there will come a time when it reaches saturation. The next phase of mobile money evolution needs to be planned. For a start, the service needs to be more competitive by reducing transaction costs.[65] This could be achieved through scaling up and diversification.[66] In Kenya, for example, mobile money has long been used to pay school fees and, therefore, positively contribute to reducing illiteracy.[67] Since schools are not restricted to rural areas, Heyer and Mas argue that:

> [This] reverses the flow of money, from rural households to dependents in larger urban centres. Young people may be schooled away from home due to a lack of schools in rural areas or due to the better quality of educational choices available in larger towns.[68]

Another opportunity lies in cross-border remittances. The African labour market is full of examples of migrant labour and if mobile money issuers were to collaborate and facilitate such remittance, it would result

[64] Ibid.

[65] Heyer and Mas (2009), p. 3.

[66] Ibid.

[67] FSA (2011) 'Going to School with M-PESA' (Financial Services Assessment), http://www.fsassessment.umd.edu/notes/education-through-mpesa.html. 23 February 2018.

[68] Heyer and Mas (2009), p. 6.

in a win-win situation. It provides a lucrative market to mobile money issuers and an important facility to the customers.[69] Africa already has a group of multinational mobile network operators who could easily facilitate this, such as MTN, Orange, Orascom and Airtel.[70] As noted earlier, Airtel Money is already offering cross-border remittance but this is restricted to Airtel Money customers.[71]*Mpamba* has collaborated with *Mukuru*, an international remittance service with a strong presence in Africa to do the same.[72] Currently, the service is restricted to inward remittances from South Africa with prospects of expansion to the UK and Europe.[73] The service also allows users to invest funds remitted through *Mukuru* in Old Mutual, an international investment and pension house with a local presence in Malaŵi through a spin-off service called *Mpamba Fesa*.[74] Both mobile money services are also actively engaging banks to allow for seamless transactions between mobile money wallets and bank accounts. *Mpamba* has teamed up with National Bank while Airtel Money has teamed up with Standard Bank. TNM has collaborated with First Capital Bank (FCB) and *Mpamba* customers can withdraw from FCB ATMs even when they do not have a bank account.[75] As a footnote, it must be pointed out that there are cross-ownership or shareholding relationships, in the TNM collaborations. I am aware as a fact that TNM itself is largely owned by Press Corporation Limited, which owns is the majority shareholder of National Bank. FCB is also the second majority shareholder in TNM. Therefore, while these collaborations illustrate innovation and diversity, the in-breeding aspect need not be lost. It would, therefore, seem that although financial inclusion has not been attained, the mobile

[69] Ibid.

[70] Ibid.

[71] Airtel (2017b) 'Airtel Money Cross Border Transfer' (Airtel Malawi), http://africa.airtel.com/wps/wcm/connect/AfricaRevamp/malawi/airtel_money/home/airtel-money-cross-border. 23 February 2018.

[72] Anon (2016) 'TNM Mpamba Partners Mukuru International Money Transfer Service: Partnership Provides for Investment in Mpamba Fesa' *Nyasa Times* (31 May 2016), http://www.nyasatimes.com/tnm-mpamba-partners-mukuru-international-money-transfer-service-partnership-provides-investment-mpamba-fesa/#sthash.Lx0BOj2H.dpuf. 23 February 2018.

[73] Ibid.

[74] Ibid. Fesa is a Cheŵa word which meanings plant or sow as in "plant or sow seeds".

[75] TNM (2018) 'TNM Mpamba', www.tnm.co.mw/mpamba. 30 December 2018.

money issuers are already planning for the next stage in the evolution of the service. The lessons of *M-Pesa* seem to have been embraced even as that service evolves. However, has regulation moved at the same pace? It is submitted that the regulatory framework is still stuck in the pre-financial inclusion phase. Moving towards the next phase, the framework will need to learn quickly and move on. As is discussed in 10.3.10, the regulatory cycle cannot remain static.

### *10.3.6 Evolution of Telecommunication Operators*

Thirty years ago, the mobile phone did not even exist. Today it is ubiquitous. With it has come add-on services such as data communication, which has enabled the short messaging service (SMS), and mobile money services, among others. However, who knows where the evolution will next head to? What is to stop a mobile network operator from buying a bank or some other business and changing the business platform from which it operates? The change of the risk profile of such an operator is an issue that regulators need to consider in the future.[76] This change would not only affect the communications regulator but the financial regulator as well. It may also affect competition should it involve mergers and acquisitions or display anti-competitive tendencies. This may require regulators to either delineate boundaries or expand their own boundaries to accommodate changes.[77] Currently, mobile money may not be systemically important yet, but may become so in future. If mobile money were to gain traction it might change, the way people pay for their goods and services thereby affecting how the current national payment system operates.[78]

### *10.3.7 Government, Institutional and Bill Payments*

As Airtel Money's Mkoloma observed, mobile money is uniquely placed to facilitate government payments to sectors such as teachers, pensioners, chiefs and other employees who are either living in rural areas or are far

[76] Porteous (2006), p. 36.

[77] Ibid.

[78] Ibid., p. 37.

from traditional banking facilities.[79] Overcoming government resistance is, therefore, a key tool to not only unlock the potential of mobile money but also to avail to the affected employees with more disposable income accrued from the reduced costs of m-money.[80] The reason why government involvement would expand the mobile money base is that it plays a pivotal and central role not only in procurement but also as a major employer.[81]

Among the middle-income earners, mobile money has been embraced more for the convenience it offers in bill payments other than remittances.[82] However, unlike in Kenya where this has gained traction with the Kenya Revenue Authority embracing mobile money payments for tax purposes, in Malaŵi, using mobile money to pay bills still has some ground to cover.[83] Currently, only the major utility service providers are linked to mobile money.[84] Both issuers have, however, been active in getting on board merchants and vendors to link them up to their customers. Hopefully, the passing of the Payments Systems Act 2016 and Electronic Transactions and Cybersecurity Act 2016 can facilitate mobile money payments over a wider coverage.[85] Heyer and Mas say, apart from bill payment, attracting "large-scale institutional payments may

[79] Mkoloma (2015).

[80] Twea (2015).

[81] Mary O'Connell and others (2016) *Case Study: Malawi* (Low-income Customer Support Units, WaterAid), p. 2, http://www.wateraidamerica.org/sites/default/files/publcations/LICSU%20Malawi%20case%20study.pdf. 23 February 2018.

Heyer and Mas (2009), p. 7.

[82] Deogracias Kalima (2016) 'Mobile Payment in Malawi: Integrating and Cost Reducing: The Mobile Money Revolution' (Journ Africa), http://journafrica.de/en/banking-economy-finance-innovation-malawi-45312. 23 February 2018.

[83] KRA (2017) 'KRA M-Service: Mobile E-Slip General & Payment User Guide' (Kenya Revenue Authority), http://www.kra.go.ke/notices/pdf2015/KRA%20m-Service%20User%20Guide%20-%20Mobile%20E-slip%20Generation%20&%20Payment.pdf. 23 February 2018.

[84] Airtel (2017a) 'What Is Airtel Money? How to Pay Bills' (Airtel Malawi), http://africa.airtel.com/wps/wcm/connect/AfricaRevamp/Malawi/home/personal/airtel-money/about-airtel-money. 23 February 2018.

TNM (2017) 'How to Use Mpamba: Pay Bills' (Telekom Networks Malawi), https://www.tnmmpamba.co.mw/index.php/user-guide. 23 February 2018.

[85] Payment Systems Act (Malaŵi, 2016).

also comprise significant markets".[86] Considering that *M-Pesa* was initially launched as a microfinance loan repayment scheme,[87] this could be revisited and expanded to include such regular payments as micro-insurance premiums.[88] Adapting the mobile money platform to interlink with other services may require a much more sophisticated ICT infrastructure on the part of such third parties, something that cannot be taken for granted.[89] However, in order to attract government and bill payments, there need to be interoperability of mobile money systems nationwide, as there may be resistance if the payment channels are fragmented.[90]

### *10.3.8 Readiness of Individual Districts to the Service*

So far, most literature has looked at mobile money in terms of country readiness,[91] but not much has been done about how mobile money has spread within countries and the readiness of districts to the service. National statistics are important but do not tell the whole story. The next frontier of research requires mapping the geographical spread of mobile money. For example, within the country, is mobile money more prevalent in some districts compared to others? Is it more prevalent among a certain age group or gender? Does it have anything to do with district literacy and financial literacy levels? As was noted, although Airtel has a slight edge of the market share over TNM, this is not evenly spread across the country's three regions. TNM leads Airtel in the North and the South but Airtel trumps TNM in the Central Region.[92] But what about the districts within these regions?

Research also needs to look at how distributed the telecommunication network is and whether this has a bearing on the subscriber base. A study of the ecosystems within the district would also be instructive in analysing and understanding why mobile money may have grown faster or gained traction in some districts compared to others. Although there is migrant labour prevalent in the country, is there uniformity among all

[86] Heyer and Mas (2009), p. 7.

[87] AFI (2010), p. 4.

[88] Heyer and Mas (2009), p. 7.

[89] Ibid., p. 7.

[90] Ibid., p. 7.

[91] Ibid., p. 20.

[92] MACRA (2016), p. 12.

the rural people who have trekked to towns to look for work? Of course, when looking at districts, factors such as rural, urban and peri-urban need to be considered. However, just like *Kibera* in Nairobi, Kenya, Malaŵi also has its ghetto suburbs on the outskirts of most cities, which are overpopulated but lack basic services. Most people who migrate from rural areas target these as the first step of their migrant life, and most never leave them. Researching the impact of mobile money within districts may, therefore, reveal more about the adoption patterns.

### *10.3.9 Insurance Protection*

Since mobile money is not a banking service, the lender of last resort facility as a safety net does not extend to it. Campbell and Lastra define the safety net as a mixture of several instruments such as a "regulatory framework, a deposit protection system, bank insolvency laws and lender of last resort role by the central bank."[93] Of course, the term safety net in its strictest use refers to those institutions, which are susceptible to contagion,[94] most notably banks.[95] Other schemes to protect consumers, therefore, need to be put in place. Insurance protection is one such scheme.[96] While such a scheme is ideal, the question of who funds it is vital.[97] The follow-up question is who bears the cost of setting it up and who runs it.[98] It must be pointed out, that no known insurance scheme provides 100% coverage of deposits.[99] Secondly, there is no assurance that such a scheme would prevent a bank run.[100] Running the bank well

[93] Campbell and Lastra (2009), p. 454.

[94] Schooner and Taylor (2010), p. 52; Herring and Santomero (2000), p. 62.

[95] Campbell and Lastra (2009), p. 462. They argue that the extension of liquidity to non-bank institutions on the USA has tested this conventional wisdom.
See also Polizatto (1992), p. 296.

[96] Di Castri (2013), p. 29.

[97] Ibid.

[98] Samuel H Talley and Ignacio Mas (1992) 'Prudential regulation and Banking Supervision' in Dimitri Vittas (ed) *Financial Regulation: Changing the Rules of the Game* (The World Bank, Washington, DC), p. 340.

[99] Ibid., p. 325.

[100] Andrew Campbell and others (2009) 'A New Standard for Deposit Insurance and Government Guarantees after the Crisis' 17 (3) *Journal of Financial Regulation and Compliance* 210, http://dx.doi.org/10.1108/13581980910972214. 20 February 2018.
See also Herring and Santomero (2000), p. 62.

from both a prudential and conduct perspective remains the best way to appease customers. There are two forms of deposit insurance schemes, the implicit one, which is discretionary, and the explicit one, which specifies whether participation is discretionary or mandatory.[101] When used, deposit insurance scheme refers to the explicit one. In summary under the deposit insurance scheme, should there be a bank failure; depositors are assured of receiving at least a certain minimum value of their money which has been insured.[102] A deposit insurance scheme that can quickly reimburse depositors is likely to gain credibility.[103] But on what basis is insurance extended to customers? After all, bank customers do not own the deposits in the strictest sense. In fact, the relationship is more of a debtor and creditor.[104] In *Foley v Hill*, it was held that:

> Money, when paid into a bank, ceases altogether to be the money of the principal ... it is then the money of the banker, who is bound to return an equivalent by paying a similar sum to that deposited with him when he is asked for it.[105]

It can, therefore, be said that the deposit insurance scheme helps to reassure customers that they will be paid (subject to any maximum set) which, when it works, can help prevent or at least contain a financial crisis. The same concept can be extended to mobile money. The fact that customers have exchanged their cash with mobile money means they may have a claim to redeem their cash but they cannot lay a claim to the deposits in the pool account. That said, although cash exchanged with mobile money is not deposits in the banking sense, it is submitted the scheme could still be tweaked to produce the same effect. The relationship between the mobile money customer and the mobile network operator is akin to one of creditor and debtor.

The concept of the DIS started in the USA. The Federal Deposit Insurance Corporation (FDIC) is the oldest DIS to date.[106] Most

[101] Talley and Mas (1992), pp. 323–4.
[102] Schooner and Taylor (2010), p. 57.
[103] Campbell and others (2009), p. 215.
[104] Ibid., p. 212.
[105] [1848] 11 H.L.C 28, p. 1005.
[106] Schooner and Taylor (2010), p. 57.

developed economies now have a DIS in place.[107] The UK has a slightly different model using what is termed the "paybox" scheme.[108] Under the UK model, participating firms pay in premiums to the Financial Services Compensation Scheme (FSCS).[109] The FCSC compensates those eligible in the event of a winding-up or bank failure.[110] Di Castri says DIS has been successfully extended to mobile money in the USA.[111] Tarazi and Breloff have also argued for an extension of the deposit insurance scheme to individual mobile money customers.[112] This involves placing the mobile money into a deposit scheme.[113] For deposits in the trust fund, the deposit insurance scheme protection passes through to each customer up to a set limit.[114] In the case of Malaŵi, such an extension may not be possible because there is no deposit insurance scheme in place. However, the central bank is in the process of introducing such a scheme,[115] and overseeing the drafting of a bill to set up a deposit insurance corporation.[116] Campbell et al. have argued that,

[A] separate, operationally independent, and accountable deposit insurance entity … may be the best practice model available to provide:

[107] Ibid.

[108] Singh (2007), p. 192.

[109] Ibid., pp. 191–2.

[110] Ibid., p. 192.

[111] Di Castri (2013), p. 30.

[112] Tarazi and Breloff (2010), p. 8.

[113] Di Castri (2013), p. 30.

[114] Ibid.

[115] FSVC (2016) 'Malawi Program Overview' (*Financial Services Volunteer Corps*), http://www.fsvc.org/node/99. 20 July 2018.

Chikondi Chiyembekeza (2014) 'Depositors' Protection Scheme in the Offing' *The Nation* (1 May 2014), http://mwnation.com/depositors%E2%80%99-protection-scheme-in-the-offing/. 24 February 2018.

[116] Goodall Gondwe (2015) 'Economic and Fiscal Policy Statement 2015' (Malaŵi Government), https://www.africanbondmarkets.org/fileadmin/uploads/afdb/Countries/Malawi/Ministry_of_Finance_of_Malawi/Malawi-Eco___Fiscal_Pol_2015.pdf. 24 February 2018.

Arthur Peter Mutharika (2016) 'Towards Recovery and Sustainable Socio-Economic Development' (Malaŵi Government), http://www.manaonline.gov.mw/index.php/analysis/item/380-state-of-the-nation-address-president-mutharika. 24 February 2018.

- the most effective incentives for the control of moral hazard affecting a deposit insurer
- the greatest protection of the interests of depositors
- more balanced and effective decision making; and
- the promotion of more extensive monitoring of potential conflicts.[117]

In setting up the deposit insurance scheme, it would be recommended that the central bank considers making it an autonomous entity within the above framework. However, it must be pointed out, that the scheme being designed by the central bank would only apply to bank deposits.[118] No thought has yet been made of extending it to mobile money. Application of the deposit insurance scheme to mobile money may, therefore, be a long way off. It is also recommended that the country immediately joins the International Association of Deposit Insurers (IADI), as an associate and become a full member once the deposit insurance scheme has been launched.[119]

### 10.3.10 *Continuous Monitoring of the Regulatory Cycle*

Developing a regulatory framework is not an end in itself. Porteous has proposed a phased approach to regulation. First is a pioneer phase which involves monitoring and engaging leading to developing a roadmap, moving on to a breakout phase, which he also refers to as the facilitation and coordination phase.[120] Next is the consolidation phase where the regulator can now start supervising in ernest.[121] However, when the service has attained maturity, the regulator needs to ensure that there is an ongoing competition.[122] Monitoring the outcomes based on the regulatory objectives is, therefore, important.[123] Ogus argues that regulation

[117] Campbell and others (2009), p. 219.

[118] Chiyembekeza (2014).

[119] IADI (2016) 'IADI Members and Participants' (International Association of Deposit Insurers), http://www.iadi.org/en/about-iadi/iadi-members-and-participants/list-of-members/. 1 May 2018.

[120] Porteous (2006), p. 15.

[121] Ibid.

[122] Ibid.

[123] Córdova-Novion and Hanlon (2002), p. 108.

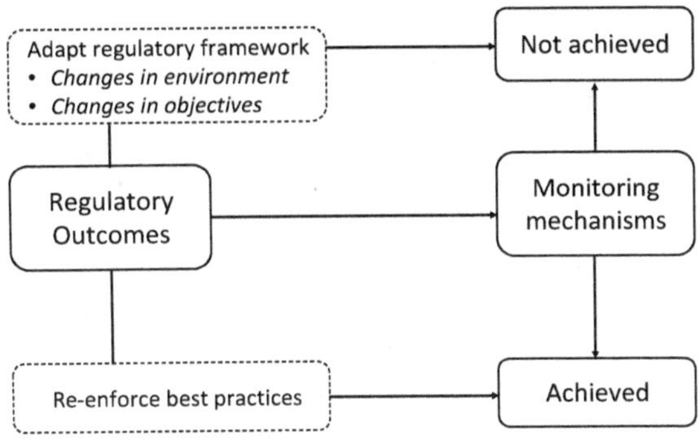


**Fig. 10.1** Regulatory cycle (*Source* Author)

is dynamic and good regulatory design needs to feed off the "behavioural responses to regulatory obligations" of the regulated industry.[124] Looked at this way, regulation is a process of continuous evolution. The regulatory outcomes operate as inputs, which are then monitored to see if they are being achieved. Where there is an achievement, they become the basis of best practices. Where they are not achieved, the regulatory framework is re-examined and reconfigured to see if it can achieve different outcomes. This could result in changes in the environment or the outcomes themselves. The figure below illustrates this regulatory cycle (Fig. 10.1).

## 10.4 Conclusion

To conclude, certain things can be said about mobile money and how it has developed since its inception. It is an emerging form of money and with time may evolve further depending on use and the channels that are used for its distribution. For now, it is considered of low systemic risk because it is fully backed up by funds deposited in a pool account. Will mobile money continue to pose a low risk to the financial system or will it explode to something, which the regulator must pay special attention to? The quest is to achieve financial inclusion, but what happens when it has been fully achieved? What next can mobile money become? As a payment system, can it start to challenge the banking payment system? With growth in pool funds, is there a need for regulatory requirements

[124]Ogus (2009), p. 344.

for mobile money issuers to diversify where their accounts are domiciled as one way of minimising risk?[125] There is already a requirement to isolate the pool funds from the mobile network operators' accounts by creating a ring fence. Should this be a double ring fence, which further isolates the trust fund from the other deposits? The only problem with this would be that it would limit the ability of the bank to intermediate. It may also mean that instead of the fund making a profit through earned interest, the bank may need to be paid as a fund manager.

Although the concept of earning interest looks attractive, the chances are mobile money will not earn interest any time soon. The pool account, however, continues to earn interest and with time, the regulator may need to look at how the trustees are using this interest. As a payment system, mobile money can operate outside the banking system and has the advantage of the instantaneous settling of obligations. Increasingly, however, mobile money and its ecosystem are being embraced by national payment systems and the more there is a convergence of these systems, the more the regulations tools of mobile money may need to be revisited. For now, most jurisdictions have adopted the light-touch approach regarding mobile money. This may be acceptable and encouraged at this phase where financial inclusion is a target. Once financial inclusion has been attained, and mobile money is in the post-financial inclusion era, a different regulatory approach would have to be adopted. This book advances the concept of really responsive regulation as the ideal approach to regulating a complex service such as mobile money, which is in a constant state of evolution. It embraces the transition from light-touch to a self-regulatory framework based on the collaboration of all stakeholders. In terms of operation, mobile money rides on the rails of the telecommunication backbone and is likely to do so as long as it retains the core of its current form and nature. Regulation needs to embrace and respond to this reality.

Regarding regulatory models, the book has considered either staying with the status quo with some changes or adopting the independent agency model. The agency model has obviously been preferred. It has its challenges, but these challenges can be overcome. Currently, mobile money is not considered systemically important and this may affect how regulators and politicians may view the proposal to have an autonomous

[125] Tarazi and Breloff (2010), p. 6.

agency. For now, what can be said is that with technology developments, mobile money will continue to evolve and may pose new regulatory challenges with such evolution. This concluding chapter has highlighted some of the issues that may form the next mobile money regulatory debate and research. For now, there is need to ensure that regulation does not stifle innovation. But this is not enough. As noted by Mkoloma, in Malaŵi, the government is a key player in the employment sector. So far, it has not joined the mobile money ecosystem as a participant. It is, therefore, recommended that the government considers doing so not only as a way of giving mobile money a boost, but also in ensuring that its payees in rural areas have more take-home pay. Whatever the future holds, one thing can be said: regulation of mobile money under the current architecture, which is based on banking, is not ideal. Neither is the architecture of having a plurality of regulators who are sector regulators. There is a danger of such regulators talking past each other. An agency may not resolve all regulatory problems, but it is the first step, it is submitted, towards having clarity from this regulatory flux.

## References


AFI (2010) *Enabling Mobile Money Transfer: The Central Bank of Kenya's Treatment of M-Pesa* (Alliance for Financial Inclusion), http://www.gsma.com/mobilefordevelopment/wp-content/uploads/2013/09/enablingmobilemoneytransfer92.pdf. 15 December 2018.

Airtel (2017a) 'What Is Airtel Money? How to Pay Bills' (Airtel Malawi), http://africa.airtel.com/wps/wcm/connect/AfricaRevamp/Malawi/home/personal/airtel-money/about-airtel-money. 23 February 2018.

Airtel (2017b) 'Airtel Money Cross Border Transfer' (Airtel Malawi), http://africa.airtel.com/wps/wcm/connect/AfricaRevamp/malawi/airtel_money/home/airtel-money-cross-border. 23 February 2018.

Andrew Campbell and others (2009) 'A New Standard for Deposit Insurance and Government Guarantees after the Crisis' 17 (3) *Journal of Financial Regulation and Compliance* 210, http://dx.doi.org/10.1108/13581980910972214. 20 February 2018.

Andrew Campbell and Rosa Lastra (2009) 'Revisiting the Lender of Last Resort' 24 (3) *Banking and Finance Law Review* 453, http://0-search.proquest.com.pugwash.lib.warwick.ac.uk/docview/218867839?accountid=14888. 10 December 2018.

Anon (2016) 'TNM Mpamba Partners Mukuru International Money Transfer Service: Partnership Provides for Investment in Mpamba Fesa' *Nyasa Times*

(31 May 2016), http://www.nyasatimes.com/tnm-mpamba-partners-mukuru-international-money-transfer-service-partnership-provides-investment-mpamba-fesa/#sthash.Lx0BOj2H.dpuf. 23 February 2018.

Anthony Ogus (2009) 'Regulation Revisited' (2) *Public Law*, http://repub.eur.nl/pub/16031/A.%20Ogus,%20Regulation%20Revisited.pdf. 19 May 2018.

Aptantech (2013a) 'M-Pesa & Its "OffSpring"—A Look at 5 "M" Payments Solutions Developed after M-Pesa', http://aptantech.com/2013/08/m-pesa-its-offsprings-a-look-at-5-m-payments-solutions-developed-after-m-pesa/. 23 February 2018.

Aptantech (2013b) 'What Does Equity's Deal with Bharti's Airtel Money Mean for Orange Money and Safaricom's M-Kesho?', http://aptantech.com/2013/07/what-does-equitys-deal-with-bhartis-airtel-money-mean-for-orangelectronic-money-and-safaricoms-m-kesho/. 23 February 2018.

Arthur Peter Mutharika (2016) 'Towards Recovery and Sustainable Socio-economic Development' (Malaŵi Government), http://www.manaonline.gov.mw/index.php/analysis/item/380-state-of-the-nation-address-president-mutharika. 24 February 2018.

César Córdova-Novion and Deirdre Hanlon (2002) 'Regulatory Governance: Improving the Institutional Basis for Sectoral Regulators' 2 (3) *OECD Journal on Budgeting*, https://www.oecd.org/gov/budgeting/43505850.pdf. 15 February 2018.

Chikondi Chiyembekeza (2014) 'Depositors' Protection Scheme in the Offing' *The Nation* (1 May 2014), http://mwnation.com/depositors%E2%80%99-protection-scheme-in-the-offing/. 24 February 2018.

Chikondi Chiyembekeza (2015) 'Court Rebuffs TNM, Airtel Over MACRA Decision' *The Nation* (1 April 2015), http://mwnation.com/court-rebuffs-tnm-airtel-over-macra-decision/. 22 February 2018.

Chris Skinner (2015) 'When Everyone on the Planet Has a Mobile Money Account, Things Will Change' (24 June 2015), http://thefinanser.com/2015/06/when-everyone-on-the-planet-has-a-mobilelectronicmoney-account-things-will-change.html/. 9 February 2018.

Communications Act (Malaŵi, 2016).

Dalvinder Singh (2007) *Banking Regulation of UK and US Financial Markets* (Ashgate Publishing, Aldershot, Hampshire).

David Porteous (2006) *The Enabling Environment for Mobile Banking in Africa* (Report Commissioned by Department for International Development [DFID], Boston), http://bankablefrontier.com/wp-ontent/uploads/documents/ee.mobil_banking.report.v3.1.pdf. 14 September 2018.

Deogracias Kalima (2016) 'Mobile Payment in Malawi: Integrating and Cost Reducing: The Mobile Money Revolution' (Journ Africa), http://journafrica.de/en/banking-economy-finance-innovation-malawi-45312. 23 February 2018.

EBL (2017) 'M-Kesho' (Equity Bank Limited), http://ke.equitybank-group.com/business/products/ways-to-bank/mobile-banking/m-kesho. 23 February 2018.

FATF (2012) *International Standards on Combating Money Laundering and the Financing of Terrorism & Proliferation (updated October 2016)* (Financial Action Task Force), http://www.fatf-gafi.org/media/fatf/documents/recommendations/pdfs/FATF_Recommendations.pdf. 20 February 2018.

Financial Crimes Act (Malaŵi, 2017).

FSA (2011) 'Going to School with M-PESA' (Financial Services Assessment), http://www.fsassessment.umd.edu/notes/education-through-mpesa.html. 23 February 2018.

FSVC (2016) 'Malawi Program Overview' (Financial Services Volunteer Corps), http://www.fsvc.org/node/99. 20 July 2018.

Goodall Gondwe (2015) 'Economic and Fiscal Policy Statement 2015' (Malaŵi Government), https://www.africanbondmarkets.org/fileadmin/uploads/afdb/Countries/Malawi/Ministry_of_Finance_of_Malawi/Malawi-Eco___Fiscal_Pol_2015.pdf. 24 February 2018.

Guidelines for Mobile Payment Systems (Malaŵi, 2011).

Heidi Mandanis Schooner and Mark W Taylor (2010) *Global Bank Regulation: Principles and Policies* (Academic Press, Burlington, MA).

Heyer A and Mas I (2009) 'Seeking Fertile Grounds for Mobile Money' *Mobile Money for the Unbanked* (GSMA), http://www.gsma.com/mobilefordevelopment/wp-content/uploads/2012/03/fertile_grounds_mobile_money55.pdf. 14 February 2018.

IADI (2016) 'IADI Members and Participants' (International Association of Deposit Insurers), http://www.iadi.org/en/about-iadi/iadi-members-and-participants/list-of-members/. 1 May 2018.

Ignacio Mas (2010) 'M-KESHO in Kenya' (GSMA) (27 May 2010), http://www.gsma.com/mobilefordevelopment/programme/mobilelectronicmoney/m-kesho-in-kenya. 23 February 2018.

Interview at Reserve Bank of Malaŵi Headquarters (RBM HQ) on 6 August 2015.

Interview with Bigboy Mkoloma Product and Development Manager, Airtel Money (7 August 2015).

Interview with Theodose Twea Pensioner (19 August 2015).

Interview with Thokozani Chimbe Deputy Director—Legal (Consumer Affairs); Malaŵi Communications Regulatory Authority (3 August 2015).

Interview with Webster Mbekeani Head, Mobile Money Division, TNM (20 August 2015).

Jabulani Kamngoya (2015) 'Teveta to Harmonise Vocational Curricula and Certification' (1 June 2015), http://allafrica.com/stories/201506011690.html. 27 February 2018.

James Nthondo (2016) 'Exclusive: New Cashgate in Malawi, How Macra Funds Are Abused' *Nyasa Times* (12 September 2016), http://www.nyasatimes.com/exclusive-new-cashgate-malawi-macra-funds-abused/#sthash.efL9KDSw.dpuf. 27 February 2018.

KRA (2017) 'KRA M-Service: Mobile E-Slip General & Payment User Guide' (Kenya Revenue Authority), http://www.kra.go.ke/notices/pdf2015/KRA%20m-Service%20User%20Guide%20-%20Mobile%20E-slip%20Generation%20&%20Payment.pdf. 23 February 2018.

MACRA (2016) *National Survey on Access to and Usage of ICT Services in Malawi* (Malaŵi Communications Regulatory Authority Blantyre), http://www.macra.org.mw/wp-content/uploads/2016/01/MACRA-Survey-Report-National-Household-and-Individual-access-to-and-usage-of-ICT.pdf. 11 March 2018.

Malaŵi Government (2015) 'Commencement of Universal and Compulsory Birth & Death Registration and Issuance of Certificates' (Government of Malaŵi), https://www.facebook.com/malawigovernment/posts/439708072882359. 21 July 2018.

Marc Quintyn and Michael W Taylor (2002) *Regulatory and Supervisory Independence and Financial Stability* (International Monetary Fund, Washington, DC), https://www.imf.org/external/pubs/ft/wp/2002/wp0246.pdf. 1 February 2018.

Mary O'Connell and others (2016) *Case Study: Malawi* (Low-Income Customer Support Units, WaterAid), http://www.wateraidamerica.org/sites/default/files/publcations/LICSU%20Malawi%20case%20study.pdf. 23 February 2018.

Michael Tarazi and Paul Breloff (2010) *Nonbank Electronic Money Issuers: Regulatory Approaches to Protecting Customer Funds* (Focus Note, CGAP, Washington, DC), https://www.cgap.org/sites/default/files/CGAP-Focus-Note-Nonbank-Electronicmoney-Issuers-Regulatory-Approaches-to-Protecting-Customer-Funds-Jul-2010.pdf. 3 February 2018.

Michael U Klein and Colin Mayer (2011) *Mobile Banking and Financial Inclusion: The Regulatory Lessons* (Policy Research Working Paper, The World Bank), http://documents.worldbank.org/curated/en/docsearch/document-type/620265. 14 February 2018.

Muhammad Aslam Hayat (2009) 'Mobile Payments: Will Colombo Keep Its leadership in South Asia?' *Sunday Times* (Colombo, Sri Lanka), http://www.sundaytimes.lk/090712/FinancialTimes/ft323.html. 14 February 2018.

Nicola Jentzsch (2012) 'Implications of Mandatory Registration of Mobile Phone Users in Africa' 36 (8) *Telecommunications Policy* 608, http://doi.org/10.1016/j.telpol.2012.04.002. 14 November 2018.

Payment Systems Act (Malaŵi, 2016).

Rasheda Sultana (2009) 'Mobile Banking: Overview of Regulatory Framework in Emerging Markets' (*4th Communication Policy Research, South Conference*) Negombo, Sri Lanka, http://papers.ssrn.com/sol3/papers.cfm?abstract_id=1554160. 14 February 2018.

Richard J Herring and Anthony M Santomero (2000) 'What Is Optimal Financial Regulation?' in Benton E. Gup (ed) *The New Financial Architecture* (Quorum Books, Westport, CT).

Robert Cull (2010) 'M-PESA: Mobile Payments, Improved Lives for Kenyans' (The World Bank), http://econ.worldbank.org/external/default/main?theSitePK=469382&contentMDK=22594763&menuPK=476752&pagePK=64165401&piPK=64165026. 23 February 2018.

Samuel H Talley and Ignacio Mas (1992) 'Prudential Regulation and Banking Supervision' in Dimitri Vittas (ed) *Financial Regulation: Changing the Rules of the Game* (The World Bank, Washington, DC).

Simone Di Castri (2013) *Mobile Money: Enabling Regulatory Solutions* (GSMA, London), http://www.gsma.com/publicpolicy/wp-content/uploads/2013/02/GSMA2013_Report_Mobilelectronicmoney-EnablingRegulatorySolutions.pdf. 20 February 2018.

Technical, Entrepreneurial and Vocational Education and Training Act, 1999 (Act No. 6 of 1999).

TEVETA (2017) 'About Us' (Technical, Entrepreneurial and Vocational Education and Training [TEVET] Authority), http://www.teveta.mw/index.php/about-us. 27 February 2018.

*The State v Malaŵi Communications Regulatory Authority (MACRA) Ex Parte TNM and Airtel*, Misc. Civil Cause No. 4 of 2010 (unreported).

Tilman Ehrbeck and Michael Tarazi (2011) *Putting the Banking in Branchless Banking: Regulation and the Case for Interest-Bearing and Insured Electronic Money Savings Accounts* (Mobile Financial Services Development Report, World Economic Forum, Geneva, Switzerland), http://www3.weforum.org/docs/WEF_MFSD_Report_2011.pdf. 20 February 2018.

TNM (2017) 'How to Use Mpamba: Pay Bills' (Telekom Networks Malawi), https://www.tnmmpamba.co.mw/index.php/user-guide. 23 February 2018.

TNM (2018) 'TNM Mpamba', www.tnm.co.mw/mpamba. 30 December 2018.

Vincent P Polizatto (1992) 'Prudential Regulation and Banking Supervision' in Dimitri Vittas (ed) *Financial Regulation: Changing the Rules of the Game* (The World Bank, Washington, DC).

# Bibliography

### *Legislation*


Malaŵi

Communications Act, Act No. 34 of 2016, Chapter 68:01 of the Laws of Malaŵi.

Competition and Fair Trading Act, Act No. 43 of 1998, http://www.itu.int/ITU-D/treg/Legislation/Malawi/act43.pdf. 18 November 2018.

Constitution of the Republic of Malaŵi (1994), http://www.malawi.gov.mw/images/Publications/act/Constitution%20of%20Malawi.pdf. 21 December 2018.

Consumer Protection Act (2003), https://www.rbm.mw/Home/GetContentFile/?ContentID=3752. 14 November 2018.

Electronic Transactions and Cybersecurity Act, No. 33 of 2016, http://www.macra.org.mw/wp-content/uploads/2014/07/E-Transactions-Act-2016.pdf. 19 July 2018.

Financial Crimes Act, Act No. 14 of 2017.

Financial Crimes (Suppression of Terrorist Financing and Proliferation) Regulations 2017.

Financial Services Act, Act No. 26 of 2010, https://www.rbm.mw/Home/GetContentFile/?ContentID=3743. 13 December 2018.

Financial Services (Fit and Proper Requirement for Persons Associated with Ownership and Management of Securities Market Players) Directive 2015, https://www.rbm.mw/Supervision/GetContentFile/?ContentID=6457. 20 July 2018.






S. Madise, *The Regulation of Mobile Money*, Palgrave Macmillan Studies in Banking and Financial Institutions,
https://doi.org/10.1007/978-3-030-13831-8

Malaŵi Bureau of Standards Act, Act No. 17 of 2012, http://www.rbm.mw/documents/legislation/RBM%20ACT%20JUNE%202013.pdf. 10 February 2018.

Money Laundering Proceeds of Serious Crime and Terrorist Financing Act, Act No. 11 of 2006, http://www.rbm.mw/documents/pisu/Money%20Laundering%20Act%202006.pdf. 31 March 2018.

National Registration Act (2010), https://www.globalintegrity.org/wp-content/uploads/2016/01/Malawi-NATIONAL-REGISTRATION-ACT.pdf. 21 July 2018.

Ombudsman Act, Act No. 17 of 1996, Chapter 3:07 of the Laws of Malaŵi, http://www.africanchildforum.org/clr/Legislation%20Per%20Country/Malawi/malawi_ombudsman_1996_en.pdf. 27 February 2018.

Payment Systems Act, Act No. 15 of 2016, https://www.rbm.mw/Home/GetContentFile/?ContentID=12256. 15 March 2018.

Penal Code, Act No. 22 of 1929, Chapter 7:01 of the Laws Malaŵi, https://www.unodc.org/tldb/pdf/Malawi_Penal_Code.pdf. 22 December 2018.

Sale of Goods Act, Act No. 14 of 1967, Chapter 48:01 of the Laws of Malaŵi, http://www.malawilii.org/mw/consolidatedlegislation/4801/48_2001_20sale_20of_20goods_1_docx_12176.pdf. 3 May 2018.

Reserve Bank of Malaŵi Guidelines for Mobile Payment Systems 2011.

Other Countries

Business Groups Incorporation Act (Papua New Guinea, 1974), http://www.paclii.org/pg/legis/consol_act/bgia1974365/. 21 July 2018.

CBK (2013) 'E-Money Regulation' (Central Bank of Kenya), https://www.centralbank.go.ke/images/docs/NPS/Regulations%20and%20Guidelines/Regulations%20-%20E-%20Money%20regulations%202013.pdf. 28 December 2018.

Central Bank of Kenya Act (1966), https://centralbank.go.ke/images/docs/The_Central_Bank_of_Kenya_Act_1st_January_2014.pdf. 28 December 2018.

Financial Services Act (United Kingdom: Chapter 21, 2012), http://www.legislation.gov.uk/ukpga/2012/21/pdfs/ukpga_20120021_en.pdf. 2 June 2018.

Kenya Information and Communications Act (1998), http://kfcb.co.ke/wp-content/uploads/2016/07/Kenya_Information_and_Communications_Act.pdf. 28 December 2018.

National Payment System Act 39 of 2011, http://kenyalaw.org/kl/fileadmin/pdfdownloads/Acts/NationalPaymentSystemsAct__No39of2011.pdf. 19 February 2018.

## *Cases*

Malaŵi

*Finance Bank of Malaŵi Ltd (In Voluntary Liquidation) v Reserve Bank of Malaŵi and Attorney General* Constitutional Cause No. 5 of 2010 (High

Court, Constitutional Division), http://www.malawilii.org/mw/judgment/high-court-general-division/2013/451. 9 March 2018.

*In the Matter of Citizen Insurance Company Limited Ex Parte the Registrar of Financial Services* Commercial Case No. 55 of 2011 (High Court), http://www.malawilii.org/mw/judgment/high-court-commercial-division/2012/5/. 27 February 2018.

*R v Kumwembe et al.* Criminal Case No. 65 of 2013 (High Court).

England

*Edward Foley v Thomas Hill* [1848] 11 H.L.C 27.

*Three Rivers DC v Bank of England* [2001] 2 All ER 513 (HOL), https://www.publications.parliament.uk/pa/ld199900/ldjudgmt/jd000518/rivers-1.htm. 27 February 2018.

International Court of Justice

*Case Concerning the Payment of Various Serbian Loans Issued in France (France v. Serbia) and Payment in Gold of the Brazilian Federal Loans Contracted in France (France v. Brazil)* PCIJ Rep Series A Nos 20–21 (Permanent Court of International Justice), http://legal.un.org/PCIJsummaries/documents/english/PCIJ_FinalText.pdf. 7 November 2018.

## *Malaŵi Government Documents and Publications*

*Commencement of Universal and Compulsory Birth & Death Registration and Issuance of Certificates* (2015).

*Financial Sector Development Strategy: 2010–2015* (2015), http://www.finance.gov.mw/fspu/index.php/financial-sector-laws/strategy-documents/55-malawi-financial-sector-development-strategy-2010-2015/file. 21 December 2015.

Gondwe G (2015) *Economic and Fiscal Policy Statement 2015* (Budget Statement, Lilongwe).

Mutharika AP (2016) *Towards Recovery and Sustainable Socio-Economic Development* (State of the Nation Address, Lilongwe).

*National ICT Policy* (2013).

Nankhumwa K (2015) *Statement on the Sale of MSB and IndeBank* (State House, Malaŵi).

'Public Appointment: Reserve Bank Governor' (2017), https://www.facebook.com/malawigovernment/?hc_ref=PAGES_TIMELINE&fref=nf. 21 April 2018.

## *United Kingdom Government Documents*

House of Commons Treasury Committee (2009) *Banking Crisis: Regulation and Supervision* (Parliament, London), https://www.publications.parliament.uk/pa/cm200809/cmselect/cmtreasy/767/767.pdf. 3 February 2018.

Kenya Government Publications

Musuni JTO (2015) 'Mobile Money: The Kenyan Experience' (Government of Kenya), http://www.cto.int/media/events/pst-ev/2015/Broadband%20 2015/Presentations/Mobile%20Money%20Service%20Joseph%20 Tiampati%20Ole%20Musuni.pdf. 28 December 2018.

## *Books, Book Chapters and Handbooks*

Agar J (2003) *Constant Touch: A Global History of the Mobile Phone* (Icon Books, Cambridge).

Alberts DS and Hayes RE (2006) 'Reader Orientation' in *Understanding Command and Control* (CCRP Publishing, Washington, DC).

Austin J (1832) *The Province of Jurisprudence Determined* (John Murray, London).

Ayres I and Braithwaite J (1992) *Responsive Regulation: Transcending the Deregulation Debate* (Oxford University Press, Oxford).

Backhouse RE (1991) 'Money' in *Applied UK Macroeconomics* (Basil Blackwell, Oxford)

Bagehot W (1873) *Lombard Street: A Description of the Money Market* (Henry S King & Co., London).

Baldwin R, Cave M and Lodge M (2011) *Understanding Regulation: Theory, Strategy, and Practice* (Second edn, Oxford University Press, Oxford).

Baron de Montesquieu CdS (1748) 'Of Laws in Relation to the Use of Money' in *The Spirit of Laws (2001 repr)* (Batoche Books, Ontario).

Bordo MD and Kydland FE (1997) 'The Gold Standard as a Rule' in Eichengreen B and Flandreau M (eds.), *The Gold Standard in Theory and History* (Routledge, London).

Braithwaite J (2002) 'Responsive Regulation' in *Restorative Justice and Responsive Regulation* (Oxford University Press, Oxford).

Braithwaite J and Drahos P (2000) 'Financial Regulation' in *Global Business Regulation* (Cambridge University Press, Cambridge).

Burton M and Brown B (2014) *The Financial System and the Economy: Principles of Money and Banking* (Routledge, Abingdon, Oxon).

Chown JF (1994) 'Some Concepts of Money' in *A History of Money from AD 800* (Routledge, London).

Cooper G (2010) 'Money, Banks and Central Banks' in *The Origin of Financial Crises: Central Banks, Credit Bubbles and the Efficient Market Fallacy* (Harriman House Limited, Petersfield, Hampshire).

Davies G (2002) 'From Primitive and Ancient Money to the Invention of Coinage, 3000–600 BC' in *A History of Money: From Ancient Times to the Present Day* (3rd edn, University of Wales Press, Cardiff).

de Soto H (2001) *The Mystery of Capital: Why Capitalism Triumphs in the West and Fails Everywhere Else* (Black Swan, London).

Dodd N (2014) *The Social Life of Money* (Princeton University Press, Princeton, NJ).

Donovan K (2012) 'Mobile Money for Financial Inclusion' in *Information and Communications for Development 2012* (World Bank, Washington, DC).

Dumez H and Jeunemaitre A (1997) 'Financial Regulation: From Economic Analysis to Practical Experience' in Jeunemaitre A (eds.), *Financial Markets Regulation* (MacMillan Press Ltd, Basingstoke).

Fleuriof P (1997) 'Financial Regulation as the Safeguard of Balances in a Global Context' in Jeunemaitre A (eds.), *Financial Markets Regulation* (MacMillan Press Ltd, Basingstoke).

Freeman ER (1984) 'Stakeholder Theory of the Modern Corporation' in *General Issues in Business Ethics* (Harper Collins, New York).

Frieden JA (1993) 'Dynamics of International Monetary Systems: International and Domestic Factors in the Rise, Reign, and Demise of the Classical Gold Standard' in Snyder J and Jervis R (eds.), *Coping with Complexity in the International System* (Westview Press, Boulder).

Goodhart C (1988) *The Evolution of Central Banks* (MIT Press Books, Cambridge).

Goodhart C and Illing G (2002) *Financial Crises, Contagion, and the Lender of Last Resort, a Reader* (Oxford University Press, OUP Oxford).

Graeber D (2011) *Debt: The First 5,000 Years* (Melville House, Brooklyn, New York).

Gunningham N and Sinclair D (2017) 'Smart Regulation' in Drahos P (ed), *Regulatory Theory: Foundations and Applications* (Australian National University Press, Canberra).

Hancher L and Moran M (1998) 'Organizing Regulatory Space' in Baldwin R, Scott C and Hood C (eds.), *A Reader in Regulation* (Oxford University Press, Oxford).

Haslett C (2008) *Essentials of Radio Wave Propagation* (Cambridge University Press, Cambridge).

Hayek FA (1990) *Denationalisation of Money—The Argument Refined: An Analysis of the Theory and Practice of Concurrent Currencies* 3rd Ed. (Institute of Economic Affairs, London).

Herring RJ and Santomero AM (2000) 'What Is Optimal Financial Regulation?' in Gup BE (eds.), *The New Financial Architecture* (Quorum Books, Westport, CT).

Huang RH and Schoenmaker D (2014) *Institutional Structure of Financial Regulation: Theories and International Experiences* (Routledge, London).

Hudson M (2004) 'The Archaeology of Money: Debt Versus Barter Theories of Money's Origins' in Wray RL (eds.), *Credit and State Theories of Money* (Edward Elgar, Cheltenham).

Humphrey DB (1995) *Payment Systems: Principles, Practice, and Improvements*, vol 23 (World Bank Publications, Washington, DC).

Jevons WS (1875) 'Barter' in *Money and the Mechanism of Exchange*, vol XVII (D. Appleton and Company, New York).

Keynes JM (1997) 'The Significance of the Gold Points' in Eichengreen B and Flandreau M (eds.), *The Gold Standard in Theory and History* (Routledge, London).

Luhmann N (1990) 'The Autopoiesis of Social Systems' in *Essays on Self-Reference* (Columbia University Press, New York).

Luhmann N (2004) 'The Location of Legal Theory' in *Law as a Social System* (Oxford University Press, Oxford).

Matthews B and Ross L (2010) *Research Methods: A Practical Guide for the Social Sciences* (Pearson Education Limited [Longman], Harlow).

Maturana HR and Varela FJ (1980) *Autopoiesis and Cognition: The Realization of the Living* (Springer Netherlands, Dordrecht).

Menger C (1892) *On the Origins of Money (2009 repr)* (Ludwig von Mises Institute, Auburn, Alabama).

Mohan R (2008) 'Economic Growth, Financial Deepening and Financial Inclusion' in Sharma M (eds.), *Dynamics of Indian Banking: Views and Vistas* (Atlantic Publishers, New Delhi).

Morawczynski O and Miscione G (2008) 'Examining Trust in Mobile Banking Transactions: The Case of M-PESA in Kenya' in Avgerou C, Smith ML and van den Basselaar P (eds.), *Social Dimensions of Information and Communication Technology Policy*, vol 282 (Springer, Boston).

Morgan B and Yeung K (2007) *An Introduction to Law and Regulation* (Cambridge University Press, Cambridge).

Mwenda KK (2006) *Legal Aspects of Financial Services Regulation and the Concept of a Unified Regulator* (World Bank, Washington, DC).

——— (2010) *Legal Aspects of Banking Regulation: Common Law Perspectives from Zambia* (PULP).

Myers CF and Crosby LS (1953) *Principles of Electricity Applied to Telephone and Telegraph Work* (American Telephone & Telegraph Company, New York).

Ogus AI (1994) *Regulation: Legal form and Economic Theory*, vol 152 (Clarendon Press Oxford, Oxford).

Padoa-Schioppa T (2003) 'Central Banks and Financial Stability: Exploring the Land in Between' in Gaspar V, Hartmann P and Sleijpen O (eds.), *Second ECB Central Banking Conference: The Transformation of the European Financial System* (European Central Bank, Frankfurt).

Persaud A (2015) 'Why Do We Regulate Finance?' in *Reinventing Financial Regulation* (Apress, New York).

Phillips R (2003) 'Stakeholder Theory and Organizational Dogma' in Phillips R (eds.), *Stakeholder Theory and Organizational Ethics* (Berrett-Koehler Publishers Inc., San Francisco, CA).

Polizatto VP (1992) 'Prudential Regulation and Banking Supervision' in Vittas D (eds.), *Financial Regulation: Changing the Rules of the Game* (The World Bank, Washington, DC).

Proctor C (2012) *Mann on the Legal Aspect of Money* (7th edn, Oxford University Press, Oxford).

Public Law Project (2013) *An Introduction to Judicial Review* (Public Law Project, London).

Reed Jr AP (1998) *Money and the Global Economy* (Woodhead Publishing, Cambridge).

Religious Tract Society (1854) *Money; Its Nature, History, Uses, and Responsibilities* (The Religious Tract Society, London).

Rogowski R (2013) *Reflexive Labour Law in the World Society* (Edward Elgar Publishing Ltd, Cheltenham).

Santos BDS (2005) 'Law, Politics, and the Subaltern in Counter-Hegemonic Globalization' in Santos BDS and César AR-G (eds.), *Law and Globalization from Below* (Cambridge University Press, Cambridge).

Schooner HM and Taylor MW (2010) *Global Bank Regulation: Principles and Policies* (Academic Press, Burlington, MA).

Scott C (2017) 'The Regulatory State and Beyond' in Drahos P (eds.), *Regulatory Theory: Foundations and Applications* (Australian National University Press, Canberra).

Selznick P and Nonet P (1978) *Law and Society in Transition: Toward Responsive Law* (Harper and Row, New York).

Senior JM. (1951) *Optical Fiber Communications* (Prentice-Hall International Inc, London).

Simon HA (1972) 'Theories of Bound Rationality' in McGuire CB and Radner R (eds.), *Decision and Organization: A Volume in Honor of Jacob Marschak*, vol 12 (North-Holland Publishing Company, Amsterdam).

Singh D (2007) *Banking Regulation of UK and US Financial Markets* (Ashgate, Aldershot, Hampshire).

Stoll RR (1961) *Set Theory and Logic* (Dover Publications, Inc., New York).

Sundararajan V and others (2005) *Financial Sector Assessment* (World Bank & International Monetary Fund, Washington, DC).

Talley SH and Mas I (1992) 'Prudential Regulation and Banking Supervision' in Vittas D (eds.), *Financial Regulation: Changing the Rules of the Game* (The World Bank, Washington, DC).

Taylor MW (1995) "Twin Peaks": A Regulatory Structure for the New Century (London : Centre for the Study of Financial Innovation, London).

Teubner G (1986) 'After Legal Instrumentalism? Strategic Models of Post-regulatory Law' in Teubner G (eds.), *Dilemmas of Law in the Welfare State*, vol 3 (Walter de Gruyter, New York).

Teubner G (1993) *Law as an Autopoietic System* (Blackwell Publishers, Oxford).

Thornton H (1939) *An Enquiry into the Nature and Effects of the Paper Credit of Great Britain (1802)* (Frank Cass & Co Ltd, London).

Tomasic R (2010) 'Beyond 'Light Touch' Regulation of British Banks After the Financial Crisis' in MacNeil IG and O'Brien J (eds.), *The Future of Financial Regulation* (Hart Publishing, Portland).

Williams I and Kwofie B (2014) 'The Impact of Liberalization on the Mobile Telephony Market in Africa' in Skouby KE and Idongesit W (eds.), *The African Mobile Story* (River Publishers, Copenhagen).

Yermack D (2015) 'Is Bitcoin a Real Currency? An Economic Appraisal' in David KC Lee (eds.) *Handbook of Digital Currency* (Elsevier), pp. 31–44.

## *Journal and Research Articles*

Aker J and Mbiti I (2010) 'Mobile Phones and Economic Development in Africa' 24 (3) *Journal of Economic Perspectives* 207, https://www.aeaweb.org/atypon.php?doi=10.1257/jep.24.3.207. 13 December 2018.

Alford R (2010) 'Some Help in Understanding Britain's Banking Crisis, 2007–2009' *LSE Financial Markets Group Paper Series* (London School of Economics), http://www.lse.ac.uk/fmg/workingPapers/specialPapers/PDF/SP193.pdf. 9 February 2018.

Ali R and others (2014a) 'Innovations in Payment Technologies and the Emergence of Digital Currencies' 54 *Quarterly Bulletin* (Bank of England, London), http://www.bankofengland.co.uk/publications/Documents/quarterlybulletin/2014/qb14q3digitalcurrenciesbitcoin1.pdf. 21 July 2018.

——— (2014b) 'The Economics of Digital Currencies' 54 *Quarterly Bulletin* (Bank of England, London), http://www.bankofengland.co.uk/publications/Documents/quarterlybulletin/2014/qb14q3digitalcurrenciesbitcoin2.pdf. 14 September 2018.

Allen F and others (2012) 'The Foundations of Financial Inclusion' *Policy Research Working Paper 6290* (The World Bank), http://documents.worldbank.org/curated/en/348241468329061640/pdf/wps6290.pdf. 20 April 2018.

Argenti J (1997) 'Stakeholders: The Case Against' *Long Range Planning*, vol 30 (3) 442, http://www.sciencedirect.com/science/article/pii/S0024630197000046 16 February 2018.

Baldwin R and Black J (2008) 'Really Responsive Regulation' 71 (1) *The Modern Law Review* 59, http://onlinelibrary.wiley.com/doi/10.1111/j.1468-2230.2008.00681.x/full. 18 November 2018.

Banda J (2007) 'Money Laundering Developments in Malaŵi, 2004 to 2006' *Confronting the Proceeds of Crime in Southern Africa: An Introspection* (Institute for Security Studies, Pretoria), https://www.issafrica.org/chapter-1-money-laundering-developments-in-malawi-2004-to-2006. 22 December 2018.

Barth JR and Wihlborg C (2016) 'Too Big to Fail and Too Big to Save: Dilemmas for Banking Reform' (235) *National Institute Economic Review*, http://journals.sagepub.com/doi/pdf/10.1177/002795011623500113. 9 February 2018.

Baxter H (1998) 'Autopoiesis and the "Relative Autonomy" of Law' 19 *Cardozo Law Rev* 1987, http://heinonline.org/hol-cgi-bin/get_pdf.cgi?handle=hein.journals/cdozo19&section=76. 2 February 2018.

Bayoumi T and Eichengreen B (1995) 'The Stability of the Gold Standard and the Evolution of the International Monetary System' *IMF Working Paper*, https://papers.ssrn.com/sol3/papers.cfm?abstract_id=883236. 1 May 2018.

Black J (1996) 'Constitutionalising Self-Regulation' 59 (1) *The Modern Law Review* 24, http://onlinelibrary.wiley.com/doi/10.1111/j.1468-2230.1996.tb02064.x/full. 19 May 2018.

——— (2005) 'The Emergence of Risk-Based Regulation and the New Public Risk Management in the United Kingdom' *Public Law* 510, https://www.academia.edu/1295947/The_emergence_of_risk-based_regulation_and_the_new_public_risk_management_in_the_United_Kingdom?auto=download. 28 April 2018.

——— (2007) 'Principles Based Regulation: Risks, Challenges and Opportunities' (Principles Based Regulation, University of Sydney, Sydney), http://eprints.lse.ac.uk/62814/. 28 April 2018.

——— (2008) 'Forms and Paradoxes of Principles Based Regulation' *LSE Law, Society and Economy Working Papers 13/2008* (London School of Economics and Political science), http://eprints.lse.ac.uk/23103/1/WPS2008-13.pdf. 28 April 2018.

——— (2010) 'The Rise, Fall and Fate of Principles Based Regulation' *LSE Law, Society and Economy Working Papers 17/2010* (London School of Economics and Political Science), http://eprints.lse.ac.uk/32892/1/WPS2010-17_Black.pdf. 27 April 2018.

——— (2013) 'Seeing, Knowing, and Regulating Financial Markets: Moving the Cognitive Framework from the Economic to the Social' *LSE Law, Society and Economy Working Papers 24/2013*, www.lse.ac.uk/collections/law/wps/WPS2013-24_Black.pdf. 19 May 2018.

Bordo MD (2007) 'A Brief History of Central Banks' *Economic Commentary (Federal Reserve Bank of Cleveland)*, https://www.clevelandfed.org/en/newsroom-and-events/publications/economic-commentary/economic-commentary-archives/2007-economic-commentaries/ec-20071201-a-brief-history-of-central-banks.aspx. 24 May 2018.

Borda-Rodriguez A and Vicari S (2014) 'Rural Co-operative Resilience: The Case of Malaŵi' 2 (1) *Journal of Co-operative Organization and Management* 43, http://oro.open.ac.uk/40390/1/Rural%20co-operative%20resilience%20The%20case%20of%20Malawi.pdf. 13 December 2018.

Braithwaite J (2005) 'Neoliberalism or Regulatory Capitalism' *Occasional Paper 5* (Regulatory Institutions Network, Australian National University), https://www.anu.edu.au/fellows/jbraithwaite/_documents/Articles/Neoliberalism_Regulatory_2005.pdf. 25 April 2018.

Briault C (1999) 'The Rationale for a Single National Financial Services Regulator' *Occasional Paper Series* (Financial Services Authority), http://citeseerx.ist.psu.edu/viewdoc/download?doi=10.1.1.468.6859&rep=rep1&type=pdf. 12 May 2018.

Buckley R, Greenacre J and Malady L (2015) 'The Regulation of Mobile Money in Malaŵi' 14 (3) *Washington University Global Studies Law Review* 435, http://openscholarship.wustl.edu/cgi/viewcontent.cgi?article=1536&context=law_globalstudies. 3 February 2018.

Campbell A (1997) 'Stakeholders: The Case in Favour' *Long Range Planning*, vol 30 (3) 446, http://www.sciencedirect.com/science/article/pii/S0024630197000034. 16 February 2018.

Campbell A and Lastra R (2009) 'Revisiting the Lender of Last Resort' *Banking and Finance Law Review*, vol 24 (3) 453, http://0-search.proquest.com.pugwash.lib.warwick.ac.uk/docview/218867839?accountid=14888. 10 December 2018.

Campbell A and others (2009) 'A New Standard for Deposit Insurance and Government Guarantees After the Crisis' *Journal of Financial Regulation and Compliance*, vol 17 (3) 210, http://dx.doi.org/10.1108/13581980910972214. 20 February 2018.

Chibba M (2009) 'Financial Inclusion, Poverty Reduction and the Millennium Development Goals' 21 (2) *The European Journal of Development Research* 213, http://10.1057/ejdr.2008.17. 20 April 2018.

Cirasino M and Malaguti M (2012) 'From Remittances to M-Payments: Understanding "Alternative" Means of Payment Within the Common Framework of Retail Payments System Regulation' *Financial Infrastructure Series* (The World Bank), http://siteresources.worldbank.org/EXTPAYMENTREMMITTANCE/Resources/WB2012_Mobile_Payments.pdf. 20 February 2018.

Clarke GR, Gebreab FA and Mgombelo HR (2003) 'Telecommunications Reform in Malaŵi' *Policy Research Working Papers* (The World Bank), http://dx.doi.org/10.1596/1813-9450-3036. 2 December 2018.

Cohen BJ (2008) 'The International Monetary System: Diffusion and Ambiguity' *International Affairs* 455, http://escholarship.org/uc/item/97r5n8jx. 4 October 2018.

Córdova-Novion C and Hanlon D (2002) 'Regulatory Governance: Improving the Institutional Basis for Sectoral Regulators' 2 (3) *OECD Journal on Budgeting*, https://www.oecd.org/gov/budgeting/43505850.pdf. 15 February 2018.

Cull R (2010) 'M-PESA: Mobile Payments, Improved Lives for Kenyans' (The World Bank), http://econ.worldbank.org/external/default/main?theSitePK=469382&contentMDK=22594763&menuPK=476752&pagePK=64165401&piPK=64165026. 23 February 2018.

Cunningham R and Friedrich C (2016) 'The Role of Central Banks in Promoting Financial Stability: An International Perspective' *Bank of Canada Staff Discussion Paper 2016–2015* (Bank of Canada), http://www.bankofcanada.ca/wp-content/uploads/2016/07/sdp2016-15.pdf. 1 May 2018.

de Koker L (2013) 'The 2012 Revised FATF Recommendations: Assessing and Mitigating Mobile Money Integrity Risks Within the New Standards Framework' 8 *WASH JL TECH & ARTS* 165.

de Regil AJ (2001) 'Neoliberalism and Its Dogma: The Implications of Its Philosophical Postulates' *TLWNSI Issue Essay Series* (Jus Semper Global Alliance), http://www.jussemper.org/Resources/Economic%20Data/The%20Neo-Capitalist%20Assault/Resources/NeoliberalismPostulates.pdf. 25 April 2018.

Demirguc-Kunt A and Klapper L (2012) 'Measuring Financial Inclusion: The Global Findex Database' *Policy Research Working Papers* (The World Bank), https://laomfa.org/wp-content/uploads/formidable/7/Measuring-Financial-Inclusion_The-World-Bank-2010.pdf. 20 April 2018.

Dev SM (2006) 'Financial Inclusion: Issues and Challenges' 41 (41) *Economic and Political Weekly* 4310, http://www.jstor.org/stable/4418799. 20 April 2018.

Diamond DW and Dybvig PH (1983) 'Bank Runs, Deposit Insurance, and Liquidity' 91 (3) *Journal of Political Economy* 401, http://www.journals.uchicago.edu/doi/pdfplus/10.1086/261155. 27 April 2018.

Di Castri S (2013) 'Mobile Money: Enabling Regulatory Solutions' *GSMA*, http://www.gsma.com/publicpolicy/wp-content/uploads/2013/02/GSMA2013_Report_Mobilelectronicmoney-EnablingRegulatorySolutions.pdf. 20 February 2018.

Dittus P and Klein M (2011) *On Harnessing the Potential of Financial Inclusion* (BIS Working Papers, Bank of International Settlements), http://www.bis.org/publ/work347.pdf. 20 February 2018.

Donovan KP (2012) 'Mobile Money, More Freedom? The Impact of M-PESA's Network Power on Development as Freedom' 6 *International Journal of Communication* 2647, http://ijoc.org/index.php/ijoc/article/view/1575. 20 May 2018.

Dupas P and others (2016) 'Banking the Unbanked? Evidence from Three Countries' *NBER Working Papers* (National Bureau of Economic Research), https://web.stanford.edu/~pdupas/BankingTheUnbanked.pdf. 9 March 2018.

Ehrbeck T and Tarazi M (2011) 'Putting the Banking in Branchless Banking: Regulation and the Case for Interest-Bearing and Insured Electronic Money

Savings Accounts' *Mobile Financial Services Development Report* (World Economic Forum), http://www3.weforum.org/docs/WEF_MFSD_Report_2011.pdf. 20 February 2018.

Evans DS and Pirchio A (2014) 'An Empirical Examination of Why Mobile Money Schemes Ignite in Some Developing Countries but Flounder in Most' 13 (4) *Review of Network Economics* 397, https://www.degruyter.com/view/j/rne.2014.13.issue-4/rne-2015-0020/rne-2015-0020.xml. 12 May 2018.

Fengler W (2012) 'How Kenya Became a World Leader for Mobile Money' *Africa Can End Poverty* (The World Bank, Washington, DC), http://blogs.worldbank.org/africacan/how-kenya-became-a-world-leader-for-mobilelectronicmoney. 7 April 2018.

Flores-Roux EM and Mariscal J (2010) 'The Enigma of Mobile Money Systems' (79) *Communications & Strategies*, ftp://ftp.repec.org/opt/ReDIF/RePEc/idt/journl/CS7903/CS79_MARISCAM_FLORES-ROUX.pdf. 14 February 2018.

Friedman M (1971) 'The Euro-Dollar Market: Some First Principles' *Review (Federal Bank of St Louis)*, https://research.stlouisfed.org/publications/review/71/07/Principles_Jul1971.pdf. 13 September 2018.

Gilman L (2016) 'The Impact of Mobile Money Interoperability in Tanzania' (GSMA), http://www.gsma.com/mobilefordevelopment/wp-content/uploads/2016/10/2016_GSMA_The-impact-of-mobilelectronicmoney-interoperability-in-Tanzania.pdf. 10 May 2018.

Goodhart CAE (1998) 'The Two Concepts of Money: Implications for the Analysis of Optimal Currency Areas' 14 *European Journal of Political Economy* 407, http://www.sciencedirect.com/science/article/pii/S0176268098000159. 29 April 2018.

Goodhart C and Schoenmaker D (1995) 'Should the Functions of Monetary Policy and Banking Supervision Be Separated?' 47 (4) *Oxford Economic Papers* 539, http://oep.oxfordjournals.org/content/47/4/539.extract. 12 February 2018.

Gray J (2009) 'Is It Time to Highlight the Limits of Risk-Based Financial Regulation?' 4 (1) *Capital Markets Law Journal* 50, https://doi.org/10.1093/cmlj/kmn035. 28 April 2018.

Greco Jr TH (1997) 'New Money: A Creative Opportunity for Business' 11 (3) *Global Development Research Centre First Published in Perspectives on Business and Global Change (World Business Academy), vol 11 No. 3*, http://www.gdrc.org/icm/new-money.html. 14 November 2018.

Greenacre J, Malady L and Buckley R (2014) 'The Regulation of Mobile Money in Malaŵi' (Centre for International Finance and Regulation), http://www.uncdf.org/sites/default/files/Documents/the_regulation_of_mobile_money_in_malawi_project_report_final_version.pdf. 30 June 2018.

Grossman R (2006) 'The Emergence of Central Banks and Banking Regulation in Comparative Perspective' *Wesleyan Economics Working Papers* (Wesleyan University, Department of Economics), http://repec.wesleyan.edu/pdf/rgrossman/2006021_grossman.pdf. 1 June 2018.

Grossman SJ and Miller MH (1988) 'Liquidity and Market Structure' 43 (3) *The Journal of Finance* 617, http://onlinelibrary.wiley.com/doi/10.1111/j.1540-6261.1988.tb04594.x/pdf. 6 October 2018.

Gunnar Camner ES, Caroline Pulver (2009) 'What Makes a Successful Mobile Money Implementation? Learnings from M-PESA in Kenya and Tanzania' (GSMA), http://www.gsma.com/mobilefordevelopment/wp-content/uploads/2012/03/What-makes-a-successful-mobilelectronicmoney-implementation.pdf. 1 March 2018.

Halliday S (2009) 'The First Common Market? The Hanseatic League' 59 (7) *History Today*, http://www.historytoday.com/stephen-halliday/first-common-market-hanseatic-league. 13 September 2018.

Harrigan P (2003) 'Tales of a Thaler' 54 (1) *ARAMCO World* 14, http://archive.aramcoworld.com/issue/200301/tales.of.a.thaler.htm. 13 September 2018.

Hawaiju G (2013) 'The Impact of Mobile Money Transfer Technology' *Clknet Policy Brief No. 12:* (CLKnet), http://docplayer.net/14873424-Curriculum-vitae-giuseppe-travaglini.html. 11 November 2018.

Hedgedus N (2012) 'An African Success Story Revealed' (2) *Ericsson Business Review* 10, http://www.ericsson.com/res/thecompany/docs/publications/business-review/2012/issue2/an_african_success_story_explained.pdf. 15 December 2018.

Heyer A and Mas I (2009) 'Seeking Fertile Grounds for Mobile Money' *Mobile Money for the Unbanked* (GSMA), http://www.gsma.com/mobilefordevelopment/wp-content/uploads/2012/03/fertile_grounds_mobile_money55.pdf. 14 February 2018.

Hilton A (1994) 'UK Financial Supervision: A Blueprint for Change' (Centre for the Study of Financial Innovation [CSFI], London).

Hughes N and Lonie S (2007) 'M-PESA: Mobile Money for the "Unbanked" Turning Cellphones into 24-Hour Tellers in Kenya' 2 (1–2) *Innovations* 63, http://www.mitpressjournals.org/doi/pdf/10.1162/itgg.2007.2.1-2.63. 15 December 2018.

Hunt C (2016) 'A Short History of Prudential Regulation and Supervision at the Reserve Bank' *Bulletin* (Reserve Bank of New Zealand), http://www.rbnz.govt.nz/-/media/ReserveBank/Files/Publications/Bulletins/2016/2016aug79-14.pdf. 1 May 2018.

Hüpkes E, Quintyn M and Taylor MW (2006) 'Accountability Arrangements for Financial Sector Regulators' 39 *IMF Economic Issues*, https://www.imf.org/external/pubs/ft/issues/issues39/ei39.pdf. 27 February 2018.

Hussein MK (2009) 'Opposition Politics in Malaŵi: Hopeful Signs Amid the Warnings' 16 (3) *South African Journal of International Affairs.*

Isern J and others (2005) 'AML/CFT Regulation: Implications for Financial Service Providers That Serve Low-Income People' 29 *CGAP Focus Note*, https://www.cgap.org/sites/default/files/CGAP-Focus-Note-AML-CFT-Regulation-Implications-for-Financial-Service-Providers-That-Serve-Low-Income-People-Jul-2005.pdf. 10 May 2018.

Isern J and De Koker L (2012) 'AML/CFT: Strengthening Financial Inclusion and Integrity' *CGAP Focus Notes* (CGAP), http://dro.deakin.edu.au/eserv/DU:30020790/dekoker-amlcft-2009.pdf. 14 November 2018.

Iwamura M, Kitamura Y and Matsumoto T (2014) 'Is Bitcoin the Only Cryptocurrency in the Town? Economics of Cryptocurrency and Friedrich A Hayek' *SSRN*, http://papers.ssrn.com/sol3/papers.cfm?abstract_id=2405790. 14 September 2018.

Jack W and Suri T (2011) 'Mobile Money: The Economics of M-PESA' (National Bureau of Economic Research), http://www.nber.org/papers/w16721. 15 December 2018.

Jack W, Suri T and Townsend RM (2010) 'Monetary Theory and Electronic Money: Reflections on the Kenyan Experience' 96 (1) *Federal Reserve Bank of Richmond Economic Quarterly* 83, https://www.richmondfed.org/publications/research/economic_quarterly/2010/q1/townsend. 15 December 2018.

Jenkins B (2008) 'Developing Mobile Money Ecosystems' (Washington, DC: International Finance Corporation and Harvard Kennedy School), http://ww.gsma.com/mobilefordevelopment/wp-content/uploads/2012/06/report_30_mobilemoney.pdf. 13 December 2018.

Jentzsch N (2012) 'Implications of Mandatory Registration of Mobile Phone Users in Africa' 36 (8) *Telecommunications Policy* 608, http://doi.org/10.1016/j.telpol.2012.04.002. 14 November 2018.

Kalima D (2016) 'Mobile Payment in Malaŵi: Integrating and Cost Reducing: The Mobile Money Revolution' (*Journ Africa*), http://journafrica.de/en/banking-economy-finance-innovation-malawi-45312. 23 February 2018.

Kane S (2002) 'Telecom Reform and Poverty Alleviation in Kenya' (3) *African Journal of Information and Communication* 31.

Kelley Jr EW (1999) 'The Future of Electronic Money: A Regulator's Perspective' 34 *Spectrum* (IEEE, New York), http://spectrum.ieee.org/telecom/standards/the-future-of-electronic-money-a-regulators-perspective. 14 September 2018.

Klein MU and Mayer C (2011) 'Mobile Banking and Financial Inclusion: The Regulatory Lessons' *Policy Research Working Paper* (The World Bank), http://documents.worldbank.org/curated/en/docsearch/document-type/620265. 14 February 2018.

Kremers J and Schoenmaker D (2010) 'Twin Peaks: Experiences in the Netherlands' December 2010 *LSE Financial Markets Group Paper Series*, http://www.lse.ac.uk/fmg/workingPapers/specialPapers/PDF/SP196.pdf. 4 October 2018.

Lall SV, Wang H and Munthali T (2009) 'Explaining High Transport Costs Within Malaŵi—Bad Roads or Lack of Trucking Competition?' *Policy Research Working Paper 5133* (World Bank Publications), http://elibrary.worldbank.org/doi/pdf/10.1596/1813-9450-5133. 11 March 2018.

Lee BC and Longe-Akindemowo O (1999) 'Regulatory Issues in Electronic Money: A Legal-Economics Analysis' 1 (1) *Netnomics* 53, http://link.springer.com/article/10.1023/A:1011445620486. 12 March 2018.

Lelieveldt SL (1996) 'How to Regulate Electronic Cash: An Overview of Regulatory Issues and Strategies' 46 *Am UL Rev* 1163, http://heinonline.org/hol-cgi-bin/get_pdf.cgi?handle=hein.journals/aulr46&section=39. 17 March 2018.

Leonard RA (1994) 'Money and Language' (55) *Money: Lure, Lore, and Literature* 1, https://www.unc.edu/~salemi/Econ006/Leonard.pdf. 13 September 2018.

Lerner AP (1947) 'Money as a Creature of the State' 37 (2) *The American Economic Review* 312, http://www.jstor.org/stable/pdf/1821139.pdf. 29 April 2018.

Lourenço A (2010) 'Autopoietic Social Systems Theory: The Co-Evolution of Law and the Economy' 35 *Austl J Leg Phil* 35, http://heinonline.org/hol-cgi-bin/get_pdf.cgi?handle=hein.journals/ajlph35&section=6. 19 May 2018.

Luhmann N (1991) 'Operational Closure and Structural Coupling: The Differentiation of the Legal System' 13 *Cardozo L Rev* 1419, http://heinonline.org/hol-cgi-bin/get_pdf.cgi?handle=hein.journals/cdozo13&section=94. 19 May 2018.

Luke C (2015) 'Critique of Microfinance Raises Questions About Efficacy, Donor Support of the Industry' (*Devex Impact*), https://www.devex.com/news/critique-of-microfinance-raises-questions-about-efficacy-donor-support-of-the-industry-85617. 20 April 2018.

Mas I and Morawczynski O (2009) 'Designing Mobile Money Services Lessons from M-PESA' 4 (2) *Innovations* 77, http://www.mitpressjournals.org/doi/pdf/10.1162/itgg.2009.4.2.77. 20 May 2018.

Mas I and Ng'weno A (2010) 'Three Keys to M-PESA's Success: Branding, Channel Management and Pricing' (GSMA), http://www.www.oneapigw.gsma.com/mobilefordevelopment/wp-content/uploads/2012/06/keystom-pesassuccess4jan69.pdf. 15 December 2018.

Mas I and Radcliffe D (2011) 'Mobile Payments Go Viral: M-PESA in Kenya' 32 *The Capco Institute Journal of Financial Transformation* 169, http://www.capco.com/sites/all/files/journal-32_article-16.pdf. 15 December 2018.

Mascini P and Wijk EV (2009) 'Responsive Regulation at the Dutch Food and Consumer Product Safety Authority: An Empirical Assessment of Assumptions Underlying the Theory' 3 (1) *Regulation & Governance* 27, http://citeseerx.ist.psu.edu/viewdoc/download?doi=10.1.1.1001.348&rep=rep1&type=pdf. 19 May 2018.

Mauree V and Kohli G (2013) 'The Mobile Money Revolution—Part 2: Financial Inclusion Enabler' *ITUT Technology Watch* (International Telecommunications Union), https://www.itu.int/dms_pub/itu-t/oth/23/01/T23010000200002PDFE.pdf. 1 May 2018.

Maurer B (2012) 'Regulation as Retrospective Ethnography: Mobile Money and the Arts of Cash' 27 (2) *Banking and Finance Law Review* 299, http://www.imtfi.uci.edu/files/docs/2012/bankingfinance_law_review_27.2_maurer.pdf. 15 December 2018.

McCubbins MD, Noll RG and Weingast BR (1989) 'Structure and Process, Politics and Policy: Administrative Arrangements and the Political Control of Agencies' 75 *Virginia Law Review* 431, http://scholarship.law.duke.edu/cgi/viewcontent.cgi?article=5950&context=faculty_scholarship. 20 February 2018.

Michael B (2014) 'The "Twin Peaks" Regulatory Model: The Future of Financial Regulation?' *Banking Today* 2, http://www.law.hku.hk/aiifl/wp-content/uploads/2014/09/Twin-Peaks.pdf. 3 October 2018.

http://www.bankofengland.co.uk/publications/Documents/quarterlybulletin/2013/qb130403.pdf. 4 October 2018.

Morawczynski O and Pickens M (2009) 'Poor People Using Mobile Financial Services: Observations on Customer Usage and Impact from M-PESA' *CGAP Brief* (August), http://www.cgap.org/publications/poor-people-using-mobile-financial-services. 29 April 2018.

Muthiora B (2015) 'Enabling Mobile Money Policies in Kenya: Fostering a Digital Financial Revolution' (GSMA), https://www.itu.int/en/ITU-T/focusgroups/dfs/Documents/2015_MMU_Enabling-Mobilelectronicmoney-Policies-in-Kenya.pdf. 17 February 2018.

Naqvi M and Southgate J (2013) 'Banknotes, Local Currencies and Central Bank Objectives' *Bank of England Quarterly Bulletin* Q4 (Bank of England, London).

Ngwu FN (2015) 'Promoting Formal Financial Inclusion in Africa: As Institutional Re-examination of the Policies with a Case Study of Nigeria' 16 (4) 306 *Journal of Banking Regulation*, http://link.springer.com/article/10.1057/jbr.2014.13. 15 December 2018.

Noko J (2011) 'Dollarization: The Case of Zimbabwe' 31 (2) *Cato Journal* 339, https://www.ciaonet.org/attachments/18686/uploads. 14 September 2015.

Norman B, Shaw R and Speight G (2011) 'The History of Interbank Settlement Arrangements: Exploring Central Banks' Role in the Payment System'

*Bank of England Working Paper* (Bank of England), http://ssrn.com/abstract=1863929. 30 May 2018.

Nyborg K (2000) 'Homo Economicus and Homo Politicus: Interpretation and Aggregation of Environmental Values' 42 (3) *Journal of Economic Behavior & Organization* 305, http://www.sciencedirect.com/science/article/pii/S0167268100000913. 21 December 2018.

Ogus A (1995) 'Rethinking Self-Regulation' 15 (1) *Oxford Journal of Legal Studies* 97, http://ojls.oxfordjournals.org/content/15/1/97.full.pdf. 19 May 2018.

——— (2009) 'Regulation Revisited' (2) *Public Law* 332, http://repub.eur.nl/pub/16031/A.%20Ogus,%20Regulation%20Revisited.pdf. 19 May 2018.

Omwansa TK (2009) 'M-PESA: Progress and Prospects' *Innovations/Mobile World Congress* 107, https://profiles.uonbi.ac.ke/tomwansa/files/innov-gs-ma-omwansa.pdf. 1 December 2018.

Palma JG (2012) 'How the Full Opening of the Capital Account to Highly Liquid Financial Markets Led Latin America to Two and a Half Cycles of "Mania, Panic and Crash"' *Cambridge Working Papers in Economics (CWPE) 1201*, http://www.econ.cam.ac.uk/dae/repec/cam/pdf/cwpe1201.pdf. 19 May 2018.

Paterson J and Teubner G (1998) 'Changing Maps: Empirical Legal Autopoiesis' 7 (4) *Social & Legal Studies* 451, http://sls.sagepub.com/content/7/4/451.short. 2 February 2018.

Peltzman S (1976) 'Toward a More General Theory of Regulation' 19 (2) *The Journal of Law and Economics* 211, http://www.journals.uchicago.edu/doi/pdfplus/10.1086/466865. 1 February 2018.

Posner RA (1974) 'Theories of Economic Regulation' 5 (2) *Bell Journal of Economics and Management Science* 335, http://www.thecre.com/oira/wp-content/uploads/2016/03/Posner.pdf. 1 February 2018.

Quaglia L (2010) 'Completing the Single Market in Financial Services: The Politics of Competing Advocacy Coalitions' 17 (7) *Journal of European Public Policy* 1007, http://aei.pitt.edu/33124/1/quaglia._lucia_(2).pdf. 17 October 2018.

Quintyn M and Taylor MW (2002) 'Regulatory and Supervisory Independence and Financial Stability' (International Monetary Fund, Washington, DC), https://www.imf.org/external/pubs/ft/wp/2002/wp0246.pdf. 1 February 2018.

Saidi E (2009) 'Mobile Opportunities, Mobile Problems: Assessing Mobile Commerce Implementation Issues in Malaŵi' 14 (1) *Journal of Internet Banking and Commerce* 1.

Sarma M and Pais J (2011) 'Financial Inclusion and Development' 23 *Journal of International Development* 613, http://onlinelibrary.wiley.com/doi/10.1002/jid.1698/pdf. 20 April 2018.

Satåo S and Humphrey DB (1995) *Transforming Payment Systems: Meeting the Needs of Emerging Market Economies (World Bank Discussion Papers, 0259–210X; 291)* (World Bank).

Saubramaniam G 'Mobile Money: A Theoretical Study of Alternative Media of Exchange, and an Empirical Study with Respect to M-Pesa in Kenya' (Toulouse School of Economics 2013), http://papers.ssrn.com/sol3/papers.cfm?abstract_id=2278679. 15 December 2018.

Schinasi GJ (2003) 'Responsibility of Central Banks for Stability in Financial Markets' WP/03/121 *IMF Working Papers*, https://www.imf.org/external/pubs/ft/wp/2003/wp03121.pdf. 1 June 2018.

Schmidt RA and others (1999) 'Deshopping-the Art of Illicit Consumption' 27 (8) *International Journal of Retail & Distribution Management* 290, http://www.emeraldinsight.com/doi/pdfplus/10.1108/09590559910288569. 4 November 2018.

Scott C (2001) 'Analysing Regulatory Space: Fragmented Resources and Institutional Design' *Public Law* 329, http://researchrepository.ucd.ie/bitstream/handle/10197/6785/AnalysingRegSpace.pdf?sequence=2. 1 December 2018.

Shin HS (2009) 'Reflections on Northern Rock: The Bank Run That Heralded the Global Financial Crisis' 23 (1) *The Journal of Economic Perspectives* 101, http://dx.doi.org/10.1257/089533009797614045. 4 October 2018.

Shleifer A (2005) 'Understanding Regulation' 11 (4) *European Financial Management* 439, http://scholar.harvard.edu/files/shleifer/files/02_eufm00121.pdf?m=1360042225. 19 May 2018.

Stigler GJ (1971) 'The Theory of Economic Regulation' *The Bell Journal of Economics and Management Science* 3, http://hsecon.tripod.com/stigler-regulation.pdf. 1 February 2018.

Tarazi M and Breloff P (2010) 'Nonbank Electronic Money Issuers: Regulatory Approaches to Protecting Customer Funds' *CGAP Focus Note*, https://www.cgap.org/sites/default/files/CGAP-Focus-Note-Nonbank-Electronicmoney-Issuers-Regulatory-Approaches-to-Protecting-Customer-Funds-Jul-2010.pdf. 3 February 2018.

Taylor MW (1995) *"Twin Peaks": A Regulatory Structure for the New Century* (Centre for the Study of Financial Innovation, London).

——— (2011) 'The Road from "Twin peaks"—And the Way Back' 16 (1) *Connecticut Insurance Law Journal* 61, http://insurancejournal.org/wp-content/uploads/2011/07/Abstract-21.pdf. 3 October 2018.

Teubner G (1983) 'Substantive and Reflexive Elements in Modern Law' *Law and Society Review* 239, http://www.jstor.org/stable/3053348. 18 November 2018.

Thatcher M (2002) 'Delegation to Independent Regulatory Agencies: Pressures, Functions and Contextual Mediation' 25 (1) *West European Politics* 125, http://0-dx.doi.org.pugwash.lib.warwick.ac.uk/10.1080/713601588. 16 February 2018.

'The Warwick Commission on International Financial Reform: In Praise of Unlevel Playing Fields' (2009) (University of Warwick), https://www2.warwick.ac.uk/research/warwickcommission/financialreform/report/uw_warcomm_intfinreform_09.pdf. 2 June 2018.

Varela FG, Maturana HR and Uribe R (1974) 'Autopoiesis: The Organization of Living Systems, Its Characterization and a Model' 5 (4) *Biosystems* 187, http://homepages.math.uic.edu/~kauffman/MUV.pdf. 19 May 2018.

Witteveen WJ (2005) 'A Self-Regulation Paradox: Notes Towards the Social Logic of Regulation' 9 (1) *Electronic Journal of Comparative Law* 1, http://www.ejcl.org/91/art91-2.PDF. 19 May 2018.

Wymeersch E (2007) 'The Structure of Financial Supervision in Europe: About Single Financial Supervisors, Twin Peaks and Multiple Financial Supervisors' 8 *European Business Organization Law Review* 237.

## *Conference Papers and Proceedings*

Aamo BS (2012) 'FATF's Focus on Financial Inclusion: Protecting the Integrity of the Global Financial System' (*Global Partnership for Financial Inclusion Conference on Standard-Setting Bodies and Financial Inclusion: Promoting Financial Inclusion Through Proportionate Standards and Guidance*, Basel), http://www.fatf-gafi.org/publications/fatfgeneral/documents/fatfsfocusonfinancialinclusionprotectingtheintegrityoftheglobalfinancialsystem.html. 20 February 2018.

Brezo F and Bringas PG (2012) 'Issues and Risks Associated with Cryptocurrencies Such as Bitcoin' (*SOTICS 2012: The Second International Conference on Social Eco-Informatics*, https://www.thinkmind.org/download.php?articleid=sotics_2012_1_40_30101. 14 September 2018.

Dass R and Pal S (2011) 'Exploring the Factors Affecting the Adoption of Mobile Financial Services Among the Rural Under-Banked' (*European Conference on Information Systems*, Helsinki), http://aisel.aisnet.org/ecis2011/246. 26 April 2018.

Eyal I and others (2016) 'Bitcoin-NG: A Scalable Blockchain Protocol' (*13th USENIX Symposium on Networked Systems Design and Implementation [NSDI' 16] March 16–18, 2016* Santa Clara, CA, USA), https://www.usenix.org/system/files/conference/nsdi16/nsdi16-paper-eyal.pdf. 3 April 2018.

Kenani JM, Kaunda SG and Chafuwa C (2014) 'Taxation Policy and Performance in Malaŵi Since Independence' (*Inaugural ECAMA Research Symposium*, Lilongwe), http://www.slideshare.net/IFPRIMaSSP/taxation-policy-and-performance-in-malawi-since-independence-by-sg-kaunda-j-kenani. 17 February 2018.

Ndiaye F (2007) 'National Strategy for Financial Inclusion: Challenges and Opportunities' (*3rd African Microfinance Conference, Kampala, 20–23 August 2007*), http://www.fsdu.or.ug/pdfs/3AMC%20Conference%20Presentations/Day%202/Morning%20Plenary%200830%20-%201100/National%20Strategy%20for%20Financial%20Inclusion%20-%20Chanlleges%20&%20Opportunities.pdf. 14 February 2018.

Nyaoma G (2009) 'Regulating Mobile Money: The Case of M-Pesa in Kenya' (*Global Policy Forum, Nairobi, 16 September 2009*), http://www.afi-global.org/sites/default/files/GPF_Gerald_Nyaoma.pdf. 20 May 2018.

Parlour R (2014) *Strategic Issues in Financial Markets Regulation* Post-Graduate Seminar, University of Warwick.

Sultana R (2009) 'Mobile Banking: Overview of Regulatory Framework in Emerging Markets' (*4th Communication Policy Research, South Conference*, Negombo, Sri Lanka), http://papers.ssrn.com/sol3/papers.cfm?abstract_id=1554160. 14 February 2018.

Tarullo DK (2016) 'Financial Regulation Since the Crisis' (*Federal Reserve Bank of Cleveland and Office of Financial Research 2016 Financial Stability Conference*, Washington, DC), https://www.federalreserve.gov/newsevents/speech/tarullo20161202a.htm. 1 May 2018.

Williams I (2013) 'Regulatory Frameworks and Implementation Patterns for Mobile Money in Africa: The Case of Kenya, Ghana and Nigeria' (*ICT Conference*, Accra, Ghana), http://www.academia.edu/download/42068100/Regulatory_frameworks_and_Implementation20160204-17000-9tcws1.pdf. 17 February 2018.

## *Interviews and Requests for Information*

Chimbe T (2015) Deputy Director—Legal (Consumer Affairs); Malaŵi Communications Regulatory Authority, (Interview) Blantyre, Malaŵi.

Mbekeani W (2015) Head, Mobile Money Division, TNM, (Interview) Blantyre, Malaŵi.

Mkoloma B (2015) Product and Development Manager, Airtel Money, (Interview) Lilongwe, Malaŵi.

Mphepo A (2018) Senior Public Relations Manager, Telekom Networks Malaŵi (RFI).

Ngwira M (2017) Spokesperson, Reserve Bank of Malaŵi (10 March 2017) (personal communication).

Ngwira M (2018) Spokesperson, Reserve Bank of Malaŵi (RFI).

NyaMoyo CCC (2015) (Interview) Madise Village, Mzimba, Malaŵi.

Nyirenda A (2015) Malaŵi Communications Regulatory Authority, (Interview) Blantyre, Malaŵi.

Phiri AT (2015) Director, Financial Intelligence Unit (FIU), (Interview) Lilongwe, Malaŵi.
Reserve Bank of Malaŵi (RBM) Headquarters (2015) (Interview) Lilongwe, Malaŵi.
Reserve Bank of Malaŵi (RBM) MicroFinance Division (2015) Reserve Bank of Malaŵi, (Interview) Blantyre, Malaŵi.
Twea T (2015) Pensioner, (Interview) Thela Village, Mzimba, Malaŵi.

### *Thesis*

Kalilombe L, 'Central Bank Governance, Accountability and Independence: The Case of Reserve Bank of Malaŵi ' (MA, University of Kwazulu-Natal 2008), http://researchspace.ukzn.ac.za/handle/10413/575. 5 May 2018.
Shima HN, 'The Concept of Economic Integration with Specific Reference to Southern Africa ' (PhD Thesis, University of Pretoria 2009), http://upetd.up.ac.za/thesis/available/etd-03282009-130922/unrestricted/00front.pdf. 17 March 2018.

### *In-House Publications and Reports*

ADB (2014) 'Comparing the Real Size of African Economies' African Development Bank, https://www.afdb.org/fileadmin/uploads/afdb/Documents/Project-and-Operations/Highlights_-_Comparing_the_Real_Size_of_Africa_Economies_%E2%80%93_Main_results_of_the_2011_round_of_the_International_Comparison_Program__ICP_.pdf. 20 July 2018.
AFI (2010) 'Enabling Mobile Money Transfer: The Central Bank of Kenya's Treatment of M-Pesa' (Alliance for Financial Inclusion), http://www.gsma.com/mobilefordevelopment/wp-content/uploads/2013/09/enablingmobilemoneytransfer92.pdf. 15 December 2018.
Anon (2013) 'Malawian Snapshot: 2013 Quarter 2' (KPMG [Malaŵi]), https://www.kpmg.com/Africa/en/KPMG-in-Africa/Documents/2013%20African%20Country%20Reports/KPMG_Malawi%202013Q2.pdf. 13 September 2018.
——— (2017) 'Index of Economic Freedom (Malaŵi)' (*The Heritage Foundation*), http://www.heritage.org/index/country/malawi. 10 March 2018.
Bank TW (2008) 'The World Bank Group in Malaŵi' *The World Bank Group*, http://siteresources.worldbank.org/MALAWIEXTN/Resources/Malawi_Brochure_2008.pdf. 8 February 2018.
Bhatia A and Mwanakatwe P (2016) 'Malaŵi 2016' (Africa Economic Outlook, OECD Development Centre), http://www.africaneconomicoutlook.org/sites/default/files/2016-05/Malawi_GB_2016%20WEB.pdf. 9 March 2018.

BIS (1997) 'The Payment System in Malaŵi' (Bank of International Settlements), https://www.bis.org/cpss/paysys/Malawi.pdf. 20 February 2018.

Chipeta C and Kanyumbu E (2015) 'Improving Access to Banking Services in Malaŵi' (Southern African Institute for Economic Research), http://aercafricaevents.org/wp-content/uploads/2015%20December/Group%20C/C3-Improving-access-to-banking-services-in-Malawi-Chinyamata-Chipeta-and-Esmie-Kanyumbu-FR.pdf. 14 November 2018.

Cisco (2012) 'MTN Mobile Money Service' *Mobile Connected Life Experiences* (Cisco), http://www.cisco.com/en/US/solutions/collateral/ns341/ns525/ns537/ns705/ns1058/Cisco_MTN_CS.pdf. 19 March 2015.

CPSS (2001) 'Core Principles for Systemically Important Payment Systems' (Bank for International Settlements [Committee on Payment and Settlement Systems]), http://www.bis.org/cpmi/publ/d43.pdf. 17 February 2018.

——— (2012) 'Innovations in Retail Payments' (Bank for International Settlements [Committee on Payment and Settlement Systems]), http://www.bis.org/cpmi/publ/d102.pdf. 20 February 2018.

de Swaan T and others (1995) 'The Supervision of Financial Conglomerates' (Tripartite Group of Bank, Securities and Insurance Regulators), https://www.iosco.org/library/pubdocs/pdf/IOSCOPD47.pdf. 3 October 2018.

Dermish A, Phiri J and Sanford C (2012) 'Mapping the Retail Payment Services Landscape Malaŵi' (FinMark Trust), http://www.finmark.org.za/wp-content/uploads/pubs/Rep_RPS_landscape_Malawi_2012.pdf. 10 February 2018.

Development of Postal Services in 2011: A Few Key Figures (2011) Universal Postal Union, http://www.alejandrobarros.com/media/users/1/50369/files/4363/Statistics_2011_UPU.pdf. 10 May 2018.

EBA (2014) 'Opinion on "virtual currencies"' (European Banking Authority, London), http://www.eba.europa.eu/documents/10180/657547/EBA-Op-2014-08+Opinion+on+Virtual+Currencies.pdf. 15 April 2015.

ECB (2002) 'The Role of Central Banks in Prudential Supervision' (European Central Bank, Frankfurt), https://www.ecb.europa.eu/pub/pdf/other/prudentialsupcbrole_en.pdf. 1 May 2018.

——— (2012) 'Virtual Currency Schemes' (European Central Bank, Frankfurt), https://www.ecb.europa.eu/pub/pdf/other/virtualcurrencyschemes201210en.pdf. 15 April 2015.

FATF (2012) 'International Standards on Combating Money Laundering and the Financing of Terrorism & Proliferation (Updated October 2016)' (Financial Action Task Force), http://www.fatf-gafi.org/media/fatf/documents/recommendations/pdfs/FATF_Recommendations.pdf. 20 February 2018.

——— (2014) 'Virtual Currencies Key Definitions and Potential AML/CFT Risks' (Financial Action Task Force), http://www.fatf-gafi.org/media/fatf/documents/reports/Virtual-currency-key-definitions-and-potential-aml-cft-risks.pdf. 14 September 2018.

FCIC (2011) 'The Financial Crisis Inquiry Report: Final Report of the National Commission on the Causes of the Financial and Economic Crisis in the United States' (The Financial Crisis Inquiry Commission), https://www.gpo.gov/fdsys/pkg/GPO-FCIC/pdf/GPO-FCIC.pdf. 1 May 2018.

Finscope (2014) 'FinScope Consumer Survey Malaŵi 2014' (Finmark Trust, Midrand, Johannesburg), http://www.finmark.org.za/wp-content/uploads/2016/08/FS-Malawi-2014-Launch-presentation.pdf. 5 May 2017.

G-10 (2001) 'Chapter III: Effects of Consolidation on Financial Risk in *Report on Consolidation in the Financial Sector*' (Group of 10, International Monetary Fund, Washington, DC), https://www.imf.org/external/np/g10/2001/01/Eng/pdf/file3.pdf. 1 June 2018.

Gibson A (2006) 'Developing Financial Services Markets for the Poor: FinMark in South Africa' *Making Markets Work for the Poor: Case Studies Series* (Schweizerische Eidgenossenschaft), http://www.value-chains.org/dyn/bds/docs/614/M4P_case_study_FinMark_april2007.pdf. 19 March 2015.

GSMA (2015) 'The Mobile Economy Sub-Saharan Africa 2015', https://www.gsmaintelligence.com/research/?file=721eb3d4b80a36451202d0473b-3c4a63&download. 12 December 2018.

IFC (2011) 'IFC Mobile Money Study 2011 - Summary Report' (International Finance Corporation), http://www.ifc.org/wps/wcm/connect/fad057004a052eb88b23ffdd29332b51/MobileMoneyReport-Summary.pdf?MOD=AJPERES. 15 December 2018.

ITU (2009) 'Information Society Statistical Profiles 2009 - Africa' (International Telecommunications Union), http://www.itu.int/dms_pub/itu-d/opb/ind/D-IND-RPM.AF-2009-PDF-E.pdf. 12 December 2018.

Jost PM and Sandhu HS (2003) 'The Hawala Alternative Remittance System and Its Role in Money Laundering' (Interpol), https://www.peacepalacelibrary.nl/ebooks/files/hawala.pdf. 14 February 2018.

Lancaster H (2015) 'Malaŵi—Telecoms, Mobile and Broadband—Statistics and Analyses' (Paul Budde Communication Pty Ltd), https://www.budde.com.au/Research/Malawi-Telecoms-Mobile-and-Broadband-Statistics-and-Analyses. 11 October 2018.

MACRA (2014) 'Strategic Plan 2015–2020' (Malaŵi Communications Regulatory Authority), http://www.macra.org.mw/wp-content/uploads/2014/09/MACRA-Strategic-Plan-2015-2020.pdf. 12 March 2018.

——— (2015) *Subscriber Trends 2000–2014* (Malaŵi Communications Regulator Authority).

——— (2016) 'National Survey on Access to and Usage of ICT Services in Malaŵi' (Malawi Communications Regulatory Authority), http://www.macra.org.mw/wp-content/uploads/2016/01/MACRA-Survey-Report-National-Household-and-Individual-access-to-and-usage-of-ICT.pdf. 11 March 2018.

Malonda CW (2016) *Approval of the Merger Between FDH Financial Holdings and Malaŵi Savings Bank (MSB)* (Competition and Fair Trading Commission 2016).

Matoi P (2016) 'M-Pesa in Tanzania: The Journey So Far' (Vodacom), https://www.udbs.udsm.ac.tz/images/ICAESB2016/M-Pesa_in_Tanzania.pdf. 10 May 2018.

NSO (2009) '2008 Population and Housing Census' (Malaŵi Government [National Statistics Office]), http://www.mw.one.un.org/wp-content/uploads/2014/04/Malawi-Population-and-Housing-Census-Preliminary-Report-2008.pdf. 29 April 2018.

O'Connell M and others (2016) 'Case Study: Malaŵi' *Low-Income Customer Support Units* (WaterAid), http://www.wateraidamerica.org/sites/default/files/publcations/LICSU%20Malawi%20case%20study.pdf. 23 February 2018.

Porteous D (2006) 'The Enabling Environment for Mobile Banking in Africa' (Report Commissioned by Department for International Development [DFID]), http://bankablefrontier.com/wp-content/uploads/documents/ee.mobil_.banking.report.v3.1.pdf. 14 September 2018.

RBM 'Monthly National Payments System Report: July 2016' (Reserve Bank of Malaŵi), https://www.rbm.mw/PaymentSystems/GetContentFile/?ContentID=7870. 12 May 2018.

——— (2008) 'Malaŵi National Payment System Vision Strategy Framework for the Period 2009–2013' (Reserve Bank of Malaŵi), http://www.rbm.mw/documents/payment_systems/NPS%20Vision%20%20Strategy%20Framework%20December%202008%20Final.pdf. 10 February 2018.

——— (2013) 'National Payment Systems Annual Report 2012' (Reserve Bank of Malaŵi), http://www.rbm.mw/documents/payment_systems/payment%20systems%20annual%20report%202012.pdf. 10 February 2018.

——— (2015) 'Payment Systems Annual Report 2014' (Reserve Bank of Malaŵi), http://www.rbm.mw/PaymentSystems/GetContentFile?ContentID=5169. 4 May 2018.

——— (2015) 'Financial and Economic Review' (Reserve Bank of Malaŵi), https://www.rbm.mw/Home/GetContentFile?ContentID=7492. 14 December 2015.

——— (2016) 'Monthly National Payments System Report: December 2016' (Reserve Bank of Malaŵi), https://www.rbm.mw/PaymentSystems/GetContentFile/?ContentID=12148pdf. 17 February 2018.

——— (2017) 'Monthly National Payments System Report: January 2017' (Reserve Bank of Malaŵi), https://www.rbm.mw/PaymentSystems/GetContentFile/?ContentID=12203. 10 March 2018.

——— (2018) 'Monthly National Payment System Report, May 2018', vol 6 No. 5, https://www.rbm.mw/PaymentSystems/GetContentFile/?ContentID=26223. 2 December 2018.

SADC (2011) 'SADC Bankers: Reserve Bank of Malaŵi' (Committee of Central Bank Governors in Southern Africa Development Community [SADC]), http://www.sadcbankers.org/SADC/SADC.nsf/LADV/E4E3EF0D1F5967B8422576740044D454/$File/Malawi-.pdf. 10 October 2018.

Safaricom (2016) 'SAFARICOM LIMITED Annual Report 2016', https://www.safaricom.co.ke/annualreport_2016/downloads/Safaricom%20Annual%20Report%202016.pdf. 10 May 2018.

Study on Informal and Non-Formal Rural Financial Services (2012) Concern Universal Malaŵi, http://concern-universal.org/wp-content/uploads/2014/07/CUMO-Study-of-Rural-Finance-Summary.pdf. 7 October 2018.

TNM (2016) 'Annual Report 2015' (Telekom Networks Malaŵi Limited), https://drive.google.com/file/d/0B9DwraK-rABVQUlRYnoyTlo0Znc/view. 11 March 2018.

UNCDF (2015) 'Malaŵi Annual Monitor 2015' *Mobile Money for the Poor (MM4P)* (United Nations Capital Development Fund), http://www.uncdf.org/sites/default/files/Documents/malawi_country_monitor_long_version_rev5.pdf. 9 March 2015.

Vodacom (2016) 'Vodacom Integrated Report for the Year Ended 31 March 2018', http://www.vodacom-reports.co.za/integrated-reports/ir-2016/pdf/full-integrated.pdf. 10 May 2018.

Vudayagiri GS and others (2016) 'World Payments Report' (Capgemini and BNP Paribas), http://www.astrid-online.it/static/upload/worl/world_payments_report_wpr_2016.pdf. 10 March 2018.

Webb M and others (2014) 'Mobile Money Regulation' (WebbHenderson), http://webbhenderson.com/wp-content/uploads/2015/06/Mobilelectronicmoney-Regulation-April-2014.pdf. 9 February 2018.

## *Organisational Websites*

'About Malswitch' (2015) (Malswitch Ltd), http://www.malswitch.mw/malswitch/index.php?option=com_content&view=article&id=30&Itemid=140. 14 December 2015.

Airtel (2013a) 'Airtel Money Launch in Malaŵi' (Airtel), http://africa.airtel.com/wps/wcm/connect/africarevamp/malawi/home/personal/airtel-money. 15 December 2018.

——— (2013b) 'Airtel—Merchants and Utilities' (Airtel Malaŵi), http://africa.airtel.com/wps/wcm/connect/AfricaRevamp/Malawi/Airtel_Money/Home/Merchants_and_utilities. 23 March 2015.

——— (2013c) 'About Airtel Money' (Airtel Malaŵi), http://africa.airtel.com/wps/wcm/connect/AfricaRevamp/Malawi/Airtel_Money/Home/Personal/About_airtel_money. 23 March 2015.

——— (2013d) 'Airtel—How It Works: Send Money' (Airtel Malaŵi), http://africa.airtel.com/wps/wcm/connect/africarevamp/malawi/airtel_money/home/personal/how_it_works/send_money. 23 March 2015.

——— (2013e) 'Agents' (Airtel Malaŵi), http://africa.airtel.com/wps/wcm/connect/AfricaRevamp/Malawi/Airtel_Money/Home/Agents. 23 March 2015.

——— (2016a) 'Me2U' (Airtel, Malaŵi), http://africa.airtel.com/wps/wcm/connect/africarevamp/malawi/home/personal/voice-and-text/phone-services/me2u. 21 May 2018.

——— (2016b) 'Airtel Malaŵi Tariffs' (Airtel), http://africa.airtel.com/wps/wcm/connect/AfricaRevamp/Malawi/Airtel_Money/Home/Personal/tariffs. 27 December 2018.

——— (2017a) 'One Network Countries' (Airtel Ghana), http://africa.airtel.com/wps/wcm/connect/africarevamp/Ghana/Home/personal/premier/one-network/PG_One-Network-Countries/. 29 May 2018.

——— (2017b) 'What Is Airtel Money? How to Pay Bills' (Airtel Malaŵi), http://africa.airtel.com/wps/wcm/connect/AfricaRevamp/Malawi/home/personal/airtel-money/about-airtel-money. 23 February 2018.

——— (2017c) 'Airtel Money Cross Border Transfer' (Airtel Malaŵi), http://africa.airtel.com/wps/wcm/connect/AfricaRevamp/malawi/airtel_money/home/airtel-money-cross-border. 23 February 2018.

——— (2017d) 'Bharti Airtel' (Bharti Airtel), http://www.airtel.in/about-bharti/about-bharti-airtel. 23 February 2018.

Anon (2007) 'Kibera UK—The Gap Year Company' (Kibera UK Charity), http://www.kibera.org.uk/Facts.html. 16 March 2015.

——— (2010) 'Mobile Cellular Subscriptions (Per 100 People) in Malaŵi' (Trading Economics), http://www.tradingeconomics.com/malawi/mobile-cellular-subscriptions-per-100-people-wb-data.html. 11 March 2018.

——— (2014a) 'Rural Population in Malaŵi' (Trading Economics), http://www.tradingeconomics.com/malawi/rural-population-wb-data.html. 19 May 2018.

——— (2014b) 'Malaŵi Unemployment Rate' (Trading Economics), http://www.tradingeconomics.com/malawi/unemployment-rate. 28 May 2018.

——— (2015a) 'Why Africa Mobile Phone Penetration Rising to 79% by 2020 Is Good News' (*Amgoo Telecom Co., Ltd.*), http://www.amgoo.com/blog/why-africa-mobile-phone-penetration-rising-to-79-by-2020-is-good-news. 12 December 2018.

——— (2015b) 'Submarine Cable Map' (PriMetrica, Inc), http://www.submarinecablemap.com/#/. 12 December 2018.

——— (2016a) 'What Is the Bristol Pound?' (Bristol City), http://bristolpound.org/what. 13 September 2018.

——— (2016b) 'Malaŵi Unemployment Rate 2005–2016' (Trading Economics), http://www.tradingeconomics.com/malawi/unemployment-rate. 4 May 2015.

——— (2016c) 'Mobile Money—M-Pesa In Kenya, 7 Things Worth Knowing' (SEPA Mobile Payments), http://www.sepaforcorporates.com/sepa-mobile-payments/mobilelectronicmoney-m-pesa-kenya-7-things-didnt-know/. 31 October 2018.

Apple (2016) 'Apple Pay' (Apple Inc), http://www.apple.com/uk/apple-pay/. 9 March 2018.

Aptantech (2013a) 'M-Pesa & Its "OffSpring"—A Look at 5 "M" Payments Solutions Developed After M-Pesa' (Aptantech), http://aptantech.com/2013/08/m-pesa-its-offsprings-a-look-at-5-m-payments-solutions-developed-after-m-pesa/. 23 February 2018.

——— (2013b) 'What Does Equity's Deal with Bharti's Airtel Money Mean for Orange Money and Safaricom's M-Kesho?' (Aptantech), http://aptantech.com/2013/07/what-does-equitys-deal-with-bhartis-airtel-money-mean-for-orangelectronicmoney-and-safaricoms-m-kesho/. 23 February 2018.

CAK (2018) 'Telecommunications Overviews' (Communications Authority of Kenya), https://ca.go.ke/industry/telecommunication/overview/. 28 December 2018.

CAMA (2016) 'Consumers Association of Malaŵi', https://www.facebook.com/Consumers-Association-of-Malawi-104178233025786/. 20 December 2018.

CFTC (2016a) 'Competition and Fair Trading Commission of Malaŵi' (Competition and Fair Trading Commission), https://www.facebook.com/CompetitionAndFairTradingCommissionOfMalawi/. 29 December 2018.

——— (2016b) 'Competition and Fair Trading Commission (Malaŵi)—History' (Competition and Fair Trading Commission), http://www.cftc.mw/index.php/about-us/history.html. 29 December 2018.

CIA (2014) 'The World Factbook' Central Intelligence Agency, https://www.cia.gov/library/publications/the-world-factbook/rankorder/2147rank.html. 20 July 2018.

CoS (2016) 'Scottish Banknotes Legal Position' (The Committee of Scottish Bankers), http://www.scotbanks.org.uk/legal_position.php. 13 September 2018.

EBL (2017) 'M-Kesho' (Equity Bank Limited), http://ke.equitybankgroup.com/business/products/ways-to-bank/mobile-banking/m-kesho. 23 February 2018.

FATF (2016) 'Financial Action Task Force' (FATF), http://www.fatf-gafi.org/. 15 December 2018.

Faulkner C (2015) 'What Is NFC? Everything You Need to Know', http://www.techradar.com/news/phone-and-communications/what-is-nfc-and-why-is-it-in-your-phone-948410. 9 March 2018.

FIU (2017) 'Malaŵi Parliament Passes Financial Crimes Bill into Law' (Financial Intelligence Unit), http://www.fiumalawi.gov.mw/Parliament%20Passes%20FC%20Bill.html. 9 March 2018.

FMB 'First Merchant Bank to Acquire Opportunity International Bank of Malaŵi' 27 June 2017, http://www.fmbmalawi.com/first-merchant-bank-to-acquire-opportunity-international-bank-of-malawi/. 18 July 2018.

FOSL (2017) 'Financial Ombudsman Service' (Financial Ombudsman Service Limited), http://www.financial-ombudsman.org.uk/. 13 March 2018.

FSA (2011) 'Going to School with M-PESA' (Financial Services Assessment), http://www.fsassessment.umd.edu/notes/education-through-mpesa.html. 23 February 2018.

FSVC (2016) 'Malaŵi Program Overview' (Financial Services Volunteer Corps), http://www.fsvc.org/node/99. 20 July 2018.

GSMA (2017) 'Brief History of GSM & the GSMA' (GSM Association), http://www.gsma.com/aboutus/history. 10 March 2017.

IADI (2016) 'IADI Members and Participants' (International Association of Deposit Insurers), http://www.iadi.org/en/about-iadi/iadi-members-and-participants/list-of-members/. 1 May 2018.

KRA (2017) 'KRA M-Service: Mobile E-Slip General & Payment User Guide' (Kenya Revenue Authority), http://www.kra.go.ke/notices/pdf2015/KRA%20m-Service%20User%20Guide%20-%20Mobile%20E-slip%20Generation%20&%20Payment.pdf. 23 February 2018.

Lyman T (2016) 'Regulation and Supervision' (CGAP), http://www.cgap.org/topics/regulation-and-supervision. 21 May, 2018.

MACRA (2016b) 'Telecommunications' (Malaŵi Communication Regulatory Authority), http://www.macra.org.mw/?cat=7. 8 February 2018.

Malswitch 'Malswitch' (Malaŵi Switch Centre Limited), http://www.malswitch.mw/malswitch/. 10 February 2018.

MLC (2016a) 'Malaŵi Law Commission', http://www.lawcom.mw/. 22 December 2018.

——— (2016b) 'About Us: How We Operate' (Malaŵi Law Commission), http://www.lawcom.mw/index.php?option=com_content&view=article&id=19&Itemid=103. 22 December 2018.

MoneyGram 'MoneyGram' (MoneyGram International Limited), https://m.moneygram.com/mgomobile/site/costEstimator.html#CostEstimatorResults. 11 March 2018.

MPC (2017) 'Financial, Retail & Agency Services' (Malaŵi Posts Corporation), http://malawiposts.com/finance.html. 10 March 2018.

MSE (2014) 'Daily Stock News' (Malaŵi Stock Exchange), http://www.mse.co.mw/current/daily.pdf. 17 June 2014.

MTN (2016) 'Mobile Money' (MTN), https://www.mtn.co.za/everyday_services/useful_extras/Banking/Pages/mobile_banking.aspx. 20 May 2018.

Nagarajan G (July 2010) 'Money in a Pot: Has OIBM Altered Savings in Rural Malaŵi?' (Financial Service Assessment), http://www.fsassessment.umd.edu/notes/savings-rural.html. 11 March 2018.

Ofcom (2001) 'Mobile Phone Base Stations—How Mobile Phone Networks Work' (Office of the Communications Regulator, UK), http://www.ofcom.org.uk/static/archive/ra/topics/mpsafety/school-audit/mobilework.htm. 12 December 2018.

'Prudential Regulation Authority' (2017) Bank of England, http://www.bankofengland.co.uk/pra/Pages/default.aspx. 1 May 2018.

RBM (2015) 'Financial and Economic Review' (Reserve Bank of Malawi). https://www.rbm.mw/Home/GetContentFile?ContentID=7492. 14 December 2018.

RBM (2017) 'Reserve Bank of Malaŵi', https://www.rbm.mw/. 24 April 2018.

SADC (2013) 'Payment Systems Progress Report to Committee of Central Bank Governors (CCBG) for the Period April 2011 to March 2012 (Malaŵi)' (Southern Africa Development Community [SADC] Bankers Association), http://www.sadcbankers.org/subcommittees/PaySystem/media/Documents/Newsletters/Vulindlela_Nov2012/Malawi.pdf. 10 February 2018.

——— (2014) 'SADC Overview' (Southern Africa Development Community [SADC]), http://www.sadc.int/about-sadc/overview/. 17 March 2018.

Safaricom (2016) 'M-PESA Rates' (Safaricom), https://www.safaricom.co.ke/personal/m-pesa/get-started-with-m-pesa/m-pesa-tariffs. 9 May 2018.

——— (2017) 'Sambaza' (Safaricom, Kenya), https://www.safaricom.co.ke/personal/calls-sms/prepay/sambaza. 17 February 2018.

Sants H (2009) 'Delivering Intensive Supervision and Credible Deterrence' (Financial Services Authority), http://www.fsa.gov.uk/pages/Library/Communication/Speeches/2009/0312_hs.shtml. 28 April 2018.

TEVETA (2017) 'About Us' (Technical, Entrepreneurial and Vocational Education and Training [TEVET] Authority), http://www.teveta.mw/index.php/about-us. 27 February 2018.

TNM (2013) 'Me2u Service' (Telekom Networks Malaŵi), http://www.tnm.co.mw/index.php/me2u.html. 21 May 2018.

——— (2014a) 'What Is Mpamba' (Telekom Networks Malaŵi), https://www.tnmmpamba.co.mw/index.php/what-is-mpamba. 20 March 2015.

——— (2014b) 'How to Use Mpamba: Customers' (Telekom Networks Malaŵi), https://www.tnmmpamba.co.mw/index.php/user-guide. 20 March 2015.

——— (2014c) 'How to Use Mpamba: Agents' (Telekom Networks Malaŵi), https://www.tnmmpamba.co.mw/index.php/user-guide/agent-user-guide. 20 March 2015.

——— (2017a) 'Mpamba, TNM Mobile Money' (Telekom Networks Malaŵi), https://www.tnmmpamba.co.mw/. 12 March 2017.

——— (2017b) 'How to Use Mpamba: Pay Bills' (Telekom Networks Malaŵi), https://www.tnmmpamba.co.mw/index.php/user-guide. 23 February 2018.

——— (2018a) 'Mpamba Customer Fees' (Telekom Networks Malaŵi), https://www.tnmmpamba.co.mw/index.php/customer-fees. 20 December 2018.

——— (2018b) 'TNM Mpamba', www.tnm.co.mw/mpamba. 30 December 2018.

UNESCO (2016) 'Malaŵi' (UNESCO Institute for Statistics), http://uis.unesco.org/en/country/mw. 17 February 2018.

UNOHRLLS (2011) 'Landlocked Developing Countries (LLDCs)' (United Nations Office of the High Representative for the Least Developed Countries, Landlocked Developing Countries and Small Island Developing States), http://www.unohrlls.org/UserFiles/File/UN_LLDCs_Factsheet.pdf. 21 May 2018.

Vodacom (2016) 'Ada za M-Pesa' (Vodacom Tanzania PLC), https://vodacom.co.tz/mpesa/consumers/mpesa_tarrifs. 9 May 2018.

WIZZIT (2016a) 'History' (WIZZIT), http://www.wizzit.co.za/?q=node/197. 14 May 2018.

——— (2016b) 'Cellphone Banking' (WIZZIT), http://www.wizzit.co.za/?q=node/68. 14 May 2018.

——— (2016c) 'Who We Are' (WIZZIT International), http://wizzit-int.com.dedi89.cpt1.host-h.net/who-we-are/. 14 May 2018.

World Bank (2015) 'Malaŵi—Overview' (World Bank), http://www.worldbank.org/en/country/malawi/overview. 21 December 2015.

## *Newspapers, Magazines and Other News Outlets*

Adepetun A (2015) 'Africa's Mobile Phone Penetration Now 67%' *The Guardian* (Kenya), http://www.ngrguardiannews.com/2015/06/africas-mobile-phone-penetration-now-67/. 12 December 2018.

Anon (2003) 'Power Failure Rocks Malaŵi's Telecoms' (*PANA Press*), http://www.panapress.com/Power-Failure-Rocks-Malawi-s-Telecoms–13-475501-18-lang1-index.html. 29 June 2018.

——— (2007) 'Malaŵi Mobile Phone Network Goes Off the Air' (*ClickAfrique*), http://www.clickafrique.com/Magazine/ST010/CP0000002372.aspx. 29 June 2018.

——— (2008) 'Celtel Morphs into Zain' (*TeleGeography*), https://www.telegeography.com/products/commsupdate/articles/2008/08/04/celtel-morphs-into-zain/. 30 May 2018.

——— (2010a) 'Out of Thin Air' (*The Economist*), http://www.economist.com/node/16319635. 15 December 2018.

——— (2010b) 'Airtel Swallows Zain' (*Vanguard Media Limited*), http://www.vanguardngr.com/2010/11/airtel-swallows-zain/. 30 May 2018.

——— (2010c) 'Consumers Demonstrate Over High Bank Rates in Malaŵi' (*Maravi blog*), http://maravi.blogspot.co.uk/2010/04/nyasatimes-consumers-demonstrate-over.html. 11 March 2018.

——— (2012) 'Light Touch No More' *The Economist* (New York), http://www.economist.com/news/21567399-britains-financial-regulators-are-getting-much-tougher-light-touch-no-more. 9 February 2018.

——— (2013a) 'Digital Currencies: A New Specie' *The Economist* (New York), http://www.economist.com/news/leaders/21576104-regulators-should-keep-their-hands-new-forms-digital-money-such-bitcoin-new-specie. 9 March 2018.

——— (2013b) 'TNM Launches Mobile Money Mpamba to Build Great Malaŵi Nation' *Nyasa Times*, http://www.nyasatimes.com/tnm-launches-mobilelectronicmoney-mpamba-to-build-great-malawi-nation/. 28 December 2018.

——— (2013c) 'Why Does Kenya Lead the World in Mobile Money?' *The Economist*, http://www.economist.com/blogs/economist-explains/2013/05/economist-explains-18. 15 December 2018.

——— (2016a) 'TNM Mpamba Partners Mukuru International Money Transfer Service: Partnership Provides for Investment in Mpamba Fesa' *Nyasa Times*, http://www.nyasatimes.com/tnm-mpamba-partners-mukuru-international-money-transfer-service-partnership-provides-investment-mpamba-fesa/#sthash.Lx0BOj2H.dpuf. 23 February 2018.

——— (2016b) 'TNM Mpamba Builds K11m School Block in Chileka' *Nyasa Times*, http://www.nyasatimes.com/tnm-mpamba-builds-k11m-school-block-chileka/. 12 March 2018.

——— (2016c) 'Airtel Leads the Way' *The Times* (Blantyre), http://www.times.mw/airtel-malawi-leads-the-way/. 11 March 2018.

Bisani L (2016) 'Airtel Proud of Airtel Money' *Malaŵi 24*, https://malawi24.com/2016/06/27/airtel-proud-airtel-money/. 11 March 2018.

Burn-Callander R (2014) 'The History of Money: From Barter to Bitcoin' *The Telegraph* (London), http://www.telegraph.co.uk/finance/businessclub/money/11174013/The-history-of-money-from-barter-to-bitcoin.html. 13 September 2018.

Chaguza K (2017) 'Opportunity International Bank of Malaŵi (OIBM) to Trim Its Staff This Year' (*Face of Malaŵi*), http://www.faceofmalawi.com/2017/01/opportunity-bank-of-malawi-oibm-to-trim-its-staffs-this-year/. 10 March 2018.

Chiyembekeza C (2013) 'National Switch: A Long Overdue Project or a Waste?' *The Nation* (Blantyre), http://mwnation.com/national-switch-long-overdue-project-waste/. 10 February 2018.

——— (2014) 'Depositors' Protection Scheme in the Offing' *The Nation* (Blantyre), http://mwnation.com/depositors%E2%80%99-protection-scheme-in-the-offing/. 24 February 2018.

——— (2015) 'Court Rebuffs TNM, Airtel Over MACRA Decision' *The Nation* (Blantyre), http://mwnation.com/court-rebuffs-tnm-airtel-over-macra-decision/. 22 February 2018.

Chutel L (2016) 'Vodacom Has Given Up on Revolutionary Mobile Money Service M-Pesa, in South Africa' (*Quartz Africa Weekly Brief*), https://

qz.com/679059/vodacom-has-given-up-on-revolutionary-mobilelectronic-money-service-m-pesa-in-south-africa/. 10 January 2018.

Crabtree J (2012) 'M-Pesa's Cautious Start in India' *Financial Times*, http://www.ft.com/cms/s/0/a09c0f68-4a9a-11e2-9650-00144feab49a.html#axzz3UGBgLWPj. 15 December 2018.

Dagada R (2015) 'Mobile Money Stalls in SA' *ITWeb in Banking*, http://www.itweb.co.za/index.php?option=com_content&view=article&id=141012. 19 March 2015.

Day P (2005) 'Mutual Benefits of Profits from Poverty' *BBC News* (London), http://news.bbc.co.uk/1/hi/business/4648049.stm. 17 February 2018.

Dzikanyanga P (2016) 'Reserve Bank of Malaŵi to Launch Financial Literacy Strategy' *Nyasa Times*, http://www.nyasatimes.com/reserve-bank-of-malawi-to-launch-financial-literacy-strategy/#sthash.vWN1Njlb.dpuf. 17 February 2018.

England A (2016) 'Zimbabwe to Print "Bond Notes" to Tackle Cash Shortage' *Financial Times* (London), http://www.ft.com/cms/s/0/90a66462-12da-11e6-91da-096d89bd2173.html#axzz4AKE4BM9k. 1 June 2018.

Etelej P (2011) 'About M-PESA' (*The Online Kenyan*), http://blog.theonlinekenyan.com/about-mpesa. 28 March 2018.

Floy S (2016) 'How and Why Mobile Money (M-Pesa) Works in Kenya' *Our Mobile World*, http://samfloy.com/how-and-why-mobilelectronicmoney-m-pesa-works-in-kenya/. 7 April 2018.

Fuller J (2010) 'The King Is Dead; Long Live the King' *Financial World*, http://fwarchive.ifslearning.ac.uk/financial_world/Archive/2010/2010_07July/Comment/Jane%20Fuller/pdf/18908.pdf. 28 February 2018.

Gondwe G (2011) 'Reserve Bank of Malaŵi Appoints New Governor' (*Biz Community*), http://www.bizcommunity.com/Article/415/87/40038.html. 3 March 2018.

Greeley B (2013) 'One Good Paper: Monopoly Power in Mobile Money' (*Bloomberg Businessweek*), http://www.businessweek.com/articles/2013-03-13/one-good-paper-monopoly-power-in-mobilelectronicmoney. 28 March, 2018.

Gwede W (2016) 'Malaŵi Parliament Rejects Financial Crimes Bill: Goodall Wants Committee Meet Weekend for Fast-Track Scrutiny' *Nyasa Times*, http://www.nyasatimes.com/malawi-parliament-rejects-financial-crimes-bill-goodall-wants-committee-meet-weekend-fast-track-scrutiny/#sthash.MZ5CaRjv.dpuf. 22 December 2018.

Hanna Ziady H (2016) 'Interest Rate Caps Are Now Effective' *The Citizen* (Johannesburg), http://citizen.co.za/business/business-news/1109479/interest-rate-caps-are-now-effective/. 5 December 2018.

Harrison R (2005) 'Cell Phones Plug Africa's Poor into Mobile Banking' *Reuters, South Africa*, https://www.mail-archive.com/telecom-cities@forums.nyu.edu/msg00327.html. 21 January, 2018.

Hayat MA (2009) 'Mobile Payments: Will Colombo Keep Its Leadership in South Asia?' *Sunday Times* (Colombo, Sri Lanka), http://www.sundaytimes.lk/090712/FinancialTimes/ft323.html. 14 February 2018.

Hill and Leahy (2009) 'FSA Bids Farewell to Light-Touch Financial Regulation' *Financial Times* (London), http://www.ft.com/cms/s/0/da208b14-1426-11de-9e32-0000779fd2ac.html?ft_site=falcon&desktop=true#axzz4YBrB-0BUq. 9 February 2018.

Kajilwa G (2015) 'Safaricom and Airtel Lose Market Share to New Comers, Regulator Report Shows' *Standard* (Nairobi), http://www.standardmedia.co.ke/business/article/2000186415/safaricom-and-airtel-lose-market-share-to-new-comers-regulator-report-shows. 31 October 2018.

Kamanga B (2016) 'Malaŵi Junior Queens Gets K10mil Airtel Money for Africa Games' *Nyasa Times*, http://www.nyasatimes.com/malawi-junior-queens-gets-k10mil-airtel-money-africa-games/#sthash.CdRa3jCd.dpuf. 12 March 2018.

Kamngoya J (2015) 'Teveta to Harmonise Vocational Curricula and Certification' (*All Africa*), http://allafrica.com/stories/201506011690.html. 27 February 2018.

Kansilanga C (2015) 'Malaŵi Savings Bank Finally Sold ' *Daily Times* (Blantyre), http://www.times.mw/malawi-savings-bank-finally-sold-2/. 20 July 2018.

Khombe G (2014) 'CAMA to Name and Shame Traders on Receipt Guarantee and Warranty' *Zodiak Online* (Lilongwe), http://zodiakmalawi.com/top-stories/cama-to-name-and-shame-traders-on-receipt-guarantee-and-waranty. 14 November 2018.

——— (2015) 'National Switch Connects ATMs to All' *Zodiak Online* (Lilongwe), http://www.zodiakmalawi.com/top-stories/national-switch-connects-atms-to-all. 15 December 2015.

Khunga S (2015) 'MSB Sale Fallout, Goes at K9.5 Billion' *The Nation* (Blantyre), http://mwnation.com/msb-sale-fallout-goes-at-k9-5-billion/. 18 November 2018.

Kihagi S (2013) 'Malawians to Pay for Fuel Services Using Airtel Money' (*HumanIPO*), http://www.humanipo.com/news/36717/malawians-to-pay-for-fuel-services-using-airtel-money/. 12 March 2018.

Krueger M (2011) 'Four Reasons M-Pesa Succeeded in Kenya' *Mobile Money Exchange*, https://mobilemoneyexchange.wordpress.com/2011/05/09/four-reasons-m-pesa-succeeded-in-kenya/. 10 March 2018.

Malakata M (2015) 'Power Problems Disrupt Africa's Telecom Sector' *PCWorld*, http://www.pcworld.com/article/2926892/power-problems-disrupt-africas-telecom-sector.html. 29 June 2018.

Manthorpe R (2017) 'Live Tracker Reveals How Much NHS Hackers Are Making from Their Ransomware Demands' *Wired*, http://www.wired.co.uk/article/nhs-hackers-bitcoin-value. 29 May 2018.

Masina L (2015) 'Controversy as Government Sells Malaŵi Savings Bank' *African Business*, http://africanbusinessmagazine.com/african-banker/controversy-as-government-sells-malawi-savings-bank/. 18 November 2018.

Masters B (2011) 'Regulator's "Light Touch" Ledto Failure' *Financial Times* (London), https://www.ft.com/content/2bf14c52-24ce-11e1-bfb3-00144feabdc0. 9 February 2018.

Mkandawire L (2014) 'Kumbatira Appointed New Macra Boss' *The Nation* (Blantyre), http://mwnation.com/kumbatira-appointed-new-macra-boss/. 8 February 2018.

——— (2015) 'Macra, MPC Bosses Swap Posts' *The Nation* (Blantyre), http://mwnation.com/macra-mpc-bosses-swap-posts/. 8 February 2015.

Monaghan A (2016a) 'Sterling Hits New 31-Year Low Against the Dollar' *The Guardian* (London), https://www.theguardian.com/business/2016/jul/06/brexit-pound-plunges-to-30-year-lows-as-eu-fears-bite-into-global-markets-again. 13 September 2018.

——— (2016b) 'First Post-Brexit Vote Data Shows UK Inflation Rose to 0.6% in July' *The Guardian* (London), https://www.theguardian.com/business/2016/aug/16/first-post-brexit-data-shows-uk-inflation-rose-to-06-in-july. 13 September 2018.

Monbiot G (2016) 'Neoliberalism—The Ideology at the Root of All Our Problems' *The Guardian* (London), https://www.theguardian.com/books/2016/apr/15/neoliberalism-ideology-problem-george-monbiot. 25 April 2018.

Mtika C (2015) 'Malaŵi Struggles with End of Western Donations' *African Independent*, http://www.africanindy.com/business/malawi-struggles-with-end-of-western-donations-1435026. 20 December 2018.

Mulligan G (2015) 'Is Fibre Optic Cable Key to Africa's Economic Growth?' *BBC Business News* (London), http://www.bbc.co.uk/news/business-32079649. 9 May 2018.

Mungai C (2015) 'The Mobile Phone Comes First in Africa; Before Electricity, Water, Toilets or Even Food' *Mail & Guardian Africa* (Johannesburg), http://mgafrica.com/article/2015-03-03-mobile-come-first-in-africa-before-electricity-water-toilets-or-even-food. 9 March 2018.

Ngigi G (2012) 'M-Pesa Linked to Rise in Inflation' *Business Daily* (Nairobi), http://www.businessdailyafrica.com/M-Pesa-linked-to-rise-in-inflation/-/539552/1327538/-/13rogmr/-/index.html. 23 February 2018.

Njiraini J and Anyanzwa J (2008) 'Unmasking the Storm Behind M-Pesa' *The Standard* (Nairobi), http://www.standardmedia.co.ke/?articleID=1144002826&story_title=. 13 March 2015.

Nthenda G (2018) 'Parliament Refers Interest Cap Bill to Joint Committee', Kulinji.com 13 December 2018, https://www.kulinji.com/article/news/2018/parliament-refers-interest-cap-bill-joint-committee. 28 December 2018.

Nthondo J (2016) 'Exclusive: New Cashgate in Malaŵi, How Macra Funds Are Abused' *Nyasa Times*, http://www.nyasatimes.com/exclusive-new-cashgate-malawi-macra-funds-abused/#sthash.efL9KDSw.dpuf. 27 February 2018.

Ombok E (2010) 'Safaricom Names Collymore as Chief Executive Officer' *Bloomberg Business*, http://www.bloomberg.com/news/articles/2010-07-22/kenya-s-safaricom-appoints-bob-collymore-as-ceo-replacing-michael-joseph. 16 March 2015.

Phimbi E (2016) 'Kapito Faults APM on "Buy Malaŵi" Campaign: "Establish Consumer Protection Council"' *Nyasa Times*, http://www.nyasatimes.com/kapito-faults-apm-on-buy-malawi-campaign-establish-consumer-protection-council/#sthash.DbigqXjh.dpuf. 28 December 2018.

Phiri A (2016) 'Finance Bank in K3 Billion Case' *The Times* (Blantyre), http://www.times.mw/finance-bank-in-k3-billion-case/. 9 March 2018.

Phiri F (2005) 'Finance Bank Closure: Precursor to Return of Forfeiture Act?' (*Malawiana*), https://groups.yahoo.com/neo/groups/MALAWIANA/conversations/topics/3175. 23 February 2018.

Phiri G (2015) 'Telecom Operators' Performance Poor' *The Nation* (Blantyre), http://mwnation.com/telecom-operators-perfomance-still-poor/. 12 March 2018.

Reuters (2018) 'Iran Currency Extends Record Fall as U.S. Sanctions Loom' (29 July 2018), https://www.reuters.com/article/us-iran-nuclear-currency/iran-currency-extends-record-fall-as-us-sanctions-loom-idUSKBN1KJ0DY. 4 November 2018.

Sabola T (2015) 'Banks Switch on Payment System' *Daily Times* (Blantyre), http://timesmediamw.com/banks-switch-payment-system/. 7 October 2018.

Safi M (2016) 'Australian Craig Wright Claims He Is Bitcoin Founder Satoshi Nakamoto' *The Guardian* (London), https://www.theguardian.com/technology/2016/may/02/craig-wright-bitcoin-founder-satoshi-nakamoto-claim. 14 September 2018.

Simango C (2015) 'Mobile Money Is New Fashion in Malaŵi' *The Nation* (Blantyre), http://mwnation.com/mobilelectronicmoney-newfashion-malawi/. 11 May 2018.

Smith D (2014) 'Internet Use on Mobile Phones in Africa Predicted to Increase 20-Fold' *The Guardian* (London), http://www.theguardian.com/world/2014/jun/05/internet-use-mobile-phones-africa-predicted-increase-20-fold. 10 March 2018.

Soko H (2015) 'Malaŵi Government Drilled Over MSB Sale' *Malaŵi* 24, http://allafrica.com/stories/201503190408.html. 18 November 2018.

Sundu Y (2016) 'APM Says National IDs Will Transform Malaŵi' *The Nation* (Blantyre), http://mwnation.com/apm-says-national-ids-will-transform-malawi/. 14 November 2018.

Tarrant H (2011) 'Why Kenya's M-Pesa Won't Work Anywhere Else' *Moneyweb*, http://www.moneyweb.co.za/archive/why-kenyas-mpesa-wont-work-anywhere-else/.

Thipa G (2016) 'Banks Faulted on Natswicth' *Daily Times* (Blantyre), http://www.times.mw/banks-faulted-on-natswitch/. 7 October 2018.

Tovrov D (2011) '5 Biggest Slums in the World' *International Business Times*, http://www.ibtimes.com/5-biggest-slums-world-381338. 16 March 2015.

Young J (2009) 'Weird & Wireless: RF "Line of Sight"' *Electronics Weekly*, http://www.electronicsweekly.com/blogs/electro-ramblings/weird-wireless/weird-wireless-rf-line-of-sight-2009-10/. 10 March 2018.

### *Blogs and Various Miscellaneous Internet Sources*

'Airtime' (2016) *Cambridge University Press*, http://dictionary.cambridge.org/dictionary/english/airtime. 27 June 2018.

Anon (2007) 'WIZZIT: Banking the Unbanked in South Africa' (World Bank, Washington, DC), (Audio Visual), https://www.youtube.com/watch?v=2SKhCYoF0Lg. 1 March 2018.

——— (2014) 'WIZZIT CEO: Reflections & Predictions for The Future of Mobile Money' *Mondato Insight*, http://mondato.com/blog/wizzit-founder/. 14 May 2018.

——— (2017) 'African Countries by Population' Wordometres, http://www.worldometers.info/population/countries-in-africa-by-population/. 20 July 2018.

Blair D (2013) 'The FSA Is Dead; Long Live the FCA, the PRA and the FPC', http://www.osborneclarke.com/connected-insights/publications/the-fsa-is-dead-long-live-the-fca-the-pra-and-the-fpc/#sthash.PzXxYUIX.dpuf. 3 March 2018.

Camner G and Sjöblom E (2009) 'Can the Success of M-PESA Be Repeated?—A Review of the Implementations in Kenya and Tanzania', http://emil.sjoblom.com/pdf/M-Pesa_implementations_Ke_Tz.pdf. 15 December 2018.

Chibwana C (2010) 'The High and the Hidden Costs of Banking in Malaŵi', http://chibwana.com/2010/04/05/costs-of-banking-in-malawi/. 11 March 2018.

'Distance from Galasi Madise to Mzuzu', http://malawi.places-in-the-world.com/929816-925475-distance-from-galasi-madise-to-mzuzu.html. 16 December 2015.

Heeks R (2012) 'Why M-Pesa Outperforms Other Developing Country Mobile Money Schemes' *ICTs for Development*, http://ict4dblog.wordpress.com/2012/11/24/why-m-pesa-outperforms-other-developing-country-mobilelectronicmoney-schemes/. 8 May 2018.

Kenya B (2018) 'Top Ten Companies in Kenya by Market Valuation 2018' 28 February 2018, https://bilichi.co.ke/top-10-companies-kenya-2018/. 27 December 2018.

Kumwenda V (2012) 'Malaŵi Posts Corporation's Fast Cash Money Transfer', http://vincekumwenda.blogspot.co.uk/2012/05/malawi-posts-corporations-fast-cash.html. 23 February 2018.

Mas I (2010) 'M-KESHO in Kenya', http://www.gsma.com/mobilefordevelopment/programme/mobilelectronicmoney/m-kesho-in-kenya. 23 February 2018.

Maurer B (2011) 'Mobile Money Regulation: A Story Arc of Best Practices and Emerging Realizations' *Notes from the Field* (December 2011), http://faculty.sites.uci.edu/wmmaurer/files/2011/12/Note_Dec2011_IMTFI.pdf. 15 December 2018.

Mutua W (2012) 'How M-Pesa Disrupts Entire Economies', http://memeburn.com/2012/03/how-m-pesa-disrupts-entire-economies/. 28 March 2018.

Nyerere J (1967) 'The Arusha Declaration' (Tanganyika African National Union), https://www.marxists.org/subject/africa/nyerere/1967/arusha-declaration.htm. 15 December 2018.

Oyebode A (2014) 'M-Pesa and Beyond—Why Mobile Money Worked in Kenya and Struggles in Other Markets' *Venture Capital for Africa*, http://vc4africa.biz/blog/2014/01/15/m-pesa-and-beyond-why-mobilelectronicmoney-worked-in-kenya-and-struggles-in-other-markets/. 15 December 2018.

Redwood J (2012) 'Was Light Touch Regulation the Cause of the Crisis?', http://johnredwoodsdiary.com/2012/05/27/was-light-touch-regulation-the-cause-of-the-crisis/. 3 February 2018.

Skinner C (2015) 'When Everyone on the Planet Has a Mobile Money Account, Things Will Change', http://thefinanser.com/2015/06/when-everyone-on-the-planet-has-a-mobilelectronicmoney-account-things-will-change.html/. 9 February 2018.

Snowdon C (2012) 'Malaŵi President Axes Central Bank Governor' *Central Banking*, http://www.centralbanking.com/central-banking/news/2170162/malawi-president-axes-central-bank-governor. 3 March 2018.

Szarowicz R (2016) 'Bringing Bristol Pound to Massive Attack at the Downs', http://bristolpound.org/blog/. 13 September 2018.

Wang K (2012) 'Replicating M-Pesa: Mobile and Cloud Technology Spur Innovation in Financial Inclusion', http://nextbillion.net/blogpost.aspx?blogid=2869.

XE (2018) 'XE Currency Converter' (XE), https://www.xe.com/currencyconverter/convert/. 28 December 2018.

# Index





S. Madise, *The Regulation of Mobile Money*, Palgrave Macmillan Studies in Banking and Financial Institutions,
https://doi.org/10.1007/978-3-030-13831-8

FSC
www.fsc.org
MIX
Papier | Fördert gute Waldnutzung
FSC® C083411

Kolibri 360 GmbH
Ferdinand-Jühlke-Straße 7
99095 Erfurt, Deutschland
produktsicherheit@kolibri360.de